智能交通信息感知理论与技术

赵池航 著

电子工业出版社·

Publishing House of Electronics Industry

北京·BEIJING

内 容 简 介

本书分上、中、下三篇,上篇、中篇用中文撰写,下篇用英文撰写。本书以交通信息感知理论与技术为主线,系统研究了交通场景中驾驶人-车辆-路面信息感知的理论与技术,主要包括:车辆信息感知理论与技术,主要有交通场景中车辆检测理论与技术、车辆品牌感知理论与技术、车辆异常行为感知理论与技术和基于车载装饰品特征的车辆检索方法;路面信息感知理论与技术,主要有基于联合检测器的路面破损检测方法、基于 Contourlet 变换的路面图像特征提取方法和基于联合特征及分类器集成的路面破损类型分类方法;驾驶人信息感知理论与技术,主要有基于 Curvelet 变换的驾驶人疲劳识别方法、基于 LMDP(Local Multiresolution Derivative Pattern)的驾驶人疲劳识别方法、基于 NC(Nonsubsampled Contourlet)变换的驾驶人异常姿态识别方法和基于融合特征的驾驶人异常姿态识别方法。

本书可作为高等院校交通运输工程、交通信息工程与控制、载运工具运用工程等专业研究生及本科生的教材,也可作为高等院校、科研院所和企事业单位从事智能交通系统研究的工程技术人员的参考书。

图书在版编目(CIP)数据

智能交通信息感知理论与技术 / 赵池航著. —北京:电子工业出版社,2019.9

ISBN 978-7-121-35622-3

Ⅰ. ①智… Ⅱ. ①赵… Ⅲ. ①交通运输管理-智能系统-信息处理-研究 Ⅳ. ①U495

中国版本图书馆 CIP 数据核字(2018)第 263644 号

策划编辑:王志宇
责任编辑:裴 杰
印   刷:北京七彩京通数码快印有限公司
装   订:北京七彩京通数码快印有限公司
出版发行:电子工业出版社
          北京市海淀区万寿路 173 信箱 邮编 100036
开   本:787×1 092 1/16 印张:13.75 字数:404.8 千字
版   次:2019 年 9 月第 1 版
印   次:2019 年 9 月第 1 次印刷
定   价:49.00 元

凡所购买电子工业出版社图书有缺损问题,请向购买书店调换。若书店售缺,请与本社发行部联系,联系及邮购电话:(010)88254888,88258888。

质量投诉请发邮件至 zlts@phei.com.cn,盗版侵权举报请发邮件至 dbqq@phei.com.cn。

本书咨询联系方式:wangzy@phei.com.cn。

前　言

随着国民经济的快速增长，交通运输业在我国国民经济和居民生活中的地位也逐步提升，驾驶人-车辆-道路信息感知理论与技术的研究已经成为智能交通系统中最重要的研究课题之一。人工智能、机器视觉和模式识别等理论与技术的最新发展使得交通智能化和现代化管理及控制成为可能，通过建立交通智能管理和控制体系，综合管理和控制驾驶人、车辆及道路等交通参与体，对于提高交通运输效率和效益、保证交通安全和促进可持续发展具有十分重要的作用。全球范围内每年度的交通事故的统计报告表明：大量交通事故是由人为因素引起的，自动理解和感知驾驶人疲劳及异常行为可有效地降低由人为引起的交通事故率；车辆信息感知是智能交通系统中车辆实时追踪的基础，车辆品牌类型感知能够在套牌车辆自动识别、交通监控场景车型的自动统计分析等领域发挥重要作用；公路路面破损严重影响了道路交通的安全性和舒适性，路面信息感知技术能够快速、准确地进行公路路况的评价。本书共 12 章，分上、中、下三篇，上篇、中篇用中文撰写，下篇用英文撰写，各章的主要内容如下。

第 1 章主要论述了车辆信息感知技术的研究现状，包括车辆检测理论与技术的研究现状、车辆品牌感知理论与技术的研究现状、车辆行为感知理论与技术的研究现状和车辆检索理论与技术的研究现状。

第 2 章主要论述了交通场景中车辆检测理论与技术，包括车辆图像采集、基于对称特征的车辆检测方法和感兴趣区域（ROI）定位方法。本章提出了一种基于车辆轮廓对称特征和车牌对称特征的融合特征的车辆区域检测方法，并与基于车辆边缘、车牌、图像灰度共生矩阵和 Gabor 变换等 5 种检测方法进行了对比研究，实验表明所提出的基于融合特征的车辆检测方法的车辆区域定位的正确率为 90.7%，有效避免了背景噪声对车辆对称轴搜索及车辆检测的影响；根据检测得到的车牌对称轴中心点搜索车牌位置，进而确定车辆前脸 ROI 区域，在使用相同实验数据测试条件下达到了 95.33% 的准确率，为车型识别提供了较为准确和全面的训练样本和测试数据。

第 3 章主要论述了车辆品牌感知理论与技术，包括基于单特征的车辆品牌感知方法和基于组合特征的车辆品牌感知方法。分析了局部能量形状直方图、局部二值模式和梯度方向直方图等 5 种特征提取方法，并采用支持向量机和 k-最近邻分类器进行车辆品牌识别实验，实验结果表明基于 HOG 特征和支持向量机的车辆品牌识别方法要优于其他组合，其识别率达到 92.40%；提出了将 HOG 和 Contourlet 两种特征的简单串联作为分类器的输入特征，并通过设计级联集成分类器方案，在保证系统可靠性的同时，提高了样本的正确识别率，设计的级联分类器的第一级由 8 个不同的分类机制组成，第二级使用 MLP 作为基分类器并结合旋转森林变换后的特征样本进行识别，实验结果表明级联集成分类器系统的可靠性为 98.15%，其中有 7.04% 的样本被"拒识"。

第 4 章主要论述了交通场景中车辆异常行为感知理论与技术，包括基于颜色空间模型的城市交通场景中信号灯的检测方法、基于车辆和车牌对称特征的车辆检测方法、基于联合特征的城市交通场景中车辆异常行为检测方法。采用中值滤波和光线补偿算法对城市交通场景图像进行预处理，并基于颜色空间模型进行城市交通场景中信号灯的状态检测，实验结果表明基于 HSV 彩色空间模型的城市交通场景中信号灯的检测方法优于其他两种彩色空间；研究了基于车辆及车牌对称特征的城市交通场景中车辆的检测方法，并与基于车牌的车辆检测方法、基于 Gabor 特征及支持向量机（SVM）的车辆检测方法和 Haar-like 特征及 AdaBoost 分类器的车辆检测方法进行了对比分析；提出了一种基于联合特征的城市交通场景中车辆异常行为检测方法，该方法基于梯度方向直方图特征和局部二值模式特征的串联联合，并采用支持向量机（SVM）进行自动分类，实验结果表明基于 HOG-LBP 模式的联合特征车辆行为识别优于其他三种单特征车辆行为识别，其识别率达到 93.6%。

第 5 章主要论述了基于车载装饰品特征的车辆检索方法，包括车载装饰品局部区域图像集的构建方法和基于车载装饰品区域图像颜色直方图的车辆检索方法。研究了基于车辆及车牌对称特征的车辆检测方法，并根据整个车辆与前挡风玻璃的相对位置定位车辆前挡风玻璃区域，实验结果表明基于车辆及号牌对称性的方法优于其他三种方法；研究了基于颜色直方图特征的车辆检索方法，并与基于局部二值模式、基于 Gabor 小波变换、基于 Contourlet 变换和基于尺度不变特征的检索方法进行了对比分析。使用基于相似度衡量方法进行了车辆图像的检索实验，实验结果表明基于颜色直方图特征的车辆检索方法优于其他四种方法，其检索综合指标为 86.7%。

第 6 章主要论述了路面信息感知技术的研究现状，包括路面图像预处理技术研究现状、路面破损检测技术研究现状和路面破损分类技术研究现状。

第 7 章主要论述了路面信息感知理论与技术，包括基于联合检测器的路面破损检测方法、基于 Contourlet 变换的路面图像特征提取方法和基于联合特征及分类器集成的路面破损类型分类。基于级联分类器的思想，提出了一种用于路面破损检测的联合检测器，理论分析和实验结果表明联合检测器的性能优于邻域灰度差分法、局部灰度最小分析法和分块标记法，其检测率达到 96.7%；对比分析了 Contourlet 变换、边缘方向直方图、梯度方向直方图和分层梯度方向直方图四种特征提取方法，采用线性核函数的 SVM 作为分类器进行了路面破损识别实验，实验结果表明 Contourlet 变换特征提取方法优于边缘方向直方图、梯度方向直方图和分层梯度方向直方图方法，检测率达到 84.32%；提出了一种基于联合特征及随机子空间交叉内核支持向量机分类器集成的路面破损自动化分类方法，实验结果表明 Contourlet 变换和 EOH 联合特征及随机子空间交叉内核支持向量机分类器集成优于单一

Contourlet 变换特征和 EOH 特征，分类正确率达到 86.61%。

第 8 章主要论述了驾驶人信息感知理论与技术的研究现状，包括驾驶人疲劳信息感知理论与技术的研究现状和驾驶人异常姿态信息感知理论与技术的研究现状。

第 9 章主要论述了基于 Curvelet 变换的驾驶人疲劳信息感知理论与技术，包括 SEU-fatigue expression 数据库构建、基于 Curvelet 变换的驾驶人疲劳信息特征提取和支持向量机分类器。与线性神经网络、k-最近邻、多层神经网络和 Parzen 进行了对比实验，实验结果证明了所提出的基于 Curvelet 变换的驾驶人疲劳信息感知方法的有效性，其识别精度达到 85%。

第 10 章主要论述了基于局部多分辨衍生模式的驾驶人疲劳信息感知理论与技术，包括 SEU-fatigue expression 数据库构建、基于局部多分辨衍生模式的驾驶人疲劳信息的特征提取方法和四种分类器方法。实验结果证明了所提出的基于局部多分辨衍生模式驾驶人疲劳信息感知方法的有效性，其识别精度达到 90%。

第 11 章主要论述了基于 Nonsubsampled Contourlet 变换的驾驶人异常姿态感知理论与方法，包括 SEU- driving postures 数据库构建、基于 Nonsubsampled Contourlet 变换的驾驶人姿态特征的提取方法和四种分类器方法。实验结果证明了所提出的基于 Nonsubsampled Contourlet 驾驶人异常姿态感知方法的有效性，其识别精度达到 88%。

第 12 章主要论述了基于融合特征的驾驶人异常姿态感知理论与方法，包括 SEU- driving postures 数据库构建及规格化、基于 Contourlet 变换和边缘方向直方图的驾驶人姿态融合特征的提取方法和基于随机子空间集成支持向量机的驾驶人异常姿态识别方法。实验结果证明了所提出的基于融合特征及随机子空间集成支持向量机的驾驶人姿态感知方法的有效性，其识别精度达到 90%。

作　者
于南京四牌楼

目　录

中篇 路面信息感知理论与技术

上 篇

车辆信息感知理论与技术

第1章
车辆信息感知技术的研究现状分析

随着国民经济的快速增长，我国的道路交通运输事业在国民经济和居民生活中的地位也逐步提升，计算机图像处理技术、通信与网络传输技术及电子技术的发展使得交通的智能化及现代化管理和控制成为可能，通过建立交通智能管理和控制体系，综合管理及控制人、车和路等交通参与体，对于提高交通运输效率和效益，保证交通安全，促进可持续发展具有十分重要的作用，已经引起世界许多国家的广泛重视。基于视频图像的车辆检测技术通过监控相机获得实时交通视频信息，结合图像处理原理和模式识别方法对图像进行实时处理和分析，计算得到交通流量、占有率、平均车速、排队长度等交通参数，并对车辆逆行、慢速、超速和交通阻塞等交通行为进行分析，并自动统计和记录相关数据。综合交通参数及交通事件等重要信息，可对交通状态进行估计和预测，及时发布诱导信息或通过交警进行调控，从而保障交通正常安全运行。

为了适应城市管理和城市治安防控的需求，"天网工程"项目实施中，大量高清视频传感器被架设在城市道路的两边和建筑物上，可以通过视频专网、互联网、移动等网络将一定范围内的监控点所拍摄的视频图像传送到监控处理中心。车牌号码是识别车辆的"身份证"，成为车辆管理的重要标识和手段，对监控处理中心的数据进行高效处理，提取视频数据中车辆车牌、车辆品牌和颜色等信息，并根据车辆车牌检索车管所车辆登记数据库中的车辆相关信息，与实时识别的车辆品牌和车辆颜色信息进行对比分析，可有效地识别出假（套）牌嫌疑车辆。因此，利用智能交通数据处理平台可以对各种刑事案件、治安事件和交通违章等处理，这为加强城市综合管理、有效预防打击犯罪和处理突发性治安事件提供了有力的解决方案。

作为智能交通管理系统中的重要内容，车辆异常行为检测属于交通事件检测的一种。从交通法规上来说，所谓车辆异常行为是指道路上的车辆违章行为，它是指道路上的偶发性事件，包括闯红灯、车轮压线、违章转向等行为。而对于车辆异常违章行为的检测，传统的检测方法多有其局限性，近年来，随着智能交通领域技术的不断发展，特别是智慧交通城市的建设，很多学者和研究机构已将计算机视觉、图像处理和人工智能等技术应用于交通管理方面。通过采集交通场景下的视频图像，对其进行处理检测，提供机器学习以实现所需功能。在降低系统成本的同时，更能提高准确检测的效率，可靠性更高，具有很高的实用价值。因此，基于计算机视觉和数字图像处理，本书对车辆闯红灯、压线、违法转向等多种异常行为进行检测识别和分类，通过选取和改进合适的算法，开展了在城市交通场景中车辆异常行为的研究，以实现车辆异常行为的自动识别和分类。这对于保障城市道

第 1 章
车辆信息感知技术的研究现状分析

路交通安全，减少人民生命财产损失和道路拥挤，建设平安智慧城市具有重要的意义。

随着数字图像处理技术、机器视觉技术和模式识别技术等的迅猛发展，自动从海量图像数据中搜索嫌疑车辆成为可能，通过对视频或图像数据的处理，公安人员可以直接利用计算机从视频或图像所包含的内容进行分析和特征提取，从而搜索到所需的有用信息。目前，从视频或图片数据中自动搜索可疑车辆信息主要根据车辆固有的车牌号码、车辆品牌和车辆颜色自动识别。但是，在现实生活中涉及车辆的违法案件中，涉案车辆往往是假（套）牌车，此时根据车辆车牌进行侦查将发挥不了任何作用；同时，根据车辆品牌和车辆颜色检索可疑车辆在减少工作量方面起到的作用微乎其微。因此，基于车辆固有属性特征的检索方法对于假（套）牌车辆达不到预期的检索效果。解决该难题的有效办法是借助可疑车辆的车载装饰品，例如车辆的摆件、年检标签等特征进行嫌疑车辆的检索。采用车辆装饰品特征进行检索对于刑事案件的侦破具有极为重要的意义。

1.1　车辆检测理论与技术的研究现状

车辆区域检测及定位是车型分类的基础，国内外学者近年来相继提出了多种车辆检测方法，对于一幅在交通路口或路段相机获取的车辆图片，检测及定位车辆区域的难点在于区分路面、阴影、天空等背景及其他杂乱的噪声。Sun 等[1]将车辆分割方法分为三类：① 基于先验知识的方法；② 基于立体的方法；③ 基于运动的方法。其中第一种方法只需要单幅图片，后两种方法需要多幅图片或视频序列。如果对多幅图片和视频进行分析，可以使用背景差分法[2,3]进行车辆检测，虽然背景差分法比较方便，但它对光照条件、摄像机颤动及阴影等问题非常敏感，如果有少许的光照或相机位置的变动就要重新获取背景。

目前使用图像先验特征进行车辆检测的研究有很多，国内外研究机构和学者相继开展了车辆检测方法的研究，车辆的先验特征包括对称、颜色、阴影、几何（如角点，边缘）、纹理及车灯等特征，如 Gao 等[4]根据车尾灯为红色特点寻找车尾部红色区域并通过检测红色尾灯的对称轴定位车辆，其检测结果表明该方法在定位夜间车辆位置时效果显著；Guo 等[5]通过提取车辆周围物体颜色特征构建颜色模型以排除不真实或偏斜颜色；Techawatcharapaikul 等[6]使用颗边缘密度区分运动车辆区域及其阴影区域，该方法能有效检测简单交通场景中的车辆及进行阴影区域提取，但当交通场景复杂和车辆及其阴影区域较小时错误率较高；Johansson 等[7]使用颜色圆柱体将车辆图像前景分为阴影和高亮区域，该方法能够在光照强度足够时进行车辆检测和追踪；Cucchiaral 等[8]通过检测夜间车辆车头灯定位车辆区域，但该方法易受地面反射物或车本身反射的影响。综上所述，车辆颜色、阴影及车灯特征对光照及背景变化比较敏感，存在阴雨天没有阴影、光照较强时颜色特征不明显及车灯主要用于夜间车辆检测等问题。

车辆区域特征提取及识别提供了一种有效的车辆检测方法。Kim[9]提取车辆图像灰度共生矩阵特征并使用支持向量机（SVM）进行车辆区域验证，根据 Kim 的分析，使用图像灰度共生矩阵（GLCM）作为纹理特征准确度较高。Kalinke[10]使用图像熵特征，图像熵特征能够有效描述感兴趣区域（ROI）内纹理特征，但检测精确度不如图像灰度共生矩阵特征。Wu[11]提取车辆区域小波变换特征并使用主成分分析（PCA）进行车辆识别。Sun[12]使用 Gabor 变换提取图像 Gabor 特征并且使用 SVM 分类器与神经网络分类器进行分类，Sun[12]

的实验结果显示，使用 Gabor 特征及 SVM 识别效果较好。

关于车辆对称特征的研究，Zielke 等[13]提出了使用基于图像亮度对称的车辆中心线的检测方法，该方法能够从背景中分割出车辆区域，但存在图像亮度对光照变化敏感的问题。Du 等[14]提出了使用车辆轮廓对称特征检测对称轴，令扫描线上每对像素"投票选取"对称轴，最后将得票最高的位置作为车辆对称轴，但由于该方法是对整幅图像进行计算，对称轴检测易受交通标志及道路边缘影响。Bin 等[15]使用对称算子同时检测车辆竖直对称轴及车辆竖直边缘，该方法需要计算不同子窗口对称轴以满足车辆定位要求，这种方法时间复杂度过高。Teoh[16]计算不同窗口中水平扫描线上的对称值，并对对称值进行聚类分析以消除道路标志及建筑物的影响，但这种方法对存在竖直对称特征的较大尺寸物体（如交通标志牌）比较敏感。

不仅限于车辆区域检测，在目标识别研究领域，Viola 和 Jones[17]提出了使用 Haar 特征结合 Adaboost 分类器进行人脸检测，他们提出使用积分图像快速计算 Haar 特征，极大地提高了训练速度和检测效率，并提出了分类器的级联方式以提高检测速度。Dalal[18]提出了使用 HOG 特征进行行人脸检测，研究表明，HOG 特征在特征描述方面具有卓越的性能，能够刻画目标局部边缘细节信息，使之能够推广到多种目标检测的应用。台湾的 Chun-Hao Chang[19]将 HOG 特征与 Gentle Adaboost 结合用于多视角车辆检测并获得了较好的检测效率及检测速度。

1.2 车辆品牌感知理论与技术的研究现状

国内研究机构和学者对车型识别技术进行了研究。2007 年，李国强等[20]依据车型外观、体积大小的不同，采用积分思想建立了车辆长度、宽度和高度 3 个参数的算法模型，并提出了基于模板匹配的特征点自动搜索法，最后利用数据聚类、神经网络和统计分析将车型分为客车、货车。2008 年，沈勇武等[21]认为车辆的外围形状能够区分不同的车型，利用改进的线求和投影法提取 8 个车辆轮廓特征参数，增加了长宽高之间的对比来描述车辆的形状特征，分类器设计采用基于 BP 神经网络对《收费公路车辆通行费车型分类》中的四类车型进行分类实验，正确率能都达到 81%。2009 年，廖海斌等[22]综合分析了常用的从车辆顶部、侧面、正面三种三维特征提取的方法，提出了一种从车辆前上方提取特征的方法，该方法通过二维到三维的维度变换，同时提取出车辆的长宽高三维信息和车牌信息，基于灰色关联分析进行大型车、中型车和小型车的分类，识别率超过 90%，且识别率与识别时间均优于 BP 神经网络和 SVM。上述方法中车辆参数均是从特定摄像头架设角度拍摄的二维图片中提取的，分类效果很大程度取决于参数，如前者存在 6%的误差。2010 年，马蓓等[23]通过背景差分等预处理提取出候选区域后，采用主成分变换定位出车型识别区域，在此基础上通过灰度共生矩阵的纹理分析提出了特征脸（Eigenfaces），然后利用灰度共生矩阵提取 5 个纹理特征值作为输入向量，最后基于最小距离判断规则设计分类器进行车型识别，实验数据显示该车型识别方法简便、快捷、有效，但是基于灰度共生矩阵的方法也存在存储空间大、实时性差等问题。2011 年，刘海明等[24]基于车脸中的特征区域进行车型识别，由于不同的车型都具有不同的排气口及车标，而排气口很可能包含车标，则选取特征区域为车辆的排气口和车标。然后根据双阈值将特征区域分割为三个部分，即车标、排气口的左边部分和右边部分，提取灰度特征和尺度空间特征。排气口部分采用简单的二值图像的相同点所占的比例作为匹配，利用 SIFT 特征提取车标，最后采用最邻近法计算向量空间距离，进行最终的 5 种车型分类，识别率达到 80%左右，识别精度易受车标定位精度影响，对含有车标污染等的噪声情况不具有健壮性。

国内研究机构和学者对车辆品牌识别技术进行了研究。2009 年，王玫等[25]在车牌和车标定位识别的基础上，截取车灯垂直幅值倍数的水平宽度作为精确车型有效区域，综合车标识别的车系和车灯识别出车辆具体车型，使用图像的不变矩距离分类器进行前车车灯识别，准确率达到 95.5%，但是该方法进行测试的样本量较少，且车灯定位精度易受车标定位和噪声（例如车头装饰物）等影响。2012 年，马军等[26]主要从轿车局部区域尾灯进行车型分类研究，采用变分水平集方法对轿车图像进行分割，提取出三个特征参数用于描述尾灯区域轮廓宽高比、矩形度和分散度，然后利用支持向量机对 31 种不同轿车车型进行分类与识别，实验结果显示准确率达到 100%。但是同样受噪声影响，还需要进一步研究提高车灯分割自动化程度，使其自动定位并准确提取。

国外研究机构和学者对车型识别进行了研究。2007 年，Kazemi 和 Samadi 等[27]采用 k-邻近（k-NN）分类器对比分析了 Fourier、Wavelet、Curvelet 变换，结果显示 Curvelet 变换可以提取到较好的特征，5 种车辆品牌的整体识别率超过 95%；缺点是特征维数较高。2012 年，Hu 和 Ye 等[28]提取了整个车身部分的 HOG 特征和多尺度下的 Harr 特征，利用 AdaBoost 将弱分类器集成为强分类器。结果显示大型车与小型车的识别率分别达到 93.3%和 98%。2014 年，Zhang 和 Zhou 等[29]提取了车身 EOH 特征，提出了一种新的分类方式，该方法由 k-均值聚类、SOM 和神经气体组成的混合模式来实现集群和内核自协助（KAA），实验表明 4 类车型的识别率可以达到 95%的准确率和 98%的可靠性。

国外研究机构和学者对车辆品牌识别技术进行了研究。2004 年，Petroviv 和 Cootes[30]基于车脸区域采用距离测量的分类方法对比分析了多种刚性结构特征，如局部归一化梯度（Locally Normed Grads）、边缘方向图（Edge Orientation）、Sobel 边缘响应、光谱相位图、Harris 角点等多种特征，结果显示基于梯度计算得到的特征如 SMG（Square Mapped Gradient）获得的精度更高，因为这种特征所包含的轮廓边缘和方向信息独立于车辆颜色，35 种车辆品牌的整体分类精度达 93.3%。2006 年，Negri 和 Clady 等[31]提出了利用面向轮廓点来描述车辆品牌的分类方法，通过阈值处理后的直方图中提取了面向轮廓点的权矩阵，然后采用基于投票算法的判断函数进行分类，20 类车辆品牌的分类精度达到 92.4%，结果显示面向轮廓点的特征对车脸的局部遮挡有健壮性。2008 年，Clady 和 Negri 等[32]利用车辆前脸区域提取了基于轮廓点的 6 个矩阵，然后设定判断函数将基于分类器的三个投票机制的结果与误差距离联系起来形成分类得分，采用了两层分类策略，最后用最邻近法生成最终分类结果，50 类车型识别率达 90%。2011 年，Zhuyu 和 Tianmin 等[33]基于 Gabor 小波的车辆识别算法，提出了与隐马尔科夫模型（HMM）车辆检测相结合的算法，然后通过主成分变换降维，15 种车辆品牌的识别率最高可达 96%以上。2012 年，Daya 和 Akoum 等[34]利用车牌作为参考标准提取了车脸区域，主要包括车灯、车标、车牌、保险杠等作为车辆类型的识别范围，利用多层神经网络提取了用于识别车型的 3 个全局特征，实验结果显示 9 种车辆品牌的识别率达到 95%，这说明局部车脸的几何特征可以对车型识别达到很好的描述。2013 年，Zhang 等[35]研究了 21 种车辆品牌的识别方法，提出了一种基于拒绝机制的级联分类器集成的高可靠性分类器，特征选择的是 Gabor 特征和 PHOG 特征作为分类器的输入。首先第一层集成包含多个分类器，如 k-NN、MLP、SVM 和 RF。通过由一个集成元学习方法 RF 的基 MLP 进行第二层集成，分类器的可靠性进一步得到增强。最后通过多数投票得到一个高信心的测量结果来滤除不确定的样本从而建立拒绝机制。实验结果显示在拒绝率为 2.5%下分类精度达到 98.65%，这表明该种级联分类器集成具有高可靠性，有潜在的实际应用价值。2012 年，Zhang 和 Zhou 等[36]提出了一种基于分类矢量量化（Classified Vector Quantization，CVQ）的车辆品牌分类方法，该方法首先提取 Harr 特征和 HOG 特征作为特征输入向量，通过高效的神经学习算法如 k-均值聚类、SOM、NG 算法生成每个类别的码本，然后通过广义最近邻进行比较，引入拒绝机制进行决策。2013 年，Zhang 等在上文的基础上引入了信心机制，实验结果显示该方法增加了 CVQ 分类的可靠性，在拒绝率为 8%时分类精度达到 95%，在拒绝率为 20%时分类精度达到 98%。

1.3　车辆行为感知理论与技术的研究现状

城市交通场景中的车辆异常行为主要包括非法占道、逆向行驶、车辆压线、闯红灯、违章变道、超速行驶等。目前对于车辆异常违章行为的检测方式主要有感应线圈检测、激光检测和微波检测等。感应线圈检测在车辆违章行为中应用很广，它是应用了电磁感应原理，在路下面埋上线圈，并通有一定电流，当车辆经过感应线圈时，会切割磁感线，造成回路电感量的变化，以此来检测出车辆通过和存在的信息，它主要应用于车辆闯红灯行为，具有性能稳定、精度高等优点，但缺点就是破坏路面，影响道路寿命。激光检测主要应用于车速检测方面，采用激光测距原理，主要包括激光发射器和接收器等硬件设备，通过对被测物体发射激光光束，并进而对该光束的反射波接收以记录时间差，从而确定被测物体与测试地点的距离，并最终得到该物体的移动速度。对于微波检测来说，其硬件系统主要由发射天线和接收器构成，其工作原理是当被测物体通过检测区域时，覆盖检测区域发射天线发射的微波波速会以不同的频率返回到天线，并被接收器接收，检测器通过这种频率的变化来判断被测车辆是否通过。这几种检测方式虽然得到一定应用，但容易被干扰，而且检测区域受限，并且只适用于闯红灯、超速等个别车辆异常行为的检测。

随着近年来智能交通领域新型技术的兴起，人们开始将计算机视觉、图像处理等技术应用到车辆违章检测领域。在车辆及其异常行为检测方面，1998 年，Alan[37]等人提出一种端到端的方法从连续视频流中提取运动目标，并且进行跟踪。他们通过连续图像帧的像素差来检测到运动目标，通过 classification 度量和时态约束一致性将行人、车辆等目标分类。最终结合时间差分法和模板匹配对车辆目标进行跟踪。2002 年，Lin[38]设计了一套可以对车辆闯红灯、速度违章、停止线违章及跟踪个别车辆的系统。通过双摄像头来检测违规行为，一个模拟摄像机用于实时跟踪，另一个数字相机用于车牌读取。并且系统与交通信号系统控制相连，来监测每个红灯、绿灯的相位。并通过两个道路循环对车辆路径和速度进行检测。最终由行驶轨迹、标线位置、信号灯状态和车速来判断车辆是否违章。实验表明该系统具有良好的健壮性。2009 年，Zhang[39]等人设计了一套在交叉路口环境下对违章车辆进行识别和跟踪的监控系统，该算法通过静态背景的混合高斯模型并使用 Hough 变换检测出道路标线，从监控图像中得到协调序列。车辆信息由背景帧差法获得，并由车辆与标线的距离和均值漂移法分别对违章车辆进行检测和跟踪。实验结果表明该方法的检测精度达 80%以上。2010 年,Iswanjono[40]等人基于 RFID 技术通过 Scilab 仿真模拟对交叉路口的红绿灯违章进行了检测,并对车流量做出了预测。该方法通过对车辆身份证标签在阅读器的移动来检测信号灯违章,通过 RFID 阅读器形成的通道距离对车辆进行预测,实验证实了该方法的检测精度。2011 年,Zhao[41]等人提出了一种在城市交通道路下基于视频的车辆追尾检测方法,基于道路交通中对违法停车的规定,作者提出了在实时视频中交通信号灯检测、车辆跟踪分析和道路拥堵检测等算法。通过测量车辆眼轨迹、速度和交通状况等用于交通违章行为的识别。该算法在实际道路上达到 90%的正确率。2012 年,Kato[42]等人通过使用多元线性关系的时空图像提取出群体行为中的车辆异常运动,当多台摄像机以不同速度在不同方向上平移运动时,多元线性时空图像才会成立。一旦车辆运动异常,将会出现速度不均的平移运动。基于此种属性,Kato SARUWATARI 通过真实场景图片检测出车辆转弯、横向运动等车辆异常运动。2013 年,对于发生红灯停止线前的违章变道行为,Klubsuwan[43]基于车辆在感兴趣区域的移动和均方位移(MSD)方法,并结合多车辆轨迹行为的评估对车辆闯红灯和变道进行检测。实验表明该方法具有较高的检测精度。2015 年,Aaron[44]等人提出了一种检测交通违章转弯和阻塞人行道机器视觉算法,通过背景差分法和系统遗传算法来检测这些行为。实验结果表明该系统适用于实时的交通检测系统。

在国内,2004 年,Jen-Chao Tai[45]等人通过在实时位置建立活动轮廓模型得到汽车的位置,然后通过 Kalman 滤波对车辆进行跟踪。使用一个特殊电路板以及一个独立图像跟踪器等硬件设备构建自动交通监控系统。系统结果表明,对于多车道上的车辆其有良好的跟踪性能。2006 年,佟守愚[46]对于交通违章行为,先选用中值滤波、增强模板和形态学边缘检测对交通场景图像进行预处理,在背景差分算法的基础上,提出了基于形态学边缘检测和背景差分结合的车辆检测算法,并在充分研究违章车辆信息的基础上,提出了基于颜色的违章车辆数据库检索方法,通过背景更新、阈值选取和阴影处理等技术,对闯红灯、违章超速和违章右转有较高的检测性能,但在复杂交通场景下,系统性能还有待进一步提高。2009 年,袁涛[47]在基于帧间差分的运动车辆检测算法上,通过车身与车宽的投影面积来消除非汽车和行人的运动影响。对于轨迹跟踪,作者通过计算运动车辆质心、运动车辆轨迹和中心线的夹角变化趋势以及运动车辆轨迹和中心线的相对近端距离的变化趋势来确定车辆的运动线路。最后作者通过基于颜色车牌、数学形态学方法和面积匹配的车辆车牌定位法来确定车牌。2009 年,西华大学的骆迪[48]采用背景差分法提取出运动目标,设定 Otsu 阈值选取法将差分图像二值化,并在后面处理中提出一种邻域统计方法去除噪声,对车辆逆行和闯红灯行为进行检测。2012 年,付城[49]等人提出了一种基于混合高斯模型和 CPU 的车辆闯红灯检测算法。先用时间均值法对根据监控系统运行的第一个红灯期间采集的视频数据构建背景图像,再利用背景图像初始化混合高斯模型参数,进而检测运动车辆,并通过 CPU 并行计算实现实时检测。实验表明该算法具有良好的实时性。2012 年,叶荣炬、李振龙、陈阳舟[50]等人采用多高斯背景模型提取出前景运动车辆及其质心,并利用 Kalman 滤波算法跟踪运动车辆,以此得到行驶车辆的时空图。通过车辆时空图对车辆轨迹进行确定分析,根据时间序列上车辆位置的变化检测车辆逆行等异常行为。2012 年,Sang Haifeng[51]等人采用背景差分法来检测运动车辆,背景差分法就是选择一参考帧作为背景图像,再用当前帧与背景帧作差分运算,如果背景帧选取得当,便可分割出运行物体。同时建立信息链跟踪车辆库来对车辆进行跟踪和行为判别，该方法很好地解决了传统方法中失去检测盒错误匹配的问题，并且能准确地计算交通流。2012年，蔡英凤[52]等人提出基于视频的虚拟传感器的设计方案，运用带有时间和空间信息的车辆轨迹对针对自组织神经网络进行训练，通过概率模型对车辆轨迹进行提取，所提算法可对超低（高）速行驶、违章停车、违规调头等异常行为实行有效监控，且系统具有直观、安装方便和维护费用低等优点。2013年，长沙理工大学的熊金艳[53]提出了一种HSV颜色空间分析和灰度帧差统计的混合检测法，以车辆左侧车轮为研究对象，建立车轮与黄线间的车辆–黄线位置模型，采用Camshift-kalman算法滤波对车辆运动过程进行跟踪判断，以此检测车辆是否压线违章。2013年，王会[54]通过背景差分、二值化、数学形态学处理等，检测运动车辆，还提出了一种自适应阈值算法，来检验算法有效性。在对车辆运动轨迹分析的基础上，对超速、闯红灯、逆行、违章停车四种行为检测，效果良好。2013年，西南大学的冯春贵[55]通过在限速牌上设置RFID标签，在车载系统上安装RFID读取装置来比较路段的限速，来检测车辆是否超速。2014年，曹凯[56]等人采用多隐马尔可夫的建模方法，识别和预测交通场景中车辆的机动行为；通过使用Baum-Welch算法和前向算法，以生成模型训练和模型评价两种输入数据；并采用机动驾驶模拟方法，建立车辆机动行为数据库，提高了HMM参数的学习效率。实验结果表明该方法具有较高的准确率。

1.4　车辆检索理论与技术的研究现状

从20世纪70年代起，许多科研机构和高校实验室相继开展了图像检索技术的研究，发展到90年代，出现了基于图像语义的检索技术[57]，相关检索技术及理论方法陆续被应用到商业的检索系统中。例如，国际商业机器公司旗下的Almanden实验室开发的QBIC[58]系统、Virage公司开发的VISE（the Virage Image Search Engine）图像搜索引擎[59]、麻省理工学院媒体实验室研制的Photobook[60]图像搜索引擎和谷歌公司开发的VideoGoogle[61]视频检索系统，在国内，"浙江大学视觉感知教育部–微软重点实验室"研究了WebscopeCBVR[62]图像检索系统等。QBIC系统的全称是Query By Image Content，是第一个在商业上成功应用的基于内容的图像信息检索系统，该系统提供的检索条件包括物体的颜色、形状和纹理属性，与此同时该系统还提供多种检索方式供用户选择，例如，根据输入查询图像或者手绘图像，通过设置分析图像的颜色百分比和形状特征查找目标图像，系统将返回符合用户要求的检索结果。Virage[59]系统支持通过纹理、形状和颜色进行图像的搜索的功能，在查询中也可以分配各个特征的权重。Photobook[60]系统提供基于纹理、形状和面部特征进行图像搜索，用户可以根据自己的需要选择这三个特征检索图片。VideoGoogle[61]视频检索系统主要满足用户在视频中检索和定位所描述发生的事件对象，该系统利用镜头的视频时间连续性跟踪对象以抑制不稳定的区域和噪声的影响，检索机理与文本检索相类似，运用预处理好的特征描述符并用倒排文件系统和文档排名进行视频的检索，可以作为感兴趣的检索对象包括人或者物体，由于与文本检索相类似，所以该系统的检索速度非常快。WebScopeCBVR[62]系统提供了通过关键字及视频片段作为检索对象的检索方式，用户可以选择输入包含与视频内容相匹配的关键字或者包含数帧的视频片段，然后系统会输出与输入关键字或者视频匹配度最高的视频。

目前，国外研究人员及机构相继开展了基于纹理特征的图像检索技术的研究，1996 年，B.S. Manjunathi 等[63, 64]提出了一种基于 Gabor 小波的纹理特征提取方法，并将其应用于图像数据的检索中，与传统的 PWT（Pyramid-structured Wavelet Transform）特征、TWT（Tree Wavelet Transform）特征和 MRSAM（Multi-Resolution Simultaneous Autoregressive Model）特征进行了对比实验。1997 年，Madirakshi 等[65]提出了一种基于颜色的多相检索系统 FOCUS（Fast Object Color-based qUery System），该系统第一相匹配的是图像的颜色直方图，第二相匹配的是图像颜色的区域空间关系，该系统的图像查全率和查准率分别达到 90% 和 75%。2002 年，Minh 等[66]提出了一种小波纹理特征提取方法，该方法根据 Kullback-Leibler 距离计算特征之间的相似度进行图像检索。2009 年，Daniele[67]对比分析了颜色特征在图像检索中的效果，实验结果表明基于全局的 HSV 空间在不同亮度和对比度下具有最出色的检索效果。2010 年，Lisa[68]提出了一种基于监控视频的车辆检索方法，该方法约束了基于报警的车辆检测分析条件及限制了车辆姿态和光照变化，实验结果表明，颜色相关图具有较好的检索效果。2012 年，Rogerio[69~71]提出了一种基于语义属性的车辆检索方法，该方法利用车辆的颜色、运行方向、速度和长宽等特征进行检索，同时，自由形状空间学习的方法被应用于解决不同车型问题。2012 年，Tsai 等[72]为了解决视野角度、光照和背景的变化问题，采用 ASM（Active Shape Model）算法将车辆三维模型拟合到二维空间图像，并提取车辆的格栅、大灯和车轮的 SIFT 和 PHOG 特征和曼哈顿距离进行车辆图像检索。2013 年，Thitiphat[73]采用 MSERs 算法进行车牌的定位，根据车牌坐标定位车标和特征脸的候选区域，并采用特征脸及其 PHOG 特征进行车辆检索，其查全率和查准率分别达到 86.7% 和 80%。2015 年，Bashirahamad 等[74]采用 Haar 特征及 Adaboost 分类器检测车辆，并根据车辆的颜色、运行速度和方向等特征进行车辆的检索，实验结果表明，采用车辆颜色和运行方向的查准率分别为 72%、92%。

车辆图像检索技术是图像检索技术研究的一个分支方向，目前，国内车辆图像检索技术的研究主要针对图片数据和视频数据两种，这两种数据检索方法的研究主要区别在于车辆检测技术的不同及提取目标特征的微小差别，视频数据不仅可以提取车辆的固有属性特征，同时也能够提取出车辆的运动轨迹特征，但是图片数据不能提取出车辆的运动特征。

2006 年，Zhang 等[75]提出了一种基于小波描述子及 R-树索引的分层图像检索模型，并将其应用于车辆图像检索中。2009 年，Chen 等[76]提出了一种利用颜色特征和多实例学习的车辆图像检索方法，该方法基于颜色变换模型来提取车辆特征，并采用 MIL 方法精确定位图像中的车辆，实验结果表明基于颜色特征的车辆检索系统具有较好的适用性和精确度。2010 年，夏等[77]采用经典背景差进行运动车辆的检测，提出了一种基于车辆外观颜色、外轮廓几何参数等特征的车辆检索方法。2011 年，LI 等[78]提出了一种基于车辆车牌识别的车辆检索系统，该系统首先从视频中检测包含车辆牌照字符的关键帧，并利用改进的雷登变化校正车牌，用户可以根据自己的需要在数据库中检索所需要的车辆图片。2011 年，Liu 等[79]研发了一种基于视频的物体颜色、型号和运动轨迹的检索系统，用户通过选择颜色或者型号来检索所需要的目标，实验结果表明该系统提供了一种有效的物体索引和检索方法。2011 年，梁等[80]研发了一种基于交通场景视频的车辆图像分析与检索系统，该系统首先提取待检索车辆图像的 SIFT 特征，系统将提取输入的待检索的车辆图像的 SIFT 特征，并采用 Bloom Filter 海量数据处理算法进行查找匹配，最后利用倒排文件技术实现图像的模糊检索。2012 年，Wu 等[81]提出了一种基于融合特征的车辆检索方法，该方法首先采用车辆颜色直方图进行粗略检索，其次采用车辆的 SIFT 特征进行精细检索，最后采用第一步的粗略检索和第二步的精细检索进行综合评估实现。实验结果表明对于车辆等刚性物体检索的精确率达到 99%，而对于行人等非刚性物体的检索精确率达到 95%。2012 年，王等[82]提出了一种基于多监控录像的车辆检索方法，该方法将车辆检索与地图匹配结合起来，并在地图上显示出车辆路径。

2013 年，Lin 等[83]提出了采用三维模型进行车辆的检索。2013 年，刘等[84]研发了一种基于车辆特征的交通视频检索系统，该系统采用基于背景建模的背景差方法检测运动物体并采用车辆外观颜色、轮廓几何特征和车辆的运行轨迹等特征进行目标检索，实验结果表明，该系统具有较高的查全率，但查准率还有待提高。2014 年，Pei[85]等采用词袋的方法进行车辆的检索，hessian-affine 检测器被用来检测车辆的特征，并采用 "TF-IDF" 方法计算每两张图片的余弦相似度及排序。2014 年，Nilsson[86]等采用相机校正和分割算法检测车辆，并基于三维车辆模型地面的采样搜索空间检索车辆，其检索精确率达到了 91.4%。2014 年，鲁等[87]提出了一种基于交通视频的车辆检索方法，该方法采用 SIFT 实现车辆特征提取及车辆检索。2013 年，魏等[88]研发了一种基于角度判别的车辆视频检索系统，该系统基于 SIFT（尺度不变特征变换）特征提取提出了一种 B-SIFT（分块不变特征变换）算法，实验结果表明，分块 B-SIFT 具有较高的检索率。2014 年，张等[89]提出一种基于改进的 SURF 算法的交通视频车辆检索方法，该算法包括 FAST（Features From Accelerated Segment Test）特征点的检测、SURF 特征向量提取及特征点的匹配，根据待检索图像与库中所有车辆图像之间的相似度并进行排序，实验结果表明，该方法能够较准确地检索并反馈结果。

参考文献

[1] Sun Z, Bebis G, Miller R. On-road vehicle detection: a review [J] .IEEE Transactions Pattern Analysis and Machine Intelligence, 2006, 28 (5): 694-711.

[2] Gupte S, Masoud O, Martin R F K, et al. Detection and classification of vehicles [J]. IEEE Transactions on Intelligent Transportation Systems, 2002, 3 (1): 37-47.

[3] Foresti G L, Murino V, Regazzon C. Vehicle Recognition and Tracking from Road Image Sequences [J]. IEEE Transactions on Vehicular Technology, 1999, 48 (1): 301-318.

[4] Gao L, Li C, Fang T, Xiong Z. Vehicle detection based on color and edge information [J] .Lecture Notes in Computer Science, 2008, 5112/2008: 142-150.

[5] Guo D, Fraichard T, Xie M, et al. Color modeling by spherical influence field in sensing driving environment [C]. Intelligent Vehicles Symposium, 2000.

[6] Techawatcharapaikul C, Kaewtrakulpong P, Siddhichai S. Outdoor vehicle and shadow segmentation by temporal edge density information of adjacent frames [J]. Telecommunications and Information Technology, 2008, 1 (3): 433-436.

[7] Johansson B, Wiklund J, Forssén P, et al. Combining shadow detection and simulation for estimation of vehicle size and position [J] .Pattern Recognition Letters, 2009, 30 (8): 751-759.

[8] Cucchiara R, Piccardi, M. Vehicle Detection under Day and Night Illumination [C]. International Conference on Networking, Sensing and Control, 1999.

[9] Kalinke T, Tzomakas C, von Seelen W. A texture based object detection and an adaptive model-based classification [J]. Proceedings of IEEE Intelligent Vehicles Symposium'98, 1998: 341-346.

[10] Kim K J, Park SM, Baek N. A texture-Based algorithm for vehicle area segmentation using the support vector machine Method [J] .Lecture Notes in Computer Science, 2007, 4482/2007: 542-549.

[11] Wu J, Zhang X, Zhou J. Vehicle detection in static road images with PCA and wavelet based classifier [C]. IEEE Intelligent Transportation Systems Proceedings, 2001.

[12] Sun Z, Bebis G, Miller R. On-road vehicle detection using Gabor filters and support vector machines[C]. International Conference on Digital Signal Processing, Greece, July 2002.

[13] Zielke T, Brauckmann M, Seelen W V. Intensity and edge-based symmetry detection with an application to car-following [J]. Image Understanding, 1993,58 (2): 177-190.

[14] Du Y, Papanikolopoulos N P. Real-time vehicle following through a novel symmetry-based approach [J]. In: Proceedings of 1997 IEEE International Conference on Robotics and Automation, 1997,4: 3160-3165.

[15] Bin D, Yajun F, Tao W. A vehicle detection method via symmetry in multi-scale windows[C]. IEEE Conference on Industrial Electronics and Applications, 2007.

[16] Teoh S S, Bräunl T. Symmetry-based monocular vehicle detection system [J]. Machine Vision and Applications, 2012,23 (5): 831-842.

[17] Viola P, Jones M. Robust Real-time Object Detection [J]. International Journal of Computer Vision, 2004,57 (2): 137-154.

[18] Dalal N, Triggs B. Histogram of oriented gradients for human detection [C]. IEEE Computer Society Conference on Computer Vision and Pattern Recognition, Montbonnot, France, 2005,1.

[19] Chang C, Wang C, Lien J. Multi-view vehicle detection using gentle boost with sharing hog features [C]. Computer Vision, Graphics and Image Processing, Taiwan, 2009.

[20] 李国强. 基于图像处理技术的车辆分类研究[D]. 西安: 长安大学, 2007.

[21] 沈勇武. 基于图像识别的车型自动分类系统[D]. 杭州: 浙江大学, 2008.

[22] 廖海斌, 王伟, 王宏勇, 等. 基于灰色理论的车型自动分类识别[J]. 微计算机信息, 2009, (10):289-291.

[23] 马蓓. 车型识别技术在视频监控中的应用[D]. 西安: 西安电子科技大学, 2010.

[24] 刘海明. 基于车脸的精确车型识别研究[D]. 武汉: 武汉理工大学, 2011.

[25] 王玫, 王国宏, 于元港, 等. 新车型识别方法及其在套牌车辆鉴别中的应用[J]. 计算机工程与应用, 2009, 45 (17): 211-214.

[26] 马军, 贺俊吉, 史立, 等. 轿车局部区域特征提取与车型识别[J]. 工业控制计算机, 2012, 25 (8): 72-74.

[27] Kazemi F M, Samadi S, Poorreza H R, et al. Vehicle recognition based on fourier, wavelet

and curvelet transforms-a comparative study[C]. IEEE International Conference on Information Technology, 2007.

[28] Hu Y, He Q, Zhuang X, et al. Algorithm for vision-based vehicle detection and classification[C]. IEEE International Conference on Robotics and Biomimetics, 2013.

[29] Zhang B, Zhou Y, Pan H, et al. Hybrid model of clustering and kernel autoassociator for reliable vehicle type classification[J]. Machine vision and applications, 2014, 25 (2): 437-450.

[30] Petrovic V S, Cootes T F. Analysis of Features for Rigid Structure Vehicle Type Recognition[C]. BMVC, 2004.

[31] Negri P, Clady X, Milgram M, et al. An Oriented-Contour Point Based Voting Algorithm for Vehicle Type Classification[C]. Proceedings of the 18th International Conference on Pattern Recognition, 2006.

[32] Clady X, Negri P, Milgram M, et al. Multi-class vehicle type recognition system[M]. Artificial Neural Networks in Pattern Recognition. Springer Berlin Heidelberg, 2008.

[33] Zhuyu Z, Tianmin D, Xianyang L. Study for vehicle recognition and classification based on Gabor wavelets transform & HMM[C]. IEEE International Conference on Consumer Electronics, Communications and Networks, 2011.

[34] Daya B, Akoum A H, Bahlak S. Geometrical Features for Multiclass Vehicle Type Recognition Using MLP Network[J]. Journal of Theoretical & Applied Information Technology, 2012, 43 (2): 285-294.

[35] Zhang B. Reliable classification of vehicle types based on cascade classifier ensembles[J]. IEEE Transactions on Intelligent Transportation Systems, 2013, 14 (1): 322-332.

[36] Zhang B, Zhou Y, Pan H. Vehicle classification with confidence by classified vector quantization[J]. IEEE Intelligent Transportation Systems Magazine, 2013, 5 (3): 8-20.

[37] Lipton A J, Fujiyoshi H, Patil R S. Moving Target Classification and Tracking from Real-Time Video[C]. 4th IEEE Workshop on Applications of Computer Vision, 1998.

[38] Dae-Woon L, Sung-Hoon C, Joon-Suk J. automated detection of all kinds of violations at a street intersection using real time individual vehicle tracking[J]. Fifth IEEE Southwest Symposium on Image Analysis and Interpretation, 2002: 126-129.

[39] Zhang J, Gao T, Liu Z G. Traffic Video Based Cross Road Violation Detection[C]. ICMTMA 2009 International Conference on Measuring Technology and Mechatronics Automation, 2009.

[40] Iswanjono B. Budiardjo, K R. Simulation for RFID-Based Red Light Violation Detection: Violation Detection and Flow Prediction[C]. 2010 Second International Conference on Computer Research and Development, 2010.

[41] Zhao Q. Video Based Vehicle Tailgate Behavior Detection in Urban Road Junction[C]. 2011 International Conference on Future Computer Sciences and Application, 2011.

[42] SARUWATARI K, SAKAUE F, SATO J. Detection of Abnormal Driving using Multiple View Geometry in Space-Time[J]. 2012 Intelligent Vehicles Symposium. IEEE, 2012:

1102-1107.

[43] Klubsuwan K, Thailand B. Traffic Violation Detection Using Multiple Trajectories Evaluation of Vehicles[C]. 2013 4th International Conference on Intelligent Systems Modeling & Simulation, 2013.

[44] Aaron C P U, Rhen A B, Ana Rizza Q. Machine vision for traffic violation detection system through genetic algorithm[C]. 2015 International Conference on Humanoid, Nanotechnology, Information Technology, Communication and Control, Environment and Management, 2015.

[45] Jen-Chao T, Shung-Tsang T, Ching-Po L, Kai-Tai S. Real-time image tracking for automatic traffic monitoring and enforcement applications[J]. Image and Vision Computing 22, 2004: 485-501.

[46] 佟守愚. 基于视频技术的交通违章检测与识别理论及方法研究[D]. 长春: 吉林大学, 2006.

[47] 袁涛. 基于图像处理的车辆闯红灯自动检测技术研究[D]. 重庆: 重庆大学, 2009.

[48] 骆迪. 基于视频技术的车辆违章行为检测[D]. 成都: 西华大学, 2009.

[49] 付城, 贾年. 基于混合高斯模型和 CPU 的车辆闯红灯快速检测算法及实现[J]. 西华大学学报, 2012, 31 (2): 9-13.

[50] 叶荣炬, 李振龙, 陈阳舟. 一种基于车辆时空图的车辆异常行为检测方法[J]. 交通信息与安全, 2012, 30 (4): 89-98.

[51] Sang Haifeng, Wang Hui, Wu Danyang. Vehicle Abnormal Behavior Detection System based on Video[C]. Fifth International Symposium on Computational Intelligence and Design, 2012.

[52] 蔡英凤, 张为公, 王海. 基于视频的城市快速路车辆异常行为检测[J]. 现代交通技术, 2012, 9 (1): 60-63.

[53] 熊金艳. 基于视频处理的道路车辆违章检测[D]. 长沙: 长沙理工大学, 2013.

[54] 王会. 基于视频的车辆异常行为检测[D]. 沈阳: 沈阳工业大学, 2013.

[55] 冯春贵. 基于 RFID 的车辆超速自动监测系统设计[D]. 重庆: 西南大学, 2013.

[56] 曹凯, 于善义, 于少伟. 基于多隐马尔可夫模型的车辆机动行为识别和预测[J]. 信息与控制, 2014, 43 (4): 506-512.

[57] Yong R, Huang T S, Chang S F. Image Retrieval: Current Techniques, Promising Directions, and Open Issues [J]. Journal of Visual Communication & Image Representation, 1999, 10 (1): 39-62.

[58] Flickner M, Sawhney H, Niblack W, et al. Yanker query by image and video content: the qbic system[J]. Computer, 2001, 28 (9): 255-264.

[59] Bach J R, Fuller C, Gupta A, et al. Virage image search engine: an open framework for image management[C]. Storage and Retrieval for Still Image and Video Databases IV, 1996.

[60] Pentland A, Picard R W, Sclaroff S. Photobook: Content-Based Manipulation of Image Databases[J]. International Journal of Computer Vision, 1996, 18 (3): 233-254.

[61] Sivic J, Zisserman A. Video Google: A Text Retrieval Approach to Object Matching in

Videos[C]. IEEE Computer Society, 2003.

[62] Wu Yi, Zhuang Yue-ting, Pan Yun-he. Image retrieval system for Web: Webscope-CBIR[C]. IEEE Computer Society, 2000.

[63] Manjunath B S, Ma W Y. Texture Features for Browsing and Retrieval of Image Data[J]. IEEE Transactions on Pattern Analysis & Machine Intelligence, 1996, 18 (8): 837-842.

[64] Movellan J R. Tutorial on Gabor Filters[J]. Open Source Document, 2002.

[65] Madirakshi D, Edward M. R, Bruce A. Draper. FOCUS : Searching for Multi-colored Objects in a Diverse Image Database[C]. IEEE Computer Society Conference on Computer Vision and Pattern Recognition, 1997.

[66] Do M N, Martin V. Wavelet-based texture retrieval using generalized Gaussian density and Kullback-Leibler distance[J]. IEEE Transactions on Image Processing A Publication of the IEEE Signal Processing Society, 2002, 11 (2): 146-158.

[67] Borghesani D, Grana C, Cucchiara R. Color Features Performance Comparison for Image Retrieval[C].Image Analysis and Processing—ICIAP 2009, Italy, September 8-11, 2009, Proceedings. 2009.

[68] Brown L M. Example-Based Color Vehicle Retrieval for Surveillance[C]. IEEE International Conference on Advanced Video & Signal Based Surveillance. IEEE Computer Society, 2010.

[69] Feris R, Siddiquie B, Zhai Y, et al. Attribute-based vehicle search in crowded surveillance videos[C].Proceedings of the 1st ACM International Conference on Multimedia Retrieval. ACM, 2011.

[70] Feris R S, Siddiquie B, Petterson J, et al. Large-Scale Vehicle Detection, Indexing, and Search in Urban Surveillance Videos[J]. IEEE Transactions on Multimedia, 2012, 14 (1): 28-42.

[71] Feris R, Pankanti S, Siddiquie B. Learning Detectors from Large Datasets for Object Retrieval in Video Surveillance[C]. 2012 IEEE International Conference on Multimedia and Expo. IEEE, 2012.

[72] Tsai M K, Lin Y L, Hsu W, et al. Content-based vehicle retrieval using 3D model and part information[C]. Acoustics, Speech, and Signal Processing, 1988. ICASSP-88., 1988 International Conference on, 2012.

[73] Anakavej T, Kawewong A, Patanukhom K. Internet-Vision Based Vehicle Model Query System Using Eigenfaces and Pyramid of Histogram of Oriented Gradients[C]. Proceedings of the 2013 International Conference on Signal-Image Technology & Internet-Based Systems. IEEE Computer Society, 2013.

[74] Momin B F, Mujawar T M. Vehicle detection and attribute based search of vehicles in video surveillance system[C]. Circuit, Power and Computing Technologies (ICCPCT), 2015 International Conference on IEEE, 2015.

[75] Zhang H M, Wang Q H, Kan Y X, et al. Researches on Hierarchical Image Retrieval Model Based on Wavelet Descriptor and Indexed by Half-Axes-Angle using R-Tree[C]. Machine Learning and Cybernetics, 2006 International Conference on IEEE, 2006.

[76] Chen S Y, Hsieh J W, Wu J C, et al. Vehicle Retrieval Using Eigen Color and Multiple Instance Learning[C].Intelligent Information Hiding and Multimedia Signal Processing, 2009. IIH-MSP '09. Fifth International Conference on IEEE, 2009.

[77] 夏洁. 交通视频中机动车辆检索关键技术研究[D]. 苏州: 苏州大学, 2010.

[78] Li X C, Li C H, Xie Y. A retrieval system of vehicles based on recognition of license plates[C].Machine Learning and Cybernetics (ICMLC), 2011 International Conference on IEEE, 2011.

[79] Liu C, Chen G, Ma Y, et al. A system for indexing and retrieving vehicle surveillance videos[C].Image and Signal Processing (CISP), 2011 4th International Congress on IEEE, 2011.

[80] 梁旭. 交通视频中的车辆分析与特征检索[D]. 杭州: 杭州电子科技大学, 2011.

[81] Wu J, Zhao Y and Zhang X, et al. A Cascaded Retrieval Method of Specified Object Based on Fusing Multiple Features[C]. 2012 Third Global Congress on Intelligent Systems, 2012.

[82] 王春明, 李会茹, 刘伟. 一种多个监控录像中的车辆检索方法. CN102799618A[P]. 2012.

[83] Lin Y L, Tsai M K, Hsu W H, et al. Investigating 3-D Model and Part Information for Improving Content-Based Vehicle Retrieval[J]. IEEE Transactions on Circuits & Systems for Video Technology, 2013, 23 (3): 401-413.

[84] 刘洋. 基于车辆特征的交通视频检索[D]. 长沙: 湖南大学, 2013.

[85] Pei W, An Z J, Zhu Y Y, et al. A rapid vehicle recognition and retrieval system[C].Systems and Informatics (ICSAI), 2014 2nd International Conference on IEEE, 2014.

[86] Nilsson M, Ardo H. In search of a car utilizing a 3D model with context for object detection[C].2014 International Conference on Computer Vision Theory and Applications (VISAPP). IEEE Computer Society, 2014.

[87] 鲁建飞. 监控视频快速车辆检索算法研究[D]. 无锡: 江南大学, 2014.

[88] 魏寻源. 基于角度判别的车辆视频检索[D]. 长沙: 中南大学, 2013.

[89] 张子龙, 薛静, 乔鸿海, 等. 基于改进 SURF 算法的交通视频车辆检索方法研究[J]. 西北工业大学学报, 2014 (2): 297-302.

第 2 章

交通场景中车辆检测理论与技术

本章主要研究内容为：首先提出一种新的车辆区域检测方法，确定车型识别感兴趣区域（ROI）；其次，分析车辆图像数据来源、筛选及预处理方法。对于一幅输入的监控图像，研究定位车辆所在位置的方法。分析车辆几何、颜色及纹理特征，进而在现有检测方法的基础上改进车辆检测方法。根据车辆区域假设和验证步骤研究两类方法进行车辆区域检测：第一类是直接使用车辆先验知识，即车牌、车辆边缘和车辆对称特征进行检测，第二类是提取车辆特征并使用分类器进行车辆区域识别。通过分别研究基于车辆边缘、车牌、车辆对称特征、车辆纹理特征及车辆图像 Gabor 特征 5 种检测算法的检测效率和计算复杂度，分析得出适于智能交通车辆监控、车型识别及车辆分类的车辆区域定位方法。根据车辆区域包围框定位出能够表征车辆品牌和型号的区域，即车前脸区域。

2.1　车辆图像采集

进行模式识别需要大量的实验数据作为支撑，本章介绍本书所使用图像数据来源及筛选过程。同时，由于车辆类型识别是根据感兴趣区域（ROI）特征结合分类器实现的，车辆前脸（包括散热器，车标及车灯等）特征能够有效描述一辆车的类型信息，因此，我们首先研究了一种车辆区域定位方法，之后根据车牌位置和车辆前脸尺寸关系定位出感兴趣区域（ROI）。为了完成本书所涉及相关图像处理和模式识别相关算法的实验验证，我们需要准备一些车辆图像数据。苏州交通局独墅湖高教区分局为我们的科学研究提供了原始的图像数据，这些数据是由交通监控相机记录一个月所产生的。图像由安装在 10 个交叉口的 CCD 相机在每天 8:00—18:00 的时间段内触发获取，包含不同的天气及光照情况。从这些大量的图像数据中（每天数据>20 000），我们选取了包含 15 种品牌的 18 种车型共 4 500 张图片，这些车型包括奥迪（Audi）、别克（Buick）（2 种）、长安（Changan）、奇瑞（Chery）（2 种）、雪佛兰（Chevrolet）、雪铁龙（Citroen）、福特（Ford）、本田（Honda）、现代（Hyundai）（2 种）、马自达（Mazda）、日产（Nissan）、标志（Peugeot）、大众（Volkswagen）、丰田（Toyota）和五菱（Wulin）。其中，有些车型是同一品牌的不同类型，如现代索纳塔（Sonata）和现代伊兰特（Elantra），这两种车型的外观有很大不同。如果一些品牌的不同车型具有类似的外观，如 Audi A7 和 Audi A8，别克凯越（Excelle）和别克 Xt，我们将他们归为一种车型。所有图像数据均包含一辆正面车辆影像，车辆到摄像头的距离远近不一。原始图像的大小为 1 024mm×1 360mm，如图 2.1 所示为车辆部分图像数据。从图 2.1

中可得，大部分车辆外观不同，在车辆前部具有丰富的边缘信息。不同位置、角度、光照条件的车辆图像如图 2.2 所示，数据库中车辆图像具有很大的不同，主要表现在车辆位置、尺度、角度及光照等方面。

图 2.1   车辆部分图像数据

图 2.2   不同位置、角度、光照条件的车辆图像

在目标识别系统中有两个重要的问题需要解决，即目标区域检测和识别问题。在车型识别系统中，车辆区域的检测和定位尤其重要，这是由于车型识别是基于车辆感兴趣区域（前脸区域）进行的，因此本书首先研究一种车辆区域检测方法，并结合车辆区域和车牌位

置定位出车辆前脸区域作为车型识别系统的输入图像。

2.2　基于对称特征的车辆检测方法

以车辆轮廓竖直对称轴作为定位车辆区域是一种有效的检测方法，但车辆轮廓对称轴易受树木、道路标线等噪声的影响。本书根据车辆轮廓存在竖直对称轴和车牌存在水平和竖直对称轴的特点，首先检测车辆轮廓竖直对称轴，以车辆轮廓对称轴位置为参考检测车牌水平和竖直对称轴，最后根据所检测到的车牌水平和竖直对称轴进行车辆区域及车型识别感兴趣区域（ROI）定位。首先生成输入灰度图像的边缘图像，采用拉普拉斯算子进行车辆边缘检测，之后对边缘图像进行中值滤波，中值滤波结果在消除噪声的同时保存了图像中的细节部分。拉普拉斯算子是不依赖于边缘方向的二阶微分算子，对于数字图像，拉普拉斯变换可以借用模板实现，模板函数可以表示为：

$$G(i,j) = \left| 4f(i,j) - f(i+1,j) - f(i-1,j) - f(i,j+1) - f(i,j-1) \right| \tag{2-1}$$

式中：$G(i,j)$为将(i,j)处的像素值$f(i,j)$使用 Laplace 算子计算后的结果；图 2.3 为输入图像灰度化后使用 Laplace 算子进行边缘检测及滤波后的结果。

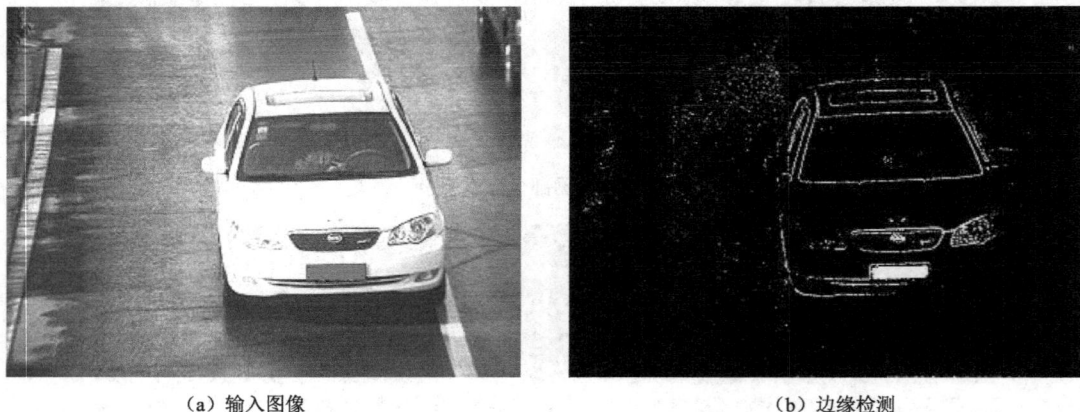

（a）输入图像　　　　　　　　　　　　（b）边缘检测

图 2.3　输入图像及车辆边缘检测结果

考虑到车辆区域在监控图像固定范围内，为减少运算量，图像边缘区域可以不做考虑，设置车辆对称轴搜索区域如图 2.4（a）所示，计算水平扫描线上每个像素点的对称值[1]：

$$V(x,y) = \sum_{x'=1}^{W/2} S(x,x',y') \tag{2-2}$$

$$S(x,x',y') = \begin{cases} 5, f(x-x',y') = f(x+x',y') = 255 \\ -1, f(x-x',y') \neq f(x+x',y') \\ 0, f(x-x',y') = f(x+x',y') = 0 \end{cases} \tag{2-3}$$

式中：$V(x,y)$为(x,y)处对称值；W为计算每个像素点对称值的幅宽，本书根据车辆图像的像素宽度假设为 300；x'为当前搜索水平扫描线上像素的横坐标；y'为当前水平扫描线上像素的纵坐标，每条扫描线上像素对称值的计算结果如图 2.4（b）所示。

根据车辆轮廓几何特征，车辆轮廓对称值在其竖直对称轴处最大而在车辆边缘处对称值最小，根据公式（2-4）计算每列对称值之和：

$$\mathrm{Vcol}(x) = \sum_{n=0}^{M} V(x, n * \mathrm{val}) \qquad (2\text{-}4)$$

（a）车辆对称轴搜索区域　　　　　　　　　　（b）扫描线对称值计算

图 2.4　车辆轮廓对称轴搜索区域及搜索区域内水平扫描线对称值计算

式中：val 为行距；$\mathrm{Vcol}(x)$ 为第 x 列对称值之和。对 $\mathrm{Vcol}(x)$ 进行排序，得到最大对称值 $\mathrm{Vcol}(x_m)$ 对应列 x_m 作为车辆轮廓的对称轴。

对称轴上决定对称值大小的像素点集中在车辆边缘信息最丰富的区域，如散热器、车灯所在区域，以此可以搜索对称轴上最大对称值区段，使用以下公式检索对称值最大区段：

$$\mathrm{Vcol}(x_m, n) = \sum_{n=i}^{i+5} V(x_m, n * \mathrm{val}), i = 1, 2, \cdots, M \qquad (2\text{-}5)$$

得到 $\mathrm{Vcol}(x_m, n)$ 最大时对应的扫描行 n_m，对应图像纵坐标为 $y_m = n_m * \mathrm{val}$。图 2.5（a）所示竖直线为实验车辆图像的对称轴，白色圆点 (x_m, y_m) 为对称值最大区段起始行，由计算结果可以看出对称轴上最大对称值区段所在行车辆轮廓信息最丰富。考虑到车辆轮廓丰富区域一般在车辆散热器和车灯等位置，本书以车辆轮廓对称轴上最大对称值区段起始行作为参考点，该参考点位于车牌上方且位置变化范围较大，若以该点作为车辆轮廓定位参考点则定位误差较大，可以此参考点为基准搜索车牌水平和竖直对称轴所在位置。

以参考点 (x_m, y_m) 作基准，在其下方搜索车牌水平和竖直对称轴。设参考点 (x_m, y_m) 到车辆轮廓对称轴搜索窗下边缘距离为 δ，车牌水平对称轴搜索区域为参考点到搜索下边缘距离 δ 的 $\beta_1 \sim \beta_2$ 倍，$\beta_1 = 0.2$，$\beta_2 = 0.8$，如图 2.5（b）中竖直扫描线区域。计算车牌水平对称轴搜索区域每条竖直扫描线上像素点对称值，将每行对称值之和最大行作为车牌水平对称轴，图 2.5（b）中水平线所示位置即车牌水平对称轴 y_s。

在由点 $(x_m - \delta_1, y_s - \delta_2)$ 和 $(x_m + \delta_1, y_s + \delta_2)$ 确定的矩形范围内搜索车牌竖直对称轴，与车牌水平对称轴计算方法相同，计算车牌竖直对称轴，图 2.5（b）中处于车辆轮廓对称轴右方的竖直线即为车牌竖直对称轴 x_s，车牌水平对称轴和竖直对称轴交点为 (x_s, y_s)。根据车辆对称轴和基准点假设车辆区域，假设车辆区域在由 $(x_s - w, y_s - h_t)$ 和 $(x_s + w, y_s + h_b)$ 确定的矩形包围框内。使用基于灰度积分投影的方法搜索车辆区域，边缘图像竖直及水平积分投影计算公式为：

$$v_i = \sum_{j=1}^{2w} f\left(x_i, y_j\right) \tag{2-6}$$

$$h_i = \sum_{i=1}^{h_b+h_t} f\left(x_i, y_j\right) \tag{2-7}$$

式中：$f(x,y)$是点(x,y)处的像素值。如图 2.6（a）所示为假设区域内车辆灰度水平和竖直投影直方图。分别计算竖直和水平积分投影的最大值 m_v 及 m_h，从上到下搜索水平投影目标像素个数超过阈值 $0.5\,m_h$ 的第一行作为上边界，从左到右搜索竖直投影目标像素个数超过阈值 $0.5\,m_v$ 的第一列作为左边界，使用同样的方法搜索得到右边界和下边界。如图 2.6（b）所示为车辆区域检测的最终结果。

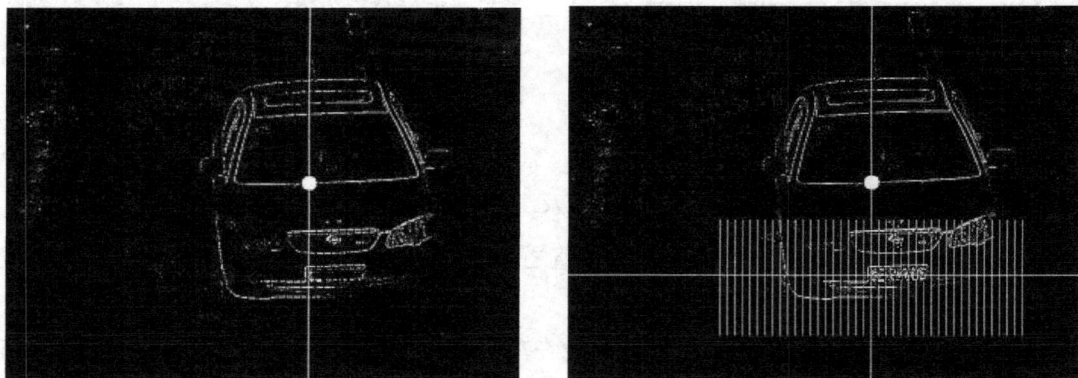

（a）轮廓对称轴　　　　　　　　　　　　（b）车牌对称轴确定

图 2.5　车辆轮廓对称轴及车牌对称轴搜索区域

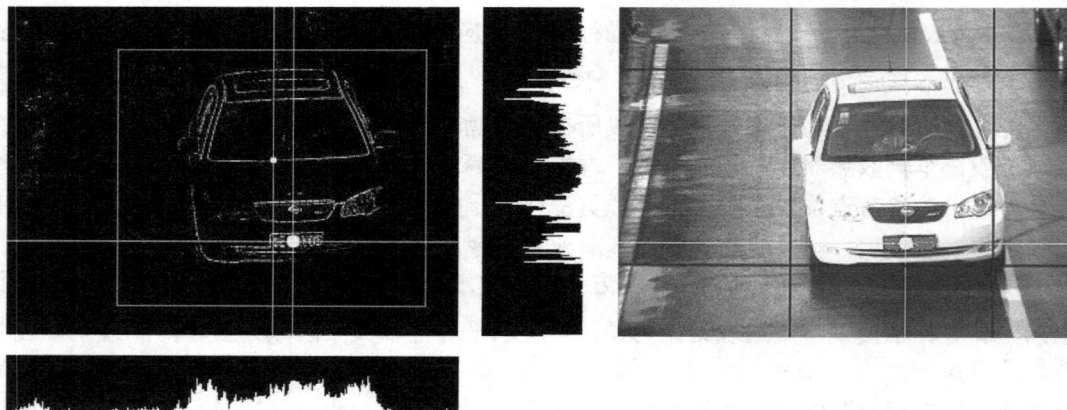

（a）车辆区域假设　　　　　　　　　　　　（b）车辆区域验证

图 2.6　车辆区域假设及车辆区域验证

2.3　其他车辆检测方法

作为与车辆对称特征检测方法的比较，本书分别使用其他 4 种方法进行车辆区域检测：第一类是直接使用车辆先验知识，即车牌、车辆边缘进行检测；第二类是首先提取车辆纹理、Gabor 特征，之后使用支持向量机（SVM）进行训练学习后进行车辆检测。

1. 基于边缘的车辆区域检测方法

Song[2]通过检测车辆虚拟上视图（virtual top-view）竖直边缘定位车辆边缘有效解决了远距离车辆边缘信息不足的问题。Ha[3]提出一种基于运动边缘检测的方法区分车辆边缘及车辆阴影边缘，有效消除了车辆阴影边缘对运动车辆追踪的影响。本书所用车辆图像使用拉普拉斯算子进行边缘检测在消除噪声的同时保存了车辆边缘，可以直接进行车辆区域搜索，使用灰度投影统计的方法搜索车辆轮廓区水平和竖直边缘。

根据行车原理，车辆靠右行驶，超车车辆在其左道行驶，监控相机所获图片右下方噪声比较少，因此可首先确定车辆区域矩形框右下角点。从下向上搜索水平投影目标像素个数超过阈值 T 的第一行作为下边界 y_b，从右向左搜索竖直投影目标像素个数超过阈值 T 的第一列作为右边界 x_r，将右下角点 (x_r, y_b) 作为参考点，假设车辆区域在由 $(x_r - w, y_b - h)$、(x_r, y_b) 两点确定的矩形包围框内（其中 w, h 分别为假设车辆区域的宽带和长度），之后在预选框内使用同样方法搜索上边界和左边界。

2. 基于车牌定位的车辆区域检测方法

Nikul[4]对图像进行形态学计算、YCbCr 颜色空间分割及边缘检测方法定位车牌区域，该方法能够有效检测印度车辆车牌区域。Zheng[5]使用竖直 Sobel 算子检测车辆图像竖直边缘并排除过长或过短的竖直边缘以筛选出车牌区域，通过对中文车牌检测实验表明该方法具有较好的健壮性。类似 Zheng[5]提出的方法，本书根据车牌区域灰度投影变化比较剧烈的特点，使用图像列与列相减的方法突出车牌区域，同时噪声点在相减的过程中得到削弱，列相减即计算图像水平方向的一阶差分：

$$f(i,j) = f(i, j+1) - f(i,j) \tag{2-8}$$

图像列与列相减后，将图像进行阈值化，阈值根据列相减后自身灰度分布确定，阈值为：

$$T = \frac{1}{2m} \sum_{i=1}^{m} \max f(x_i, y) \tag{2-9}$$

式中：m 为列数；$f(x,y)$ 为输入图像。统计边缘图像的灰度投影，从下往上搜索到第一行目标像素个数大于阈值 T 时作为车牌下边界 y_b，根据车牌高度估计上边界 y_t，之后在上下边界内使用同样方法搜索左边界 x_l 和右边界 x_r。根据车牌颜色 RGB 三分量差别较大的特点，在输入彩色图像中验证估计车牌区域内颜色差异较大的区域作为车牌的最终区域。车牌尺寸与车辆尺寸存在一定的比例关系，可以根据车牌位置和尺寸估计车辆区域。

3. 基于车辆纹理及支持向量机（SVM）的检测方法

将输入图像灰度化后网格化为 $M \times N$ 个尺寸为 $W \times H$ 的子图，将子图灰度级量化为 16级，提取每个窗口图像灰度共生矩阵，其灰度共生矩阵为 16×16 维，以列优先将其重排为256 维的支持向量机（SVM）[6, 7]输入向量，选取车辆区域和背景区域样本子图提取其纹理特征，使用支持向量机（SVM）进行训练。使用 SVM 训练结果对输入测试图像的每个子图像的灰度共生矩阵特征向量进行识别，判断每个矩形格是否属于车辆区域。由于相邻矩形格之间的灰度相关性，识别结果会产生一些噪声，通过计算所有被识别为车辆区域方格中心坐标的均值 (x_{mean}, y_{mean})，遍历每个被识别为车辆区域方格中心坐标 (x,y)，计算其与中心坐标 (x_{mean}, y_{mean}) 的距离：

$$\delta = \sqrt{\left(x_i - x_{\text{mean}}\right)^2 + \left(y_i - y_{\text{mean}}\right)^2} \tag{2-10}$$

真实车辆窗口应为与中心距离小于某阈值 T 的区域，若某窗口与中心距离较大则为噪声。

4. 基于 Gabor 特征及支持向量机（SVM）的检测方法

将输入车辆图像划分为 $M \times N$ 个网格，用 $m \times n$ 个网格表示车辆或背景区域，以行优先规则遍历每个 $m \times n$ 窗口，计算每个 $m \times n$ 窗口的 Gabor 响应特征，如取 $M=N=8$，$m=3$，$n=4$，则每幅图片共有 30 个子窗口。将每个子窗口中图像分布与 Gabor 滤波器函数[8, 9]计算卷积，得到每个窗口的 Gabor 响应，将 Gabor 响应的统计量均值、方差和偏态作为 Gabor 特征，假设使用 3 尺度、4 方向滤波器组，将每个滤波器与图像卷积，则特征向量维数为 $3 \times 4 \times 3 = 36$ 维。分别选取若干车辆区域和背景区域计算 Gabor 特征，将样本 Gabor 特征使用 SVM 进行训练，将每张测试图片的所有交叠窗口均作为假设车辆区域，使用 SVM 训练结果识别每张图片的 30 个子窗口，识别出车辆区域和背景区域。

2.4　感兴趣区域（ROI）定位

车辆引擎盖下方包含车标、车灯及散热器的前脸区域反映了车辆类型的主要信息，而不同类型车辆引擎盖上方的挡风玻璃部位则大同小异，因此车型分类的感兴趣区域（ROI）是车辆前脸区域。结合本章提出的对称轴检测方法及车牌检测方法定位车牌，首先定位到车牌对称中心，以对称中心假设车牌搜索区域，假设区域如图 2.7 所示。

图 2.7　车牌位置搜索

由于监控相机角度及位置固定，所拍摄图像中车牌尺寸固定，假设车牌大小为 $W \times H$，在车牌搜索区域内进行遍历匹配，统计每个大小为 $W \times H$ 窗口内的目标像素个数，当目标像素个数超过某一阈值时将对应窗口标记为车牌区域，否则排除该窗口，像素个数阈值满足以下要求

$$t = \rho \sum_i \sum_j f(i, j) \tag{2-11}$$

式中：$\sum_i \sum_j f(i, j)$ 为搜索区域内所有目标像素个数，ρ 为系数，决定阈值 t 的大小。搜索遍历的示意图如图 2.7 所示。考虑到车辆前脸图像尺寸与车牌图像尺寸之间的固定关系，假设车牌的宽度为 w_p，使用如图 2.8（a）所示的方法确定车辆前脸感兴趣区域，如图 2.8

（b）所示是最终获取的车脸 ROI 区域。作为车型识别及分类的基础，选取品牌分别为 Audi、Buick、Changan、Chery、Chevrolet、Citroen、Ford、Honda、Hyundai、Mazda、Nissan、Peugeot、Toyota、Volkswagen 及 Wulin 的 15 种不同品牌车辆实验图片，每种类型 30 张共450 张由监控相机获取的车辆图片。

（a）车辆图像 ROI 区域检测　　　　　　　　（b）车脸 ROI 区域

图 2.8　根据车牌位置确定感兴趣区域

本书所述算法在 VC 6.0 环境下开发，使用 Open CV[10]（开源计算机视觉库）实现图像处理操作，计算机配置（Intel Core Duo 2.0 GHz）。分别使用基于边缘、基于车牌和基于车辆对称特征三种方法对 450 张实验图片进行检测，并与 Teoh[11]提出的车辆轮廓对称轴检测方法进行比较，输入图片尺寸为 1 024×1 360 mm，当车辆包围框覆盖车辆90%以上区域且包围框尺寸与车辆尺寸相差不超过 10%时为正确识别。随机选取 150 张图片作为基于 GLCM 特征和 SVM 车辆检测、基于 Gabor 特征和 SVM 车辆检测的训练图片，对于基于 GLCM 特征的检测，将图片网格化，提取每个子窗口的灰度共生矩阵，使用 SVM 对样本图片进行训练，之后用训练后的结果对数据库中其余 300 张图片进行识别；对于基于 Gabor 特征的检测，按 2.3.4 节的方法划分图像，则 150 张图片共划分为 1 500 张子图像，选取训练样本中车辆子图像作为车辆目标图像，另外选取 500 张背景子图像，使用 Gabor 滤波器组分别提取车辆和背景子图像的 Gabor 特征，本书 Gabor 滤波器组为 4 尺度、6 方向，则 Gabor 特征为 72 维，之后将样本特征使用 SVM 训练，使用训练结果检测其余 150 张图片。6 种车辆检测方法的检测率及检测时间如表 2.1 所示。

表 2.1　6 种车辆检测方法的检测率及检测时间

方　法 结　果	融合特征	轮廓特征	车　牌	GLCM	Gabor	Teoh[11]
检测率	90.7%	82.8%	80.9%	86.4%	80.8%	87.6%
检测时间(ms)	125	140	125	6 513	17 609	109

实验结果表明本书所提出基于对称特征的车辆检测方法检测率为 90.7%，比 Teoh[11]中基于轮廓对称特征的检测准确率高 3.1%，同时我们的方法在检测率和检测时间上优于其他的方法，如基于 GLCM、Gabor 特征和 SVM 进行分类的方法。从表 2.1 中可以看出，本书的方法在检测时间上是最短的，这对车辆实时检测和识别等应用具有重要意义。

在车型识别中，我们首先要根据车辆位置确定感兴趣区域即车辆前脸区域，采用 2.4 节感兴趣区域定位的方法，对实验数据进行处理得到车辆前脸区域。考虑到车型识别的训练样本应覆盖多种光照条件、不同车辆姿态等图像样本，我们规定当所截取的车辆前脸图像与实际前脸包围框相差不超过 20%时即可作为训练样本，如图 2.9 所示为几张正确获取 ROI 及偏差较大 ROI 图像示意图。通过对相同实验数据进行处理，能正确获取 ROI 的图像占所有测试图像的百分比为 95.33%，因此，该方法可以为车型识别提供实时准确的输入图像数据。

图 2.9　偏差较大 ROI 及正确获取 ROI（示意图）
（第一行为偏差加大 ROI，第二行为正确获取 ROI）

2.5　小结

通过分析交通监控视频车辆图像几何、颜色及纹理等特征，本章提出了一种基于车辆轮廓对称特征和车牌对称特征的特征融合的两种车辆区域检测方法，通过检测车辆轮廓对称轴及以车牌水平和竖直对称轴，之后以车牌水平和竖直对称轴交点为基准检测车辆区域。此外，论文使用基于车辆边缘、车牌、GLCM 和 Gabor 变换等 5 种检测方法进行了对比研究。经过对实验图片检测表明，论文提出的基于特征融合的车辆检测方法对实验图片进行车辆区域定位的正确率为 90.7%，有效避免了背景噪声对车辆对称轴搜索及车辆检测的影响。另外，根据检测得到的车牌对称轴中心点搜索车牌位置，进而确定车辆前脸 ROI 区域，在使用相同实验数据测试条件下达到了 95.33%的准确率，为车型识别提供了较为准确和全面的训练样本和测试数据。车辆检测的实现是车型识别及车辆分类等新兴应用领域的技术基础，在下一章的工作中，我们将涉及这方面的内容。

参考文献

[1] Teoh S S, Bräunl T. Symmetry-based monocular vehicle detection system [J]. Machine Vision and Applications, 2012, 23 (5), 831-842.

[2] Song G Y, Lee K Y, Lee J W. Vehicle Detection by Edge-Based Candidate Generation and Appearance-based Classification [C]. IEEE Intelligent Vehicles Symposium, 2008.

[3] Ha D M, Lee J M, Kim Y D. Neural-edge-based vehicle detection and traffic parameter extraction [J]. Image and Vision Computing, 2004, 22 (11), 899-907.

[4] Nikul U, Mehta H. An accurate method for license plate localization using morphological operations and edge processing [J] .Image and Signal Processing, 2010, 5 (12), 2488-2491.

[5] Zheng D, Zhao Y, Wang J. An efficient method of license plate location [J]. Pattern Recognition Letters, 2005, 26, 2431-2438.

[6] Wu J D, Liu C T. Finger-vein pattern identification using SVM and neural network

technique [J]. Expert Systems with Applications, 2011, 38 (11), 14284-14289.

[7] Zhao C, Zhang B, Lian J, et al. Classification of driving postures by support vector machines [C]. Image and Graphics (ICIG), Hefei, 2011.

[8] Sun Z, Bebis G, Miller R. On-road vehicle detection using evolutionary Gabor filter optimization [J]. IEEE Transaction on Intelligent Transportation Systems, 2005, 6 (4), 125-137.

[9] Cheng H, Zheng N, Sun C. Boosted Gabor Features Applied to Vehicle Detection.[C]. Pattern Recognition, 2006. ICPR 2006. 18th International Conference on. IEEE, 2006.

[10] 陈利利. 基于多尺度图像分析的路面病害检测方法研究与分析[D]. 南京: 南京理工大学, 2009.

[11] Teoh S S, Bräunl T. Symmetry-based monocular vehicle detection system [J]. Machine Vision and Applications, 2012, 23 (5), 831-842.

第 3 章

车辆品牌感知理论与技术

首先，分析了局部能量形状直方图、局部二值模式和梯度方向直方图等 5 种特征提取方法，并采用支持向量机和 k-最近邻分类器进行车辆品牌识别实验。

其次，分别提取图像梯度方向直方图（HOG）和 Contourlet 特征，使用不同特征融合的方法描述车前脸特征，通过实验比较得出能够有效表征车前脸独特性的特征描述方法。研究特征降维及特征融合方法，直接使用特征描述所提取的特征维数都比较高，并且分类器的训练会占用大量时间。

最后，研究具有"拒识"功能的级联集成分类器，级联分类器的第一级集成分类器由不同的基分类器组成，选用的四种基分类器包括朴素贝叶斯，k-最近邻（k-NN），支持向量机（SVM），多层神经网络（MLP），分别使用 HOG 和 Contourlet 变换特征作为输入特征进行训练，对比每种特征及分类器结合的识别效率，同时建立基于多数表决分类机制的集成分类器，拒绝识别没有达到多数表决阈值的输入特征，并将该特征对应的模糊图像送入第二级级联分类器进行识别；第二级集成分类器是基于神经网络的旋转森林集成分类器，基分类器使用相同的 MLP 网络，对被第一级拒绝识别的样本进行识别，第二级分类器也带有"拒识"功能，我们通过设计两级分类器级联将被拒绝识别的样本降低到一个可以被人工处理接受的水平，同时又保证了系统的可靠性。

3.1 基于单特征的车辆品牌感知方法

3.1.1 车辆品牌纹理特征提取

1）局部能量形状直方图

局部能量形状直方图（LESH）是在局部能量模型的基础上演变而来的，在论文[1, 2]中有相关的研究工作。

Morrone 和 Owens 在论文[3]中首先提出局部能量模型，是指一幅图像的相位中局部频率成分最大的点的特征，通过式（3-1）计算，即：

$$E(x) = \max_{\overline{\varphi}(x) \in [0,2\pi]} \frac{\sum_n A_n \cos\left(\phi_n(x) - \overline{\phi}(x)\right)}{\sum_n A_n} \tag{3-1}$$

式中：A_n 和 ϕ_n 代表第 n 个傅里叶成分的幅度和相位，该频率信息利用一组 n 个空间频率和 v 个方向的 Gabor 滤波核对图像做卷积运算。在图像的每个尺度每个方向上，它产生的复杂值包括偶对称与奇对称的滤波输出，即关于该像素的幅度和相位：

$$G\left(\mathrm{e}_n, o_{n,v}\right) = I\left(x, y\right) * \Psi_{n,v}\left(z\right) \tag{3-2}$$

式中：$G(\cdot)$ 是图像 (x, y) 像素点在 n 尺度 v 方向的偶对称和奇对称滤波的实部与虚部的响应函数；$\Psi_{n,v}$ 代表在 n 尺度 v 方向上的一组 Gabor 滤波核。式（3-1）中的幅度 A_n 和相位 ϕ_n 可以写成：$A_n = \sqrt{e_n^2 + o_n^2}$ 和 $\phi_n = \tan^{-1}\dfrac{\mathrm{e}_n}{o_n}$。在本书中，尺度 n 分别取 1、2、3、4、5，方向取 8 个方向，分散出来的不同 Gabor 滤波核对大众车脸卷积图如图 3.1 所示。图中每行表示同一尺度上的不同方向上的 Gabor 滤波核，每一列表示不同尺度上的同一方向上的 Gabor 滤波核。

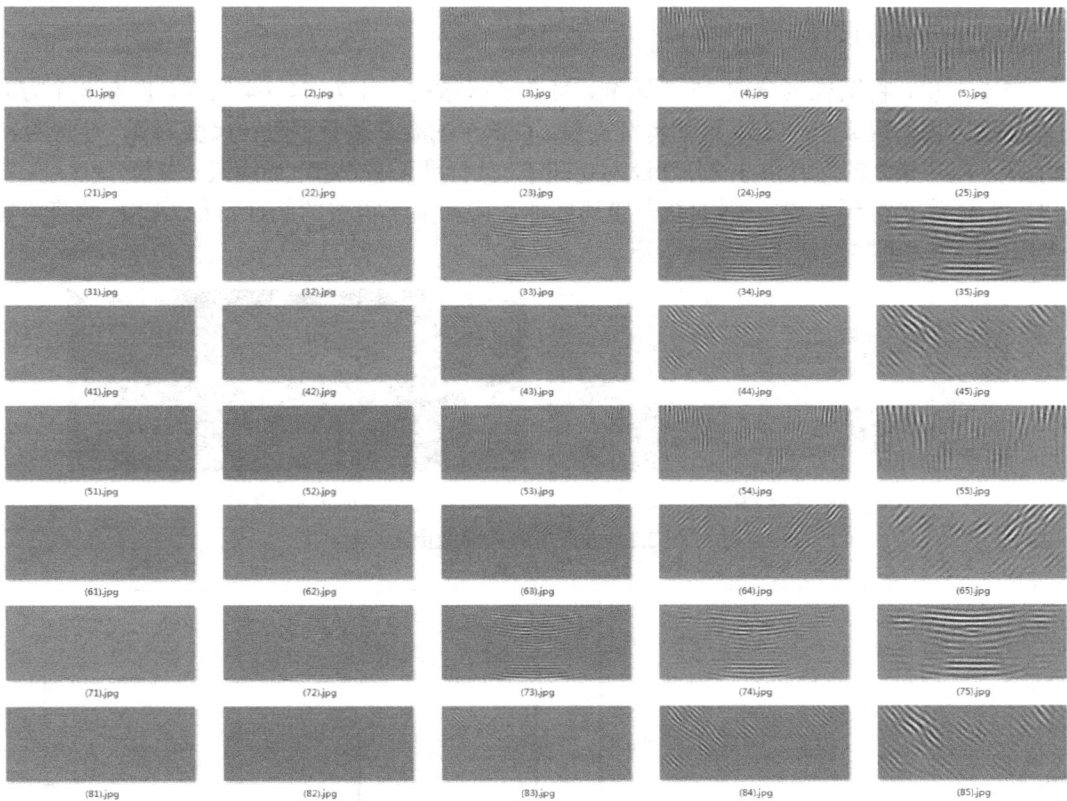

图 3.1　不同 Gabor 滤波核对大众车脸卷积图

分析局部能量模型发现在图像中的兴趣点存在对于光线和噪声具有高可靠性。基于形状是由底层的角、边或轮廓所代表这一原理，利用原始的能量信息可以进行形状编码。沿着每个滤波器的方向进行不同子区域图像的能量累积，这样可以使得模型对尺度变化具有不变性。局部直方图提取自图像的不同子区域的组合来保持图像每个部分的空间关系。首先提取方向标签图，即每个像素值被给予不同尺度上最大方向的标签。通过式（3-3）提取局部直方图 h，即：

$$h_{r,b} = \sum w_r \times E \times \delta_{Lb} \tag{3-3}$$

式中：b 代表当前的级数；L 代表方向边缘图；E 可以通过式（3-4）计算，代表局部能量；T 代表瑞利分布的噪声；ε 代表阈值；δ_{Lb} 代表克罗内克 δ 函数；w_r 是以半径 r 为中心区域的 Gaussian 权重函数。通过式（3-5）计算，该权重用于提供领域里小区域软边缘来克服尺度变化带来的问题。

$$E=\frac{\sum_n W(x)\left\lfloor A_n(x)\left(\cos\left(\phi_n(x)-\bar\phi(x)\right)-\left|\sin\left(\phi_n(x)-\bar\phi(x)\right)\right|\right)-T\right\rfloor}{\sum_n A_n(x)+\varepsilon} \tag{3-4}$$

$$w_r=\frac{1}{\sqrt{2\pi}\sigma}e^{\left[(x-r_{x0})^2+(y-r_{y0})^2\right]/\sigma^2} \tag{3-5}$$

式（3-4）中，相位频率函数权重 $W(x)$ 为 sigmod 函数。分别通过 $T=\mu_G\sqrt{\frac{\pi}{2}}+k\left(\frac{4-\pi}{2}\sigma_G\right)$ 和 $W(x)=\frac{1}{1+e^x}$ 计算而得。

在本书里，将图像划分成 32 个区域，每个子区域的大小为 64×64 像素，提取 8 个方向的局部直方图，组成一个 256 维的特征向量。Gabor 滤波参数设置为：尺度为 5，方向为 8，Gaussian 噪声模型的均值和方差分别设为 0 和 1，为标准正态分布，当阈值 ε 取值 1e-3，k 取值 3 后，计算 T 得到 3.187。则大众车脸局部能量图和最终提取的统计特征 LESH 的直方图分别如图 3.2 和图 3.3 所示。

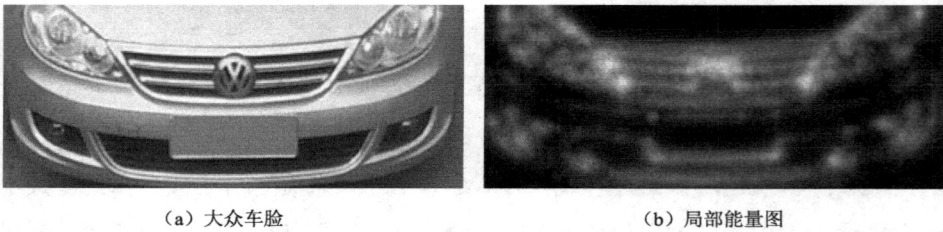

（a）大众车脸　　　　　　　　（b）局部能量图

图 3.2　大众车脸局部能量图

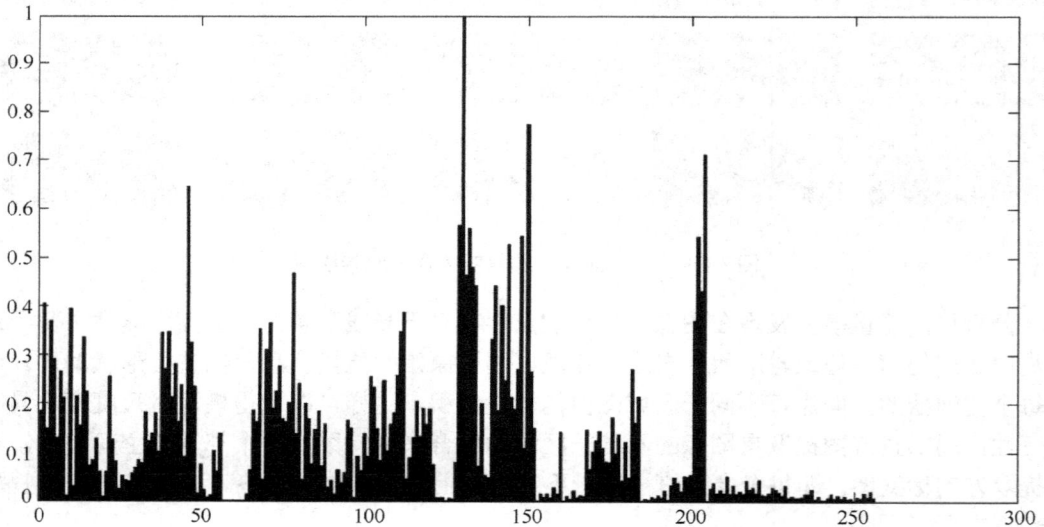

图 3.3　大众车脸 LESH 直方图

2）局部二值模式

局部二值模式（LBP）首先是由 Ojala 和 Pietikäinen 等[4]提出用来描述纹理的局部结构性的特征提取算子。该算子通过比较图像中某一像素点与周围其他相邻像素点之间的灰度变化来确定该像素点所在位置的纹理变化模式，它可以检测出图像局部纹理变化的值，可较好地提取图像边缘、角点等局部变化特征，对光照变化和图像旋转具有不变性。图像中像素点 m 的 LBP 特征值 $\text{LBP}(m)$ 的计算方法可以通过式（3-6）来计算，即：

$$\text{LBP}(m) = \sum_{i=0}^{7} s(n_i, m) \cdot 2^i \tag{3-6}$$

式中：n_i 是像素点 m 的八邻域像素点；i 自 m 的左上像素点起沿顺时针方向依次取 $0,1,\cdots,7$；$s(n_i, m)$ 表示 n_i 与 m 的阈值化结果；g_{n_i} 与 g_m 分别表示 n_i 与 m 的灰度值，其中，

$$s(n_i, m) = \begin{cases} 1, & g_{n_i} \geqslant g_m \\ 0, & g_{n_i} < g_m \end{cases}$$

假设定义 3×3 的窗口，传统的 LBP 算子提取的基本思想是：以窗口中心像素为比较阈值，逐一将中心像素与周围相邻 8 个像素的灰度值的进行，如果相邻像素值比中心像素值大，那么该像素点的位置则被设为 1，否则设为 0。然后将这 8 个像素点比较的二值结果进行串联，形成一个含有 8 位的二进制数，即表示该窗口中心像素点的 LBP 值，并用这个值来代表该区域的纹理信息。最后再将图像中每个像素点的 LBP 特征值依次按照首尾顺序串联成一个向量，同时利用 l_2 范数对该向量进行归一化后即可得到该图像的 LBP 特征。本书中将整个检测范围划分为 64×64 像素的小区域，形成了一个特征维数为 256 维的向量。对于每个小区域中的一个像素，按照上述 3×3 窗口大小计算中心像素点的 LBP 值。然后形成每个小区域里的直方图，即统计每个数字出现的频率，对该直方图进行归一化处理后再将得到的每个小区域的统计直方图进行连接成为一个特征向量，这样就提取出整幅图像的 LBP 特征向量，如图 3.4 所示。

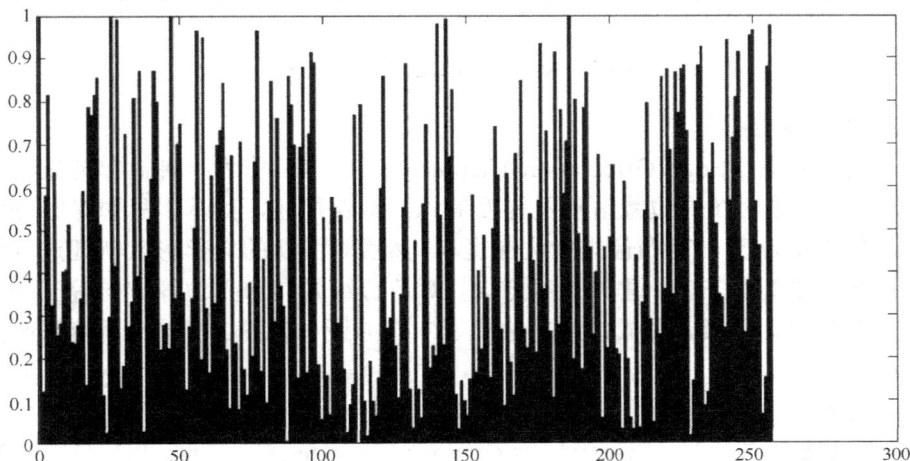

图 3.4 大众车脸 LBP 直方图

a）梯度方向直方图

梯度方向直方图（HOG）特征最初是由 Dalal 和 Triggs[5]提出的一种用于行人检测的特征，

其主要思想是在梯度或边缘的特定位置不确定的情况下，借用图像的局部梯度变化的方向的分布来实现对图像局部的纹理外观的描述。该特征对图像的微小几何形变和局部光学对比度变化都能保持很好的不变性。HOG 采用一组局部直方图来描述物体，通过把一张图片分割为多个细胞单元进行特征提取，然后对这些直方图统计图片中特定区域的梯度方向出现的次数。

HOG 特征提取的主要流程是：首先将图像分割成大小相同的单元格，利用梯度提取算子对每一个单元格进行卷积计算，得到每个像素点的梯度值的大小和方向，然后将图像的 360° 方向划分成所需的级数，再根据图像中像素点的梯度方向的梯度值进行累加，形成不同方向的直方图。可以将图像分成若干个包含小单元格的块，对单元格采用 Gamma 矫正法调节对比度来滤除光线阴影等因素的影响。最后将每个单元格提取到的 HOG 特征进行首尾串联，组成整个车脸图像的一维特征向量。本书所采用的 HOG 特征的参数检测窗口大小为 512×256 像素，块大小为 64×64 像素，细胞单元大小为 64×64 像素，细胞单元增量横向纵向均为 64 个像素，应用梯度滤波器 [−1,0,1] 获取梯度直方图，每个像素点的梯度 0°～180° 内分为 9 级，则特征维数为 9×4×8=288，最终提取的大众车脸 HOG 特征直方图如图 3.5 所示。

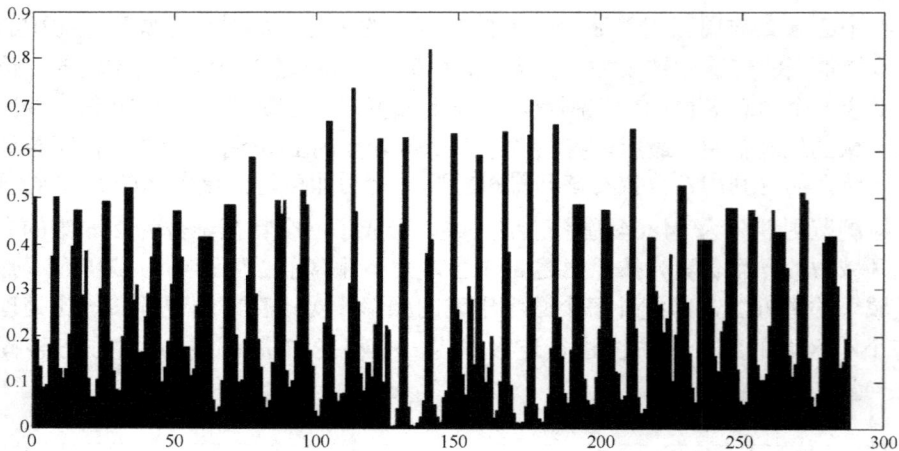

图 3.5　大众车脸 HOG 特征直方图

b）边缘方向直方图

边缘方向直方图（Edge Orientation Histogram，EOH）作为一种简单的统计特征，是 HOG 的前身，是对图像边缘信息及梯度信息的综合描述，其基本思想是首先利用边缘检测算法如 Canny 算子对图像进行边缘提取，然后对图像的局部形状特征进行边缘梯度和方向按照水平边缘方向、垂直边缘方向、对角边缘方向和无边缘方向等五个方向进行梯度直方图的统计分类，形成最终的边缘方向直方图（见图 3.6），空间特征向量的维数为 256 维。

c）金字塔梯度方向直方图

金字塔梯度方向直方图（Pyramid Histograms of Oriented Gradient，PHOG）是在 HOG 特征提取的基础上，通过四叉树分解将图像分成多层，形成金字塔状的采样方式，从低分辨率到高分辨率对每块区域进行直方图统计，对每个金字塔小块的区域提取的形状统计特征分别求直方图交核函数，最终形成图像的金字塔梯度方向直方图。在本书中，PHOG 分层层数设为 2（见图 3.7），即第 0 层进行整幅图像的特征统计，第 1 层将图像分层 4 块子区域，第三层将图像分层 16 块子区域。每个区域统计八个方向的边缘方向直方图（见图 3.8），最终形成的空间维数为 8×(1+4+16)=168 维的特征向量。

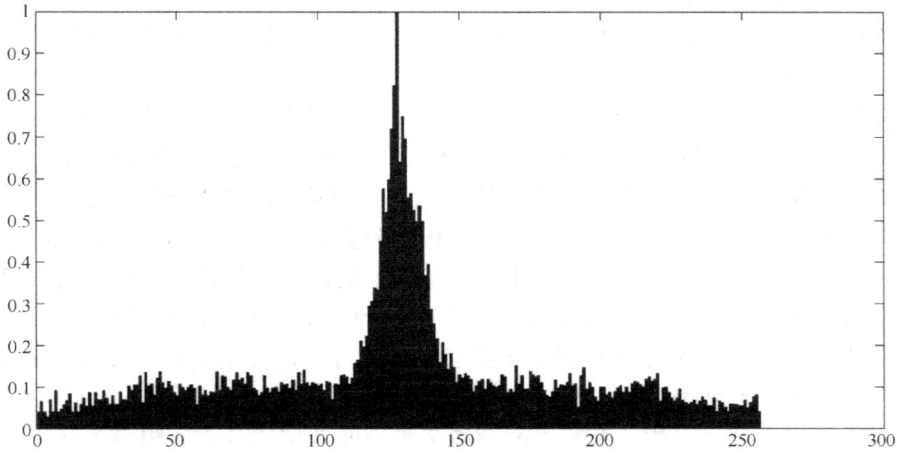

图 3.6 大众车脸 EOH 特征

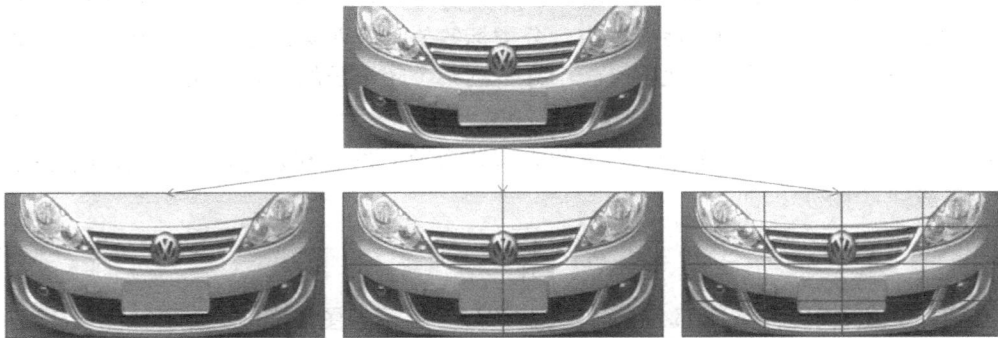

图 3.7 PHOG 采样分层示意图

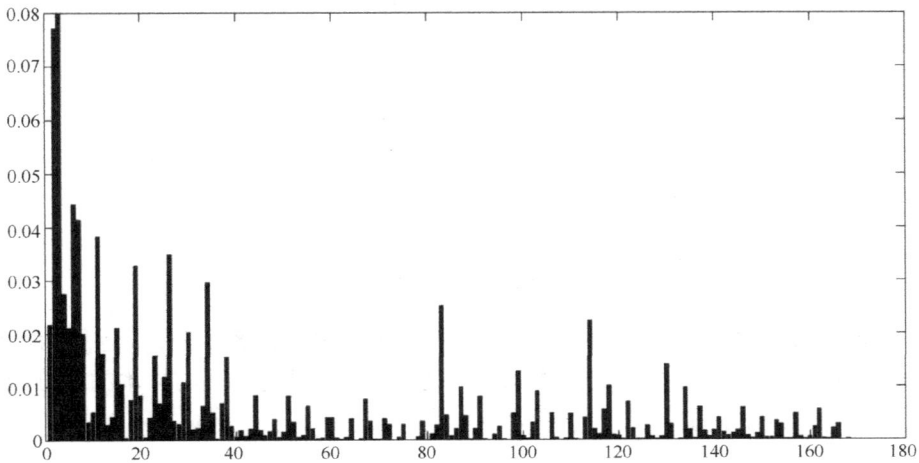

图 3.8 大众车脸 PHOG 特征

3.1.2 分类器

模式识别通过对大量数据进行样本学习，然后根据输入的测试样本，利用分类器设计不同的分类原则进行样本分类。本书着重研究了支持向量机和 k-最近邻两种分类器。

1. 支持向量机

支持向量机（Support Vector Machine，SVM）最早是由 Cortes 和 Vapnik 等在 1995 年提出的，其最重要的特性就是模型参数的确定对应着凸优化问题，是全局最优的解决方案，它能够较好地解决小样本、非线性及高维等模式识别问题[6]。支持向量机是从线性规划可分情况下解决两类分类中演变而来，选择一个最优分类面使得分类间隔最大化，是建立在统计学习理论的高维理论和结构风险最小原理基础上的。支持向量机是一种决策机制，不提供后验概率，它根据有限的样本信息在模型的复杂性和学习能力之间寻求最佳折中，以期获得最好的推广能力。SVM 处理样本数据线性不可分的情况主要是通过松弛变量（或惩罚变量）和核函数技术来实现的。

支持向量机的原理是寻找一个分类面使得多维空间数据的分类间隔最大化。假设训练数据中每个样本都是由一个向量和一个类别标签组成的，令其为 $D_i = (\boldsymbol{x}_i, y_i)$，其中 $\boldsymbol{x}_i$ 代表第 i 个样本特征所组成的向量，y_i 代表第 i 个样本所属的类别标签。多类分类可以看成多个二元分类的组合，在二元的线性分类中，分类标签值只有两类，分别为 1 和-1。假设新的数据点根据方程进行分类。由此定义一个样本到某个超平面的间隔，见式（3-7）：

$$\delta_i = y_i(w\boldsymbol{x}_i + b) \tag{3-7}$$

式中：w 代表某种功能的空间变换；b 代表偏置参数。把 w 和 b 进行归一化，则分类间隔可以表示成式（3-8），即：

$$\delta_i = \frac{1}{\|w\|}|g(\boldsymbol{x}_i)| \tag{3-8}$$

其中，$g(\boldsymbol{x}_i) = w\boldsymbol{x}_i + b$，那么 SVM 分类间隔几何示意图如图 3.9 所示。

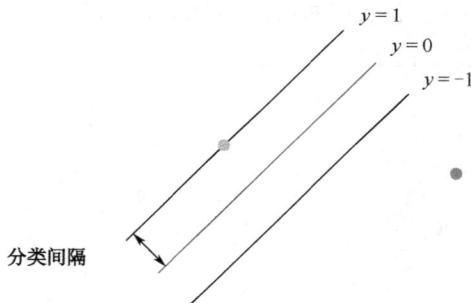

图 3.9 SVM 分类间隔几何示意图

图中，$y=0$ 是分类面，$y=1$ 和 $y=-1$ 是平行于 $y=0$ 且过离 $y=0$ 最近的两类样本的直线，$y=1$ 与 $y=-1$ 到 $y=0$ 之间的距离就是几何间隔。而几何间隔与样本的误分次数间 τ 存在关系，见式（3-9），即：

$$\tau \leqslant \left(\frac{2R}{\delta}\right)^2 \tag{3-9}$$

其中，R 是所有样本中向量长度最长的值，要使得误差上界越小，则需要求几何间隔越大的解，从式（3-9）可以看出几何间隔与 $\|w\|$ 是成反比的，所以即寻找最小的 $\|w\|$。求一个函数的最小值的问题都可以称为寻优问题，可以用等价的目标函数来代替，如式（3-10），即：

$$\min \frac{1}{2}\|w\|^2 \qquad (3\text{-}10)$$

理论证明满足 Mercer 条件的函数都可以作为核函数，而核函数的基本作用是用来接受两个低维空间里的向量，可以计算出经核函数变换后在高维空间里的向量的内积值，从而使得样本数据变得线性可分。几种常见的核函数有线性核函数、多项式核函数和 RBF 核函数。

2. k-最近邻法

k-最近邻法[7]（k-Nearest Neighbor，k-NN）最早是由 Cover 和 Hart 在 1968 年提出的，是一种比较系统的成熟理论方法，它是对最小距离法和最近邻法的推广形式。

假设要对 N 类样本进行分类，类别分别为 $w_1, w_2, \cdots, w_N$，则每一类标准样本设为 $P_1, P_2, \cdots, P_N$。基于最小距离分类的思想是计算待测试的样本 X 与所有的训练样本之间距离，然后基于所计算的距离进行比较，如若样本 X 与训练样本 P_i 之间的距离最短，那么测试样本 X 则属于 P_i。基于最小距离原理的分类机制是建立在一个理想的条件下，就是所有训练数据都可以准确地表达每类样本的模型，但是在实际应用中，样本数据可能会受到噪声对其造成的影响，使得一个类别的数据分布于一个比较大的空间范围里，这样基于最近距离的分类方法就无法准确地对测试样本进行分类。

为了解决最近距离方法受噪声对其分类影响的问题，仍然能实现较高精度的分类目的，最近邻分类方法因此产生，在上述方法中进行了改进。该方法是在所有训练样本集合中寻找到与待测试的样本所属的样本类别，首先是求出各类别集合与待测样本的最短距离，即式（3-11），其中 D_i 为第 i 类的样本数，即：

$$d_{\min}(X, w_i) = \min_{j=1,2,\cdots,D_i} d(X, P_{i,j}), i = 1, 2, \cdots, N \qquad (3\text{-}11)$$

最近邻法的分类原理是当 $i \neq j$ 时，$d_{\min}(X, w_i) < (X, w_j)$，$i = 1, 2, \cdots, N$，则将样本 X 判别为类 w_i。最近邻法是一种比较简单实用的分类方法，但是同样存在计算量大，耗费计算机存储资源等缺点，同时也受到训练数据的噪声污染、畸变点等影响较大，造成对分类结果的误判可能性较大。因此在最近邻法上进行改进与扩展为 k-最近邻法。k-最近邻法首先是计算出待测样本 X 到所有训练样本集合中每一个训练样本的距离，并对其按照距离值从大到小进行排序。然后从中选取 k 个与测试样本 X 最近的训练样本，并对这 k 个最近的训练样本进行分类统计，那么 k 个训练样本中属于同一种类别的且票数最多的标签则为测试样本的类别。假设有 N 类，所得到 k 个样本中第 i 类有 k_i，判别规则可以表示为式（3-12），即：

$$k_i > k_j \Rightarrow X \in w_i, \quad i \neq j, \quad i, j = 1, 2, \cdots, N \qquad (3\text{-}12)$$

其中 $\sum_{j=1}^{N} k_j = k$。k-最近邻法对于未知类别标签的样本，按照一定距离判断规则找出未知样本在训练集中的 k 个最近邻样本，如果这 k 个最近邻中的多数样本属于某一个类别，就将它判别为那个类别。k-最近邻分类方法在一定程度上减小了噪声样本对分类的干扰。

3.1.3 实验结果与分析

本节采用所构建的东南大学车脸数据库进行实验与分析,该数据库包含 12 000 张图片、30 种车辆品牌,涵盖如大众、别克、奥迪、宝马等品牌系列。实验硬件为研华 610H 型工控机,并采用 matlab7.0 运行环境。支持向量机采用的是台湾大学 Lin 教授等开发的 LIBSVM 工具包,其中最大迭代次数设为 1 000,惩罚因子设为 10,核函数选择的是线性核。选择线性核是因为线性预测函数形式比较简单,对于类别比较多的分类速度比较快,并且线性 SVM 的分类器具有推广性,实用价值比较高,不像非线性核函数如 RBF 核可能存在过学习等问题。k-最近邻分类器的参数 k 设为 20。

实验中每种车辆品牌车脸图片分别随机分成两部分:250 张训练样本和 150 张测试样本,并分别进行 10 次实验取平均值,作为车辆品牌分类的最终结果,以排除偶然性给实验带来的干扰。利用支持向量机和 k-最近邻 2 种分类器分别对纹理特征 LESH 特征、LBP 特征、HOG 特征、EOH 特征和 PHOG 特征进行实验。实验统计结果如表 3.1 所示。

表 3.1 SVM 和 k-NN 对 5 种纹理特征的分类精度

识别率 分类器	EOH(%)	HOG(%)	PHOG(%)	LBP(%)	LESH(%)
k-NN	65.34	82.51	76.54	72.44	80.70
SVM	73.53	92.40	83.91	85.67	88.96

由表 3.1 可知,实验结果表明支持向量机的分类效果整体优于 k-NN 分类器,在常见的 5 种纹理特征中,基于支持向量机的 HOG 的整体识别率比其他特征的分类效果好,并且分类精度从低到高的特征分别是 EOH、PHOG、LBP、LESH 和 HOG,这说明这 5 种特征所提取的纹理特征越丰富,越有利于分类。HOG 与 SVM 的训练样本分别选 50 张、100 张、150 张、200 张、250 张,测试样本分别选 14 张、50 张、100 张、150 张的最终测试的识别率统计结果如图 3.10 所示。

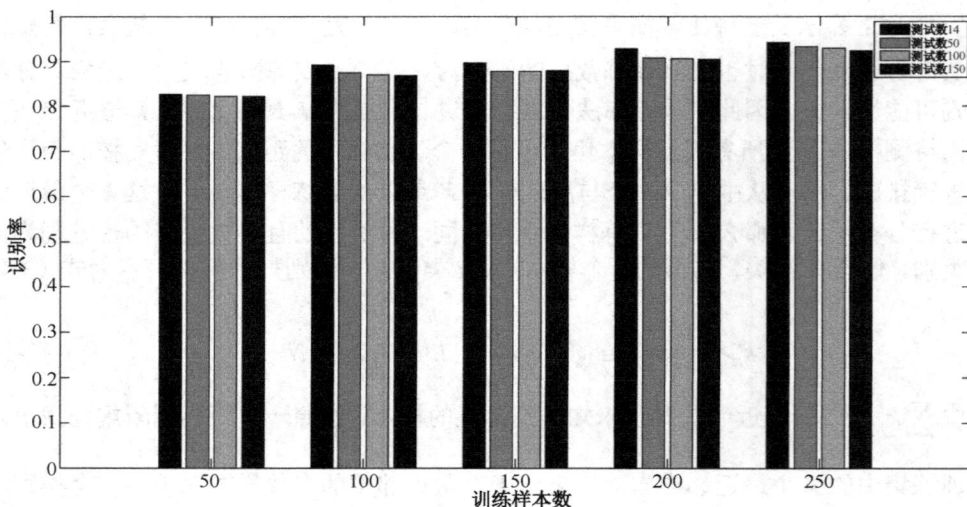

图 3.10 不同训练与测试样本数的 HOG 和 SVM 的识别率

由图 3.10 可知，随着训练样本数目的增加，分类精度在整体上升。这说明如果要提高分类精度，增加训练样本的数量以包含同一类样本集中的多种样本数据。并且随着测试样本数越来越多，分类精度在以缓慢的速度降低，表明这种分类方法具有一定的可靠性。

3.2 基于组合特征的车辆品牌感知方法

本书中所提出的车型识别系统包括两个步骤，第一步是从训练样本中提取特征训练分类器，第二步使用分类器对测试样本进行识别。图像特征提取应该能提供图像识别所需要的内在的、结构化的信息，现在有多种不同类型定义图像特征的方法，如图像颜色、灰度直方图，Gabor 滤波器和小波变换等方法。对于车辆图像来说，几何特征和边缘特征同等重要，如几何特征包括平方映射梯度[8]和梯度方向点[9]等。图像边缘的空间分布可以作为车辆识别有效的"指纹"信息。本章根据车辆类型识别需要引入两种边缘信息描述子，即 HOG 和 Contourlet 特征，为了避免维数灾难，论文提出使用主成分分析（PCA）进行数据降维，同时，本章探讨了使用特征融合提升识别率的可能性，并提出使用两种特征简单串联作为融合特征，在车型识别阶段通过实验分析了几种不同特征的识别效果。

3.2.1 梯度方向直方图（HOG）

梯度方向直方图（HOG）特征是由 Dalal[10]提出并应用于静态图像中的行人检测上，后来推广到静态图像中的车辆、行人及常见动物等目标的检测。该特征计算局部图像梯度方向信息的统计值，与尺度不变特征变换（SIFT）、边缘方向直方图（EOH）以及形状上下文方法等特征在计算方法上有相似之处，但 HOG 描述器是在一个网格密集的大小统一的细胞单元（Cells）上计算，同时还采用了重叠的对比度归一化技术提高性能。HOG 的具体实现方法是：首先将图像分成小的连通区域，即细胞单元（Cells）；然后根据 Cells 中各像素点的梯度方向和幅值计算得到其梯度方向直方图；最后把这些直方图组合起来构成特征描述器。为了提高性能，把这些 Cells 的梯度方向直方图在图像的更大区间（Block）内进行归一化，即先计算各直方图在区间中的密度，然后根据密度对区间中的各细胞单元进行归一化，通过归一化能够消除光照和阴影的影响。HOG 特征提取算法流程图如图 3.11 所示。

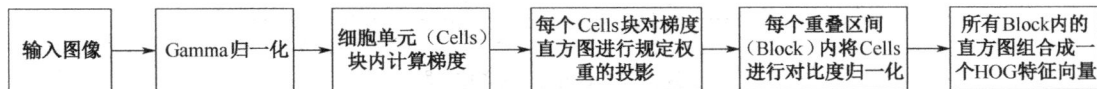

输入图像 → Gamma 归一化 → 细胞单元（Cells）块内计算梯度 → 每个 Cells 块对梯度直方图进行规定权重的投影 → 每个重叠区间（Block）内将 Cells 进行对比度归一化 → 所有 Block 内的直方图组合成一个 HOG 特征向量

图 3.11　HOG 特征提取算法流程

3.2.2 Contourlet 变换

Contourlet 变换是结合拉普拉斯塔形分解（LP）和方向滤波器组（DFB）实现的一种多分辨率、多方向的、局域的图像表示方法，是由 Do[11]提出的。Contourlet 变换用随尺度变化长宽比的"长条形"基结构来逼近图像，具有方向性和各向异性。Contourlet 变换对曲线的描述如图 3.12 所示。

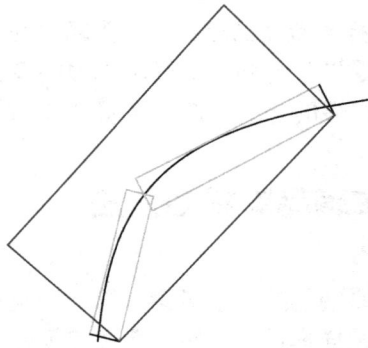

图 3.12　Contourlet 变换对曲线的描述

LP 分解是实现图像多分辨率分析的一种有效方式。每一层 LP 分解将产生一个下采样的低通部分和一个该图像与预测图像的差图像。对低通图像继续分解得到下一层的低通图像和差值图像。二维方向滤波器组（DFB）应用于 LP 分解得到的每一级高频分量上，在第 l 层上得到 2^l 个方向子带，图像每次经 LP 子带分解产生的高通子带输入 DFB，逐渐将点奇异连成线结构，从而捕获图像中的轮廓。Do 提出的 DFB 包括两个模块，即梅花滤波器组和平移操作。两通道的梅花滤波器组（Quincunx 滤波器，见图 3.13）是用扇形滤波器将 2-D 光谱分成两个主要方向：水平方向和垂直方向。其中，H 和 G 为分解和合成滤波，$\boldsymbol{Q}$ 为采样矩阵，有两种形式：

$$\boldsymbol{Q}_0 = \begin{Bmatrix} 1 & -1 \\ 1 & 1 \end{Bmatrix} \quad \boldsymbol{Q}_1 = \begin{Bmatrix} 1 & 1 \\ -1 & 1 \end{Bmatrix} \tag{3-13}$$

其中，$\boldsymbol{Q}$ 的作用是将图像旋转并下采样，$\boldsymbol{Q}_0$ 和 $\boldsymbol{Q}_1$ 分别将图像旋转 45° 和 -45°。平移操作（Shearing）是在 Quincunx 滤波分解阶段前进行。Shearing 操作对图像进行旋转并将其宽度变为原来的两倍。Shearing 操作可采用如下四种采样矩阵：

$$\boldsymbol{R}_0 = \begin{Bmatrix} 1 & 1 \\ 0 & 1 \end{Bmatrix} \quad \boldsymbol{R}_1 = \begin{Bmatrix} 1 & -1 \\ 0 & 1 \end{Bmatrix} \quad \boldsymbol{R}_2 = \begin{Bmatrix} 1 & 0 \\ 1 & 1 \end{Bmatrix} \quad \boldsymbol{R}_3 = \begin{Bmatrix} 1 & 0 \\ -1 & 1 \end{Bmatrix} \tag{3-14}$$

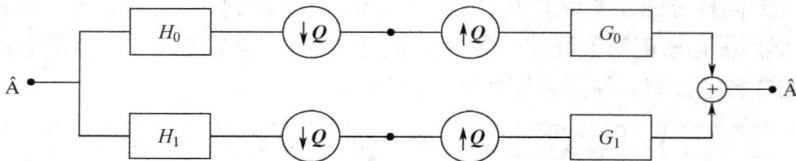

图 3.13　Quincunx 滤波器

将金字塔分解和方向滤波器结合起来，就实现了 Contourlet 变换。LP 分解不具有方向性，而 DFB 能够较好理解高频部分，对低频部分分析程度不够，二者的结合弥补了对方的不足，从而得到了很好的图像描述。图 3.14 显示了一幅输入车辆前脸图像的三层 Contourlet 分解，其中第 l 层分解的方向子带数为 2^l，最细致层上的方向子带数为 16，图中将每层的所有子带拼成了一张图片。在实际的车型识别过程中，将子带图像直接作为输入特征会造成特征向量维数过高，但直接将每个子带的均值和方差作为输入特征又会忽略掉比较多的细节信息，本书提出采用每一层所有子带合并后的图像的每行的均值和方差作为特征，对于一张输入大小为 256×256 的图像，Contourlet 变换后的三层子带合并图像大小分别为

16×16 像素， 64×64 像素， 128×128 像素。则该图像的 Contourlet 特征维数大小为 $2 \times (16 + 64 + 128) = 416$。

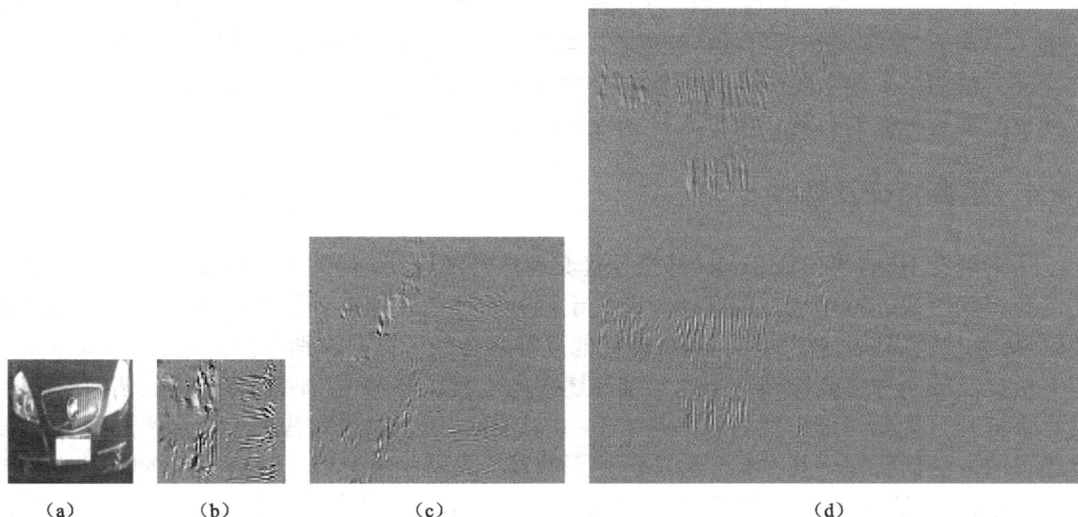

图 3.14　输入车辆前脸图像的三层 Contourlet 分解

3.2.3　特征降维

在机器学习中，对于高维特征向量经常采用一些降低维数的方法来避免维数灾难[12]，在训练样本固定的情况下，一些分类器（如贝叶斯网络、k-最近邻）的预测能力通常随着特征向量维度的增加而减小。所以在将样本输入分类器之前通常采取一些降低维数的措施，降低特征向量维数的方法有主成分分析（PCA），线性判别分析（LDA）[13]和典型相关分析（CCA）[14]等，同时支持向量机（SVM）中的核函数[15]也可以有效地解决高维到低维的映射问题。

前两节所介绍的两种特征描述子取出的图像特征维数都比较高，如不对获取的特征向量进行维数降低处理，那么分类器对信息处理的效率和精确度都会下降。主成分分析（PCA）是一个高普适用方法，通过 PCA 方法求出数据集的主元，将其余的维数省去，从而达到维数降低和简化模型的目的。PCA 方法是将数据空间通过正交变换映射到低维子空间的过程，通过求得一个低维的投影矩阵，用高维的特征乘以这个投影矩阵，便可以将高维特征的维数下降到指定的维数。假设有 N 个样本数据 $X_i = \{x_1^i, x_2^i, \cdots, x_D^i\}, 1 \leqslant i \leqslant N$，其中 D 为样本特征维数，PCA 的目标是寻找 r（$r < D$）个新变量，使它们反映事物的主要特征，具体实现过程如下所述：

（1）计算所有样本的均值向量

$$\mu = \left\{ \frac{1}{N} \sum_{i=1}^{N} x_1^i, \frac{1}{N} \sum_{i=1}^{N} x_2^i, \cdots, \frac{1}{N} \sum_{i=1}^{N} x_D^i \right\} \tag{3-15}$$

（2）计算协方差矩阵

$$S = \frac{1}{N} \sum_{i=1}^{N} (X_i - u)(X_i - u)^{\mathrm{T}} \tag{3-16}$$

（3）计算矩阵 S 的特征值 λ_i 和对应的特征向量 v_i；

（4）对特征值进行递减排序，并将特征向量重排为和排序后的特征值一致；

（5）定义贡献率为主要特征值（主成分）在所有特征值之和中占的比重，取前 r 个主要特征值（主成分）代替原来所有的特征值时，累计贡献率的大小反映了这种取代的可靠性。

（6）最后，用输入特征向量乘以 r 个主成分所对应的特征向量构建的投影矩阵，即可达到数据维数降低的目的，将输入样本特征维数从 D 维降低到 r 维。

3.2.4　组合特征及降维

尽管现在 HOG 和 Contourlet 特征已经具有广泛的应用，但关于它们实用性的许多问题还没有得到解决。特别地，现在还没有关于两种特征是否能够获取图像潜在的、不同的互补信息。如果情况是这样的话，两种特征的互补融合能否提升识别率值得关注。大体来说，本书所提及的两种特征能够从不同角度描述图像内容。同时使用两种特征得到图像的综合信息来提升分类器识别车型的效率是个不错的选择。近年来也有些关于组合两种不同特征描述子的方法的研究。其中有一种广泛使用的基于典型相关分析（CCA）[16]的特征融合方法。但是 CCA 是一种无监督的特征提取方法并且它不采用样本的类型信息，这就限制了识别功能。另外一种颇具影响力的特征融合方法是支持向量机（SVM）框架中的多核学习[15]，这种方法通过线性组合来开发不同特征的核。基于核的方法相对于其他特征融合方法的最大优势是它能够组合不同来源数据的信息。由于我们所涉及的车型数据来源单一，所以本书使用了一种较为简单的特征组合方法。

如何有效地进行多特征融合仍是一个开放问题，但多特征融合能够提升系统的可靠性和健壮性得到了学者们的共识。直接将两种特征如 HOG 和 Contourlet 特征简单串联是一种有效的提升识别率的方法，其中多层神经网络（MLP）对融合特征的识别效率的提升尤其显著，而且使用 MLP 多分类器集成和融合特征结合能够进一步提升识别率。本书所使用的第一个特征是 HOG 特征，将一幅输入图像归一化为 64×64 像素，设置细胞单元大小为 8×8，在每个细胞单元内统计 9 个直方图通道的无向梯度（即将 $0 \sim 180°$ 的梯度方向划分为 9 个区间），同时设置归一化块（Block）的大小为 16×16（即包含四个细胞单元），块在水平和竖直方向的步进大小均为 8，如图 3.15 所示为各尺寸之间的相对关系，最后将所有细胞单元的直方图组合起来形成 HOG 特征描述子，得到的特征描述子大小为 $9 \times 4 \times 7 \times 7 = 1764$。

对于 Contourlet 特征，对输入车辆图片进行三层分解，将每一层对应的所有子带拼成一张图片，统计 Contourlet 在每层子带拼接图像的每行均值方差作为特征描述子。由于车辆图像横向信

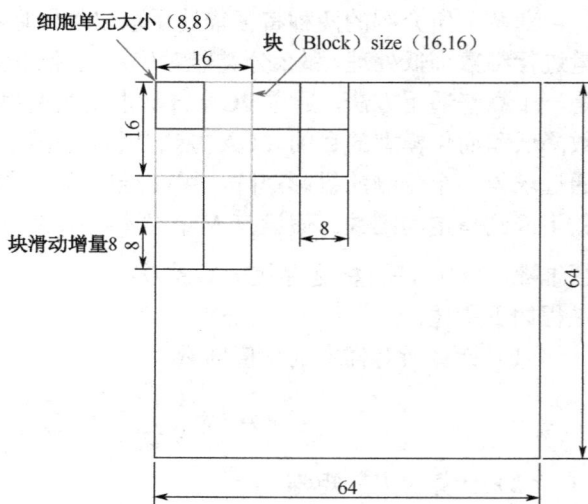

图 3.15　HOG 参数示意图

息存在冗余，将输入图像归一化为 256×256 像素，则得到每层 Contourlet 分解子带拼接图像大小分别为 16×16，64×64 和 128×128 像素，统计每行的均值方差作为特征描述子，最终得到特征向量的大小为 $(64 + 128 + 256) \times 2 = 896$ 维。

分类器中朴素贝叶斯分类器和 k-最近邻对高维特征都比较敏感，当维数比较高时，神经网络的参数设计也比较复杂，可能需要比较多的隐含层结点，训练时间也比较长，因此对特征进行降低维数是必要的。分别对 HOG 和 Contourlet 特征进行 PCA 分析，取累计贡献率为 95%对应的投影矩阵，将训练样本和测试样本特征使用投影矩阵进行变换，得到投影后的 HOG 和 Contourlet 特征维数分别为 570 维和 130 维，对应之前的高维特征数据维数降低较为明显。

3.2.5　基于级联集成分类器的可靠分类

特征分类的过程是通过建立样本集经分类器学习后，可将输入测试样本自动分类到已知类别。模式识别中有很多成熟的分类器如神经网络、k-最近邻和支持向量机[17]，但现在关于分类器可靠性问题的研究还比较少，可靠性即分类器做出某个决定的置信度。尽管现在已有的分类器可以达到很高的识别效率，但是对于交通监控中嫌疑车辆的识别来说需要更高的可靠度。目前道路上运行的车辆类型很多，很难将所有的车型都包含的数据库中，对于未知车型的强行分类显得毫无意义；另外，在车辆检测过程中也无法做到每一辆车都能精确提取感兴趣区域，将背景作为车辆区域进行分类显然会得到不好的结果。这时，如果能在分类器中加入"拒识"功能，即拒绝识别置信度不高的输入样本（模糊图片、新车型、背景区域等），而将这些样本拣出由人工识别，这样就显然提高了分类器的可靠性。本章首先介绍几种成熟的分类器，分别使用不同的分类器对两种特征和融合特征进行识别，同时引入一种带有"拒识"功能的级联集成分类器方案。

一个能够最小化错误率并且能将不确定类型的测试样本归属到"拒识"类中的分类器是衡量分类器是否最优的简单规则。Chow[18]提出了一个具有"拒识"功能的最优规则，它应满足下面两个条件：

对于一个输入样本向量 v，分类器对它识别并将其归属到第 k 类，根据贝叶斯公式，应满足：

$$p(k)p(v|k) \geqslant p(i)p(v|i) \tag{3-17}$$

$$p(k)p(v|k) \geqslant \rho \sum_{i=1,i \neq k}^{C} p(i)p(v|i) \tag{3-18}$$

在满足以下条件时，分类器拒绝识别输入样本向量 v：

$$\max_k [p(k)p(v|k)] \leqslant \rho \sum_{i=1,i \neq k}^{C} p(i)p(v|i) \tag{3-19}$$

式中，C 为类型数目，$p(i)$ $(i=1,\cdots,C)$为每一类的先验概率，$p(v|i)$ 为给定类型的条件概率，可以根据输入样本计算得到，在决策规则中的 ρ 被称为"决策阈值"，且 $0 \leqslant \rho \leqslant 1$。降低"拒识"率及错误率的方法有以下几种：

（1）为了降低错误率，我们需要通过增加式（3-18）和式（3-19）中的 ρ 来扩大"拒绝区域"。这样，被拒绝的样本会增多而被正确或错误识别的样本都会减少。

（2）根据式（3-18）为了降低"拒识"率，首先可以通过提高 $\max\left[p(k)p(v\,|\,k)\right]$ 的值，在此同时可以降低 $\rho\sum_{i=1,i\neq k}^{C}p(i)p(v\,|\,i)$ 的值。这就是说，在实际的识别过程中，一个输入样本应该具有与其对应类型最高的条件概率，并且相对于其他类型的条件概率最小。这意味着能够有效描述图像的特征在识别过程中扮演重要的角色。

引入"拒识"功能后，我们采用论文[19]中的方法如下定义识别率（Recognition Rate，RR），"拒识"率（Rejection Rate，ReR），错误率（Error Rate，ER）以及系统可靠性：

$$RR = \frac{正确识别的样本数}{所有测试样本数} \tag{3-20}$$

$$ReR = \frac{"拒识"的样本数}{所有测试样本数} \tag{3-21}$$

$$可靠性 = RR + ReR \tag{3-22}$$

$$ER = 100\% - 可靠性 \tag{3-23}$$

根据识别系统可靠性的定义，在合适权衡"拒识"率（ReR）和错误率（ER）之间的关系后，我们可以得到一个可靠性比较高的车型识别系统。

分类器集成的思想是分别训练一系列单个的分类器，之后选择合适的方法组合它们的分类结果。集成分类器不仅仅依靠某一单一训练集的特点，能够学习样本更具表现力的内容，解决单个分类器的分类偏好问题。建立集成分类器有很多方法。一个主流的方法是分别使用训练样本的不同子集训练每个分类器，可以通过对训练数据重新采样（Bagging，"Bootstrap aggregation"的简称）[20]、赋予新权值（Boosting）[21]来实现。Bagging 使用一种统计重采样技术"bootstrap"生成多个训练子集和集成分类器中的分类器组件。Boosting 的每个分类器组件的训练样本是由在它之前的分类器决定的，在前一个分类器中被误分的样本将在下一个分类器中扮演重要的角色。另外一个比较有前景的集成分类器是随机子空间（Random Subspace）[21]，它使用从所有特征中随机选取的子集作为训练样本。因此，集成分类器是由基分类器使用特征空间中随机选取的特征子集进行训练实现的。本节我们介绍一个集成分类器级联方案通过降低"拒识"率及提高识别率来实现一个高可靠性的分类系统。多层识别系统可以由若干个两级级联识别系统组成，因此我们仅介绍一个两级级联方案。如图 3.16 所示，第二级的集成分类器的输入测试样本是在第一级级联分类器中被拒绝识别的样本。

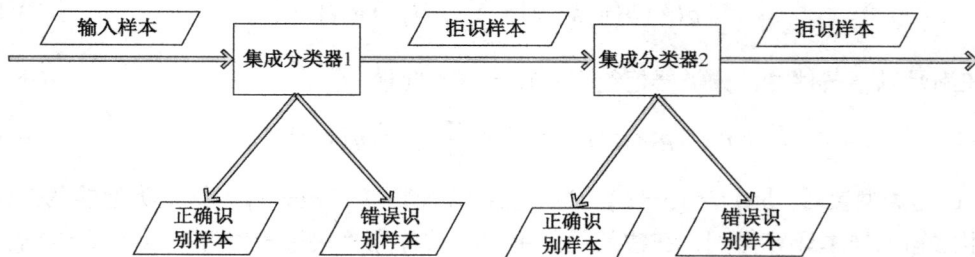

图 3.16　级联集成分类器方案

对于两层集成分类器，相应的识别率、"拒识"率和误识率满足以下关系：

$$总识别率 = \frac{第一级识别数 + 第二级识别数}{总样本数};$$

$$总误识率 = \frac{第一级误识数 + 第二级误识率}{总样本数};$$

$$第二级"拒识"率 = \frac{第一级"拒识"数 - 第二级误识数 - 第二级识别数}{第一级"拒识"数}。$$

相对于单级的集成分类器，经过两级级联的处理，被"拒识"的样本会减少。即两级的"拒识"率小于单级的"拒识"率。另外两级级联的识别率要高于单级分类器的识别率，同时，两级级联的误识率要高于单级的误识率。

本书所分析的级联分类器的第一级是由四种不同的分类器〔朴素贝叶斯（Naive Bayes），k-NN，MLP 及 SVM〕集成的，分别使用朴素贝叶斯、k-最近邻（k-NN）、多层神经网络（MLP）及支持向量机（SVM）对输入的 HOG 和 Contourlet 特征进行训练，训练后得到 8 组决策机制。级联分类器的第二级是使用旋转森林（Rotation Forest）并以 MLP 作为基分类器实现，以下就两级级联分类器的原理及方案分别介绍。

本节将首先分析朴素贝叶斯、k-最近邻（k-NN）、多层神经网络（MLP）及支持向量机（SVM）四种分类器的原理，并使用两种输入特征进行训练得到 8 组决策机制，之后使用 8 组决策机制以投票的方式构建集成分类器对输入测试样本进行表决，表决通过的样本分为正确识别和错误识别两类样本，表决没有通过即 8 种机制未达成一致的样本将送入下一级集成分类器进行识别。

1）朴素贝叶斯分类器

对于一个二值分类问题，设样本由 n 维特征向量 $\boldsymbol{x}(\boldsymbol{x} \in \boldsymbol{R}^n)$ 和类型值 $y(y \in C)$ 表示，其中 $C = \{-1, +1\}$。根据贝叶斯定理，后验概率定义如下：

$$p(C_i \mid \boldsymbol{x}) = \frac{p(C_i) p(\boldsymbol{x} \mid C_i)}{p(\boldsymbol{x})}, \quad i=1,2 \tag{3-24}$$

式中，$p(C_i)$ 为类型值 C_i 的先验概率，$p(\boldsymbol{x} \mid C_i)$ 是给定类型值 C_i 下 $\boldsymbol{x}$ 的条件概率，$p(\boldsymbol{x}) = \sum_{i=1}^{2} p(C_i) p(\boldsymbol{x} \mid C_i)$ 为 $\boldsymbol{x}$ 的边缘概率或证据。

朴素贝叶斯分类假设特征向量的每个属性是条件独立的，根据贝叶斯定理可给出朴素贝叶斯的定义：设 $\boldsymbol{X} = (x_1, x_2, \cdots, x_n)$ 为某待分类样本的特征向量，n 为特征维数，其中每个 $x_i (1 \leq i \leq n)$ 为一个特征属性，特征对应的类别集合为 $C = \{c_1, c_2, \cdots, c_m\}$，$m$ 为类型值个数，则根据贝叶斯定理，给定特征 $\boldsymbol{X}$ 下的类型值的条件概率 p 为：

$$p(C_k \mid x_1, x_2, \cdots, x_n) = \frac{p(x_1, x_2, \cdots, x_n \mid C_i) p(C_i)}{p(x_1, x_2, \cdots, x_n)}, \quad (1 \leq k \leq m) \tag{3-25}$$

其中用于计算的证据 $p(x_1, x_2, \cdots, x_n)$ 是相同的，我们不考虑这个条件，如果有很多类型，则需要找到分子最大的才能实现分类。分子是特征的类型值和特征向量的联合概率：$p(C_i, x_1, x_2, \cdots, x_n)$，重复使用链式法则，可以使用条件概率表示这个联合概率：

$$p(C_k, x_1, x_2, \cdots, x_n)$$
$$= p(C_k) p(x_1, x_2, \cdots, x_n \mid C_k)$$
$$= p(C_k) p(x_1 \mid C_k) p(x_2, x_3, \cdots, x_n \mid C_k, x_1) \quad (3\text{-}26)$$
$$= p(C_k) p(x_1 \mid C_k) p(x_2 \mid C_k, x_1) p(x_3, x_4, \cdots, x_n \mid C_k, x_1, x_2)$$
$$= p(C_k) p(x_1 \mid C_k) p(x_2 \mid C_k, x_1) p(x_3 \mid C_k, x_1, x_2) \cdots p(x_n \mid C_k, x_1, x_2, \cdots, x_{n-1})$$

基于"朴素"条件独立的假设，每个特征 x_i 相对于其他特征 $x_j (j \neq i)$ 是条件独立的，即 $p(x_i \mid C, x_j) = p(x_i \mid C)$，所以对于 $i \neq j$，联合概率模型可以表示为：

$$p(C_k, x_1, x_2, \cdots, x_n) = p(C_k) p(x_1 \mid C_k) p(x_2 \mid C_k) p(x_3 \mid C_k) \cdots = p(C_k) \prod_{i=1}^{n} p(x_i \mid C_k) \quad (3\text{-}27)$$

式（3-27）即为朴素贝叶斯分类器模型，使用这个分类器的时候，需要学习车辆类型对应的类型值，计算每个类别在训练样本中的出现频率以及每个特征属性划分对每个类别的条件概率估计，并将结果记录。识别过程中，对于输入向量 X 使用式（3-27）寻找联合概率最大时对应的类型值，即可实现样本自动分类。

2）k-最近邻分类器

k-最近邻分类算法是所有的机器学习算法中最简单的算法之一：给定一个常数 k，若某个样本在特征空间中的 k 个最相似样本中大多数属于某一类，则将输入样本分配给该类。判断相似度的规则一般使用欧拉距离，已知样本特征集合 D，其中包含 m 个样本，对于某一特定的输入特征向量 $X = (x_1, x_2, \cdots, x_n)$，使用 k-最近邻分类的算法是：

（1）使用欧拉公式计算输入特征与特征集合中 m 个样本的欧拉距离，即：

$$g_i = \|X - D_i\| = \sqrt{\sum_{j=1}^{n} (x_j - d_j)^2}, \quad 1 \leqslant i \leqslant m \quad (3\text{-}28)$$

（2）将 $g_i (1 \leqslant i \leqslant m)$ 从小到大排序，并根据设定的常数 k 取前 k 个最相似的样本；

（3）采用投票表决的方式确定最终的分类结果，在 k 个最相似样本中寻找最多的某一类对应的类型值，这里的 k 一般取奇数，避免两种票数相等难以决策。

3）多层神经网络（MLP）

人工神经网络充分吸收了人识别物体的特点，除了图像本身的统计、空间几何特征，它在被分类图像特征信息的指导下，通过自学习，修改网络结构及识别方式，达到提高分类精度和速度的目的。目前，在模式识别中使用最多的为多层前馈网络，其中又以 BP 网络为代表。BP（Back-Propagation）网络即反向传播算法，其实质是使用非线性优化问题解决样本输入输出之间关系映射问题，并通过梯度下降算法结合迭代运算来求解网络传播权值的一种学习方法。BP 神经网络模型如图 3.17 所示。

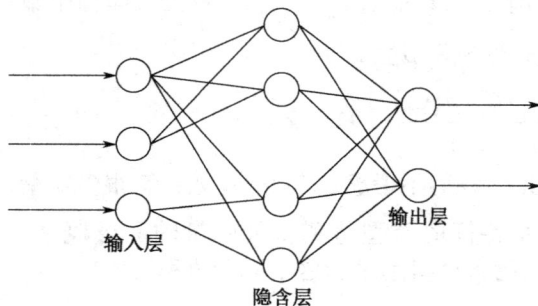

图 3.17　BP 神经网络模型

BP 网络通常选用三层结构，除了输入层、输出层结点，还可增加一个到多个隐含层结点，但增加网络层数并不能提升网络的分类能力。对于输入信号，要先向前传播到隐含层结点，经过作用函数后，再把隐含层结点的输出信号传播到输出结点，最后得到输出结果，映射函数一般采用 Sigmoid 函数：

$$f(x) = \frac{1}{1 + e^{-x}} \tag{3-29}$$

BP 算法的实质是一个均方最小误差问题，对于训练样本 $X(x_k, k = 1, 2, \cdots, n)$，期望输出为 $t = (t_1, t_2, \cdots, t_c)$，实际输出为 $z = (z_1, z_2, \cdots, z_c)$，隐含层输出为 $y = (y_1, y_2, \cdots, y_h)$，其中 c 为输出层结点个数，h 为隐含层结点个数，第 k 个神经元的输出为 net_k。则 BP 算法的目标函数为最小化误差函数，即：

$$J = \frac{1}{2} \sum_{i=1}^{c} (t_i - z_i)^2 \tag{3-30}$$

权值的迭代公式为：

$$W_{ij} = W_{ij} - \mu \frac{\partial J}{\partial W_{ij}} \tag{3-31}$$

式中，μ 为学习速率，$\mu > 0$。对于输出层结点，定义 $\delta_k = \frac{\partial J}{\partial net_k}$，于是：

$$\frac{\partial J}{\partial W_{ij}} = \frac{\partial J}{\partial net_k} \frac{\partial net_k}{\partial W_{ij}} = \frac{\partial J}{\partial net_k} y_j = \delta_k y_j \tag{3-32}$$

$$\delta_k = \frac{\partial J}{\partial net_{jk}} = \frac{\partial J}{\partial z_k} \frac{\partial z_k}{\partial net_k} = -(t_k - z_k) f'(net_k) \tag{3-33}$$

对于非输出层结点，即隐含层结点，有：

$$\frac{\partial J}{\partial y_j} = \frac{\partial}{\partial y_j} \left[\frac{1}{2} \sum_{k=1}^{c} (t_k - z_k)^2 \right] = -\sum_{k=1}^{c} (t_k - z_k) \frac{\partial z_k}{\partial y_j}$$

$$= -\sum_{k=1}^{c} (t_k - z_k) \frac{\partial z_k}{\partial net_k} \frac{net_k}{\partial y_j} = -\sum_{k=1}^{c} (t_k - z_k) f'(net_k) W_{kj} \tag{3-34}$$

于是可得：

$$\frac{\partial J}{\partial W_{ji}} = \frac{\partial J}{\partial y_j} \frac{\partial y_j}{\partial net_j} \frac{\partial net_j}{W_{ji}} = -\left[\sum_{k=1}^{c} (t_k - z_k) f'(net_k) W_{kj} \right] f'(net_k) x_i = \delta_j x_i \tag{3-35}$$

$$\delta_j = \frac{\partial J}{\partial net_j} = \frac{\partial J}{\partial y_j} \frac{\partial y_j}{\partial net_j} = f'(net_k) \sum_{k=1}^{c} \delta_k W_{kj} \tag{3-36}$$

BP 网络算法的学习过程由正向传播和反向传播组成，对于具有 M 层的 BP 网络来说，设置网络的初始权值 W 后，对于所有样本 $k = 1, \cdots, N$，首先正向计算隐含层输出 y，神经元输出 net_k 和网络实际输出 z；然后对各层从 M 到 2 进行反向计算，用式（3-33）和式（3-36）计算 δ_j，之后根据权值迭代公式（3-31）修正权值，直至网络收敛。

4）支持向量机（SVM）

支持向量机（SVM）是 Cortes 和 Vapnik[22]首次提出的，它在解决小样本、非线性及高维数等方面表现出较大的优势。对于两类的情况，支持向量机假设训练集可被一个超平面线性划分，对于 n 维输入特征向量 $\boldsymbol{x}$ 和标记 $y = \{-1, +1\}$，定义一个点到超平面的间隔为：

$$\delta_i = y_i(wx_i + b) \tag{3-37}$$

设 H_1 和 H_2 分别为各类中离超平面最近的样本且平行于分类超平面的平面，对于线性可分的情况，假设：

$$\begin{cases} H_1 : wx_i + b \geqslant 1, y_i = 1 \\ H_2 : wx_i + b \leqslant -1, y_i = -1 \end{cases} \tag{3-38}$$

将 w 和 b 进行归一化，可得分类间隔为 $\dfrac{2}{\|w\|}$，使得分类间隔最大，即使 $\dfrac{\|w\|}{2}$ 最小的超平面即最优分类超平面，如图 3.18 所示，H 是分类面，H_1 和 H_2 平行于 H，且过离 H 最近的两类样本的点的直线，在 H_1 和 H_2 上的样本点即支持矢量。

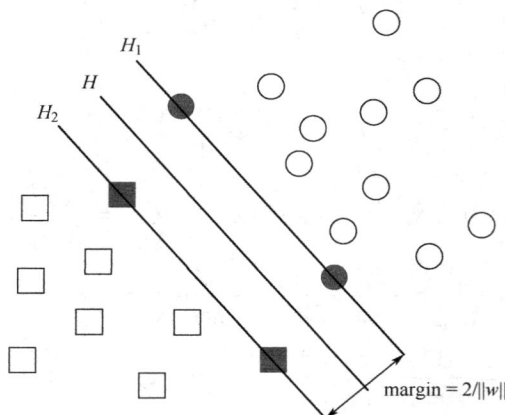

图 3.18 最优分类超平面

为了避免所有样本点都集中到 H_1 和 H_2 之间的无法分类地带，将最小分类间隔 y_i 固定为 1，则问题转化为具有目标函数和约束条件的二次规划问题：

$$\begin{cases} \min \dfrac{\|w\|}{2} \\ y_i(wx_i + b) \geqslant 1, i = 1, 2, \cdots, n \end{cases} \tag{3-39}$$

通常求解上述问题的想法是使用非负拉格朗日乘子 α_i，得到该问题的对偶问题：

$$\min \left\{ \frac{1}{2}\|w\|^2 - \sum_{i=1}^{n} \alpha_i \left[y_i(wx_i + b) - 1 \right] \right\} \tag{3-40}$$

为了避免通过将 α_i 趋向于 $+\infty$ 得到最小值，而不是原问题的最优解，忽略能够被 $y_i(wx_i + b) - 1 \geqslant 0$ 分离的点，设置相应的 α_i 为零，只有少部分 α_i 不为零，这些点即位于平面 H_1 和 H_2 上的样本点，对应的 x_i 即为支持矢量。则向量 w 为训练向量的线性组合，对应的 b 亦可求得：

$$w^* = \sum_{i=1}^{n} \alpha_i y_i x_i \tag{3-41}$$

$$b^* = y_i - w^* x_i \tag{3-42}$$

对应输入的测试样本 x，此时分类决策函数为：

$$g(x) = \left\langle w^*, x \right\rangle + b^* = \sum_{i=1}^{n} \alpha_i y_i \left\langle x_i, x \right\rangle + b^* \tag{3-43}$$

对于非线性情况，需要采用满足 Mercer 条件的核函数（kernel function）将输入向量映射到一个高维特征空间中，核函数对应某一空间中的内积：

$$K\left(x_i, x_j\right) = \psi\left(x_i\right) \cdot \psi\left(x_j\right) \tag{3-44}$$

此时相应的决策函数为：

$$g(x) = \sum_{i=1}^{n} \alpha_i y_i K\left(x_i, x_j\right) + b^* \tag{3-45}$$

第一级集成分类器基于简单的概念建立具有"拒识"功能的分类器："拒识"并没有正误之分，只是分类器对当前的输入样本保持中立的态度。我们通过使用上述四种不同的分类器对两种不同的输入特征进行训练建立集成分类器，对于某个置信度不够高的输入样本集成分类器将放弃对它的识别。使用 8 种分类机制对每个输入样本进行投票表决，建立具有"拒识"功能的集成分类器如图 3.19 所示。

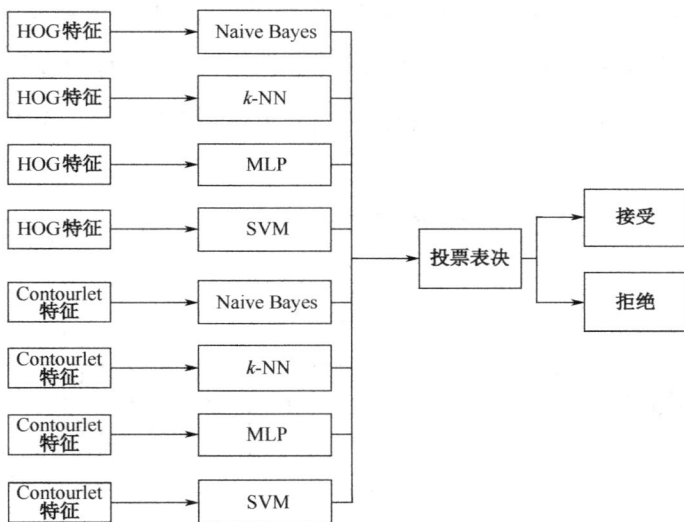

图 3.19 集成分类器表决机制

对于一个给定的测试样本 $x\left(x \in R^n\right)$，集成分类器中每个决策机制将得出一个识别结果。假设集合中分类器的个数为 M_1，每个分类器预测的结果分别为 $l_1, l_2, \cdots, l_{M_1}$。在通过 M_1 个分类结果决策时，样本最终类型是由所有分类器投票决定的，当最少有 t 个分类器同意某一分类结果时，才将样本赋予该值，其中 t 的一种取法可以为：

$$t \geqslant \begin{cases} \dfrac{M_1}{2} + 1, & M_1 \text{为偶数} \\ \dfrac{M_1 + 1}{2}, & M_1 \text{为奇数} \end{cases} \tag{3-46}$$

在其他情况下，集成分类器放弃对样本的识别。当进行多类样本分类时，只有当大多数分类器是正确时才进行分类，当大多数分类器结果不统一时放弃分类。如前所述，我们希望构建一个高可靠性、低"拒识"率、低误识率的分类器，为了达到降低"拒识"率的目的，将第一级被"拒识"的样本送入第二级进行再次识别。根据第一级集成分类器相同的理念，第二级分类器仍采用集成分类器来实现表决的目的。与第一级使用不同的基分类器进行集成不同，第二级采用相同的基分类器集成。我们选取多层神经网络（MLP）作为第二级的基分类器，这首先是基于提供充足的隐含层结点 MLP 可以拟合任何连续函数的考虑。另外，神经网络对不同的网络结构及输入特征向量一般具有不稳定的输出。

MLP 集成分类器得益于不同的基分类器对输入测试样本有不同的反映，为了进一步提升基分类器的多样性，我们使用一种新的被称为"元学习"算法的分类器集成方法——旋转森林（RF）[23]。与随机森林类似，旋转森林通过使用旋转特征空间来建立每一个基分类器。首先将输入特征集 F 划分为 K 个特征子集，然后对 K 个特征子集分别进行线性变换。之后使用 MLP 结合变换后的特征子集进行训练建立基分类器，这里线性变换的方法采用 PCA 分析。每次经过随机分割后得到的数据都被变换到不同的空间中，因而形成差别较大的分类子集。MLP 使用这些子集进行训练可以得到差异性较大的分类器，这样就进一步提升了集成分类器中 MLP 的多样性。第二级集成分类器的表决机制如图 3.20 所示，与第一级集成分类器类似，最终样本类别由多个 MLP 通过投票决定。假设集成分类器中基分类器的个数为 M_2，当最少有 t 个分类器同意某一分类结果时，将输入测试样本类型值赋予该分类结果。这里的 t 是决策阈值，当 M_2 是偶数时，$t \geqslant \dfrac{M_2}{2}+1$；$M_2$ 是奇数时，$t \geqslant \dfrac{M_2+1}{2}$。如果分类器对某样本的预测没有达成一致，则仍然拒绝对它的识别，显然这里 t 仍是决定"拒识"率的阈值。

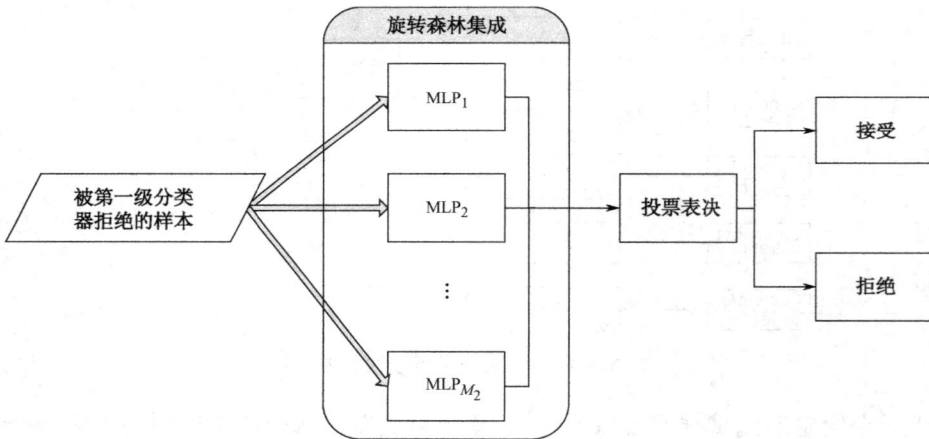

图 3.20　基于 MLP 的旋转森林集成分类器

旋转森林的实现原理为：给定包含 N 个样本的训练特征集 X，每个训练样本特征向量为 $\boldsymbol{x}=(x_1,\cdots,x_n)$，其中 n 为特征向量维数。对应特征向量的类型值分别为 $y=\{y_1,\cdots,y_N\}$，其中 y_i 的值为 $\omega_1,\cdots,\omega_C$ 中的一个，C 为类型总数。F 表示特征集。使用 $D_1,\cdots,D_L$ 表示每个基分类器，L 为基分类器个数，每个基分类器并行地进行训练。对于每个基分类器 D_i，按照以下步骤生成训练集：

（1）设定参数 K，将 F 随机分为 K 个特征子集，特征子集可以互不相交或有交错。为了最大化多样性，我们选择互不相交的特征子集。K 通常设为维数 n 的因子，则每个特征子集包含的特征个数为 $M=n/K$。

（2）设 F_{ij} 为基分类器 D_i 的第 j 个特征子集，X_{ij} 为 X 中只包含 F_{ij} 的特征子集，对于每个特征子集进行随机不放回抽取 75% 的样本，得到样本子集 X'_{ij}。对 X'_{ij} 进行 PCA 分析并存储主成分系数，即特征向量 $a_{ij}^{(1)},\cdots,a_{ij}^{(M_j)}$，由于求取的协方差矩阵的特征值有些为 0，则 $M_j \leqslant M$。

（3）将对 K 个特征子集进行主成分分析得到的系数向量使用一个稀疏"旋转"矩阵 R_i 表示：

$$R_i = \begin{bmatrix} a_{ij}^{(1)},\cdots,a_{ij}^{(M_1)} & [0] & \cdots & [0] \\ [0] & a_{ij}^{(1)},\cdots,a_{ij}^{(M_2)} & \cdots & [0] \\ \vdots & \vdots & \vdots & \vdots \\ [0] & [0] & \cdots & a_{ij}^{(1)},\cdots,a_{ij}^{(M_k)} \end{bmatrix} \tag{3-47}$$

旋转矩阵 R_i 的维数为 $n \times \sum_j M_j$。由于旋转矩阵的特征顺序在随机抽样的过程中被打乱，在计算分类器 D_i 的训练特征之前，需要将 R_i 按原始的特征顺序重排，重排后得到的旋转矩阵为 R_i^a。则分类器 D_i 的训练样本为 XR_i^a。训练完分类器后，在没有"拒识"的情况下，给定测试样本 x，假设 $d_{i,j}(xR_i)$ 为分类器 D_i 判断其为 ω_j 类的概率，则样本分配给每个类别 ω_j 的可信度为：

$$u_j(x) = \frac{1}{L}\sum_{i=1}^{L} d_{i,j}(xR_i), \quad j=1,\cdots,C \tag{3-48}$$

（4）最后将 x 分配给可信度最大值所对应的类别。

在分类器具有"拒识"选项的情况下，给定测试样本 x，按照图 3.20 所示分类决策方案，每个基分类器预测出一个类型值，最后使用多数投票的方法决定样本应属的类型。

本部分实验所使用的车辆前脸图像数据是使用第一章提出的基于对称特征融合方法获取对输入样本进行处理获取，所使用的样本集为 18 种类型车辆共 4 140 张图像，随机选择其中的 85%作为训练样本，其余 15%作为测试样本，为达到比较好的识别结果，训练样本尽可能包含了各种光照、颜色及不同角度的车辆前脸图像，部分车辆前脸图像如图 3.21 所示。

图 3.21　部分车辆前脸图像

3.2.6 实验结果及分析

本书所涉及的模式识别算法由 OpenCV 中机器学习（ML）[24]库实现，ML 库中集成了 Boosting、随机森林、神经网络等成熟算法，我们根据 ML 库中算法对输入输出特征向量的要求设置相应的参数，如神经网络中设置输入节点个数为特征向量维数，输出节点个数与类型个数相等，根据第 2 章所述方法设置中间层节点个数，训练步长为 1 000，训练误差收敛时小于 0.000 1，其他算法所使用的参数在以下内容有详细介绍。本书所有程序在 VS2008 下实现，所使用计算机为研华工控机，配置为 Intel Core Duo2.0 GHz。在实验中不同分类器的参数设置介绍如下。对于朴素贝叶斯分类器，分别计算训练样本中特征向量每个特征对于类型值的条件概率以及每个类别的先验概率，对测试样本使用联合概率计算公式（3-26）寻找联合概率最大时对应的类型值，实现样本的自动分类。对于 k-NN 分类器，在保证 k 为奇数和投票表决公正的条件下设置 k 的大小为 9。

对于多层神经网络（MLP）分类器，实验中设计了一个三层的 BP 网络，其中输入层结点个数 n_i 为样本特征向量维数，输出层结点个数 n_o 为车辆类型总数 18，因此需要建立一个大小为 18 维的矢量，在神经网络的训练模式中，首选是"双极"模式，我们使用 0.5 赋值给相应位置的模式，其他位置被赋值为-0.5，比如说第 8 类车辆对应的神经网络输出向量为：

$$\begin{bmatrix} -0.5,-0.5,-0.5,-0.5,-0.5,-0.5, \\ -0.5,0.5,-0.5,-0.5,-0.5,-0.5, \\ -0.5,-0.5,-0.5,-0.5,-0.5,-0.5 \end{bmatrix} \tag{3-49}$$

从向量（3-49）中可以看出，输出向量只有第 8 个位置被设置成 0.5，其余都为-0.5。根据经验，网络隐含层结点个数 n_h 取：

$$n_h = \sqrt{n_i + n_0} + m \tag{3-50}$$

其中，m 为常数，且 $m \in [1,10]$。在支持向量机（SVM）分类器中，我们使用了线性核函数进行特征从低维到高维的映射，线性核函数的表示形式为：

$$K(x_i, x_j) = x_i^{\mathrm{T}} \cdot x_j \tag{3-51}$$

在本书所使用的四种分类器中，只有 MLP 的输出标签是特征向量，其他三种分类器所对应的样本特征值分别为 0~17 的 18 个整数。

1. 单个分类器实验

对于所有的分类检测实验，我们每种车型随机选择 200 张图片作为训练样本，其余 30 张作为测试样本。第一个实验是对不同分类器使用不同特征进行训练的识别结果的比较，按照之前所述的使用两种特征以及它们的简单串联融合特征进行实验，每种分类机制所对应的识别结果如表 3.2 和图 3.22 所示。

表 3.2　朴素贝叶斯、k-NN、MLP 和 SVM 结合 HOG、Contourlet 特征分类

特　　征 ＼ 分 类 器	朴素贝叶斯	k-最近邻	MLP	SVM
HOG	92.4%	90.6%	89.6%	94.6%

续表

分类器 特征	朴素贝叶斯	k-最近邻	MLP	SVM
Contourlet	77.0%	80.4%	76.3%	78.5%
HOG+Contourlet	86.3%	81.7%	90.6%	94.6%

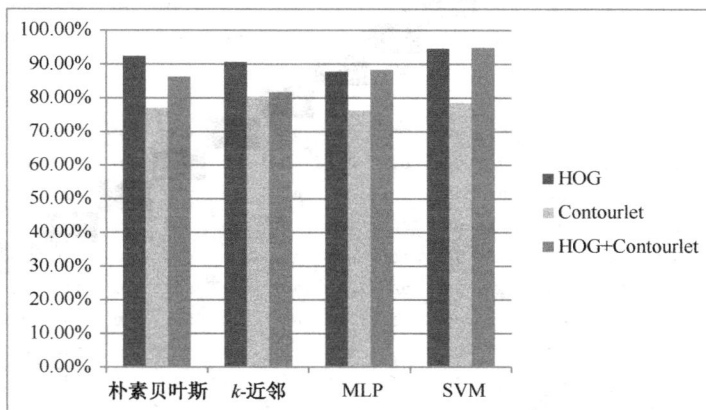

图 3.22　四种分类器和两种特征的分类识别结果比较

观察结果我们可以得到如下结论：

（1）首先，HOG 特征较之于 Contourlet 特征能够提取车辆图像较为丰富的信息并能提供不同车型更具分辨率的特征，因为由结果中可以看出四种分类器——朴素贝叶斯、k-最近邻、MLP 和 SVM 使用 HOG 特征都得到了比较好的结果。

（2）其次，使用 SVM 作为分类器，较之于其他分类器的识别结果最好。

（3）最后，采用两种特征的串联特征作为融合特征对于朴素贝叶斯分类器，k-NN 和 SVM 来说并不能显著提高识别效果，甚至还会使识别效果变差，论文[25]中提到了这种现象。这可能是由于不同的特征描述子提供不相同的信息，特征向量元素之间并不平衡，简单串联两种特征对多数分类器来说效果并不好。比较好的方法是保存两种特征之间的关联信息。MLP 似乎能通过将两种特征进行非线性组合得到关键特征，并且通过调节隐含层结点和网络结构能够较好地提取两种特征之间的互补关系，进而得到较好的识别结果，给这种说法以严格证明还有一定难度。

在多类分类问题中，通常使用混淆矩阵对每一类的识别效果及每一类与其他类别的相似性进行分析，混淆矩阵的行和列分别为样本实际和预测的类型，对角线上的元素为每一类样本正确识别的概率，非对角线上的元素为该类识别成其他类型的概率，HOG 特征车型使用 SVM 分类器训练得到的分类器对测试样本的识别效果最好，对其进行分析，得到对应样本识别结果的混淆矩阵如图 3.23 所示。从图 3.23 可得，18 种类型的车辆有 8 种车型的识别率为 100%，包括 Audi、Chery II 型及 Citroen 等。其中 Changan、Volkswagen I 型的识别率比较低，图 3.24 分别为 Chery I 型识别为 Chery II 型、Hyundai 及 Wulin 车的例图，其中所列的例图只是该种车型的代表。

	Audi	Buick I	Buick II	Changan	Chery I	Chery II	Chevrolet	Citroen	Ford	Honda	Hyundai I	Hyundai II	Mazda	Nissan	Peugeot	Volkswagen	Toyota	Wulin
Audi	1.00	0.00	0.00	0.00	0.00	0.00	0.00	0.00	0.00	0.00	0.00	0.00	0.00	0.00	0.00	0.00	0.00	0.00
Buick I	0.00	0.90	0.00	0.00	0.00	0.03	0.00	0.00	0.00	0.03	0.00	0.00	0.00	0.00	0.03	0.00	0.00	0.00
Buick II	0.00	0.10	0.90	0.00	0.00	0.00	0.00	0.00	0.00	0.00	0.00	0.00	0.00	0.00	0.00	0.00	0.00	0.00
Changan	0.00	0.13	0.03	0.73	0.03	0.00	0.00	0.00	0.00	0.00	0.00	0.00	0.00	0.00	0.00	0.00	0.00	0.07
Chery I	0.00	0.00	0.00	0.00	0.90	0.03	0.00	0.00	0.00	0.00	0.03	0.00	0.00	0.00	0.00	0.00	0.00	0.03
Chery II	0.00	0.00	0.00	0.00	0.00	1.00	0.00	0.00	0.00	0.00	0.00	0.00	0.00	0.00	0.00	0.00	0.00	0.00
Chevrolet	0.00	0.00	0.00	0.00	0.00	0.00	0.97	0.00	0.00	0.03	0.00	0.00	0.00	0.00	0.00	0.00	0.00	0.00
Citroen	0.00	0.00	0.00	0.00	0.00	0.00	0.00	1.00	0.00	0.00	0.00	0.00	0.00	0.00	0.00	0.00	0.00	0.00
Ford	0.00	0.00	0.00	0.00	0.00	0.00	0.00	0.00	1.00	0.00	0.00	0.00	0.00	0.00	0.00	0.00	0.00	0.00
Honda	0.00	0.00	0.00	0.00	0.00	0.00	0.00	0.00	0.00	1.00	0.00	0.00	0.00	0.00	0.00	0.00	0.00	0.00
Hyundai I	0.00	0.03	0.00	0.03	0.00	0.00	0.00	0.00	0.00	0.00	0.93	0.00	0.00	0.00	0.00	0.00	0.00	0.00
Hyundai II	0.00	0.00	0.00	0.00	0.00	0.00	0.00	0.00	0.00	0.00	0.00	1.00	0.00	0.00	0.00	0.00	0.00	0.00
Mazda	0.00	0.00	0.00	0.00	0.00	0.03	0.00	0.00	0.00	0.00	0.00	0.00	0.97	0.00	0.00	0.00	0.00	0.00
Nissan	0.00	0.00	0.00	0.00	0.00	0.00	0.03	0.00	0.00	0.00	0.00	0.00	0.00	0.97	0.00	0.00	0.00	0.00
Peugeot	0.00	0.00	0.00	0.00	0.00	0.00	0.00	0.00	0.00	0.00	0.00	0.00	0.00	0.00	1.00	0.00	0.00	0.00
Volkswagen	0.00	0.03	0.00	0.00	0.00	0.03	0.00	0.00	0.00	0.07	0.00	0.00	0.00	0.00	0.00	0.87	0.00	0.00
Toyota	0.00	0.00	0.00	0.00	0.00	0.03	0.00	0.07	0.00	0.00	0.00	0.00	0.00	0.00	0.00	0.00	0.90	0.00
Wulin	0.00	0.00	0.00	0.00	0.00	0.00	0.00	0.00	0.00	0.00	0.00	0.00	0.00	0.00	0.00	0.00	0.00	1.00

图 3.23　使用 SVM 分类器结合 HOG 特征车型识别结果混淆矩阵

（a）Chery I 识别为 Hyundai

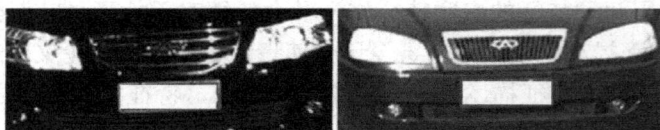

（b）Chery I 识别为 Chery II

（c）Chery I 识别为 Wulin

图 3.24　Chery I 型车识别成其他类型车辆例图，第一列为原车型，第二列为识别目标类型

从 3.24 可得，被错误识别的车辆存在几个问题：一是与其他类型车辆相似度比较高，如图 3.24（a）两种车型具有相同的散热器；二是光照条件的影响，如 3.24（b）中车辆图像是晚间拍摄，边缘细节信息已经模糊，对识别显然有影响；三是截取感兴趣区域的位置，如果所截取的车辆前脸区域包含较多的非车辆区域，则会对车型的识别产生影响。对于第一个问题，需要有能够描述车辆更详细的特征，如 HOG 和 Contourlet 的融合特征，对于第二个和第三个问题，可以本书所提出使用"拒识"的方式避免，即放弃对模糊车辆和包含

非车辆区域图像的识别，以提高系统的可靠性，"拒识"方法在级联集成分类器中会有进一步的分析。

2. 级联集成分类器实验

进一步的实验是采用本书中所提出的级联集成分类器方法进行带有"拒识"功能的分类实验，即放弃对置信度不高的输入样本的识别。根据两级集成分类器级联方案，首先将输入样本送入级联分类器的第一级即具有不同基分类器的集成分类器中识别，之后将被第一级集成分类器"拒识"的样本送入级联的第二级分类器进行进一步识别，表 3.3 和图 3.25 分别为两层级联分类器对样本的识别性能指标和级联分类器的识别性能指标。

表 3.3　两层级联分类器对样本的识别性能指标

	识别率（RR）	拒识样本数	误识样本数	拒识率（ReR）	可　靠　性
第一级	76.30%	127	1	23.52%	99.80%
第二级	62.99%	38	9	29.92%	92.91%
识别系统	91.11%	38	10	7.04%	98.15%

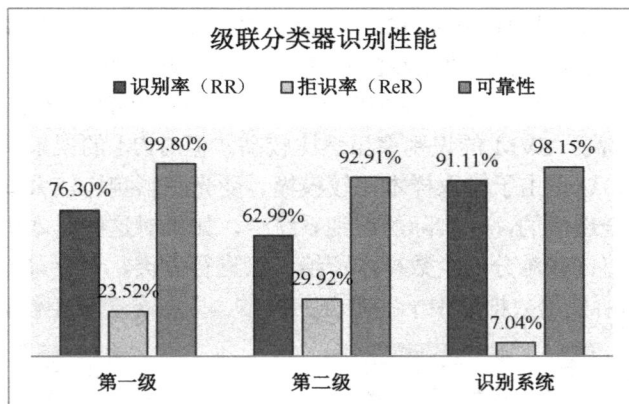

图 3.25　级联分类器的识别性能指标

根据之前的介绍，在级联的第一级中，集成分类器中有 8 种分类机制，即分别使用朴素贝叶斯、k-NN、MLP 和 SVM 结合 HOG 和 Contourlet 特征进行训练。分类识别最终结果是根据 8 种决策机制进行 $k/8$ 多数投票决定，其中 k 为对测试样本接受识别和拒绝识别的阈值，根据之前所述的表决方法，我们取 $k = 6$，即当有 6 种分类决策机制达成一致时接受对该样本的识别，否则拒绝对该样本的识别。使用上一节相同的实验数据进行分类识别，对 8 种决策机制的识别结果进行统计分析，当有 6 种以上决策机制的识别标签达成一致时，则将对应的样本归属于该类车辆。18 种车型每种测试样本为 30 个，总共有 540 个测试样本。在第一级被拒绝识别的样本为 127 个，识别错误的样本为 1 个。则被拒绝识别的样本占总样本的百分比即"拒识"率（ReR）为 23.52%，检测错误率（ER）为 0.19%，检测率（RR）为 76.30%，根据公式（3-23）可得检测系统的可靠性为 99.81%。

被第一级分类器拒绝识别的样本是较难识别的样本，我们设计了第二级级联分类器对其进行进一步处理。第二级集成分类器的设计主要根据表 3.2 中的结果，表 3.2 中的结果表明大部分分类器对简单融合 HOG 和 Contourlet 特征并不能得到更好的识别效果，更好的解决方法是能够保存两种特征之间的相互关系。从上一节的分析中得出 MLP 能够通过对 HOG 和 Contourlet 特征进行非线性组合提取关键特征进而达到提升识别率的效果，另外基于神经网络对不同输入和网络结构能够体现多样性的考虑，我们在第二级级联分类器中使用 MLP 作为基分类器。

MLP 基分类器的训练数据是使用旋转森林方法经过对特征集进行随机分割、线性变换及构造稀疏矩阵得到，这里原始训练集是 HOG 和 Contourlet 特征的简单串联特征。分别使用变换后的 M_2 个训练集对 MLP 进行训练。在识别阶段，第二级集成分类器将对被第一级拒识的样本进行识别。与第一级类似，第二级识别的最终结果采用 k/M_2 多数投票的方式决定，其中 k 为决定"拒识"率的阈值。最后系统的总识别率将根据第一级和第二级的识别结果综合得到。根据 Zhang[26] 对集成分类器个数的实验，我们设置 MLP 基分类器的个数为 $M_2 = 5$，当有 3 个基分类器结果达成一致时接受对样本的识别，否则依然拒绝对其的识别。通过对样本进行测试，将被第一级拒绝识别的 127 个样本使用第二级分类器进行识别，第二级拒绝识别样本个数为 38 个，错误识别样本 9 个。则第二级系统识别率为 62.99%，误识率为 7.08%，"拒识"率为 29.92%，系统可靠性为 92.91%。根据之前的分析可知，系统"拒识"样本共有 38 个，误识样本共 10 个，系统的总识别率为 91.11%，总"拒识"率为 7.04%，总误识率为 1.85%，则可得系统的总的可靠性为 98.15%。

对比表 3.2 和表 3.3 的结果，在正确识别率上，级联集成分类器比朴素贝叶斯、k-最近邻及单个 MLP 分类器都高，SVM 的识别率虽然比较高，但 SVM 的误识率比级联集成分类器高，即可靠性比较低，这是由于输入样本比较模糊、受光照影响比较大或由于程序自动获取的车脸区域位置不完全造成的，在实际的识别系统中，如果对这些样本进行强分类，会对统计工作造成影响，而将比较难分的少数样本留给人工进行分类，则会降低误识带来的风险，如图 3.26 所示为本书所使用数据库中一些难分的样本，即被分类器拒绝识别的样本。

图 3.26　部分被"拒识"的样本，主要受 ROI 区域获取不当及光照影响

图中第一行显示的被拒绝识别样本主要是由于所截取的感兴趣区域位置包含背景区域造成的，第二行的样本主要受白天光照的影响，导致前脸区域上出现反光和边缘模糊现象，第三行显示的测试样本为傍晚时采集，此时光照强度不够，导致所采集的车辆图片信息比较模糊。分析图 3.26 所示的被拒绝识别的样本，本书所设计的模式识别系统放弃了对它们的识别，但这些样本可以由人工来完成识别，如果使用程序对他们进行强分，显然会得到不太理想的结果，进而可能在盗拍车辆检索过程中漏掉重要信息。

在级联集成分类器的第二级中，有 47 个车辆前脸样本（38 个被"拒识"+9 个误识）

没有被系统正确识别。上一章提出的基于神经网络的旋转森林集成分类器有一种不带"拒识"选项的识别方式，即使用每个 MLP 预测输入测试样本属于每个类型的概率，将样本归属于对应的具有最大概率总和的类型。为了进一步探讨"拒识"和误识之间的关系，我们采用不带"拒识"功能的判别方式将 38 个被拒绝识别的样本进行硬分类，识别结果为：正确识别的样本数目为 17 个，错误识别的样本数目为 21 个。由于系统在第一级有一个误识的样本，则系统总误识样本数目为 21+9+1=31 个，此时系统的正确识别率为 94.26%，不具有"拒识"选项的识别系统的所有误识样本及误识目标类型如图 3.27 所示。

Buick I ->Hyundai II	Buick I ->Hyundai I	Buick I ->Honda	Buick II ->Buick I	Buick II ->Buick I
Changan->Nissan	Changan->Nissan	Changan->Chery I	Chery I ->Hyundai I	Chery II ->Chery I
Chery II ->Hyundai II	Chery II ->Mazda	Chery II ->Audi	Chevrolet->Honda	Citroen->Buick I
Honda->Mazda	Hyundai I ->Buick I	Hyundai I ->Buick I	Hyundai I ->Ford	Hyundai I ->Chery II
Hyundai I ->Chery I	Hyundai II ->Buick II	Hyundai II ->Peugeot	Hyundai II ->Buick II	Mazda->Citroen
Nissan->Chevrolet	Peugeot->Volkswagen	Volkswagen->Peugeot	Volkswagen->Nissan	Toyota->Changan
Toyota->Volkswagen				

图 3.27　不具有"拒识"选项的识别系统的所有误识样本及误识目标类型

从图 3.27 可以看出，误识的样本多为光照条件及 ROI 区域中有背景干扰的样本，而通过设计有"拒识"选项的识别系统则可放弃对这些样本的识别，由人工对模糊样本处理会提高整个系统的可靠性。当我们使用带有"拒识"选项的系统方案进行识别时，总的误识率为 1.85%，当我们不使用"拒识"项时，总的误识率为 5.74%。

3.3　小结

为了解决交通监控系统中交通流量统计分析、假牌车辆识别和自动收费系统对不同车型进行自动计费等问题，本章研究了静态图像中车辆区域定位及车辆类型识别两种技术。

首先分析了局部能量形状直方图、局部二值模式和梯度方向直方图等 5 种特征提取方法，并采用支持向量机和 k-最近邻分类器进行车辆品牌识别实验，实验结果表明基于 HOG 特征和支持向量机的车辆品牌识别方法要优于其他组合，其识别率达到 92.40%。

其次，为了有效描述车脸图像，本书采用高可分辨性图像特征提升识别效果，如 HOG 和 Contourlet 特征。同时为了避免维数灾难问题，文中提出了使用主成分分析（PCA）对特征进行降维。另外，为了探讨两种不同特征融合互补提高识别率的可能性，本书提出了将 HOG 和 Contourlet 两种特征的简单串联作为分类器的输入特征，并通过实验验证了该方法的可行性。

通过设计级联集成分类器方案在保证系统可靠性的同时提高了样本的正确识别率。不单纯的追求系统的高识别率，引入"拒识"选项降低了误识带来的风险。级联集成分类器是一个串行的方法，第二级的输入样本是第一级被拒绝的样本，可以通过引入多级级联分类器进一步降低被"拒识"的样本的数目。我们设计的级联分类器的第一级由 8 个不同的分类机制组成，第二级是使用 MLP 作为基分类器并结合旋转森林变换后的特征样本进行的识别。两级集成分类器都具有拒绝识别不确定或模糊样本的功能。在平衡"拒识"样本数目和系统可靠性的关系后，我们得到了一个高可靠性并且高识别率的系统，最后系统的可靠性为 98.15%，其中有 7.04%的样本被"拒识"。

参考文献

[1] Sarfraz M S, Hellwich O. On Head Pose Estimation in Face Recognition[M]. Computer Vision and Computer Graphics. Theory and Applications. Springer Berlin Heidelberg, 2009.

[2] Sarfraz M S, Hellwich O. An efficient front-end facial pose estimation system for face recognition[J]. Pattern Recognition and Image Analysis, 2008, 18 (3): 434-441.

[3] Morrone M C, Owens R A. Feature detection from local energy[J]. Pattern Recognition Letters, 1987, 6 (5): 303-313.

[4] Ojala T, Pietikäinen M, Harwood D. A comparative study of texture measures with classification based on featured distributions[J]. Pattern recognition, 1996, 29 (1): 51-59.

[5] Dalal N, Triggs B. Histograms of oriented gradients for human detection[C]. IEEE Computer Society Conference on Computer Vision and Pattern Recognition, 2005.

[6] Cortes C, Vapnik V. Support-vector networks[J]. Machine learning, 1995, 20 (3): 273-297.

[7] 边肇祺, 张学工. 模式识别 (第二版)[M]. 北京: 清华大学出版社, 2001.

[8] Petrović V, Cootes T. Analysis of features for rigid structure vehicle type recognition [C]. British Machine Vision Conference, 2004.

[9] Negri P. An Oriented-Contour Point Based Voting Algorithm for Vehicle Type Classification[C]. Proceedings of the 18th International Conference on Pattern Recognition, 2006.

[10] Dalal N, Triggs B. Histogram of oriented gradients for human detection [C]. IEEE Computer Society Conference on Computer Vision and Pattern Recognition, Montbonnot, France, 2005.

[11] Do M, Vetterli M. Contourlets: a directional multiresolution image representation [C].

International Conference on Image Processing, New York, USA, 2002.

[12] Mario K. The curse of dimensionality [C]. Fifth Online World Conference on Soft Computing in Industrial Applications (WSC5) Held on the Internet , 2000.

[13] Hespanha J P, Kriegman D. Eigenfaces vs. Fisherfaces: Recognition using class specific linear projection[J]. IEEE Transactions on Pattern Analysis and Machine Intelligence,1997, 19 (7): 711-720.

[14] Sun Q, Zeng S, Liu Y P, et al.A new method of feature fusion and its application in image recognition[J], Pattern Recognition. 2005, 38 (12): 2437-2448.

[15] Cortes C, Vapnik V. Support-Vector Networks [J]. Machine Learning, 1995, 20 (3): 273-279.

[16] 欧阳琰. 道路信息自动检查中的路面破损识别方法及其实现研究[D]. 武汉: 武汉理工大学, 2009.

[17] Duda R O, Hart P E, Stork D G. Pattern Classification[M]. 2nd edition,New York: Wiley, 2001.

[18] Zhang P, Bui T D, Suen C Y. A novel cascade ensemble classifier system with a high recognition performance on handwritten digits [J]. Pattern Recognition, 2007, 40 (12): 3415-3429.

[19] Breiman L. Bagging predictors [J]. Machine Learning. 1996, 24: 123-140.

[20] Freund Y, Schapire R. A decision-theoretic generalization of on-line learning and an application to boosting [J].Computational Learning Theory Lecture Notes in Computer Science, 1997,55: 119-139.

[21] Kuncheva L, Rodriguez J, Plumpton C, et al. Random subspace ensembles for fMRI classification [J], IEEE Transactions on Medical Imaging, 2010 ,29 (2): 531-542.

[22] Rodrí guez J, Kuncheva L, Alonso C. Rotation forest: A new classifier ensemble method[J]. IEEE Transactions on Pattern Analysis and Machine Intelligence, 2006, 28 (10): 1619-1630.

[23] OpenCV(open source computer vision) wiki[EB/OL]. http://opencv.willowgarage.com/wiki. Accessed on 1st June 2010.

[24] 沈花玉, 王兆霞, 高成耀, 等. BP神经网络隐含层单元的确定[J]. 天津理工大学学报, 2008, 24 (5): 13-15.

[25] Fu Y, Cao L, Guo G. Multiple feature fusion by subspace learning[C]. Proceedings of the 2008 international conference on Content-based image and video retrieval, Niagara Falls, Canada, 2008.

[26] Zhang B. Reliable Classification of Vehicle Types Based on Cascade Classifier Ensembles [J]. IEEE Transactions on Intelligent Transportation Systems, 2013,14 (1): 322-332.

第4章

交通场景中车辆异常行为感知理论与技术

本书研究城市交通场景中车辆异常行为的检测方法，具体内容如下。

首先，研究了基于颜色空间模型的城市交通场景中信号灯的检测方法。采用中值滤波和光线补偿算法对城市交通场景图像进行预处理，并采用交通信号灯的颜色直方图和巴氏系数进行交通信号灯模板匹配；基于颜色空间模型进行城市交通场景中信号灯的状态检测，实验结果表明基于 HSV 颜色空间模型的城市交通场景中信号灯的检测方法优于其他两种彩色空间。

其次，研究了基于车辆及车牌对称特征的城市交通场景中车辆检测的方法，并与基于车牌的车辆检测方法、基于 Gabor 特征及支持向量机（SVM）的车辆检测方法和基于 Haar-like 特征及 AdaBoost 分类器的车辆检测方法进行了对比分析，实验结果表明基于车辆及车牌对称特征的城市交通场景中车辆检测的方法优于其他三种方法，其检测率达到 91.2%。

最后，构建了东南大学城市交通场景中车辆行为图像库，并提出了一种基于联合特征的城市交通场景中车辆异常行为的检测方法，该方法基于梯度方向直方图（Histograms of Oriented Gradient，HOG）特征和局部二值模式（Local Binary Pattern，LBP）特征的串联联合，并采用支持向量机（SVM）方法进行自动分类。采用东南大学城市交通场景中车辆行为图像库进行了对比实验，实验结果表明：在选取线性核函数的条件下，基于 HOG-LBP 的联合特征的车辆行为识别优于其他三种单特征，其识别率达到 93.6%；车辆异常行为中闯红灯行为判定率最高，非法转向行为最难判定。

4.1 基于颜色空间模型的城市交通场景中信号灯的检测方法

在城市交通场景中，行车环境的实时感知对于行驶的车辆十分重要，而交通信号灯作为交叉路口中最重要的信号标识，其信号状态直接影响着车辆行驶的具体行为。因此要准确判断车辆的具体行为，首先要对道路场景下的交通信号灯的状态进行检测识别。因此本章主要研究基于颜色空间模型的交通信号灯状态实时检测方法。

4.1.1 图像预处理

4.1.1.1 图像去噪

本书的实验原始数据由山东省济宁市交警支队提供，这些数据是由电子警察系统记录一个月产生的。图像由安装在济宁市洸河路和供销路交叉口的监控相机在每天 8:00—17:00 的时间段触发获取，包含了不同的天气和光照情况。文章筛选出定位精度高、图像清晰度高的 340 张图片作为原始数据库，包括了车辆闯红灯、压线、非法转向及正常行驶四种车辆行为，原始图像分辨率为 2 048×1 536 像素，部分样本库图像如图 4.1 所示。

图 4.1　部分样本库图像

在交通场景图像的获取过程中，难免会存在一些噪声，不利于图像的后续处理。由于噪声频谱通常集中在高频阶段，因此可以采用低通滤波的方法来减少噪声。但由于交通场景下信号灯区域以及车辆边缘轮廓包含了大量的高频信息，低通滤波在过滤噪声的同时，会使图像的边缘信息变得模糊；若经低通滤波后再使用高通滤波来加强图像边缘轮廓，则又会加强图像的噪声。在图像学中，常常根据噪声的不同特性来选择适合的图像平滑方法，一般在频率域或者空间域采取不同的去噪措施。对空间域滤波而言，它是在图像空间借助模板进行邻域操作完成，其滤波方式一般分为线性和非线性两类。局部均值滤波就是一种常见的比较简单的线性滤波器，其基本思想是对图像中每个像素的灰度值由其局部邻域内各个像素灰度的均值替代，对噪声的消除效果比较好，但却容易丢失图像的边缘信息。因此，为了在图像平滑时降低模糊的负面影响，保护好原图像的边缘轮廓信息，同时又能够很好地过滤噪声，本书采取了中值滤波来对图像进行去噪处理。

中值滤波是一种图像处理中广泛使用的非线性滤波器，它是由 Jukey 在 1971 年提出的，并应用在一维信号处理技术（时间序列分析）中，后来被二维图像信号处理技术所引用[1~3]。

中值滤波的基本思想是对已经选好的窗口内所有像素的灰度值进行排序，然后取出排序结果的中间值作为原窗口中心点处像素的灰度值。中值滤波是使用一个滑动窗口在图像上进行扫描，假设对一个一维序列 $f_1, f_2, \cdots, f_n$，取其窗口长度为 m（m 为奇数），对此序列进行中值滤波，即从输入序列中相继抽出 m 个数，$f_{i-V}, \cdots, f_{i-1}, \cdots, f_1, \cdots, f_{i+1}, \cdots, f_{i+V}$，其中 i 表示窗口的中心位置，$V = \dfrac{m-1}{2}$，然后按照数值将这 m 个数从大到小进行排列，取其排列序号为正中间的数值作为输出值，则用公式表达为：

$$Y_i = \text{Med}\{f_{i-V}, \cdots, f_i, \cdots, f_{i+V}\} \ (i \in \mathbf{Z}, V = \dfrac{m-1}{2}) \tag{4-1}$$

对于二维序列 $\{X_{ij}\}$ 进行中值滤波，则滤波窗口也变为二维窗口，但其可以有不同的形状，例如方形、线状形、十字形以及圆环形等，二维数据的中值滤波可表示为：

$$Y_{i,j} = \underset{A}{\text{Med}}\{X_{ij}\}, \ A \text{ 为滤波窗口} \tag{4-2}$$

本章所采取的中值滤波窗口大小为 3×3 像素，先利用冒泡排序法对窗口中 9 个点进行排序，然后取其中值，如对图 4.2 中四种车辆行为原始含噪图像采用中值滤波处理后的效果图如图 4.3 所示，从图中可以看出，经过中值滤波处理后，图像中孤立的噪声点明显减少，图像变得更为平滑，而对车辆边缘等细节的影响不大。

（a）

（b）

（c）

（d）

图 4.2　原始含噪图像

（a）

（b）

（c）

（d）

图 4.3　中值滤波处理后的效果图

4.1.1.2　光线补偿

光线补偿算法流程图如图 4.4 所示。

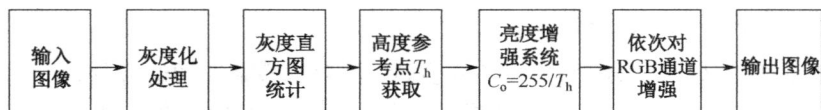

图 4.4　光线补偿算法流程图

由于采集的城市交通图像中包含不同光照和天气的情况，例如在一些阴暗或者黄昏天气条件下，整幅图像会偏暗，导致交通信号灯的检测过程容易忽略信号灯区域，从而导致漏检率的增加，因此需要对灰暗图像进行光线补偿。消除光线影响最常用的是图像增强技术，图像增强技术的作用主要有两点：一是采取一些技术手段来改善图像的视觉效果；二是将图像转化为一种更适合人或者计算机进行处理和分析的形式，增强感兴趣区域以便于后续处理。在本章中，采用光线补偿[4, 5]来解决上述问题。光线补偿的基本思想是：首先对图像进行灰度化处理，并对整幅灰度图像的直方图进行统计；其次，将图像中所有像素的亮度由高到低排列；再次，取前 15% 的亮度最大的像素，将这些像素的平均亮度线性放大为 255，此时该亮度的临界值就称为亮度参考点；最后，根据求得的系数再把整幅图像的亮度线性放大，实际上就是增强图像中部分像素的 RGB 值。光线补偿算法的具体步骤如图 4.4 所示。在图 4.3 中，将 RGB 彩色图像转化为灰度图，即：

$$I_{\text{gray}} = 0.299 \otimes I_R + 0.587 \otimes I_G + 0.114 \otimes I_B \tag{4-3}$$

式中：I_R、I_G 和 I_B 分别为原图像 R、G、B 三个分量的表示，I_{gray} 是图像中相应的灰度值。

如图 4.5 所示为对上述去噪图像经光线补偿算法处理后的效果图。

(a)　　　　　　　　　　　　　　　　(b)

(c)　　　　　　　　　　　　　　　　(d)

图 4.5　经光线补偿算法处理后的效果图

4.1.1.3　感兴趣区域划分

由于原始图像的分辨率为 2 048×1 536 像素，如果对整幅图像进行处理，势必会大大增加计算机运算的时间，因此需要确定图像中的部分感兴趣区域。在本章中，交通信号灯区域是我们的感兴趣区域。通过对大量样本图像进行分析，我们发现图像中的交通信号灯都位于图像上方的 1/4 区域，感兴趣区域划分结果如图 4.6 所示。

（a）　　　　　　　　　　　　　　　　（b）

图 4.6　感兴趣区域划分结果

(c)   (d)

图 4.6 感兴趣区域划分结果（续）

4.1.2 色彩空间模型

色彩是人类视觉感知中十分重要的一部分，它既是客观存在的，也是主观感知的。对于城市交通场景中的信号灯来说，由于它是一种发光的物体，并且颜色特征在图像中十分显著，因此能否合理地采用交通信号灯的颜色特征成为交通信号灯检测的关键所在。在色彩学中，研究人员建立了多种色彩模型，以一维、二维、三维甚至四维空间坐标来表示某单一色彩，常用的色彩空间模型有 RGB、HSV、YCbCr 颜色空间等。

4.1.2.1 RGB 颜色空间

RGB 颜色空间[6]是由 T. Yong 在 1802 年提出的，他在色度学基础理论中表示，任何颜色都可以由三种基本颜色（红 Red、绿 Green、蓝 Blue）按照不同的比例混合而成，其表达式为：

$$f = aR + bG + cB \tag{4-4}$$

式中：R 为红色分量；G 为绿色分量；B 为蓝色分量；a、b、c 分别为各分量的权值；f 为合成后的色彩颜色。在 RGB 颜色空间模型中，每种颜色出现在红、绿、蓝的原色光谱分量中，该颜色模型是基于笛卡尔坐标系统的，其颜色空间模型如图 4.7 所示，不同的颜色处在立方体上或者其内部，并可用从原点分布的向量来定义，为了方便理解，假定所有的颜色都归一化至[0,1]范围内取值。在数字图像处理中，RGB 色彩空间得到了广泛的应用，但是在该颜色模型中，R、G、B 各分量存在着很大的相关性，且容易受到光照影响，因此 RGB 色彩空间并不适用于彩色图像的精确分割。

4.1.2.2 HSV 颜色空间

HSV 颜色空间[7]也称六角椎体颜色模型，是合乎人眼对色彩空间感知的颜色空间，也是在图像分割中最常用的颜色空间之一。其中 H、S、V 分别是三个颜色通道的色调、饱和度和明度，H 表示颜色类别，如红色、蓝色、绿色；S 表示颜色的深浅程度；而 V 表示颜色的明度。

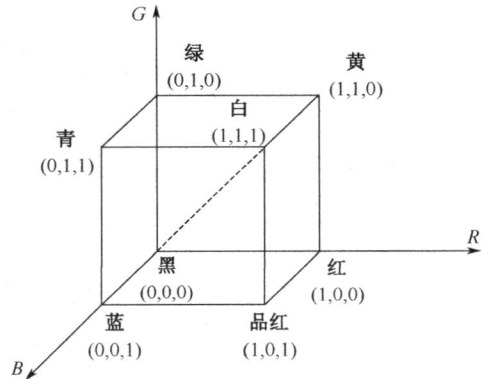

图 4.7 RGB 颜色空间模型

现实世界中任一种颜色都可以用这三个通道的不同组合来表示，HSV 颜色空间的三维模型如图 4.8 所示。

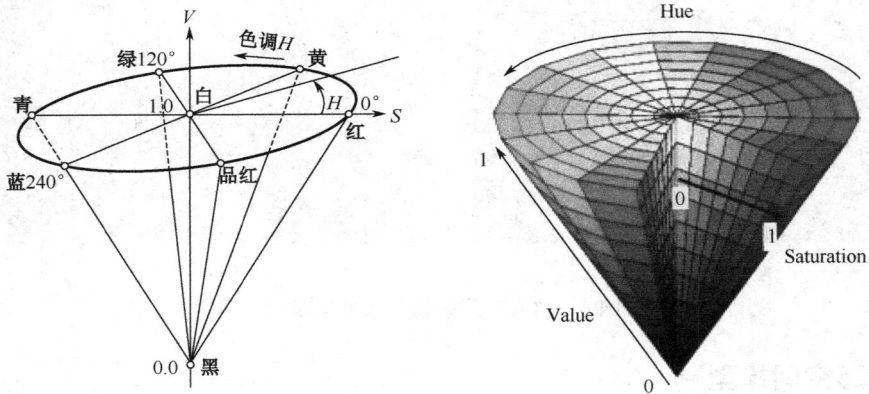

图 4.8　HSV 颜色空间的三维模型

HSV 的空间模型是一个倒圆锥，H、S、V 在模型上表示的是三个轴，其中 V 是倒圆锥的中心轴，范围从 0 到 1，圆锥顶面代表是明度为 1 的情况；色调 H 围绕 V 轴用一定角度来表示，其中红、绿、蓝分别间隔 120°，互补色分别相差 180°。圆锥顶面半径为 1，表示饱和度 S 的范围从 0 到 1，原点即圆锥的顶点表示黑色（V=0，H 和 S 无定义），顶面中心表示白色（V=1，S=0，H 无定义），从顶点到原点，明度逐渐降低。在 RGB 色彩空间中，每一种颜色都可以用 HSV 色彩空间来表示，其转换公式为：

$$H = \begin{cases} \theta, & B \leq G \\ 2\pi - \theta, & B > G \end{cases} \tag{4-5}$$

$$S = \begin{cases} 0, & \max = 0 \\ \dfrac{\max(R,G,B) - \min(R,G,B)}{\max(R,G,B)}, & \text{其他} \end{cases} \tag{4-6}$$

$$V = \frac{\max(R,G,B)}{255} \tag{4-7}$$

其中，θ 的表达式为：

$$\theta = \arccos \left\{ \frac{\frac{1}{2}\left[(R-G)+(R+G)\right]}{\left[(R-G)^2 + (R-G)(G-B)^{\frac{1}{2}}\right]} \right\} \tag{4-8}$$

HSV 颜色空间在图像处理学中有以下优点。

（1）HSV 颜色模型与人眼的颜色感觉相适应，更加接近人的视觉特性，可以有针对性地进行处理。

（2）HSV 颜色空间对光照不敏感，这一点极其重要，因为在复杂的外界环境中获取的图像，必然会受到光照的影响。基于这种情况，能够选择对光照不敏感的色彩空间是十分关键的。

（3）在 HSV 颜色空间中，H、S、V 三分量相互比较独立，相关性不大，这样的话，即

便 H、S、V 三个分量中如果有一个分量的规律不符合，也不会影响其他分量，可以保证整体规律不受太大影响，另外 H、S、V 三分量也能在较大范围内满足彩色图像处理的需求。

4.1.2.3 YCbCr 颜色空间

基于 YCbCr 颜色空间[8]的图像易于压缩、方便传输和处理，所以 YCbCr 颜色空间被广泛应用于机器视觉和图像传输领域，其中 Y 为颜色的亮度信息，Cb 为颜色与蓝色亮度的差值，Cr 为颜色与红色亮度的差值。当输入信号为 RGB 图像时，Cb 为蓝色分量与信号亮度的差值，Cr 为红色分量与信号亮度的差值，其转换公式为：

$$\begin{bmatrix} Y \\ Cb \\ Cr \end{bmatrix} = \begin{bmatrix} 0.257 & 0.564 & 0.098 \\ -0.148 & -0.291 & 0.439 \\ 0.439 & -0.368 & -0.071 \end{bmatrix} \begin{bmatrix} R \\ G \\ B \end{bmatrix} + \begin{bmatrix} 16 \\ 128 \\ 128 \end{bmatrix} \tag{4-9}$$

基于上述三种常用的颜色空间的转换参数及方程分析，下面将分别采用这三种颜色空间对交通场景中的信号灯颜色进行表征，比较在三种颜色空间下信号灯的识别效果，以确定最佳颜色空间。

4.1.3 信号灯模板匹配

4.1.3.1 颜色直方图

颜色直方图[9, 10]是在图像检索系统中被广泛采取的颜色特征，它描述的是不同色彩在整幅图像中所占的比例，而并不关心每种色彩所处的空间位置。在交通信号灯灯板中，颜色发光区域所占灯板区域的比例是固定的，因此采用颜色直方图来描述交通信号灯的特征。R 通道的颜色直方图如图 4.9 和图 4.10 所示，对于红色信号灯，我们采用 R 通道的颜色直方图。

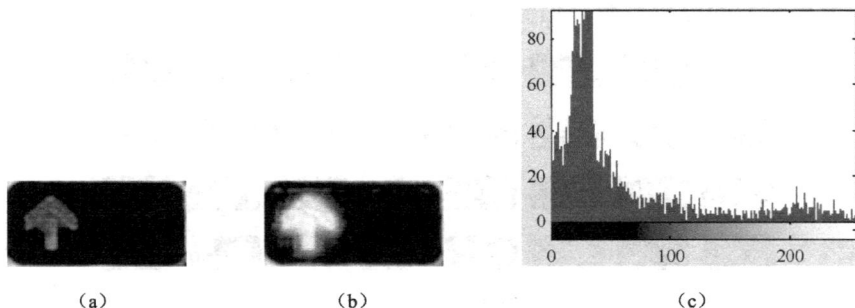

（a）　　　　　　　（b）　　　　　　　（c）

图 4.9 R 通道的颜色直方图一

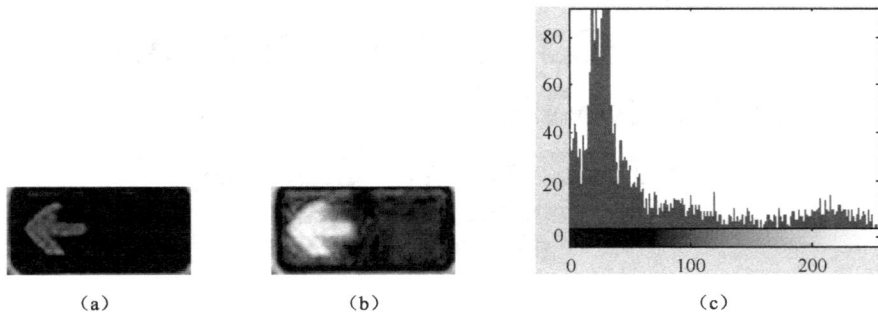

（a）　　　　　　　（b）　　　　　　　（c）

图 4.10 R 通道的颜色直方图二

从颜色直方图可以看出，尽管在信号灯板中红色信号灯的位置不同，但它的红色区域所在灯板区域的比例是一样的，因而颜色直方图具有极高的相似度。下面将通过巴氏系数来计算颜色直方图之间的相关系数。

4.1.3.2　巴氏系数

图像相似度计算主要通过对两幅图像之间内容的相似程度进行打分，根据分数的高低来判断图像的相似程度。在上节感兴趣区域的划分中，我们以交通信号灯的灯板为模板，在感兴趣区域中计算与模板相似的图像，也就是我们所需要识别的信号灯灯板，采用颜色直方图匹配的巴氏系数作为匹配模板的标准。

在统计学中，巴氏距离[11~13]（Bhattacharyya distance）用于分类中测量类的可分离性。巴氏[14]系数（Bhattacharyya Coefficient）是对两个统计样本的重叠量的近似计算，巴氏系数可用来对两组样本的相关性进行测量。巴氏系数的计算涉及对两个样本的重叠部分进行基本形式的积分。两个样本值的积分被分成指定数目的部分，而每一个样本的每一个部分的成员数被用于下式中：

$$\text{Bhattacharyya Coefficient} = \sum\{i=1|n\}\sqrt{\left(\sum a_i\right) \cdot \left(\sum b_i\right)} \tag{4-10}$$

式中：a，b 为两个样本；n 是分块数；a_i，b_i 分别是在 a，b 中第 i 部分的成员数。分块数的选定依赖于样本中的成员数量，如果分块数太少会因过估了重叠区域而失去精确性；分块数太多会因造成空块而失去精确性。对于计算后的巴氏系数，完全匹配时其值为 1，完全不匹配时其值为 0，因为这表示两个样本完全没有重叠，导致每一个分块都被 0 乘。

4.1.3.3　信号灯的模板匹配

城市交通场景中的信号灯一般包括红灯、绿灯和黄灯三种颜色，通过采集部分的信号灯样本，来计算它们的巴氏系数，信号灯样本如图 4.11 所示。

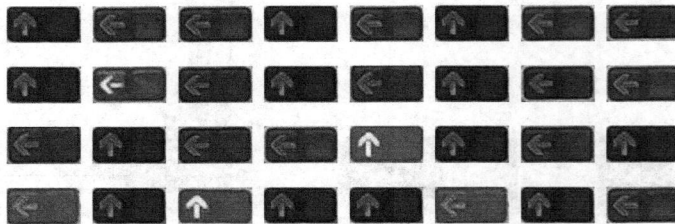

（a）红色信号灯样本

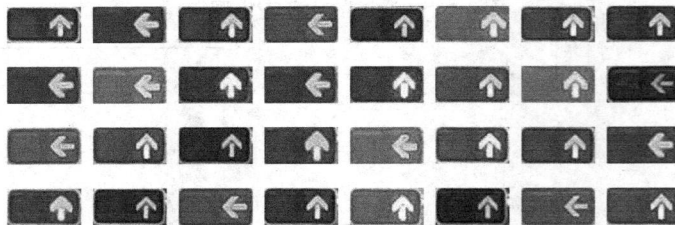

（b）绿色信号灯样本

图 4.11　信号灯样本

（c）黄色信号灯样本

图 4.11　信号灯样本（续）

　　信号灯样本中，红灯、黄灯和绿灯的样本各 32 张，通过分别对颜色信号灯的样本进行计算，取其平均值，得到城市交通场景中交通信号灯巴氏相关系数统计，如表 4.1 所示。得到三种信号灯的巴氏系数后，分别以三张信号灯的样本为模板，依次匹配图像中与其相似的图像，依据原始数据的图像尺寸关系，在实验中以 35×70 像素的窗口遍历图像。在含有红色信号灯的输入图像中进行运算，所匹配相似的图像如图 4.12 所示，经过处理所得到的图像相似度匹配结果如图 4.13 所示。

表 4.1　交通信号灯巴氏系数统计

交通信号灯	巴 氏 系 数
红灯	0.752 5
绿灯	0.786 0
黄灯	0.835 2

（a）信号灯样板　　　　　　　　（b）输入图像

图 4.12　匹配图像

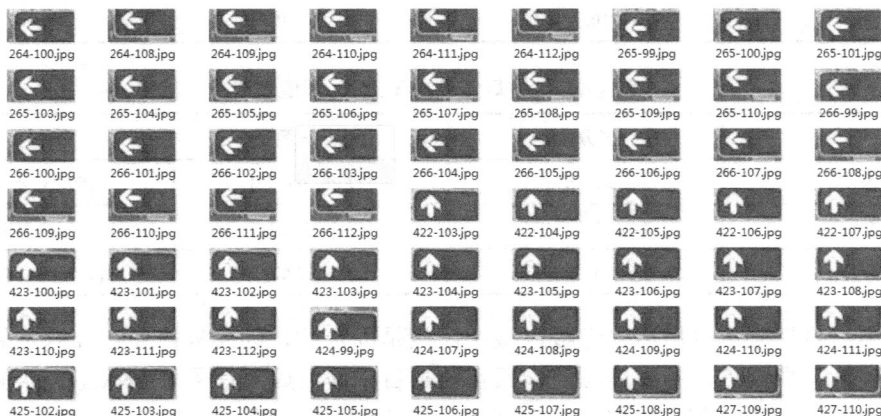

图 4.13　图像相似度匹配结果

相似图像的序号为所在感兴趣图像中的坐标，通过平均计算，最终得到输入图像中机动车道上红灯的位置坐标为[872,180,70,35]，[1 024,182,70,35]，确定的红色信号灯最终区域如图 4.14 所示。

图 4.14 红色信号灯最终区域

4.1.4 基于颜色空间模型的信号灯检测

确定信号灯区域后，需要对信号灯状态进行检测识别。根据颜色空间模型的相关知识，在颜色空间中每种颜色都具有独特的表征，因此本书采用颜色阈值分割算法对信号灯状态进行检测。阈值分割法是在颜色空间中设定阈值，并与图像像素的实际分量值进行比较，从而对满足阈值范围内的信号灯进行检测。对于 HSV 颜色空间，阈值的确定需要对三种交通信号灯的 H、S、V 各分量值进行统计分析，本书通过对 340 张信号灯样本统计，所确定的三种信号灯颜色的 HSV 阈值如表 4.2 所示；对于 RGB 颜色空间，根据颜色 RGB 对照表以及样本统计确定的信号灯颜色的"RGB"阈值如表 4.3 所示；根据 YCbCr 颜色空间与 RGB 颜色空间的转换公式，确定的信号灯颜色的 YCbCr 阈值如表 4.4 所示。

表 4.2 信号灯颜色的 HSV 阈值表

	色调（Hue）	饱和度（Saturation）	亮度（Value）
绿色	[120, 190]	[0.5, 1]	[0.6, 1]
红色	[0, 15]∪[350, 360]	[0.5, 1]	[0.5, 1]
黄色	[20, 50]	[0.5, 1]	[0.5, 1]

表 4.3 信号灯颜色的 RGB 阈值表

	R 分量	*G* 分量	*B* 分量
绿色	[0, 90]	[80, 250]	[0, 80]
红色	[110, 250]	[0, 90]	[10, 70]
黄色	[110, 250]	[110, 250]	[0, 90]

表 4.4 信号灯颜色的 YCbCr 阈值表

	Y 分量	Cb 分量	Cr 分量
绿色	[61.12, 187.97]	[77.05, 104.72]	[69.83, 98.56]
红色	[45.25, 137.87]	[95.54, 116.11]	[175.58, 199.66]
黄色	[106.31, 230.07]	[57.76, 79.71]	[135.81, 139.36]

实验中信号灯颜色区域所占灯板区域的比例是固定的，因此只需要统计满足阈值范围内信号灯颜色的像素点，并根据颜色像素点的数目来最终确定信号灯的状态。实验中选取了 200 张交通场景图像用于检测信号灯状态，其中含红色信号灯 90 张、含绿色信号灯 80

张，含黄色信号灯 30 张，三种颜色空间信号灯识别率统计如表 4.5 所示。由表 4.5 可得，基于 HSV 颜色空间模型的信号灯检测方法具有较高的识别率。同 RGB 颜色空间相比，HSV 颜色空间中 H、S、V 三分量相互独立，相关性不大，因此，H、S、V 三个分量中若有一个分量的规律不符合，也不会影响其他分量，从而可以保证整体规律不受太大影响；另外 HSV 颜色空间对光照不敏感，对不同光线下的交通场景图像是适用的。综上所述，HSV 颜色空间为城市交通场景中信号灯检测的最佳颜色空间。

表 4.5　三种颜色空间信号灯识别率统计

	RGB	HSV	YCbCr
红色信号灯	81.11%	96.67%	78.89%
绿色信号灯	73.75%	95.00%	78.75%
黄色信号灯	70.00%	88.67%	73.33%

4.2　基于车辆和车牌对称特征的车辆检测方法

为实现对车辆行为类型的自动化识别，除了检测影响车辆行为的交通信号灯外，车辆无疑是最重要的研究对象。而车辆异常行为检测的前提是对车辆本身区域的定位，在本章中，通过分析车辆轮廓和车牌的对称特征，研究了基于车辆轮廓和车牌对称特征的车辆检测方法，通过检测车身和车牌的三条对称轴来对车辆区域进行定位，并与基于车牌、Gabor 特征以及 Haar-like 特征等的车辆检测方法进行对比实验。

4.2.1　基于车辆和车牌对称特征的车辆检测

4.2.1.1　车辆边缘检测

边缘可被定义为两个根据某种特征（如灰度、彩色或纹理）存在显著特点的图像区域之间的边界，边缘检测的目的是找出一副图像或场景中最相关的边界，从而根据边界分割图像为两个或多个区域。

边缘检测方法常基于对沿亮度剖面的一阶或二阶导数的计算[15~17]，一阶导数具有直接正比于跨越边缘的亮度差别的期望性质，因此一阶导数的幅度可用来检测在图像中某个点处边缘的存在性；二阶导数可用来确定一个像素是在一个边缘的暗的一边还是亮的一边，在正的和负的波峰之间的零交叉可用来定位粗边缘的中心。本章中我们选取拉普拉斯（Laplace）算子对车辆边缘进行检测。拉普拉斯算子[18]是 n 维欧几里得空间中的一个二阶微分算子，定义为梯度（∇f）的散度（$\nabla \cdot f$）。因此，如果 f 是二阶可微的实函数，则 f 的拉普拉斯算子定义为：

$$\Delta f = \nabla^2 f = \nabla \cdot \nabla f \qquad (4\text{-}11)$$

f 的拉普拉斯算子也是笛卡尔坐标系 x_i 中的所有非混合二阶偏导数：

$$\Delta f = \sum_{i=1}^{n} \frac{\partial^2 f}{\partial x_i^2} \qquad (4\text{-}12)$$

并且，拉普拉斯算子并不依赖边缘方向，在数字图像中，拉普拉斯变换可借助模板来实现，模板函数可表示为：

$$G(i,j) = \left| 4f(i,j) - f(i+1,j) - f(i-1,j) - f(i,j+1) - f(i,j-1) \right| \qquad (4\text{-}13)$$

式中：$f(i,j)$ 为灰度图像中 (i,j) 处的像素值；$G(i,j)$ 是经过拉普拉斯变换后的结果。

为了减少图像的运算量，我们设置 ROI 区域，对人行斑马线以下区域的车辆进行处理，如图 4.15 所示。首先，对图 4.15 进行灰度化处理，然后采用拉普拉斯算子对车辆进行边缘检测，检测结果如图 4.16 所示。

图 4.15　ROI 处理区域

 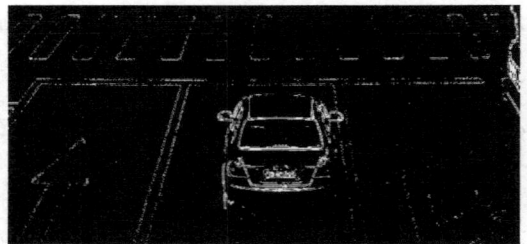

（a）输入图像　　　　　　　　　　　　　　　　（b）边缘检测

图 4.16　采用拉普拉斯算子进行边缘检测的结果

4.2.1.2　车辆轮廓对称轴检测

由于所需要检测的车辆只会出现在 ROI 区域的三个车道上，因此设置车辆竖直对称轴搜索区域要基本覆盖三个车道，且图像边缘区域可以忽略。如图 4.17（a）所示，按照公式（4-14）来计算搜索区域中水平线上的每个像素点的对称值，即：

$$V(x,y) = \sum_{x'}^{W/2} S(x,x',y') \qquad (4\text{-}14)$$

$$S(x,x',y') = \begin{cases} 5, & f(x-x',y') = f(x+x',y') = 255 \\ -1, & f(x-x',y') \neq f(x+x',y') \\ 0, & f(x-x',y') = f(x+x',y') = 0 \end{cases} \qquad (4\text{-}15)$$

式（4-14）中：$V(x,y)$ 为图像中点 (x,y) 处的对称值；W 是计算像素点对称值的幅宽。假设车辆图像像素宽度为 100，x' 为搜索区域水平线上的横坐标，y' 为纵坐标，则水平扫描线上像素对称值的计算结果如图 4.17（b）所示。

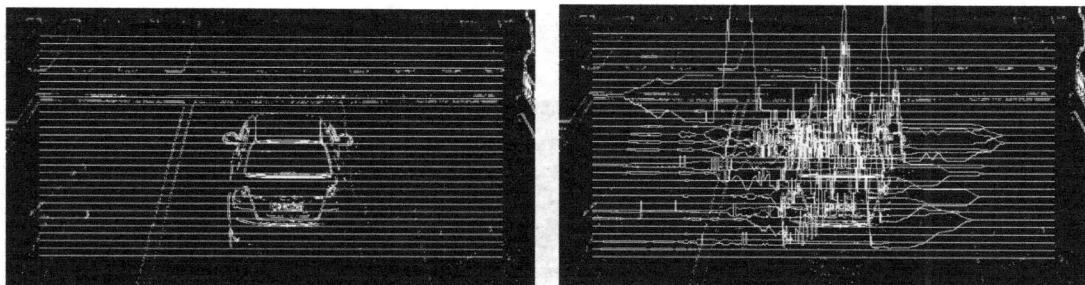

(a) 车辆对称轴搜索区域　　　　　　　(b) 水平扫描线对称值计算

图 4.17　车辆对称值搜索区域及水平扫描线对称值计算

根据几何特征，在车辆轮廓竖直对称轴处车辆轮廓对称值最大，在车辆轮廓边缘处轮廓对称值最小，根据公式（4-16）来计算每列对称值之和，即：

$$\text{Vcol}(x) = \sum_{n=0}^{M} V(x, n \otimes \text{val}) \qquad (4\text{-}16)$$

式中：val 为每行的行距，$\text{Vcol}(x)$ 为第 x 列对称值之和。对 $\text{Vcol}(x)$ 进行计算排序，计算对称值 $\text{Vcol}(x_m)$ 的最大对应列 x_m，则为车辆轮廓的竖直对称轴。在车辆边缘信息丰富的区域，如车灯等区域，集中了影响对称值大小的像素点，使用公式（4-17）来搜索对称轴上的最大区段，即：

$$\text{Vcol}(x_m, n) = \sum_{n=i}^{i+5} V(x_m, n \otimes \text{val}), \quad i = 1, 2, \cdots, M \qquad (4\text{-}17)$$

式中：n_m 是 $\text{Vcol}(x_m, n)$ 最大时所对应的扫描行，对应图像的纵坐标为 $y_m = n_m \otimes \text{val}$，这样就得到车辆轮廓的竖直对称轴，即如图 4.18 所示的竖直线，白色圆点 (x_m, y_m) 为对称值最大区段起始行。

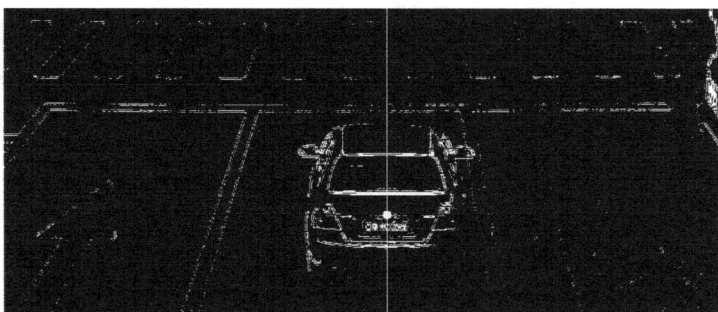

图 4.18　车辆轮廓对称轴

4.2.1.3　车牌对称轴检测

为了检测车尾的车牌，以车辆轮廓对称轴的最大区段起始行作为参考点，由于此参考点位于尾部车牌上方并且位置变化范围比较大，如果把这个点作为定位车辆轮廓范围的参考点的话必然使误差增大，因此我们以该点为基准来定位车牌对称轴位置[19]。以白色圆点 (x_m, y_m) 为基准，在其下方设置搜索区域定位车牌水平和竖直对称轴。假定点 (x_m, y_m) 到车辆轮廓对称轴搜索区域的底部距离为 δ，车牌水平对称轴搜索区域为点 (x_m, y_m) 到下边缘距离 δ 的 $\beta_1 \sim \beta_2$ 倍，本章中我们取 $\beta_1 = 0.1$，$\beta_2 = 0.2$，车牌水平对称轴搜索区域如图 4.19

所示。计算搜索区域每条竖直扫描线上像素点的对称值，以行对称值之和最大的行作为车牌水平对称轴。

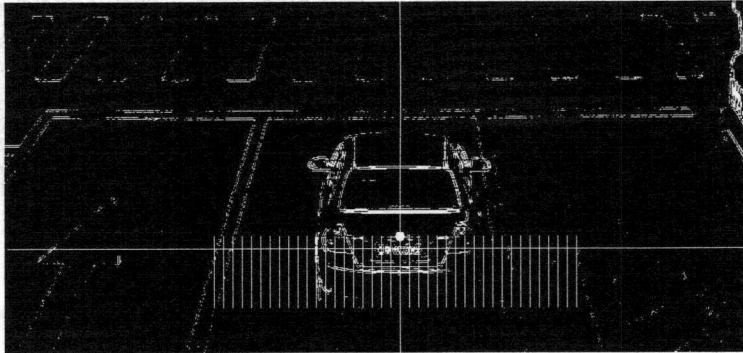

图 4.19　车牌水平对称轴搜索区域

如此，在由点 $(x_m - \delta_1, y_s - \delta_2)$ 和 $(x_m + \delta_1, y_s + \delta_2)$ 所确定的矩形框内定位车牌竖直对称轴，方法同车牌水平对称轴一样，计算车牌竖直对称轴，图中位于车辆轮廓对称轴右面的即为车牌竖直对称轴 x_s，车牌水平与竖直对称轴的交点为 (x_s, y_s)。

4.2.1.4　车辆区域定位

由于车辆位置区域包含在由点 $(x_m - \delta_1, y_s - \delta_2)$ 和 $(x_m + \delta_1, y_s + \delta_2)$ 所确定的矩形框内。使用灰度积分投影法来定位车辆，则图像竖直及水平积分投影的计算公式为：

$$v_i = \sum_{j=1}^{2w} f(x_i, y_i) \tag{4-18}$$

$$h_i = \sum_{i=1}^{h_b + h_t} f(x_i, y_i) \tag{4-19}$$

式中：$f(x, y)$ 是点 (x, y) 处的像素值，分别计算水平和竖直方向积分投影的最大值 m_h 和 m_v，从上到下搜索水平投影像素个数超过阈值 $0.5m_h$ 的第一行作为上边界，从左到右搜索竖直投影目标像素个数超过阈值 $0.5m_v$ 的第一列作为左边界，同理确定右边界和下边界。车辆区域的最终检测结果如图 4.20 所示。

图 4.20　车辆区域的最终检测结果

4.2.2　其他车辆检测方法

4.2.2.1　基于车牌的车辆检测

车辆牌照是车辆的一项重要特征，2005 年，D. Zheng[20]通过 Sobel 边缘检测定位出车辆图像的竖直边缘，并通过设定阈值来排除那些过长和过短的竖直边缘来筛选出车牌区域；2010 年，U. Nikul[21]通过对车辆进行形态学处理、YCbCr 彩色空间分割以及边缘检测算法定位车牌区域，这种方法对车牌检测有较高的准确率。和 D. Zheng 的方法相似，由于车辆牌照区域的灰度投影变化较为剧烈，根据这一特点，可通过减法使图像列和列之间相减来凸显出车牌区域，与此同时图像中的噪声会在相减过程中被削弱。所谓的列与列相减就是计算图像水平方向的一阶差分，即

$$f(i,j) = f(i,j+1) - f(i,j) \tag{4-20}$$

然后，对图像进行阈值处理，阈值由列相减后自身的灰度分布决定，阈值的表达式为：

$$T = \frac{1}{2m} \sum_{i=1}^{m} \max f(x_i, y) \tag{4-21}$$

式中：$f(x,y)$ 为相减后的图像；m 为列数。确定好阈值 T 后，对边缘图像的灰度投影进行统计。首先，从下向上搜索行目标像素，当行目标像素个数大于阈值 T 时，此行作为车牌的下边界；其次，同样从左至右搜索列目标像素，当列目标像素个数大于阈值 T 时，此列作为车牌的左边界；最后，根据车牌的高度和宽度估计车牌上边界和右边界。实验中，令车牌的宽度和高度分别为 w 和 h，则对应的车辆区域的宽度和高度分别为 $3.8w$ 和 $17h$，最终根据车牌位置和尺寸得到车辆区域。

4.2.2.2　基于 Gabor 特征及支持向量机（SVM）的车辆检测

Gabor 特征[22]是由 Dennis Gabor 在 1946 年首次提出的一种特征。Gabor 变换已被证明是在 2D 测不准的状况下，对信号空间域和时间域的最优描述。二维 Gabor 滤波器得到一组具有高斯包络的平面波，能够精准地提取出图像局部特征，对位移、形变及光照变化具有一定的容忍能力，其数学表达式为：

$$\Psi_{u,v}(z) = \frac{\|k_{u,v}\|^2}{\delta^2} \cdot \exp\left(-\frac{\|k_{u,v}\|^2 \|z\|^2}{2\delta^2}\right) \left(\exp(ik_{u,v} \cdot z) - \exp\left(-\frac{\delta^2}{2}\right)\right) \tag{4-22}$$

式中：参数 u 和 v 分别表示 Gabor 滤波器的方向和尺度；$z=(x,y)$ 表示图像像素的位置；δ 表示窗口宽度和波长的比例关系；第二个括号中第一项决定了振荡部分，第二项为补偿直流分量，用于消除滤波器响应对图像亮度绝对值变化的依赖性。

首先，将车辆图像划分为 $M \times N$ 个网格，其中用 $m \times n$ 个网格来表示车辆或背景区域，按行为优先的规则对每个 $m \times n$ 窗口进行遍历，然后计算每个窗口的 Gabor 响应特征，计算过程中令 $M=N=8$，$m=3$，$n=4$，那么每张图片有 30 个子窗口；其次，根据子窗口中的图像分布和 Gabor 滤波器函数来计算卷积，以此得到每个窗口的 Gabor 响应，以其中的偏态、均值和方差作为 Gabor 特征。在计算过程中，采用尺度为 3、方向为 4 的滤波器组，将不同尺度和方向的滤波器与图像卷积，得到的特征向量维数为 3×4×3=36 维；最后，选取包含车辆区域的正样本和不含车辆区域的负样本分别计算它的 Gabor 特征，并使用支持向量机（SVM）对得到的样本 Gabor 特征进行训练，采用训练好的分类器对车辆区域进行最终检测。

4.2.2.3 基于 Haar-like 特征及 AdaBoost 分类器的车辆检测

Haar-like 特征最早由 Papageorgiou[23]等应用于人脸表征，他们在研究正面人脸和在人体检测中使用两种类型的三种特征的形式以获得更佳的空间分辨率。随后 Licnhart 以此为基础做了特征库扩展。而目前常用的 Haar-like 特征有以下几类：边缘特征、线性特征、点特征和对角特征。每一种特征都是由 2 个或多个全等的矩形相邻组合而成的，在特征模板内有白色和黑色两种矩形，其特征值的定义为黑色矩形内所有像素值的和减去白色矩形内所有像素值的和。Haar-like 特征如图 4.21 所示。

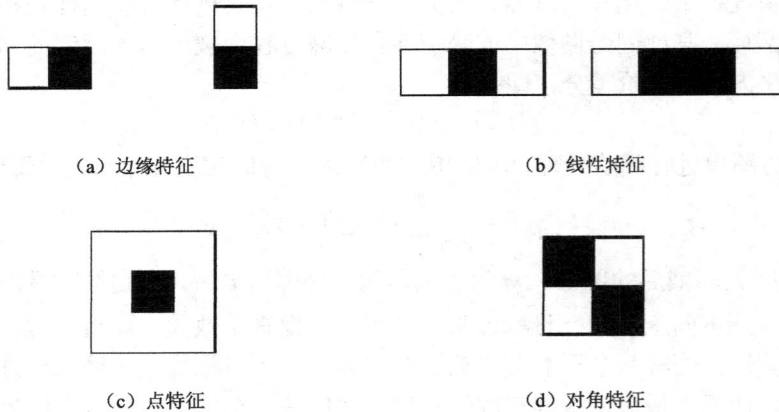

（a）边缘特征　　　　　　　　　　　（b）线性特征

（c）点特征　　　　　　　　　　　（d）对角特征

图 4.21　Haar-like 特征

AdaBoost（Adaptive Boosting）算法是 1995 年由 Schapire 和 Freund[24]在 Boosting 算法基础上开发出的一种迭代算法。其基本思想为：首先通过利用相同的训练样本得到不同的弱分类器，最后弱分类器集合构成更强的分类器。根据每次训练正确与否，以及训练前一次的正确分布，进而确定样本的权值算法，因此，AdaBoost 算法是通过改变数据分布来实现其功能的。在此基础上，更新的新权值会再次送给下层分类器不断进行训练，最后组合数次训练得到的分类器，作为最终的决策分类器。AdaBoost 算法适用于二分类或多分类的场景。在车辆检测中，我们采用 Haar-like 特征训练 AdaBoost 分类器来检测车辆，首先读取训练正负样本，其中正样本 272 张、负样本 272 张，然后提取其 Haar 特征进行强分类器的训练，最后运用训练好的强分类器进行车辆的检测。

4.2.3 实验结果

实验中我们采用数据库的原始数据，在基于 C++语言的 VS2008 及 MATLAB 软件编译环境下，使用 OpenCV[25]（开源计算机视觉库）实现图像处理操作，使用基于对称特征的车辆检测方法、基于车牌车辆轮廓和车牌的车辆检测方法、基于 Gabor 特征及 SVM 的车辆检测方法和基于 Haar-like 特征及 AdaBoost 分类器的车辆检测这四种检测方法做对比。输入图像尺寸为 2048×1536 像素，当车辆包围框覆盖车辆 90%以上区域且包围框尺寸与车辆尺寸相差不超过 10%时为正确识别。在基于 SVM 和 AdaBoost 分类器的车辆检测中，我们选取原始数据的 80%为训练样本、20%为测试样本。四种方法最终检测结果统计如表 4.6 所示。由表 4.6 可得，基于车辆轮廓和车牌对称特征的车辆检测方法具有 91.2%的检测率，优于其他三种车辆检测方法,证明了所提方法的有效性。在接下来的实验操作中,我们都选取对称特征方法来检测车辆区域,部分最终车辆区域定位结果如图 4.22 所示。

表 4.6　检测结果统计

检 测 方 法	检 测 率
对称特征	91.2%
车牌方法	82.5%
Gabor 特征	80.6%
Haar-like 特征	81.4%

图 4.22　部分最终车辆区域定位结果

4.3　基于联合特征的城市交通场景中车辆异常行为检测方法

为了实现车辆异常行为的自动识别,首先需要采用合适的特征提取方法来描述样本,其次是使用分类器对测试样本进行分类。本章中,首先构建了车辆行为数据库;其次对比分析了 HOG 特征、LBP 特征和 EOH 特征三种特征提取方法,并提出了基于 HOG 特征与 LBP 特征联合的车辆行为描述方法,然后采用 SVM 分类器进行了车辆行为识别实验,最后结合城市交通场景中交通信号灯状态检测,进行了车辆异常行为识别实验。

4.3.1 构建车辆行为图像集

车辆行为的判断，不仅需要定位出车辆区域，而且需要清楚标出车辆与道路标线所处的位置关系。本章在车辆区域定位的基础上，构建车辆行为数据库，以最终进行判定。

通过对城市交通场景中车辆图像的分析，我们发现交通场景中车辆与道路标线包含四种位置关系：（a）在车道线内，车辆轮廓线未与车道线及斑马线相交；（b）车辆前轮越过停止线，并与行人斑马线平行相交；（c）车辆轮廓线与车道分界线相交压线；（d）车辆转弯，轴线方向偏转，并与车道线或斑马线相交。四种位置关系如图 4.23 所示，这四种位置关系在不同交通信号灯状态下便形成了不同的车辆行为。例如，车辆闯红灯这一异常行为是在红色信号灯状态下，车辆前轮越过或超出道路停止线，并且车辆区域和行人斑马线有一定程度的相交。若是在绿灯或黄灯状态下，该场景下车辆行为便是正常行为，因此，获取车辆与道路位置的类别关系对车辆行为的判定至关重要。在上一章车辆区域检测的基础上，扩大车辆的区域定位，便可获得车辆与道路标线的位置关系。我们构建的东南大学车辆行为图像集包括图 4.23 中的四类车辆行为，每类 50 张图片，共 200 张，该图像集的部分图片如图 4.24 所示。

（a）在车道线内 　　　　　　　　（b）越过停止线

（c）压车道分界线 　　　　　　　（d）轴线方向偏转

图 4.23　四种车辆与道路标线的位置关系

图 4.24　车辆与道路标线扩大区域定位结果

图 4.24　车辆与道路标线扩大区域定位结果（续）

4.3.2　梯度方向直方图

梯度方向直方图，即 HOG（Histograms of Oriented Gradient）[26, 27]特征，是法国国家计算机科学及自动控制研究所的 Dalal 等人提出的一种解决人体目标检测的图像描述方法。开始 HOG 特征主要应用于静态图像的行人检测，后来逐渐推广到静态图像中车辆和其他常见物体的检测，并取得良好的效果。HOG 特征向量的核心思想是所检测的局部物体外形可以被光强梯度或边缘方向的分布所描述，它并不是从图像的整体出发来考察图像的特征，而是通过将整幅图像细分为一个个大小相同的细胞单元（cell），每个细胞单元（cell）生成一个梯度方向直方图或者细胞单元中像素点的边缘方向，这些直方图的组合可表示为描述子；同时为了提高准确率，局部直方图可以通过计算图像中一个较大的块（block）的梯度方向作为标准，然后用这个标准值归一化这个块中的所有细胞单元，这个归一化过程实现了光照不变性。HOG 特征的提取过程如图 4.25 所示。

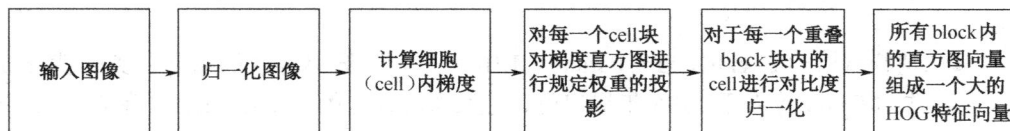

| 输入图像 | → | 归一化图像 | → | 计算细胞（cell）内梯度 | → | 对每一个cell块对梯度直方图进行规定权重的投影 | → | 对于每一个重叠block块内的cell进行对比度归一化 | → | 所有block内的直方图向量组成一个大的HOG特征向量 |

图 4.25　HOG 特征的提取过程

HOG 特征的优势主要有：① 由于 HOG 特征是在图像的局部方格单元上操作，所以它对图像几何和光学的形变都能保持很好的不变性；② 通过细胞方式进行梯度方向量化，使特征描述子具有一些平移和旋转不变性。因此，对于行人、车辆等静态物体，即使有一些细微的动作和形状的变化，也不会影响到 HOG 特征最终的检测效果。本实验中，首先将车辆行为图像归一化为 512×512 的标准尺寸，将其细胞单元设为 128×128，并在每个细胞单元内统计 9 个直方图通道的无向梯度（在 0～180°之间的梯度方向划分为 9 个区间）；然后，设置归一化块（block）的大小为 256×256（4 个细胞单元组成独立的一个块），块在水平和竖直方向的步进大小均为 128；最后，将所有细胞单元的直方图组合起来形成 HOG 特征描述子，得到的特征描述子维数为 9×4×3×3=324 维。对图 4.23 中的车辆四种位置关系图片进行 HOG 特征提取，其相应结果如图 4.26 所示。

(a)   (b)

(c)   (d)

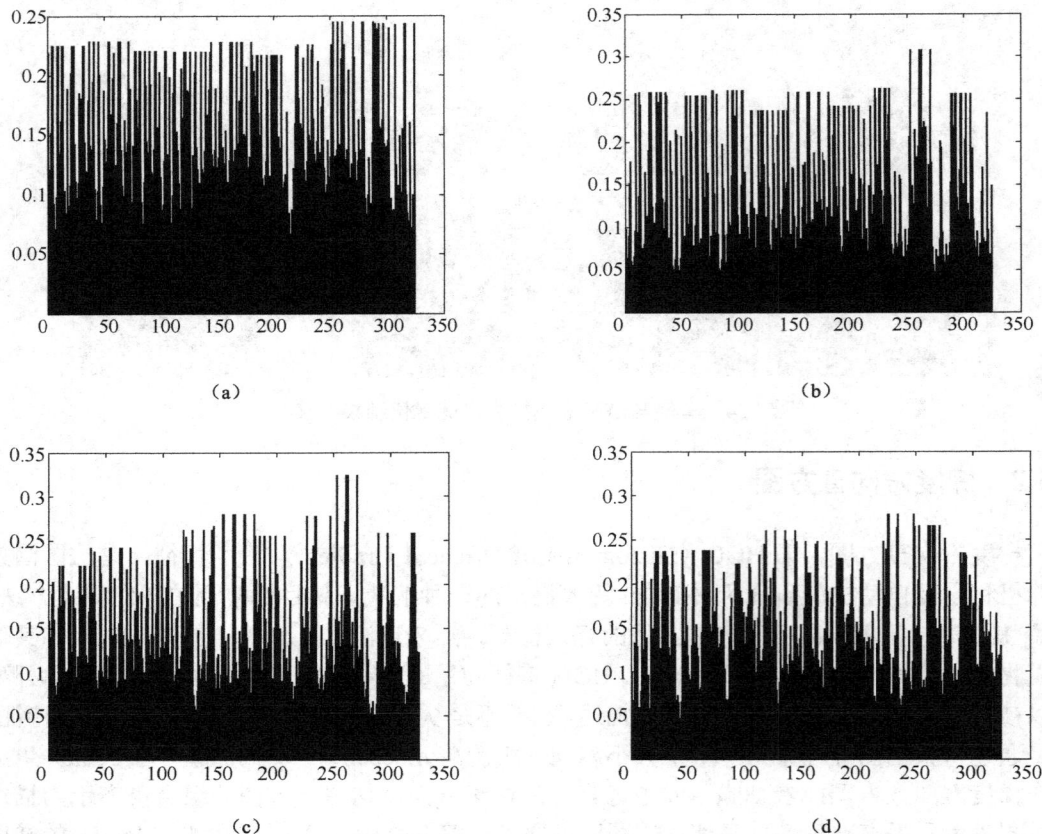

图 4.26　四种车辆位置图像的 HOG 特征直方图

4.3.3　局部二值模式

局部二值模式[28]（Local Binary Pattern，LBP）是一种简单有效的纹理分类的特征提取算法，该方法由 Ojala 等人于 1996 年提出的，用来描述纹理的局部结构性的特征提取算子。从纹理分析的角度来看，图像上某个像素点的纹理特征大多数都是指这个点和周围像素点的关系，也就是说这个点和它邻域内点的关系，从不同角度对这种关系提取特征，便形成了不同种类的特征。而 LBP 算子就是通过比较图像中某一像素点与其周围相邻像素点之间的灰度变化来确定该点所在位置的纹理变化模式，LBP 算法的优点是对光照变化和图像旋转具有不变性，能够较好地提取出图像边缘、角点等局部特征。对于基本的 LBP 算子，它是定义在 3×3 像素的邻域内，以邻域中心像素为阈值，将相邻的 8 个像素点的灰度值与其进行比较，若周围像素值大于中心像素值，则该像素点的位置被记为 1，否则为 0。这样，3×3 邻域内的 8 个点经过比较就产生了 8 位二进制数（通常转化为十进制数即 LBP 码，共256 种），即得到该邻域中心像素点的 LBP 值，并用这个值反映该区域的纹理信息，LBP算子原理如图 4.27 所示。

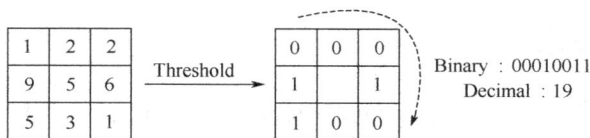

图 4.27　LBP 算子原理

LBP 特征值用公式可以定义为：

$$LBP(x_C, y_C) = \sum_{P=0}^{P-1} 2^P s(i_P - i_C) \tag{4-23}$$

式中：(x_C, y_C) 表示 3×3 邻域内的中心元素；它的像素值为 i_C；i_P 表示邻域内其他像素的值；$s(x)$ 是符号函数，即：

$$s(x) = \begin{cases} 1 & x \geqslant 0 \\ 0 & 其他 \end{cases} \tag{4-24}$$

实验中，将车辆行为图像划分为 64×64 的小区域，这样就形成了一个特征维数是 256 的特性向量。对于每一个小区域的每一个像素，采用 3×3 窗口大小来计算中心像素点的 LBP 值，然后形成每个小区域的直方图，并统计每个数字出现的频率，再对直方图归一化处理后，将每个小区域的统计直方图进行连接，最终生成了图像的 LBP 特征向量。对图 4.23 中的车辆四种位置关系图片进行 LBP 特征提取，其相应结果如图 4.28 所示。

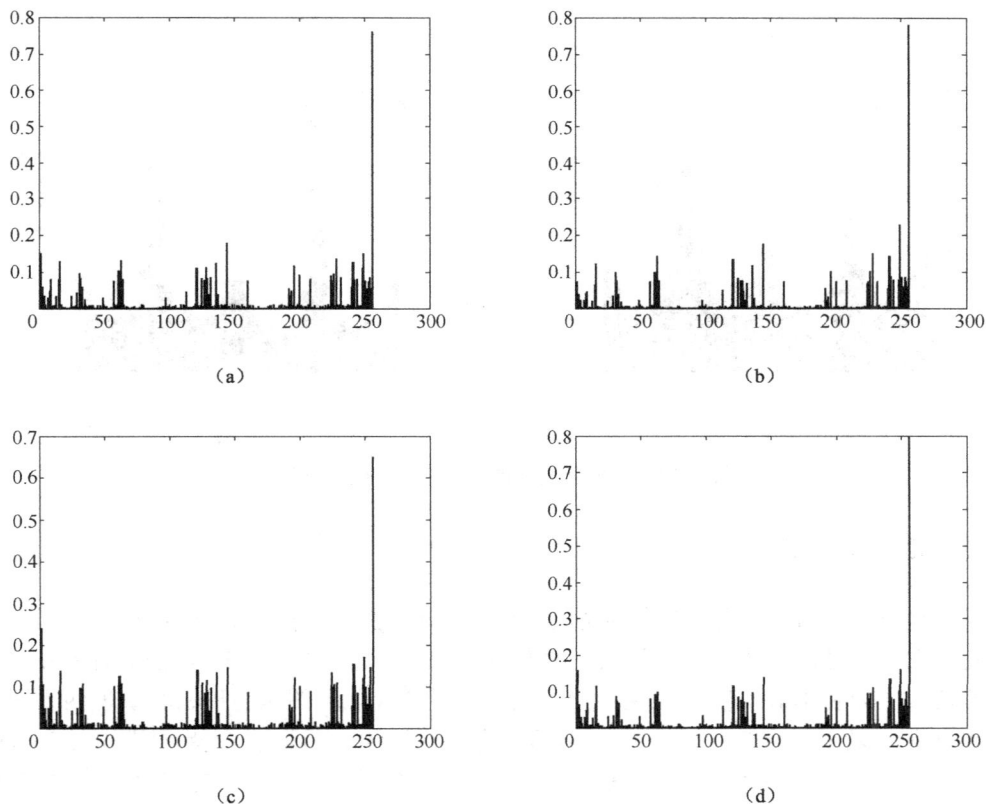

图 4.28　四种车辆位置图像的 LBP 直方图

4.3.4　边缘方向直方图

边缘方向直方图[29]（Edge Orientation Histogram，EOH）是一种针对图像边缘信息及梯度信息的特征描述算子。其具体算法流程是：首先，对图像进行灰度化处理，并通过边缘算子例如 Canny 算子对图像进行边缘提取；其次，对各个像素的梯度和方向，包括水平边缘方向、垂直边缘方向、对角边缘方向（包括两个斜对角）和无边缘方向，对其梯度直方图进行统计分类，最终得到边缘方向直方图。实验中，输入归格化为 512×512 的车辆行为图像，最终得到的 EOH 特征向量维数是 36 维，对图 4.23 中的车辆四种位置关系图进行 EOH 特征提取，其相应结果如图 4.29 所示。

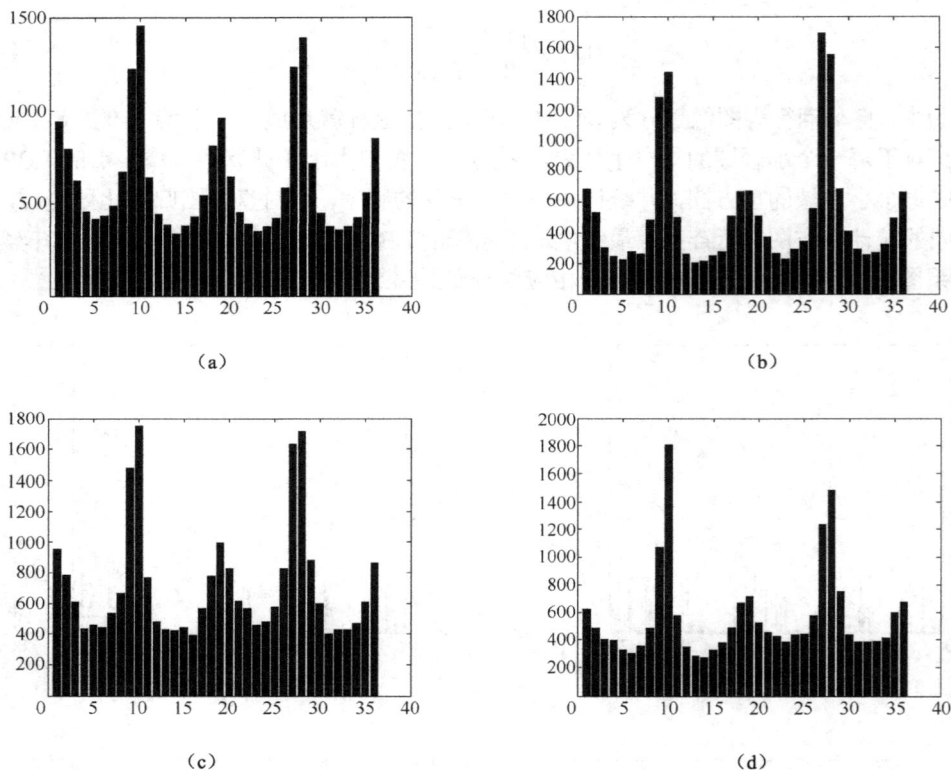

(a)　　　　　　　　　　　　　(b)

(c)　　　　　　　　　　　　　(d)

图 4.29　四种车辆位置图像的 EOH 特征表示

4.3.5　联合特征提取

采用单一特征对车辆行为的描述在性能上各有优劣[30]。例如，HOG 特征在光学变换和几何变换方面有显著优势，而在图像纹理方面却不尽人意；同时 LBP 特征却有着较好的局部纹理表达能力和单调灰度不变性。为了能够同时有效兼顾图像的形状和纹理两方面的特征，本章提出采用联合特征的方法对车辆行为进行描述。所谓联合特征[31~32]（Combined Features）就是多种特征的融合，一般情况下，比较常用的特征联合方法为特征加权联合和特征串联联合。由于特征加权联合需要对各个特征的加权进行计算从而使问题变得更复杂，因此本章采用特征串联规则提取车辆行为的联合特征。

采用 HOG 特征和 LBP 特征的联合特征[33]，其具体步骤为：首先，分别对同一张车辆行为样本图片的 HOG 特征和 LBP 特征进行特征提取；其次，将第 i 个样本的 HOG 特征和 LBP 特征首尾串联形成该样本的联合特征 f_i（$1 < i < N$，N 为训练样本数），则 f_i 是一个 580(324+256)维的特征向量。在联合特征向量中，f_i 的第 1 列至 324 列为特征数据为第 i 个样本的 HOG 特征，第 325 列至 580 列为第 i 个样本的 LBP 特征，对图 4.23 的车辆四种位置关系图采用 HOG+LBP 联合特征提取的结果如图 4.30 所示；采用 EOH+HOG 联合特征提取的结果如图 4.31 所示；采用 EOH+LBP 联合特征提取的结果如图 4.32 所示。

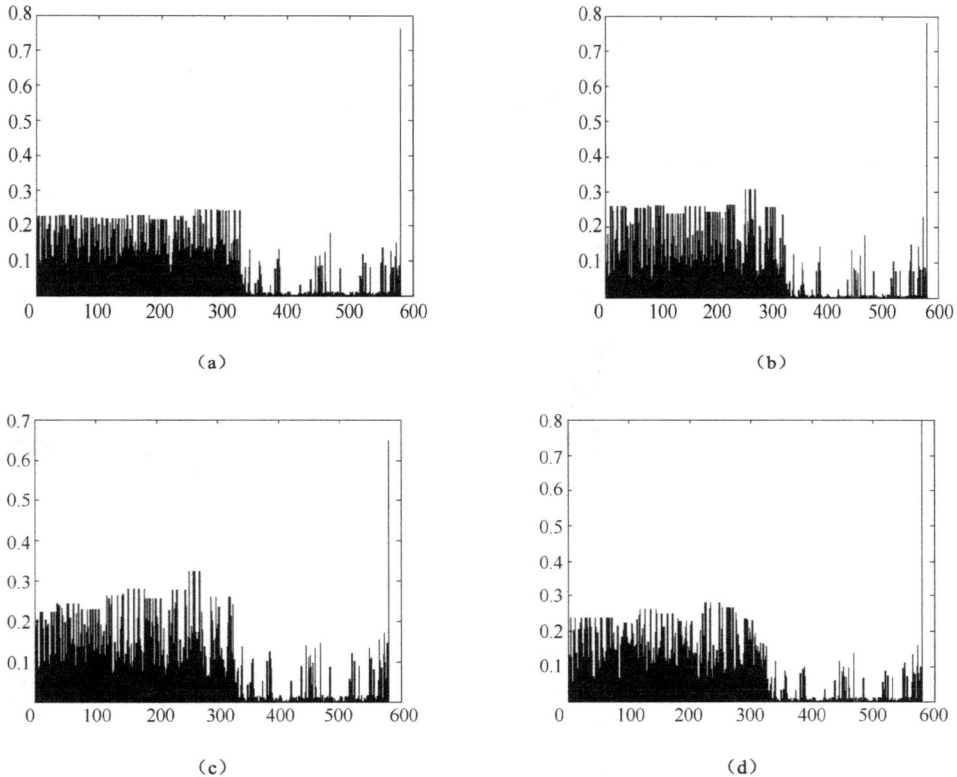

(a)

(b)

(c)

(d)

图 4.30　四种车辆位置图像的 HOG+LBP 联合特征表示

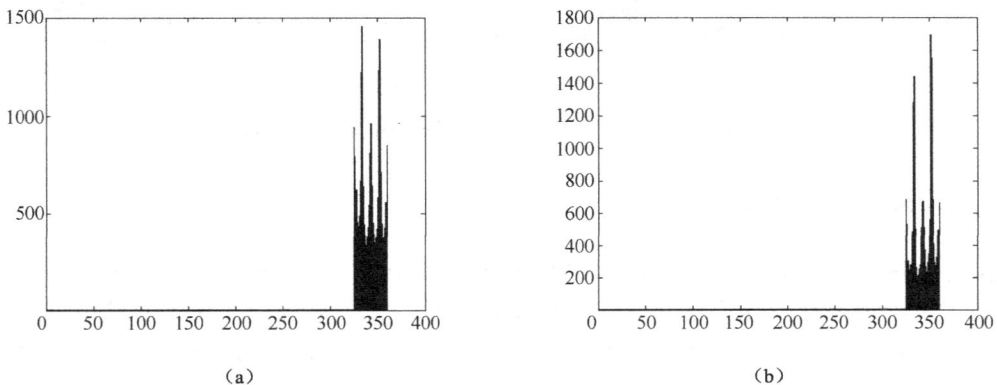

(a)

(b)

图 4.31　四种车辆位置图像的 EOH+HOG 联合特征表示

079

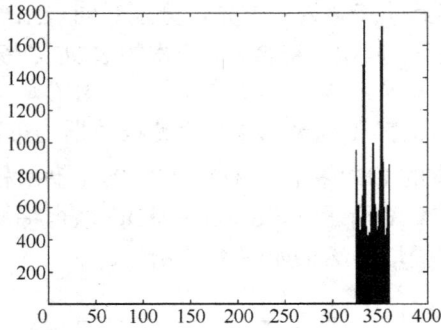
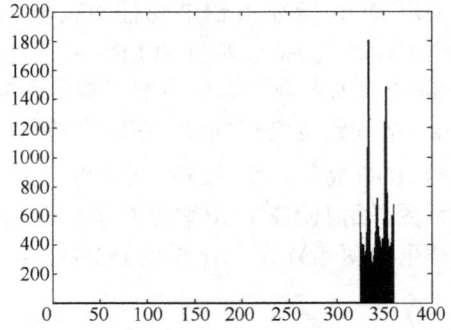

（c） （d）

图 4.31 四种车辆位置图像的 EOH+HOG 联合特征表示（续）

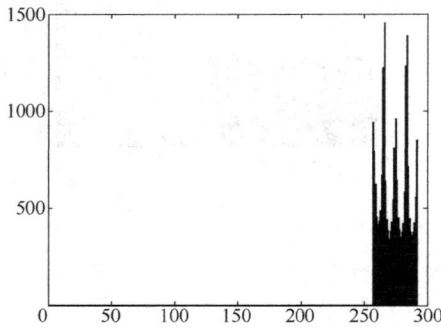
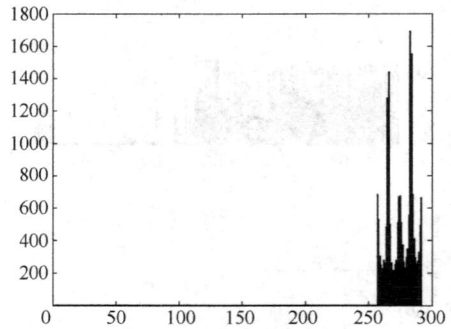

（a） （b）

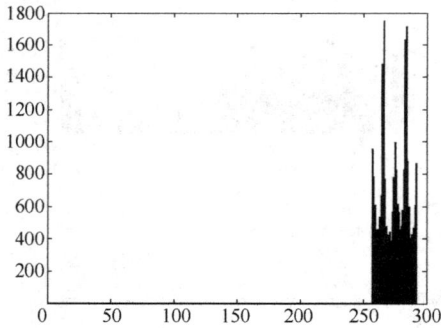
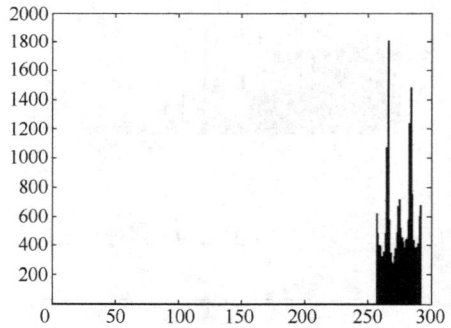

（c） （d）

图 4.32 四种车辆位置图像的 EOH+LBP 联合特征表示

4.3.6 支持向量机分类器

支持向量机（SVM）分类器最初由 Corinna Cortes 和 Vapnik[34~36]等人提出的一种新型模式识别学习方法，该方法在解决小样本、非线性以及高维模式识别问题中表现出许多特有的优势。SVM 的主要思想是针对两类分类问题，寻找一个超平面作为两类样本点的分割，以保证最小的分类错误率。在线性可分的情况下，存在一个或多个超平面能将训练样本完全分开，SVM 的目标就是找到其中的最优分类面。如图 4.33 所示，空心点和实心点分别表示两类样本，H 为正确分开两类样本的最优分类线。H_1、H_2 分别为过各类中离分界线最近的样本并且平行于分界线的直线，他们之间的距离称为分类间隔，H_1、H_2 上的点称为支持向量。最优分类面不仅要使分类线能将两类正确分开（训练错误率为 0），而且要让分类间隔达到最大，并要保证经验风险最小（为 0）。

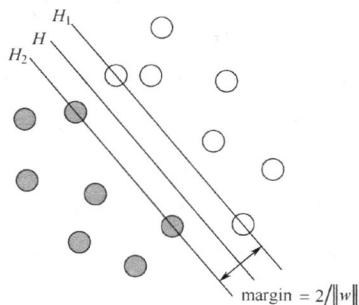

图 4.33　最优分类线

SVM 数学模型的样本模式集合 $\{x[i]\} \in R_n$ 是由两类点组成的，如果 $x[i]$ 属于第一类，则 $y[i]=1$；如果 $x[i]$ 属于第二类，则 $y[i]=-1$。训练样本集合 $\{x[i], y[i]\}$，$i=1,2,3,\cdots,n$，d 维空间的线性判别函数为：

$$g(x) = w \cdot x + b \tag{4-25}$$

最优分类面可表示为：

$$w \cdot x + b = 0 \tag{4-26}$$

该最优分类面应满足条件如下：

（1）$f(x_i) = y_i$，$i=1,2,3,\cdots,n$；

（2）$2/\|w\|$ 在所有分类面中达到最优；

（3）支持向量 x 满足 $f(x)=0$，非支持向量 x 满足 $|f(x)| \geqslant 0$。

根据上述条件可把求解二分类的最优分类面转换成求解 w、b 的凸二次问题，即求：

$$\min_{w,b} \frac{1}{2} \|w\|^2 \tag{4-27}$$

$$y_i[(w \cdot x_i) + b] \geqslant 1, i=1,2,3,\cdots,n \tag{4-28}$$

然而在多数情况下，数据样本并不是线性可分的，即并不完全满足式（4-26）。此时可以在条件 $y_i[(w \cdot x_i) + b] \geqslant 1, i=1,2,3,\cdots,n$ 上增加一个松弛项 $\xi_i \geqslant 0$，则公式（4-28）转换为：

$$y_i[(w \cdot x_i) + b] - 1 + \xi_i \geqslant 0, \ i=1,2,3,\cdots,n \tag{4-29}$$

将目标改为求 $\left[\frac{1}{2} \|w\|^2 + C(\sum_{i=1}^{n} \xi_i) \right]$ 最小，其中，C 是一个常数，它控制对分错样本惩罚的程度。根据泛函的相关理论，只要一种核函数 $K(x_i, y_i)$ 满足 Mercer 条件，它就对应某一空间变换的内积，因此，在最优分类面中采用合适的核函数 $K(x_i, y_i)$ 就能实现某一非线性变换后的线性分类。本章中，支持向量机采用以下三类核函数。

（1）线性核函数：$k(x, x_i) = (x \cdot x_i)$。

（2）多项式核函数：$k(x, x_i) = [s(x \cdot x_i) + c]^d$，其中，$s$，$c$，$d$ 为参数。

（3）径向基核函数：$k(x, x_i) = \exp(-\gamma |x - x_i|^2)$，其中，$\gamma$ 为参数。

4.3.7　实验结果

本章基于构建的车辆行为图像库开展相关实验，该图像库包括 200 张图片，图像尺寸大小均归一化为 512×512 像素，包括车辆在车道线内、车辆与斑马线平行重合、车辆碾压车道标线和车辆轴线方向偏转四种车辆行为，每种类型均 50 张。在样本图像中随机选取 80%作为训练样本，余下 20%作为测试样本，分别使用 HOG 特征、LBP 特征、EOH 特征、HOG-LBP 联合特征、HOG-EOH 联合特征和 EOH-LBP 联合特征来表征车辆行为图像，并采用支持向量机进行分类识别。实验基于台湾大学林智仁教授开发的 libsvm 软件包与 matlab 平台进行。其中，支持向量机的核函数分别选取线性核函数、多项式核函数和径向基核函数，一共进行 100 次随机实验，取 100 次实验的平均结果为最终结果，六种特征提取方法的实验结果如表 4.7 所示。

表 4.7　六种特征提取方法的实验结果

特征 核函数	HOG	LBP	EOH	HOG-LBP	EOH-HOG	EOH-LBP
线性	83.5%	79.8%	73.4%	93.6%	84.4%	87.3%
多项式	79.8%	78.7%	69.6%	87.7%	80.2%	82.3%
径向基	82.1%	77.5%	71.2%	90.1%	82.4%	85.6%

由表 4.7 中实验结果可得，三种核函数中，线性核函数的表现相对稳定，优于其他两种核函数。而在特征识别中，基于 HOG 特征与 LBP 特征串联的联合特征提取方法优于其他五种方法，可见 HOG-LBP 联合特征兼顾了图像的纹理和形状信息，使得分类识别的准确率整体提高。而在 HOG-EOH 和 EOH-LBP 联合特征中，由于 EOH 特征本身是由 HOG 特征演化而来的，并不具备 HOG 特征的梯度信息，故整体准确率不如 EOH 特征。EOH 特征的识别率最低，主要原因是 EOH 特征注重对图像边缘的表达，而车辆图像中的边缘区域整体而言都处于停止线与斑马线的区域，故不同类型之间的边缘差异不大，导致识别效果较低。

由于在不同的交通信号灯状态下，车辆与道路标线的位置关系会产生不同的车辆行为，因此，在对车辆与道路标线位置类型识别的基础上，需要结合信号灯状态来判定车辆的异常行为。不同信号灯状态下的车辆与道路位置关系所对应的具体行为如表 4.8 所示。对于获取的城市交通场景下的原始图像，首先，采用基于 HSV 颜色空间对其交通信号灯状态进行检测，并在车辆感兴趣区域内采用基于对称特征方法定位车辆区域；其次，扩大车辆检测区域，提取出车辆与标线位置关系区域图像；然后，对输出区域，提取其 HOG-LBP 联合特征，并使用支持向量机对其进行分类；最后，根据表 4.8 判定城市交通场景下的车辆行为。对于济宁市洸河路和供销路交叉路口，其三车道均为直行车道（右车道虽然可以右转，但不受交通信号灯约束），并均受交通直行信号灯约束。采用上述方法对 340 张城市交通场景中原始图像的车辆行为进行判定，其结果如表 4.9 所示。

表 4.8　不同信号灯状态下的车辆与道路位置关系所对应的具体行为

车辆正常	车辆压线	车辆闯红灯	非法转向
1. 不同信号灯状态下，车在车道线内，未与车道线和斑马线重合； 2. 绿灯状态下，车辆越过斑马线直行	不同信号灯状态下，车辆与车道线相压	红灯状态下，车辆越过停止线与斑马线重合	绿灯状态下，车辆轴线方向偏转，且与车道线重合

表4.9　四种车辆行为判定准确率

行 为 类 型	准 确 率
正常	91.30%
压线	85.46%
闯红灯	92.52%
非法转向	82.70%

由表 4.9 可得，四种车辆行为中车辆闯红灯的判定率最高，正常行为次之，这是因为车辆闯红灯和正常行为与道路标线分别有较明显的位置关系；非法转向行为的判定率最低，这是因为车辆在转向时转向幅度不一，且与压线行为出现一定程度的混合，从而导致判定率较低。

4.4　小结

为有效地管理城市交通场景中的车辆违章、违法行为，本章研究了城市交通场景中车辆异常行为的检测方法，具体成果如下。

（1）研究了基于色彩空间模型的城市交通场景中信号灯的检测方法。采用中值滤波和光线补偿算法对城市交通场景图像进行预处理，并采用信号灯的颜色直方图和巴氏系数进行信号灯模板匹配；基于颜色空间模型进行城市交通场景中信号灯的状态检测，实验结果表明基于 HSV 彩色空间模型的城市交通场景中信号灯的检测方法优于其他两种彩色空间。

（2）研究了基于车辆及车牌对称特征的城市交通场景中车辆的检测方法，并与基于车牌的车辆检测方法、基于 Gabor 特征及支持向量机（SVM）的车辆检测方法和 Haar-like 特征及 AdaBoost 分类器的车辆检测方法进行了对比分析，实验结果表明基于车辆及车牌对称特征的城市交通场景中车辆的检测方法优于其他三种方法，其检测率达到 91.2%。

（3）构建了东南大学城市交通场景中车辆行为图像库，并提出了一种基于联合特征的城市交通场景中车辆异常行为检测方法，该方法基于梯度方向直方图（Histograms of Oriented Gradient，HOG）特征和局部二值模式（Local Binary Pattern，LBP）特征的串联联合，并采用支持向量机（SVM）进行自动分类。采用东南大学城市交通场景中车辆行为图像库进行了对比实验，实验结果表明：在选取线性核函数的条件下，基于 HOG-LBP 联合特征的车辆行为识别优于其他三种单特征，其识别率达到 93.6%；车辆异常行为中闯红灯行为判定率最高，非法转向行为最难判定。

参考文献

[1] Huang T, Yang G and Tang G. A fast two-dimensional median filtering algorithm[J]. IEEE Transactions on Acoustics, Speech, and Signal Processing, 1979: 13-18.

[2] R Kirlin. Median filter and $1024^2$2D FFT with an FPS AP-120B array processor[C]. IEEE International Conference on ICASSP, 1980.

[3] Ataman E, Aatre V and Wong K. Some statistical properties of median filters[J]. IEEE Transactions on Acoustics, Speech, and Signal Processing, 1981: 1073-1075.

[4] 曾玉龙. 交通信号灯的识别[D]. 长沙: 中南大学, 2014.

[5] 贾灵芝, 李岚, 钱坤喜. 基于自适应光线补偿的人脸检测算法[J]. 计算机技术与发展, 2008, 18 (12): 120-126.

[6] Dutta S, Chaudhuri B B. A color edge detection algorithm in RGB color space[C]. 2009 International Conference on Advances in Recent Technologies in Communication and Computer, 2009.

[7] Su C H, Huang S C and Hsieh T M. An efficient image retrieval based on HSV color space[C]. 2011 International Conference on Electrical and Control Engineering, 2011.

[8] 温小勇, 乔林, 武津城. 基于 FPGA 和 YCrCb-RGB 色彩空间转换[J]. 信息技术, 2007 (10): 109-112.

[9] Novak C L and Shafer S A. Anatomy of color histogram[C]. 1992 IEEE Computer Society Conference on Computer Vision and Pattern Recognition, 1992.

[10] Tan T S C and Kittler J. Colour texture analysis using colour histogram[J]. IEE Proceedings - Vision, Image and Signal Processing, 1994: 403-412.

[11] Youn S, Lee C. Edge Detection for Hyperspectral Images Using the Bhattacharyya Distance[C]. 2013 International Conference on Paraller and Distributed Systems, 2013.

[12] Mak B and Barnard E. Phone Clustering Using the Bhattacharyya Distance[C]. Fourth International Conference on Spoken Language, 1996.

[13] Zhang M, Wang Q and Shen Y. Bhattacharyya distance based kernel method for hyperspectral data multi-class classification[C]. 2011 IEEE Instrumentation and Measurement Technology Conference, 2011.

[14] Zheng Y and Jin J. A novel image scrambling degree blind evaluation scheme based on Bhattacharyya Coefficient[C]. 2014 9th International Symposium on Communication Systems, Networks & Digital Signal Processing, 2014.

[15] 段瑞玲, 李庆祥, 李玉和. 图像边缘检测方法研究综述[J]. 光学技术, 2005, 31 (3): 415-419.

[16] 高朝阳, 张太发, 曲亚男. 图像边缘检测研究进展[J]. 科技导报, 2010, 28 (20): 112-117.

[17] P. Wang, X. Meng, K. Zhang. Research on edge detection algorithm for plate image[C]. 2013 25th Chinese Control and Decision Conference, 2013.

[18] 田素云, 王小明, 赵雪青. 基于拉普拉斯算子和图像修补的图像去噪算法[J]. 计算机应用, 2012, 32 (10): 2793-2797.

[19] Lian J, Zhao C, Zhang B, et al. Vehicle detection based on information fusion of vehicle symmetrical contour and license plate position[J]. Journal of Southeast University, 2012, 28 (2): 240-244.

[20] Zhang D, Y Zhao and Wang J. An Efficient Method of License Plate Location[J]. Pattern Recognition Letters, 2005: 2431-2438.

[21] Nikul U and Mehta H. An Accurate Method for License Plate Localization Using Morphological Operations Edge Processing[J]. Image and Signal Processing, 2010, 5 (12):

2488-2491.

[22] Manjunath B S, Ma W Y. Texture feature for image classification[J]. IEEE Transactions on Systems, Man and Cybernetics, 1973, 3 (6): 768-780.

[23] Papageorgiou C and Poggio T.. A trainable system for object detection[J]. International Journal of Computer Vision, 2000, 38 (1): 15-33.

[24] Ferund Y, Schapire R. A Decision - Theoretic Generalization of On-line Learning and An Application to Boosting[J]. Journal of Computer and System Sciences, 1997, 55 (1): 119-139.

[25] OpenCV(open source computer vision) wiki[EB/OL]. http://opencv.willowgarage.com/wiki. Accessed on 1st June 2010.

[26] Datal N, Triggs B. Histograms of Oriented Gradients for Human Detection[C]. IEEE Computer Society Conference on Computer Vision and Pattern Recognition, 2005.

[27] Zhu Q, Yeh M C, Cheng K T, et al. Fast human detection using a cascade of histograms of oriented gradients[C]. IEEE Computer Society Conference on Computer Vision and Pattern Recognition, 2006.

[28] Meena K and Suruliand A.. Local binary pattern and its variants for face recognition[C]. 2011 International Conference on Recent Trends in Information Technology, 2011.

[29] Yang Y, Wang Z and Sun D, et al. Automatic Object Tracking Using Edge Orientation Histogram Based Camshift[C]. 2010 Third International Conference on Information and Computing, 2010.

[30] 韩宏, 杨静宇. 神经网络分类器的组合[J]. 计算机研究与发展, 2000, 37 (12): 1488-1492.

[31] 杨先风, 杨燕. 一种基于 HOG-LBP 的高效车辆检测方法[J]. 计算机工程, 2014, 40 (9): 210-214.

[32] Liu P, Jia K and Wang Z.. A New Image Retrieval Method Based on Combined Features and Feature Statistic[J]. Image and Signal Processing, 2008: 635-639.

[33] 郭顺超. 基于特征联合和偏最小二乘降维的手势识别[D]. 秦皇岛: 燕山大学, 2012.

[34] Zhang P, Bui T D and Suen C Y. A Novel Cascade Ensemble Classifier System with A High Recognition Performance on Handwritten Digits[J]. Pattern Recognition, 2007, 40 (12): 3415-3429.

[35] 丁世飞, 齐丙娟, 谭红艳. 支持向量机理论与算法研究综述[J]. 电子科技大学学报, 2011, 40 (1): 2-10.

[36] Osuna E, Freund R and Girosit F. Training support vector machines: an application to face detection[C]. 1997 IEEE Computer Society Conference on Computer Vision and Pattern Recognition, 1997.

第5章

基于车载装饰品特征的车辆检索方法

为了惩处交通违法犯罪行为，我国公安系统采取了一系列的技术手段进行违法犯罪后的取证工作，其中"天网工程"通过图像采集、传输、显示和存储等一系列设备对交通路口进行监控和信息记录。但是，每天在交叉路口安装的监控设备将生成成千上万的图像数据，在这些图像数据中查找目标车辆的工作量非常巨大，目前解决这个问题的有效方法是根据车辆车牌等固有属性进行目标车辆识别查找，而这些方法对于假（套）牌车辆却没有很好的效果。通过研究我们发现，车辆前挡风玻璃处的摆件、标签等车载装饰品特征比较明显，因此本章研究基于车载装饰品特征的车辆检索方法。

首先，研究了基于车辆及车牌对称特征的车辆检测方法，并根据整个车辆与前挡风玻璃的相对位置定位车辆前挡风玻璃区域。对比分析了基于车辆及其车牌对称特征的车辆检测方法、基于 Adaboost 及 Haar 特征的车辆检测方法、基于灰度共生矩阵及支持向量机的车辆检测方法和基于梯度方向直方图及支持向量机的车辆检测方法，实验结果表明基于车辆及车牌对称特征的方法优于其他三种方法，其检测精度达到 90.7%，并且构建了基于东南大学的车载装饰品局部区域图像集。

其次，研究了基于颜色特征的车辆检索方法，并与基于局部二值模式、基于 Gabor 小波变换、基于 Contourlet 变换和基于尺度不变特征的检索方法进行了对比分析。基于相似度衡量方法进行了车辆图像的检索实验，实验结果表明基于颜色特征的车辆检索方法优于其他四种方法，其检索综合指标为 86.7%，平均检索时间为 29 730 ms。

5.1 车载装饰品局部区域图像集的构建方法

进行图像检索相关实验需要大量的实验数据作为支撑，本章研究构建车载装饰品局部区域图像集的方法。车辆检索的目标是车辆的前挡风玻璃部分，但是直接定位前挡风玻璃部分是一个比较困难的问题，如何进行前挡风玻璃的有效定位是本章研究的一个关键点。根据前挡风玻璃与车辆整体图像的先验相对关系可得：前挡风玻璃部分与车辆存在一定的几何位置关系，可以根据车辆的检测及其几何关系进行前挡风玻璃的精确定位。本章对比研究了几种图像中定位车辆的方法，结合前挡风玻璃部分与车辆的几何关系，研究前挡风玻璃粗定位的方法，并对前挡风玻璃图像进行一系列的预处理，以精确定位前挡风玻璃的感兴趣区域，最后，建立了基于东南大学的车载装饰品局部区域图像集。

5.1.1　车辆图像数据采集

为了进行图像处理及图像检索等相关算法的实验验证，本章采用由山东省济宁市公安局提供的原始图像数据，该图像数据由安装在城市道路交叉口的卡口相机于每天 8:00—18:00 的时间段内获取，从这些图像数据中（大于 20 000 张），我们选取了 1 500 张作为车辆图像数据集，该图像数据集包含不同的天气、光照及车辆角度等情况，并且每张图片包含完整的车辆图像。原始图像大小均为 2 048×1 536 像素，部分原始图像数据如图 5.1 所示。

图 5.1　部分原始图像数据

5.1.2　基于车辆及其车牌对称特征的车辆检测方法

基于车辆及其车牌对称特征的车辆检测是根据车辆本身的几何关系进行车辆检测，与基于车辆轮廓的车辆检测方法相比，基于车辆轮廓的方法容易受到背景中树木、车道标识线的影响，因此，本方法对不同的交通场景都具有较强的适应性。根据车辆的竖直对称轴及其车牌的竖直及水平对称轴的车辆定位，首先进行图像预处理，其次检测车辆轮廓的竖直对称轴，并根据竖直对称轴划定区域检测车牌的水平及竖直对称轴，从而根据对称轴确定车辆的区域，其流程如图 5.2 所示。

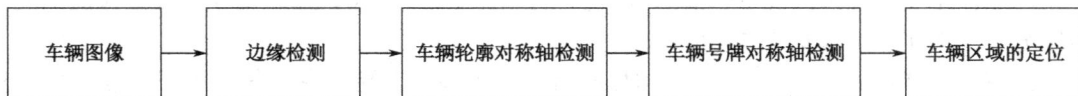

图 5.2　基于车辆及其车牌对称特征的车辆检测方法流程

本章采用的图像都是三通道彩色图像，在进行车辆边缘检测前首先对车辆图片进行灰度化处理，并采用 Laplace 算子进行车辆边缘的检测；其次，采用中值滤波算子对车辆图像进行中值滤波，以消除图像中的噪声部分。从图像边缘检测后的图像中可以看出，车辆的轮廓已清晰地显示出；在进行车辆对称轴检测时，根据扫描线上的对称值计算可以统计得出对称值最大点的位置[1]，从而可以确定车辆的对称轴；在确定了车辆对称轴以后，以车辆对称轴最大的点作为参考点，在其下方搜索车辆车牌的对称轴，搜索区域为参考点下方到车辆图片底部的 0.2～0.4 倍，作为候选区域，采用与搜索车辆对称轴相类似的方法计算车牌竖直方向和水平方向的对称值，从而得到车牌的横纵对称轴。确定了上述的对称轴后，在对称轴的周围选择候选区域，并计算其灰度积分投影，从而精确定位车辆的位置，基于车辆及其车牌对称特征的车辆检测过程如图 5.3 所示。

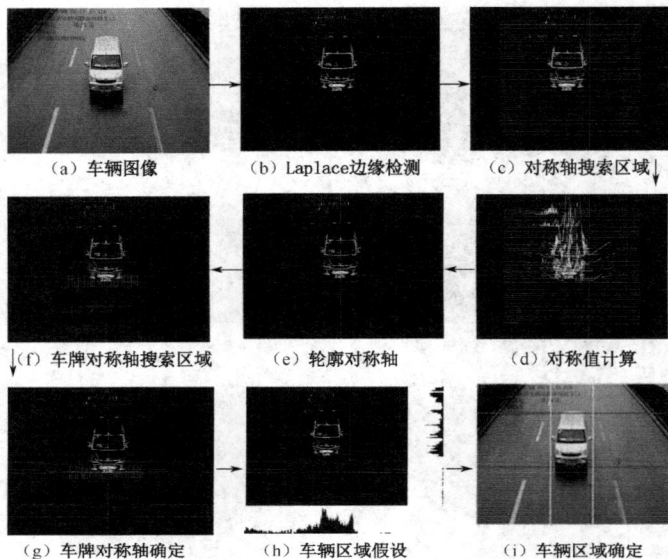

(a) 车辆图像　　　　　(b) Laplace边缘检测　　　　　(c) 对称轴搜索区域

(f) 车牌对称轴搜索区域　　　　(e) 轮廓对称轴　　　　(d) 对称值计算

(g) 车牌对称轴确定　　　　(h) 车辆区域假设　　　　(i) 车辆区域确定

图 5.3　基于车辆及其车牌对称特征的车辆检测过程

5.1.3　基于级联分类器及 Haar 特征的车辆检测方法

2001 年，Viola&Jones[1, 2]首次提出将 Adaboost 分类器与 Haar 特征用于人的检测。Adaboost 是一种自适应的基于级联分类器模型的分类器[3]，该分类器的每一级弱分类器都会及时返回学习的结果并根据反馈的结果自适应地调整预先假设的错误率。级联分类器就是将多个强分类器级联在一起进行数据的分类，组成级联分类器的各级分类器又是由若干弱分类加权后组成的。级联分类器的分类速度快的原因是组成级联分类器的各级分类器对负样本的判断准确度高、速度快，当检测到目标中含有负样本时就不会传送到下一级分类器。例如，一幅图像的绝大部分是背景，即负样本部分，该负样本部分的复杂检测将被抛弃，只有正样本才被传送到下一级强分类器中进行进一步检验，因而减少了很多检测时间。级联分类器的工作流程如图 5.4 所示。

1998 年，Papageorgiou[4]提出了 Haar 特征用于描述人脸图像，各类特征示意如图 5.5 所示。特征值的计算是根据图中描述的模板将白色矩形区域内像素值的和减去黑色矩形区域内像素值的和得到的值作为特征，由于目标在不同方向上存在灰度变化，所以将 Haar 特征分为图 5.5 中的边缘特征、线性特征、中心特征和对角线特征四类。由特征值的计算和统计方式可以看出，特征值在一定程度上反映了目标局部灰度的变化。在车辆检测应用中，为了提高 Haar 特征值的计算速度，在计算上采用了积分图。将车辆检测与人脸检测相类比，可以将整张图片中包含的车辆部分看作人脸的相似部分，并且在整张图中，背景部分局部灰度变化不明显，而在车辆目标区域灰度变化比较大。

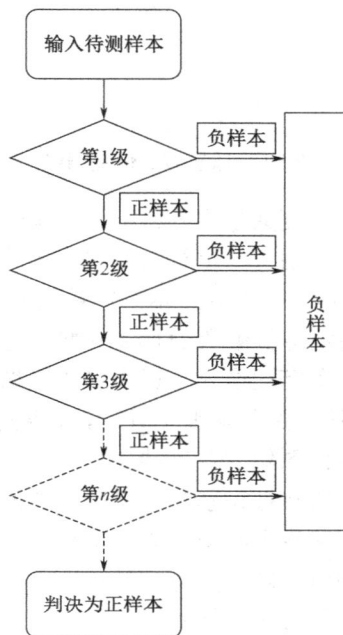

图 5.4　级联分类器的工作流程

图 5.5　边缘特征、线性特征、中心特征和对角线特征示意

　　基于级联分类器及 Haar 特征的车辆检测中，首先准备足够数量的包含目标的正样本，并准备 2～3 倍于正样本数量的负样本，然后提取样本的 Haar 特征进行强分类器的训练，最后运用训练好的强分类器进行车辆检测。

5.1.4　基于灰度共生矩阵（GLCM）的车辆检测方法

　　1973 年，灰度共生矩阵（Gray Level Co-occurrence Matrix，GLCM）首先由 Haralick 等[5]提出，并被应用于图像纹理特征的描述。2013 年，Fardin 等[6]将 GLCM 应用于全色影像的识别。灰度共生矩阵的本质是概率分布，其定义是图像中灰度值的差异为 0 或者满足一定阈值的像素对的联合分布概率。在计算共生矩阵的像素对中存在一定的空间关系，在一定的偏移角度和像素距离下，像素对出现的频数可以用概率进行标记，在统计像素对出现频数的距离 d 时，可以根据图像的大小选取任意的距离，角度值 θ 通常取 $0, \frac{\pi}{2}, \pi$ 和 $\frac{3\pi}{2}$ 四个方向。灰度值分别为 i 和 j 的像素对，当距离为 $d = (\Delta x, \Delta y)$ 和角度为 θ 时的位置偏移如图 5.6 所示。

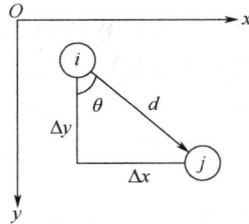

图 5.6　像素对的位置偏移

本章中，基于支持向量机及灰度共生矩阵特征进行车辆检测。首先选取只包含车辆正样本的图片和只包含背景负样本的图片，进行灰度共生矩阵特征提取，并进行训练，得到检测的特征库；其次将图像的灰度进行量化，本章中量化的等级分为 16 等级，由于像素对存在相对关系，所以其灰度共生矩阵的维数为 16×16 维，选取 $\theta = 3\pi/2$ 的对角关系计算其相对位置偏移的概率分布。由于车辆图像为三通道彩色图像，而灰度共生矩阵的计算是针对灰度值，所以首先需要对输入图像进行灰度化处理，并将图像网格化为 $M \times N$ 个 $W \times H$ 大小的子图；其次计算每个网格窗口图像的灰度共生矩阵特征，利用训练好的特征库预测该网格图像是否属于车辆部分，对所有被识别为车辆区域的网格中心的坐标进行统计，得到网格中心坐标的均值；再次根据网格中心坐标与每个被识别为车辆区域的坐标均值进行欧式距离的计算，并设定一定的阈值，若计算得到的距离大于设定的均值则被认定为背景噪声；最后根据坐标的均值得到检测的车辆图像。

5.1.5　基于支持向量机（SVM）及纹理特征的车辆检测方法

HOG 特征是由 Dalal[7]于 2005 年提出，并应用于行人检测的一种纹理特征描述子，此特征描述子通过计算局部图像的梯度和方向并利用梯度和方向构成直方图的方法来描述图像的纹理变化。HOG 特征提取的主要步骤为：第一步，将整幅目标图像分割成若干个小的连通区域，该连通区域称为"细胞单元（Cells）"；第二步，进行各个细胞单元内所有像素点方向梯度的计算，并将梯度值作为测量值，统计各个细胞单元的梯度直方图；第三步，由于对图像进行细胞单元的划分计算得到的是局部较精细的特征，所以需要将多个相邻的细胞单元组合起来形成较大的块（Block），并将块内的细胞单元的直方图进行对比度归一化；第四步，将组成图像所有块的直方图按先行后列串联后即得到目标的 HOG 特征，其详细流程如图 5.7 所示。

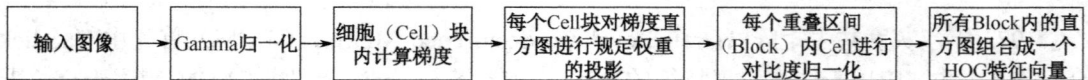

图 5.7　HOG 特征提取算法流程

支持向量机（Support Vector Machines，SVM）是由 Cortes 和 Vapnik[8]提出的机器学习方法，该方法能够将低维空间非线性的不可分类问题映射到高维空间，将问题转化为线性可分的问题，从而降低算法的复杂度。支持向量机分类器的优势在于能有效地解决样本不足、非线性和特征维数较高的问题，在分类时得到的最优解是基于现有的有限数量样本和现有条件的情况，而不是提供无穷多样本时的最优解，并且能够将低维空间转换到高维空间，并在高维空间构造判别条件和决策函数，这样就能够实现算法的推广。在车辆检测问题上，与 Haar 特征类似，在目标车辆区域也存在比较丰富的纹理特征，而与车辆区域相比，背景区域的纹理特征并不是特别明显，所以在车辆区域与背景区域的纹理特征上将存在较大的差异。在分类器问题上，利用 SVM 提供的优异性能，对正样本（目标车辆图像组成的数据集）和负样本（图像的背景区域）进行 SVM 训练将能够很好地区分车辆和背景区域。在整幅图像中运用多尺度的检测方法将能够较好地检测车辆。

5.1.6　车辆前挡风玻璃区域的定位

车辆摆件、标签等车载装饰品主要位于车辆的前挡风玻璃区域，所以在检测到车辆以后需要进行车辆前挡风玻璃区域定位，即感兴趣区域（ROI）的定位。车辆前挡风玻璃定位需要根据其与车辆整体的相对位置进行定位。例如，检测到的车辆图片如图 5.8（a）所示，起始坐标位于整张图片的左下角，整张车辆图片的宽度设为 Width，整张车辆图片的高度设为 Height，车辆前挡风玻璃的起始位置为到车辆图片底端的距离（0.4×Height），整个感兴趣区域的高度为 0.35×Height，宽度为 0.85×Width。根据其相对位置关系最终得到的粗定位前挡风玻璃部分如图 5.8（b）所示。在获取到前挡风玻璃区域的粗略定位以后，将对其进行精确定位。在精确定位之前需要对图像进行一系列的预处理：

（1）对前挡风玻璃部分进行灰度化处理；

（2）对图像运用 Canny 算子进行边缘检测；

（3）计算图像的横纵方向的投影。

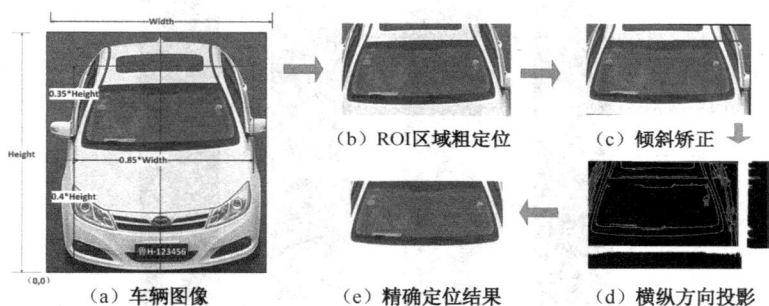

（a）车辆图像　　　（b）ROI 区域粗定位　　　（c）倾斜矫正

（e）精确定位结果　　　（d）横纵方向投影

图 5.8　车辆前挡风玻璃 ROI 定位过程

由于在前挡风玻璃的左右和上下边界存在明显边缘，投影直方图中存在突变，因此根据统计横向和纵向的投影直方图，可以清晰地找到前挡风玻璃部分的左右和上下边界。然而，在一些车辆前挡风玻璃图像中，通过坐标定位找到的前挡风玻璃部分存在一定角度的旋转，所以在得到前挡风玻璃的部分图像后需要进行一定的矫正，从而恢复前挡风玻璃部分到水平位置。在矫正图像时，需要计算出车辆前挡风玻璃部分的倾斜角度，本章采用 Hough 变换进行前挡风玻璃边缘图像的直线拟合，并计算出图像的旋转角度，然后对原始的车辆前挡风玻璃图像进行旋转，从而得到水平的前挡风玻璃图像。

5.1.7　车载装饰品局部区域图像集的构建

基于选取的 1 500 张车辆原始图像，采用所研究的车辆检测方法和车辆前挡风玻璃区域的定位方法构建车载装饰品局部区域图像集。本书所述的算法都是在 VS2013 环境中基于 C++ 开发语言及 OpenCV2.4.9 开源视觉库进行的。计算机配置为 Intel Dual Core 2.6 GHz、RAM 4.0 GB 和 ROM 500 GB。首先进行基于车辆及其车牌对称特征的车辆定位算法、基于 Adaboost 分类器及 Haar 特征的车辆检测算法、基于灰度共生矩阵的车辆检测方法和基于支持向量机及 HOG 特征的车辆检测算法的对比实验，输入图像的尺寸为 2 048×1 536 像素。在实验中，采用车辆原始图像的 70% 作为训练图片，剩余的 30% 作为测试图片，当车辆包围框覆盖车辆 90% 以上区域且包围框尺寸与车辆尺寸相差不超过 10% 时，判断为正确检测。四种车辆检测方法的检测率及检测时间如表 5.1 所示。四种车辆检测方法的检测率如图 5.9 所示。

表 5.1　四种车辆检测方法的检测率及检测时间

方法 / 结果	基于车辆及车牌对称特征	基于 Adaboost 和 Haar 特征	基于 SVM 和 HOG 特征	基于 SVM 和 GLCM 特征
检测率	90.70%	80.40%	88.50%	85.88%
检测时间（ms）	125	705	150	7 055

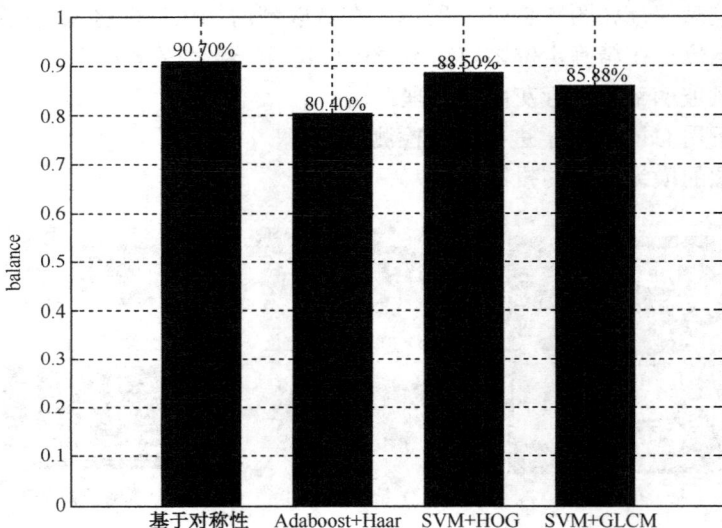

图 5.9　四种车辆检测方法的检测结果

从表 5.1 和图 5.9 中可以看出，基于车辆及其车牌对称特征的车辆定位算法检测时间较短且定位的精确率较高，且检测率达到了 90% 以上，在性能上优于其他三种检测方法。采用 Adaboost 分类器及 Harr 特征检测车辆时，类比的是人脸特征的检测方法，检测效果并不理想；采用 HOG 特征检测车辆时，图片的背景对检测结果影响较大；采用 GLCM 特征检测时，其特征的计算复杂度较大，在计算上耗费了大量的时间，在精确定位车辆时，统计中心坐标只考虑了坐标的均值和各车辆坐标之间的关系，所以检测结果也存在较大的偏差。因此，本书采用基于对称特征的车辆检测方法定位图像中的车辆区域。

本章对采集的 1 500 张图像进行了车辆区域检测实验并构建了车载装饰品区域图像集，在构建车载装饰品区域图像集时去除了一些检测效果较差的图像，如图 5.10 所示，在前挡风玻璃区域小于检测区域的 90% 即视为效果较差的检测，最后得到的数据集包含 1 300 张精确定位的车辆前挡风玻璃图像。

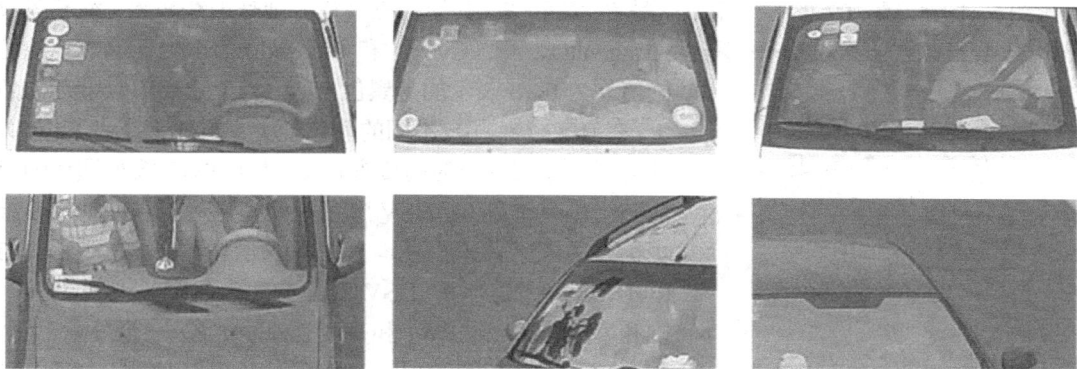

图 5.10　ROI 区域定位结果，第一行为正确定位，第二行为偏差较大

5.2　基于车载装饰品区域图像颜色直方图的车辆检索方法

　　图像的特征提取是图像检索的关键步骤之一，图像特征选取的好坏将在很大程度上决定车辆检索的性能和精确率。图像的特征不仅能够描述物体的最直观几何、颜色等特征，同时还能够描述内在的、结构化的信息。例如，直观的颜色可以采用颜色直方图进行描述；图像细节的纹理特征可以采用局部二值模式（Local Binary Pattern，LBP）、Gabor 特征、图像梯度方向直方图（HOG）特征和 Contourlet 特征等进行描述。由于车辆的摆件和标签部分存在较明显的边缘信息，所以图像的边缘空间信息可以作为前挡风玻璃的"指纹信息"进行车辆检索。

5.2.1　基于颜色直方图的车载装饰品区域图像特征表征

　　图像的颜色特征与尺寸及图像的旋转角度没有较高的相关性，对于固定的目标，颜色特征具有较高的健壮性，并且颜色特征的统计过程比较简单，计算的复杂度很低。图像颜色特征的表示是基于不同的颜色空间的，同一幅图像在不同的颜色空间中特征的表现形式也不一样，同时，目前图像特征描述多采用 RGB 颜色空间、HSV 颜色空间和 LAB 颜色空间。

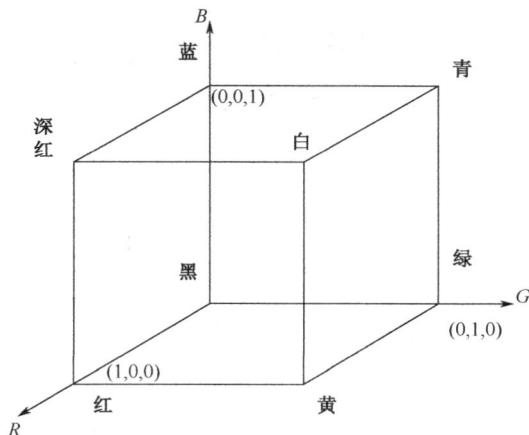

图 5.11　RGB 颜色空间表示

5.2.1.1　RGB 颜色空间

　　RGB 颜色空间采用 R、G 和 B 三原色进行颜色的描述。RGB 颜色空间可以用一个三维立方体直观地表现，如图 5.11 所示。

5.2.1.2　HSV 颜色空间

图 5.11 中，立方体的三个角依次是 R、G 和 B，其他的三个角分别是由红和蓝、绿和蓝及红和绿混合构成的二次色——深红（Magenta）、青（Cyan）和黄（Yellow），坐标原点三原色的值均为 0，0 表示的是黑色，白色为位于离原点最远的角上。在 RGB 模型中，不同的颜色处于立方体上或者其内部，并可用从原点分布的向量来定义。本书 RGB 模型通道的值被归一化成 1 到 0。HSV 颜色空间模型可以直观地用三维坐标系中圆锥体来描述，其空间表示如图 5.12 所示。与 RGB 颜色空间类似，HSV 颜色空间由色度（Hues，H）、饱和度（Saturation，S）和亮度（Value，V）三个分量表示。图 5.12 中，在圆锥的顶面中心亮度 $V=1$，色度 H 由绕 V 轴的角度大小决定，0°、120° 和 240° 分别代表红、绿和蓝，饱和度的取值范围是从 0 到 1，在圆锥下顶点处 $V=0$。在 HSV 颜色空间模型中，V 轴与 RGB 颜色空间模型中的主对角线相对应，因此这两个颜色空间模型可以互相转换。

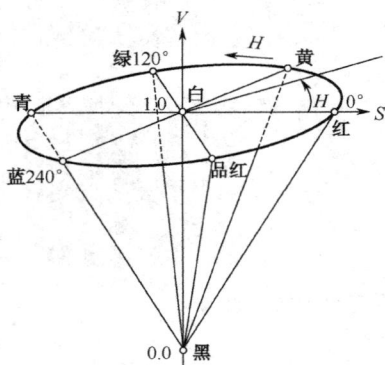

图 5.12　HSV 颜色空间表示

5.2.1.3　基于颜色直方图的特征描述

图像的颜色特征表征主要有颜色直方图和颜色矩两种方法。颜色直方图反映的是各种按一定阶数划分的颜色值在图像中出现概率的大小。颜色直方图的应用是在 2001 年由 Ballard[9] 提出来的，1995 年，Orengo[10] 提出运用颜色矩来进行颜色特征的描述。颜色直方图对物体的旋转、缩放和模糊变换具有比较好的健壮性，例如，图像在进行旋转缩放时，其颜色分布情况并没有发生较大变化，从而图像的直方图变化不大，同时，颜色直方图对于物体的物理变换也具有较强的健壮性，因此本书采用颜色直方图来表征车载装饰品区域的图像特征。车辆及其灰度图对应的颜色直方图如图 5.13 所示，图 5.13（c）、（d）分别表示的是一张车载装饰品区域对应的 RGB 三个通道和灰度化后对应的颜色直方图。由于颜色直方图是针对整张图，因此其丢失了颜色的位置分布信息，并且颜色直方图受光照的影响也比较大。

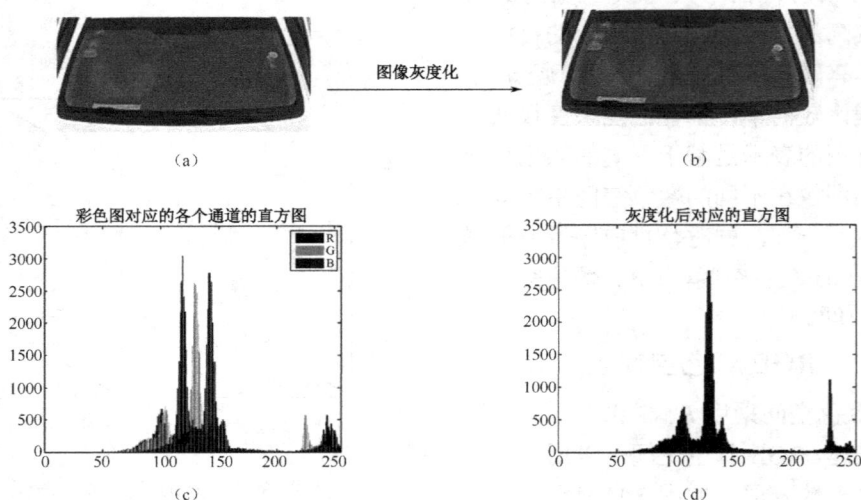

图 5.13　车辆及其灰度图对应的颜色直方图

5.2.2　基于其他图像特征的描述方法

5.2.2.1　基于局部二值模式的特征提取

局部二值模式（Local Binary Pattern，LBP）是由 Ojala 和 PietikaÈinen[11]提出的，该方法能够有效地突出描述图像的局部纹理特征，采用 LBP 算子进行处理得到原图像的 LBP 图谱，LBP 算子是一个3×3的矩阵，采用该矩阵对原图像进行以行优先的遍历，每一步遍历时取矩阵的中心像素值作为阈值并与该像素点的邻域像素值进行比较，若邻域的值大于阈值，则将该邻域的像素值标记为1，否则标记为0，在处理完某一中心像素点的所有邻域像素点之后，将标记值从左上角经顺时针串联成一串二进制编码，并将该二进制编码转换为十进制数，以得到该中心像素点的 LBP 值。假设中心像素值被标记为 m，则该像素点的 LBP(m)特征值为：

$$\text{LBP}(m) = \sum_{i=0}^{7} s(n_i, m) \cdot 2^i \tag{5-1}$$

式中：n_i 是像素点 m 的八邻域内的 8 个像素点；i 是自 m 的左上角的像素点顺时针方向旋转依次标记的值；而 $s(n_i, m)$ 表示 n_i 与中心像素点阈值比较后的结果，其计算公式为：

$$s(n_i, m) = \begin{cases} 1, g_{n_i} \geqslant g_m \\ 0, g_{n_i} < g_m \end{cases} \tag{5-2}$$

式中：g_{n_i} 与 g_m 分别表示 n_i 与 m 像素点的值。采用 LBP 算子对某一车载装饰品区域图像的一个像素点进行处理的过程如图 5.14 所示。矩形区域的 LBP 算子的缺点是其区域固定在一定的范围内，不能有效地描述不同尺寸和频率的纹理需求。为了解决不同尺寸的纹理需求，圆形 LBP 算子被提出，该算子可以扩充到不同的半径，改进后的圆形 LBP 算子可以包含任意多像素点，如图 5.15 所示。当图像旋转一定的角度后，其特征值将会发生改变，因此 LBP 算子不具备旋转不变性。为了解决旋转不变问题，Maenpaa 等[12]提出了一种旋转不变 LBP 算子，该旋转不变 LBP 算子的计算过程为：以中心像素点为圆心不断旋转圆形邻域区域，以得到一系列 LBP 值，并计算这些值的最小值作为 LBP 特征值。对于固定的中线点，无论图像的旋转角度如何，计算得到的 LBP 最小值是不变的，将该最小值作为中心像素点的 LBP 特征值，该特征值即具备了旋转不变特性。由于 LBP 特征描述的是邻域内的局部特征，其特征值的提取是邻域内像素值比较后得到的，所以无论光照如何变化，其相对值的大小保持不变，具有光照不变特性。在进行旋转不变处理以后，所提取图像的 LBP 特征还具有旋转不变性，采用旋转不变 LBP 算子得到的特征图像检测效果图如图 5.16 所示。

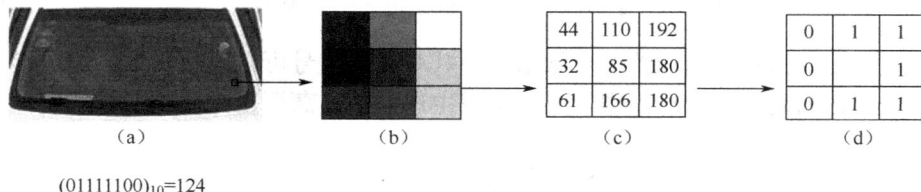

（a）　　　　　　　　（b）　　　　　　　　（c）　　　　　　　　（d）

$(01111100)_{10} = 124$

图 5.14　LBP 特征形成过程

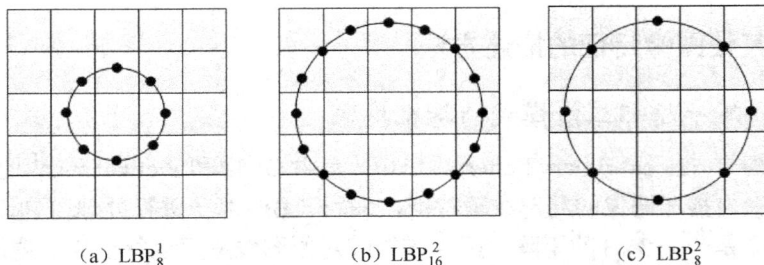

(a) LBP$_8^1$ (b) LBP$_{16}^2$ (c) LBP$_8^2$

图 5.15 圆形 LBP 算子

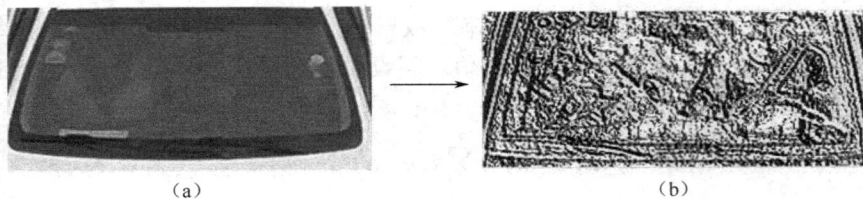

（a）   （b）

图 5.16 LBP 检测效果图

5.2.2.2 基于 Gabor 小波变换的特征提取

Gabor 小波滤波是将空域图像处理问题转换成频域问题。Gabor 特征与人类的视觉系统对视觉刺激的响应十分类似，在提取局部信号方面弥补了傅里叶变换的不足，从而在提取目标的局部空间频域信息方面具有很好的性能，Gabor 小波的核函数可以提供方便的方向和尺度选择，并且光照的变化对于 Gabor 边缘信息的提取影响不明显，该特征提取方法对光照变化具有较高的健壮性。Gabor 小波滤波的工作中心在于基函数频率的确定，其变换过程如下：

$$G_f(a;b,w) = \int_{-\infty}^{+\infty} f(t)g_a(t-b)e^{-i\omega t}dt \tag{5-3}$$

$$g_a(t) = \frac{1}{2\sqrt{\pi a}}\exp(-\frac{t^2}{4a}) \tag{5-4}$$

式中：$f(t)$ 是待处理的输入信号表达，且 $f \in L^2(R)$；$g_a(t)$ 为时间间隔 t 的高斯函数，在 Gabor 变换中被称为窗函数；$g_a(t-b)$ 是一个将时间按间隔分割后局部化的"窗函数"；$a>0$，$b>0$ 并且参数 b 用于平行移动窗口，对参数 b 进行积分得

$$\int_{-\infty}^{+\infty} G_f(a,b,w)db = \hat{f}(\omega), \omega \in \mathbf{R} \tag{5-5}$$

根据 $\hat{f}(\omega)$ 可以重构原信号，对 $\hat{f}(\omega)$ 进行积分计算实现重构，即：

$$f(t) = \frac{1}{2\pi}\int_{-\infty}^{+\infty}\int_{-\infty}^{+\infty} G_f(a;b,\omega)g_a(t-b)e^{i\omega t}d\omega db \tag{5-6}$$

上述 Gabor 变换过程处理的是连续信号，针对离散信号可以采用以下方式进行求解。

（1）核函数的选取。针对图像信号，本书中选取的是高斯窗口函数，即：

$$g(t) = \left[\frac{\sqrt{2}}{T}\right]^2 e^{-\pi(\frac{t}{T})^2} \tag{5-7}$$

则其对偶函数 $\gamma(t)$ 为：

$$\gamma(t) = \left[\frac{1}{\sqrt{2}T}\right]^{\frac{1}{2}}\left[\frac{K_0}{\pi}\right]^{-\frac{3}{2}}e^{\pi\left[\frac{t}{T}\right]^2}\sum_{n+1/2>1/T}(-1)^n e^{-\pi(n+1/2)^2} \tag{5-8}$$

（2）根据连续信号的 Gabor 变换公式，得到离散变换公式为：

$$G_{mn} = \int_{-\infty}^{+\infty}\phi(t)g\otimes(t-mT)e^{-jn\omega t}\mathrm{d}t = \int_{-\infty}^{+\infty}\phi(t)g_{mn}\otimes(t)\mathrm{d}t \tag{5-9}$$

$$\phi(t) = \sum_{m:-\infty}^{+\infty}\sum_{n:-\infty}^{+\infty}G_{mn}\gamma(t-mT)e^{jnwt} = \sum_{m:-\infty}^{+\infty}\sum_{n:-\infty}^{+\infty}G_{mn}\gamma_{mn}(t) \tag{5-10}$$

$$g_{mn}(t) = g(t-mT)e^{jn\omega t} \tag{5-11}$$

与一维 Gabor 变换相比，二维 Gabor 变换不仅能够分析局部信号，而且能够在空域和频域同时分析信号，即能够更好地描述信号的频率、空间位置和信号方向等局部信息。二维 Gabor 变换可以看作预先选定的高斯窗口核函数和正弦平面波的乘积，其复数形式如下所示：

$$g(x,y;\lambda,\theta,\psi,\sigma,\gamma) = \exp(-\frac{x'^2+\gamma^2 y'^2}{2\sigma^2})\exp[i(2\pi\frac{x'}{\lambda}+\psi)] \tag{5-12}$$

该核函数对应的实部如下所示：

$$g(x,y;\lambda,\theta,\psi,\sigma,\gamma) = \exp(-\frac{x'^2+\gamma^2 y'^2}{2\sigma^2})\cos(2\pi\frac{x'}{\lambda}+\psi) \tag{5-13}$$

该核函数对应的虚部如下所示：

$$g(x,y;\lambda,\theta,\psi,\sigma,\gamma) = \exp(-\frac{x'^2+\gamma^2 y'^2}{2\sigma^2})\sin(2\pi\frac{x'}{\lambda}+\psi) \tag{5-14}$$

式中：$x' = x\cos\theta + y\sin\theta$；$y' = -x\sin\theta + y\cos\theta$；$\lambda$ 为正弦函数的波长；θ 为核函数的方向；ψ 为相位偏移；σ 为高斯函数的标准差；γ 为空间的宽高比。

本书中，核函数的尺度和方向分别选取为 5 和 8，Gabor 核函数的图像如图 5.17 所示。利用该核函数求得输入图像的滤波图像如图 5.18 所示。

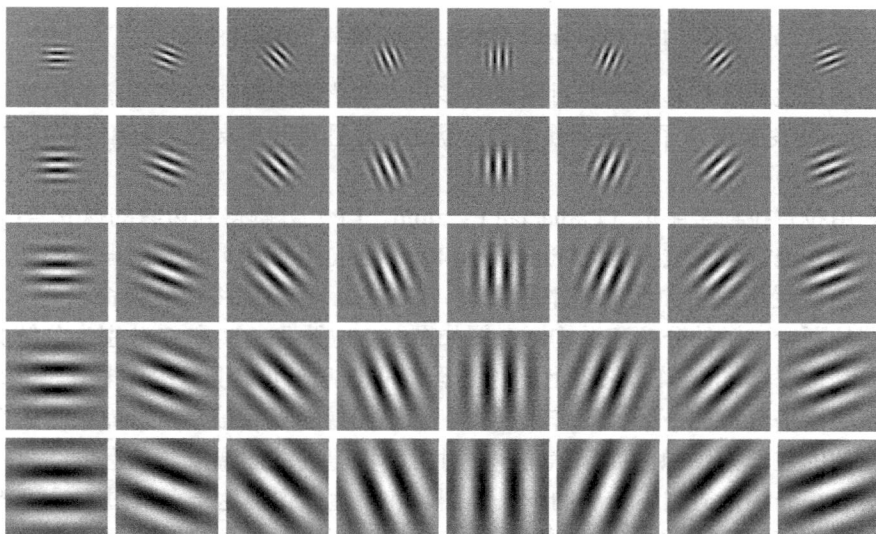

图 5.17 Gabor 核函数的图像

（a）原图

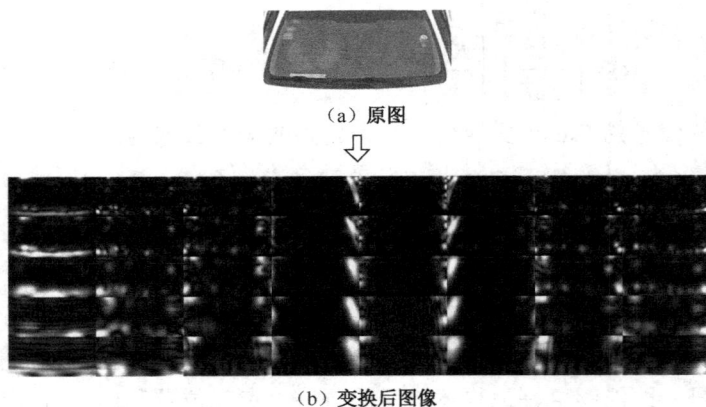

（b）变换后图像

图 5.18　利用 Gabor 核函数求得输入图像的滤波图像

5.2.2.3　基于 Contourlet 变换的特征提取

2002 年，Contourlet 变换由 Minh [13, 14]提出，Contourlet 变换采用大小和长宽比可以变化的矩形轮廓段来逼近曲线，并且具有方向性和各向异性，图 5.19 描述了 Contourlet 变换对曲线的逼近过程，因此，Contourlet 变换可以在高频段上做多个方向的任意分解。

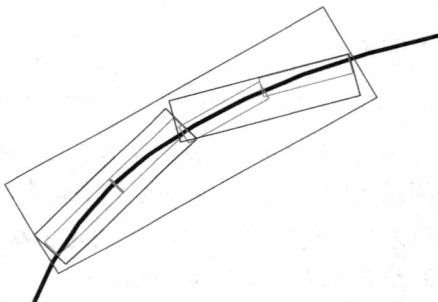

图 5.19　Contourlet 变换在不同分辨率下的描述曲线

小波变换通过伸缩和移动运算对图像的多尺度细化来实现对空间频率的局部化分析和细化，Contourlet 变换继承了小波变换的这一优点，并且将其扩展至多高维空间，Contourlet 变换的实现步骤为：

（1）利用拉普拉斯金字塔（Laplacian Pyramid，LP）分解得到边缘的孤立点；

（2）使用二维方向滤波器组（Directional Filter Bank，DFB）将方向一致的断点连接成线，这些连接线就形成了曲线的基本轮廓段（Contour），因此将该变换命名为 Contourlet 变换。拉普拉斯金字塔的分解和重构示意图如图 5.20 所示，H 和 G 分别为分解滤波器和合成滤波器，M 为采样矩阵，采用上述滤波器和采样矩阵可实现对图像多分辨率采样。经过拉普拉斯金字塔分解的下采样矩阵采样得到的是图像的低频信息 a，而预测图像与下采样得到的图像的差即为图像的高频信息 b，对上一步得到的图像低频信息继续采用该拉普拉斯金字塔进行分解，得到下一层的下采样图像和差值图像，这一分解过程重复 N 次后将会形成第 N 层的低通部分和 N 张差值图像（高频部分）。二维方向滤波器组用于图像的多向性分析，已得到的每一层高频分量上，该滤波器组采用一个 l 层的二叉树将输入图像进行分解，在第 l 层分解得到 2^l 个子带，并将拉普拉斯金字塔分解得到的每一层高频分量采用二维方向滤波器组分解得到的点奇异连接起来，从而捕获到图像的轮廓结构。二维方向滤波器组包含梅花滤波器组和平移操作两个模块，梅花滤波器组（Quincunx 滤波器，如图 5.21 所示）采用扇形滤波器将 2D 光谱分解为水平和垂直两个方向。

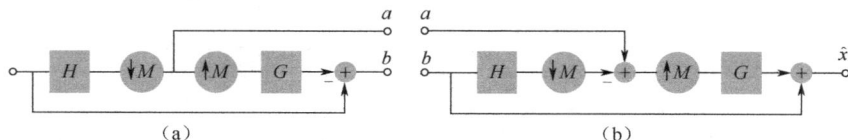

图 5.20　拉普拉斯金字塔的分解和重构示意图

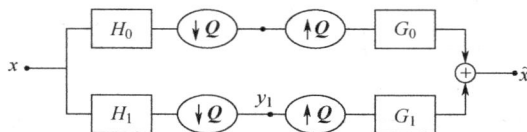

图 5.21　梅花滤波器组

图 5.21 中：H 为分解滤波器；G 为合成滤波器；Q 为采样矩阵，采样矩阵存在两种形式，如式（5-15）所示。上述两种形式的区别在于旋转的角度不同，Q_0 和 Q_1 旋转角度分别为 45° 和 −45°。在 Quincunx 滤波分解之前需要进行平移操作（Shearing），其作用是对图像的采样进行重新排序，并将图像进行旋转以将宽度变为原来的 2 倍；在合成阶段采用与采样相反的平移操作进行图像的合成，其操作可采用式（5-16）中的四种采样矩阵。

$$\begin{cases} \boldsymbol{Q}_0 = \begin{Bmatrix} 1 & -1 \\ 1 & 1 \end{Bmatrix} \\ \boldsymbol{Q}_1 = \begin{Bmatrix} 1 & 1 \\ -1 & 1 \end{Bmatrix} \end{cases} \tag{5-15}$$

$$\begin{cases} \boldsymbol{R}_0 = \begin{pmatrix} 1 & 1 \\ 0 & 1 \end{pmatrix} \\ \boldsymbol{R}_1 = \begin{pmatrix} 1 & -1 \\ 0 & 1 \end{pmatrix} \\ \boldsymbol{R}_2 = \begin{pmatrix} 1 & 0 \\ 1 & 1 \end{pmatrix} \\ \boldsymbol{R}_3 = \begin{pmatrix} 1 & 0 \\ -1 & 1 \end{pmatrix} \end{cases} \tag{5-16}$$

Contourlet 变换过程有效地结合了金字塔分解和方向滤波器，其变换过程如图 5.22 所示。金字塔分解和方向滤波器能够很好地弥补各自的不足，因此 Contourlet 变换弥补了对低频信号理解不足和金字塔分解不具备方向性的缺点。

输入车载装饰品区域图像的三层 Contourlet 分解如图 5.23 所示，在第 l 层金字塔分解的方向子带数为 2^l，最细致层上的方向子带数为 16，图中将每层的所有子带拼成了一张图像。在实际的特征提取过程中，将子带图像直接作为输入特征会造成特征向量维数过高，但直接将每个子带的均值和方差作为输入特征又会忽略掉比较多的细节信息，因此本书提出采用每一层所有子带合并后的图像的每行的均值和方差作为特征。例如，对于一张输入大小为 256×256 的图像，其 Contourlet 变换后的三层子带合并图像大小分别为 64×64、128×128 和 256×256，则该图像的 Contourlet 特征维数大小为 2×(64+128+256)=896 维。

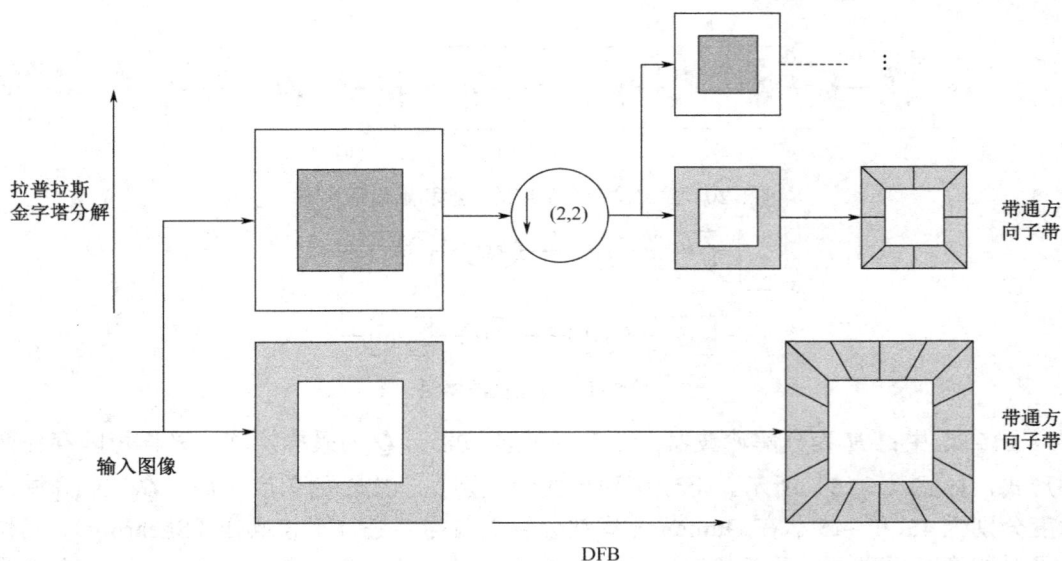

图 5.22　Contourlet 变换过程

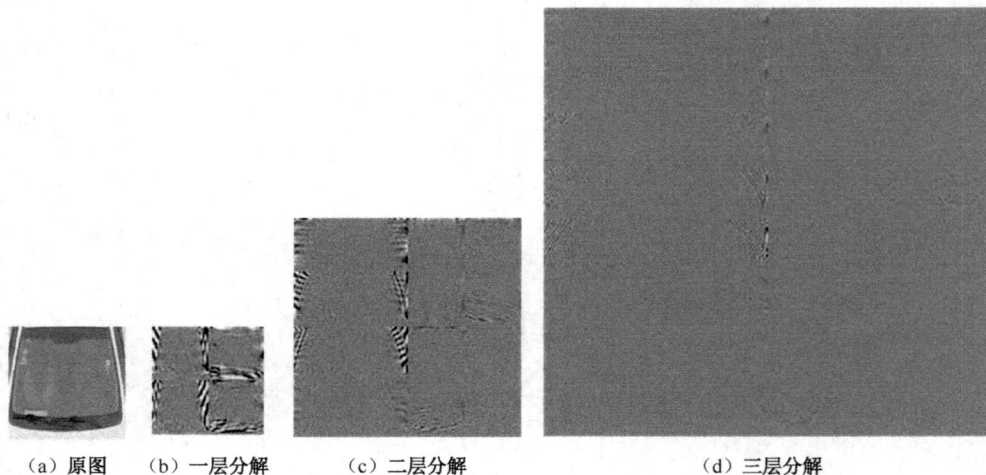

（a）原图　　（b）一层分解　　（c）二层分解　　　　（d）三层分解

图 5.23　输入车载饰品区域图像的三层 Contourlet 分解

5.2.2.4　基于尺度不变特征变换（SIFT）的特征提取

尺度不变特征变换（Scale Invariant Feature Transform，SIFT）能够有效地描述图像的局部特征，由 David[15]于 2004 年提出。该变换不仅具有尺度不变特性，而且还具有对旋转和亮度变化保持较高检测率的特点；该变换包含尺度空间的构建、关键点的检测、关键点大小及方向的计算和关键点描述子的形成四个过程。尺度空间构建的目的是得到一系列图像构成金字塔，实现该构建的方法是对图像进行下采样，得到下一尺度空间的图像后进行平滑操作，去除噪声并不断地重复上述下采样和平滑操作。图像的下采样操作通过高斯卷积核对源图像进行卷积来实现。例如，对于一幅大小为 $N \times N$ 的图像 $I(x, y)$，采用卷积公式（5-17）得到的高斯图像为：

$$L(x, y, \sigma) = G(x, y, \sigma) \times I(x, y) \tag{5-17}$$

其中，$G(x, y, \sigma)$ 是可变高斯函数，即：

$$G(x, y, \sigma) = \frac{1}{2\pi\sigma^2} e^{-(x^2 + y^2)/2\sigma^2} \tag{5-18}$$

式中：参数 σ 被称为尺度空间因子，其值的大小决定了图像的精细程度，σ 取大值时卷积得到的图像表征了整幅图的概貌特征，而 σ 取小值时将更好地描述图像的细节信息。尺度空间构建完成后将检测该空间下的关键点，根据尺度空间得到高斯差分空间（DOG scale-space）是关键点求取的关键步骤，其构建函数为：

$$D(x, y, \sigma) = [G(x, y, k\sigma) - G(x, y, \sigma)] * I(x, y) = L(x, y, k\sigma) - L(x, y, \sigma) \tag{5-19}$$

建立图像金字塔的过程如图 5.24 所示，对于输入源图像 $I(x, y)$，首先建立不同尺度的采样图像，第一个尺度图像的大小即为原图的大小，后面的每一尺度都是上一尺度图像的下采样的结果，从而构建新的尺度图像；其次，为了检测差图像的局部极值点，需要比较差图像中每个像素与其近邻的 26 个像素的值，也就是比较其与相邻上下尺度的 9 个相邻点和本尺度 8 个相邻点的值；最后，为了使算子具备旋转特性，根据梯度方向直方图计算确定关键点的主方向，在点 (x, y) 处的模和方向的计算公式如式（5-20）所示。

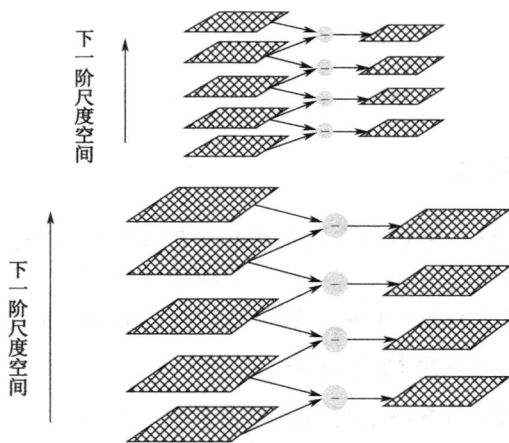

图 5.24 建立图像金字塔的过程

$$\begin{cases} m(x, y) = \sqrt{(L(x+1, y) - L(x-1, y))^2 + (L(x, y+1) - L(x, y-1))^2} \\ \theta(x, y) = \tan^{-1}\{[L(x-1, y) - L(x, y+1)^2] / [L(x+1, y) - L(x-1, y)]\} \end{cases} \tag{5-20}$$

SIFT 特征描述子的计算过程如图 5.25 所示，关键点为图 5.25（a）的中线点，采用式（5-20）求得每个像素梯度的模和梯度方向，图中的箭头方向即为计算所得方向，箭头的长度表示模的大小，每个像素点的主方向和模的大小通过所有方向和模的加权计算得到，其权值大小根据高斯函数确定。高斯加权的范围根据图像的大小确定，即如图中圆所标注的范围，与关键点的距离越近，权重越大。将图 5.25（a）分割成 4×4 的小块，在每个小块上计算 8 个方向的梯度方向直方图，即可形成一个种子点。图 5.25（b）表示的一个关键点由 2×2 共 4 个种子点组成，每个种子的特征信息包含 8 个方向的特征向量。针对车载装饰品区域图像，采用16×16大小的窗口进行计算，最终形成的特征描述子的特征维数为4×4×8＝128维。对图 5.26（a）车载装饰品区域图像进行尺度不变特征点检测的结果如图 5.26（b）所示，由检测结果可以看出，车载装饰品区域的尺度不变特征关键点主要集中在前端挡风玻璃的标签、摆件等区域，该特征提取方法能够有效地提取车载装饰品特征。

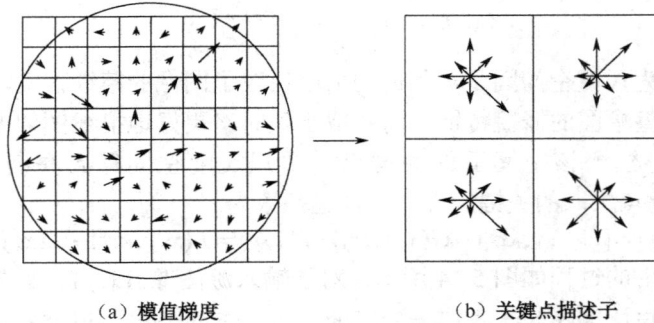

（a）模值梯度　　　　　　　　　（b）关键点描述子

图 5.25　SIFT 特征描述子的计算过程

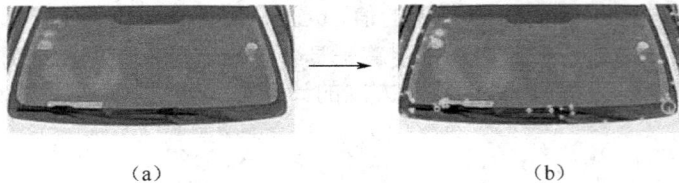

（a）　　　　　　　　　（b）

图 5.26　SIFT 关键点的检测

5.2.3　特征相似度的衡量

除特征选取及提取之外，衡量图像检索的好坏是计算候选图像与库中图像特征之间相似度的匹配。本书中，特征提取的表现形式除了颜色是以直方图形式表示，其他特征都是以向量形式表示，从而图像的相似程度就等价地转换为向量与向量的距离参数计算。

5.2.3.1　直方图的相似度衡量方法

计算颜色直方图相似度的方法主要包括相关系数、开方和直方图相交等，两幅直方图的相关系数计算公式如下。

$$d(H_1,H_2)=\frac{\sum_I(H_1(I)-\bar{H}_1)(H_2(I)-\bar{H}_2)}{\sqrt{\sum_I(H_1(I)-\bar{H}_1)^2\sum_I(H_2(I)-\bar{H}_2)^2}} \tag{5-21}$$

图像像素灰度值的平均值 $\bar{H}_k$ 的计算公式为：

$$\bar{H}_k=\frac{1}{N}\sum_J H_k(J) \tag{5-22}$$

式中：N 表示图像灰度直方图颜色区间的总和。直方图的相似度与相关系数的大小成正比。两幅直方图开方的计算为：

$$d(H_1,H_2)=\sum_I\frac{(H_1(I)-H_2(I))^2}{H_1(I)} \tag{5-23}$$

5.2.3.2　特征值的相似度衡量方法

衡量特征相似度的主要原则是依据特征之间的距离确定，所采用的方法都是以向量空间模型计算特征之间的接近程度，常用特征之间距离的度量方法主要有：街区距离、欧式距离、二次式距离、马氏距离、汉明距离和直方图相交等。

令输入待检索的车辆前挡风玻璃区域图像提取的特征向量为 $I = (i_1, i_2, i_3, \cdots, i_N)$，图像库中任意一张图像计算所得特征向量 $S = (s_1, s_2, s_3, \cdots, s_N)$，将这两个特征向量进行欧式距离的计算，计算公式如下：

$$D_{IS} = \sqrt{\sum_{i=1}^{N}(I_i - S_i)^2} \qquad (5\text{-}24)$$

式（5-24）还可以采用式（5-25）将计算距离归一化至 $[0,1]$ 区间内，所得的结果越大表明两张图像的相似度越高；反之，说明图像之间的相似度越低。

$$\text{sim}(I,S) = \frac{1}{N}\sum_{i=1}^{N}\left(1 - \frac{|i_i - s_i|}{\max(i_i, s_i)}\right) \qquad (5\text{-}25)$$

本章采用欧式距离进行图像关键点的特征向量之间的相似度匹配。

（1）在待查询图像和图像库中检测到关键点；

（2）取待查询图像的某个关键点，并按照欧式距离最近准则匹配出图像库中某一张图像中相似度最高的关键点作为匹配点。

为了减少错误的匹配或者剔除已经错误的匹配点，采用 k-最近邻搜索算法进行错误点的剔除。k-最近邻搜索算法是一种基于类比学习的搜索方法，是在特征空间中查找出与待查询的关键点最为接近的 k 个关键点。本章中将 k 的值设置为 2，如果这两个关键点中最相似的关键点与待查询图像中的关键点距离和次相似的关键点之间距离的比值大于预先设定的阈值，则接受这两个关键点作为匹配关键点。如果将这个比值确定的数值增大，则检测到的总的关键点的数量会减少，但是匹配的精度会大大地增加，这里根据匹配的经验值，设置阈值为 0.8。

5.2.4　检索效果评价标准

目前针对检索效果的评价有直接对每一张图像检索返回结果进行数据分析得到针对该图像的检索成功率，还有对所有待检索图像的数据综合分析得到检索算法的性能。查全率和查准率的数据集合之间的包含关系如图 5.27 所示。

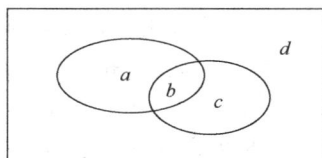

图 5.27　数据的集合关系定义图

图 5.27 中，$a+b+c+d=Z$，$a+b=S$，$b+c=T$，Z 为所有图像的集合，S 为图像库中所有真正与待检索对象相似的图像集合，T 为运用检索算法得到的检索结果集合。根据集合之间的关系可以得到查全率（recall）的计算公式：

$$recall = p(T \mid S) = \frac{P(S \cap T)}{P(S)} = \frac{b}{a+b} \tag{5-26}$$

同时，查准率（precision）的定义为：

$$precision = p(S \mid T) = \frac{P(S \cap T)}{P(T)} = \frac{b}{b+c} \tag{5-27}$$

由式（5-26）、式（5-27）可得，查全率反映了检索性能的全面性，即算法是否可以比较完整地将满足条件的对象检索出；而查准率则主要反映了检索的准确性，即返回的对象中正确的结果占所有输出检索结果的比重。同时，查准率和查全率存在负相关的对应关系，当设定的阈值使得到的查准率较高时，返回的检索结果数量就会减少，从而导致查全率相应地降低，否则，查全率就会呈上升趋势，所以，需要找到平衡的方法来综合这两个指标，式（5-28）中的 balance 代表的就是两者之间的综合指标。

$$balance = \frac{2 \times precision \times recall}{precision + recall} \tag{5-28}$$

在检索性能的评价中还有一个重要的评价方法，即排序评价。假设 R 表示检索结果中所有与待检索图像相关的图像数目，在进行检索结果输出前对图像之间的相似度进行了排序；P 表示返回检索结果中相关图像的序号；T 表示图像库中与待检索图像真正相关的图像数目，评价指标的计算如式（5-29）、式（5-30）所示。

$$AVRR = \frac{1}{R} \sum_{i=1}^{R} P_i \tag{5-29}$$

$$IAVRR = \frac{T}{2} \tag{5-30}$$

$$MT = \frac{R}{T} \tag{5-31}$$

式中：AVRR 称为平均排序值，IAVRR 称为理想排序值，这两个指标之间差值越小，表示检索算法越优秀；MT 则表示图像的漏检率，其值越小表示方法的检索性能越好。

5.2.5 实验结果

针对第 2 章构建的车载装饰品区域图像集，分别采用基于颜色直方图的特征提取方法、基于局部二值模式的特征提取方法、基于 Gabor 小波变换的特征提取方法、基于 Contourlet 变换的特征提取方法和基于尺度不变特征变换的特征提取方法对车载装饰品区域图像进行特征提取，并进行检索及评价实验。针对车辆前挡风玻璃区域的颜色特征，图像在读入内存时以 RGB 颜色模型方式，所以首先进行 RGB → HSV 颜色空间的转换，在 HSV 空间的三通道的颜色区间个数取 50、60 和 60 进行直方图的统计；针对图像的局部二值模式（LBP）特征，对于所有的图像都将得到对应的 LBP 图谱；对于 Gabor 小波变换，首先是根据图像求得 Gabor 核，本书定义 5 个尺度和 8 个方向的核函数，并用这个核函数对输入图像进行 Gabor 变换，将得到 40 个 Gabor 变换图，最终求得这 8 张图像中每一张图的均值和方差作为原图的特征；对于 Contourlet 变换特征，首先对车载装饰品图像进行三层分解，得到对应的子带图像，其次分别计算这层子带图像的均值和方差，最终得到图像的特征向量的维数为 896 维；对于 SIFT 变换特征，将得到尺度变换不变的关键点，每个点的特征维数为 128 维。

第 5 章
基于车载装饰品特征的车辆检索方法

在车载装饰品图像的检索中，对于颜色直方图特征，采用直方图的相似度衡量方法；由于 LBP 只是将原图转化为纹理的 LBP 图谱，所以在进行相似度衡量时，统计 LBP 图谱各像素值的直方图进行相关的比较；而 Gabor 变换特征和 Contourlet 变换特征是统计将原图进行相关变换后得到图像的每一行的均值和方差作为检索的特征，所以在进行检索时直接进行特征之间的欧式距离计算，从而得到相似度。在本章的实验中，只是进行车载装饰品图像的相似度比较，而没有考虑车辆前挡风玻璃检测部分对检索结果造成的影响。采用颜色直方图、Gabor 变换、Contourlet 变换、LBP 变换和 SIFT 变换所得到的检索效果和检索性能分别如表 5.3、表 5.3 所示，其中检索时间是在图像被读入程序中后开始计时，当所有图像被遍历完成后得到结果，计时结束，根据计时的起始和终止节点计算检索的整体耗时，精度精确到毫秒（ms）。不同特征的检索效果和检索性能对比直方图分别如图 5.28 和图 5.29 所示。

表 5.2　不同特征的检索效果

指标 ＼ 特征	查准率 (precision)	查全率 (recall)	综合指标 (balance)	检索时间 (ms)
ColorHistogram	0.766	1.000	0.867	29 370
Gabor	0.842	0.883	0.862	1 283 800
Contourlet	0.608	0.633	0.665	140 000
LBP	0.420	0.750	0.562	138 700
SIFT	0.487	0.867	0.767	237 300

表 5.3　不同特征的检索性能

指标 ＼ 特征	平均排序值 (AVRR)	理想排序值 (IAVRR)	图像的漏检率 (MT)	排序值的差值 (IAVRR-AVRR)
ColorHistogram	1.875	2	1.000	0.125
Gabor	1.782	2	1.250	0.218
Contourlet	1.657	2	1.677	0.343
LBP	1.400	2	1.650	0.600
SIFT	1.750	2	1.348	0.250

由图 5.28、图 5.29 和表 5.2、表 5.3 可得：基于颜色直方图特征的检索效果要优于其他四种特征，由于本章选取了 8 个方向和 5 个尺度的 Gabor 小波变换，所以导致整体的检索时间最长；采用 LBP 方法对车载装饰品图像处理后得到的标签、摆件的纹理特征与车辆前挡风玻璃其他部分的相似度比较大，所以其综合指标的检测率较低；Contourlet 变换的检索效果优于 LBP 特征，但远低于基于颜色直方图和 Gabor 变换的特征提取方法；对于基于颜色直方图的特征提取方法，其计算简单，而且标签摆件的颜色相差较大，所以根据颜色直方图得到的查全率比较高；由于查准率和查全率存在一定的负相关关系，所以基于颜色直方图的特征提取方法查准率就比较低。结合排序性能指标中的漏检率与查全率之间的关系也可以得出，当查全率与漏检率之间存在一定的负相关特性时，根据排序性能指标，去除平均排序与理想排序差距最大和漏检概率最大的特征提取方法，并结合查准率、查全率和检索时间，从而使基于颜色直方图的车辆装饰品区域图像的检索

效果最好。

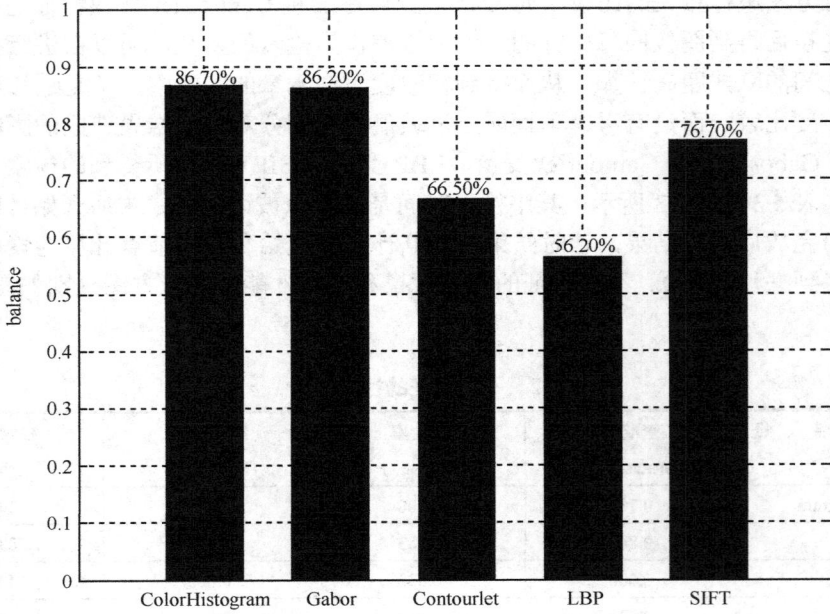

图 5.28　不同特征的检索效果对比直方图

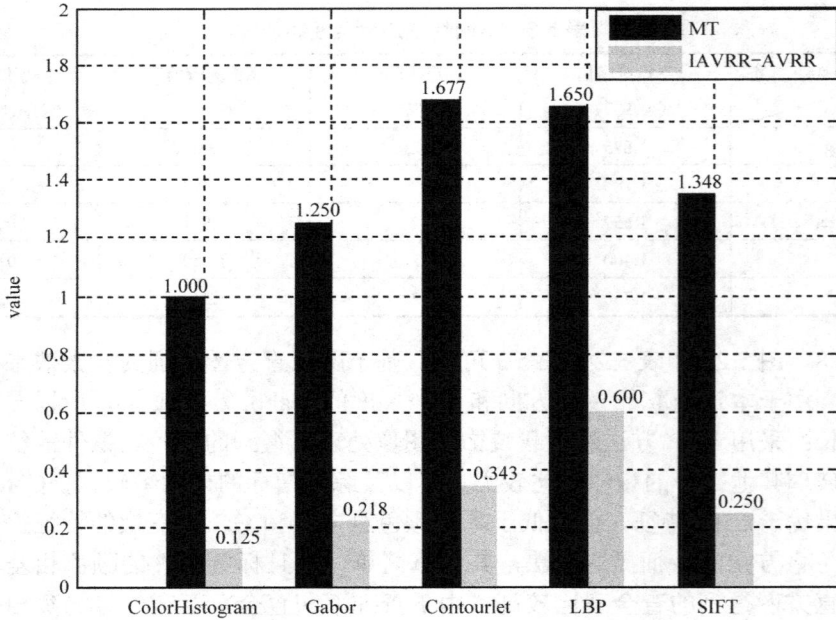

图 5.29　不同特征的检索性能对比直方图

5.3 小结

为了解决从海量交通场景图像中搜索目标车辆的问题，本章研究了基于车载装饰品特征的车辆检索方法，具体的研究成果如下。

（1）研究了基于车辆及车牌对称特征的车辆检测方法，并根据整个车辆与前挡风玻璃的相对位置定位车辆前挡风玻璃区域。对比分析了基于车辆及其车牌对称特征的车辆检测方法、基于 Adaboost 及 Haar 特征的车辆检测方法、基于灰度共生矩阵及支持向量机的车辆检测方法和基于梯度方向直方图及支持向量机的车辆检测方法。实验结果表明基于车辆及车牌对称特征的方法优于其他三种方法，其检测精度达到 90.7%，并且构建了车载装饰品局部区域图像集。

（2）研究了基于颜色特征的车辆检索方法，并与基于局部二值模式、基于 Gabor 小波变换、基于 Contourlet 变换和基于尺度不变特征的检索方法进行了对比分析。基于相似度衡量方法进行了车辆图像的检索实验，实验结果表明基于颜色特征的车辆检索方法优于其他四种方法，其检索综合指标为 86.7%，平均检索时间为 29 730 ms。

（3）提出了一种基于车载装饰品区域图像稀疏编码的车辆检索方法。对比分析了稀疏编码的几种稀疏向量的求解方法，基于车载装饰品局部区域图像构建超完备字典，并根据输入的待检索图像和建立的字典采用稀疏度自适应匹配追踪（Sparsity Adaptive Matching Pursuit，SAMP）算法求解待检索图像的稀疏表征向量；基于构建的车载装饰品局部区域图像集进行了对比实验，实验结果表明基于稀疏编码的车辆检索效果优于其他三种车辆检索方法，在重构容许误差时，其综合指标达到 88.0%，平均检索时间为 114 100 ms。

参考文献

[1] 连捷，赵池航，张百灵，等. 基于车辆轮廓对称与车牌定位信息融合的车辆检测方案[J]. Journal of Southeast University:english Edition, 2012, 28 (2): 240-244.

[2] Viola P, Jones M J. Robust Real-Time Object Detection[C]. Int. J. Computer Vision, 2014.

[3] Viola P, Jones M. Rapid object detection using a boosted cascade of simple features[C]. IEEE Computer Society, 2001.

[4] Papageorgiou C P, Oren M, Poggio T. General framework for object detection[J]. Clinical Neurology and Neurosurgery, 2013, 108 (6): 573.

[5] Haralick R M, Shanmugam K, Dinstein I. Textural Features for Image Classification[J]. Systems Man & Cybernetics IEEE Transactions on, 2010, smc-3 (6): 610-621.

[6] Mirzapour F, Ghassemian H. Using GLCM and Gabor filters for classification of PAN images[C]. Electrical Engineering (ICEE), 2013 21st Iranian Conference on IEEE, 2013.

[7] Dalal N, Triggs B. Triggs, B.: Histograms of Oriented Gradients for Human Detection. In: CVPR[C].Proceedings&CVPR, IEEE Computer Society Conference on Computer Vision and Pattern Recognition. IEEE Computer Society Conference on Computer Vision and Pattern Recognition, 2005.

[8] Cheng H, Zheng N, Sun C. Boosted Gabor Features Applied to Vehicle Detection[C]. Pattern Recognition, 2006. ICPR 2006. 18th International Conference on IEEE, 2006.

[9] Redfield S, Nechyba M, Harris J G, et al. Efficient Object Recognition Using Color[J]. Dissertation Abstracts International, Volume: 63-05, Section: B, page: 2514.;Chair: John G. Harris., 2001.

[10] Stricker A M A, Orengo M. Similarity of Color Images[J]. Proceedings of SPIE - The International Society for Optical Engineering, 1970, 2420: 381-392.

[11] Ojala T, Pietikäinen M, Mäenpää T. Multiresolution gray-scale and rotation invariant texture classification with local binary patterns[J]. IEEE Transactions on Pattern Analysis & Machine Intelligence, 2002, 24 (7): 971-987.

[12] Pietikäinen M. TEXTURE ANALYSIS WITH LOCAL BINARY PATTERNS[J]. Handbook of Pattern Recognition & Computer Vision Edition, 2005 (3): 197-216.

[13] Do M N, Vetterli M. Contourlet: A Directional Multiresolut ion Image Representation[J]. IEEE Icip, 2002, 1:I-357 - I-360.

[14] Do M N, Vetterli M. Contourlets: a new directional multiresolution image representation [C].Circuits, Systems and Computers, 1977. Conference Record. 1977 11th Asilomar Conference, 2002.

[15] Lowe D G. Distinctive Image Features from Scale-Invariant Keypoints[C]. International Journal of Computer Vision, 2004.

中 篇

路面信息感知理论与技术

第6章

路面信息感知技术的研究现状

　　随着国民经济的快速增长，我国的道路交通运输业在国民经济和居民生活中的地位也开始逐步提升，特别是高等级公路已成为衡量一个国家经济水平和现代化程度的标志之一，其建设、管理和运营也极大地促进了我国经济的发展。与此同时，随着社会的进步、居民生活水平的提高，汽车保有量也开始大幅度提升，由于交通量的增加及受车辆大型化、超载严重等现象的影响，高等级公路在使用过程中经受了严峻的考验，导致出现路面破损状况，严重影响道路交通的安全性和舒适性。因此，实施公路养护工作是公路管理部门的工作重点。目前，我国高速公路呈现建设和养护双高峰重合的特点。高速公路的年养护量（大、中修工程）在 8 000 千米以上。对于公路养护管理者来说，面临的养护任务越来越重，压力越来越大，如何搞好高速公路的养护管理工作已是一个不可回避的现实问题。

　　路面养护是公路养护的重点，其质量的好坏直接影响道路交通的安全性和舒适性，而路面破损状况作为路面养护管理工作的依据，在路面养护决策中占据重要地位。传统的路面破损检测方法是采用人工检测，但该方法工作效率低，劳动强度大，作业危险程度较高，对裂缝的检测判别仅凭借检测人员的主观经验，存在较高的主观性，且受天气条件等影响较为严重，已不适应高等级公路快速发展的需求。因此，研究设计智能化的路面破损检测方法成为提高路面养护管理工作的关键热点问题之一。数字图像处理技术、传感技术与电子信息技术在交通领域的应用为交通的智能化和信息化做出了巨大的贡献。为有效地实现路面破损的智能化检测，许多研究机构及学者对路面破损的自动检测技术进行了积极的探索和实验，相继提出了利用超声波、激光和数字图像处理技术实现对路面破损的检测识别。而目前应用最广泛的是基于数字图像处理技术的路面破损检测，该技术的应用是通过采集路面图像，对图像进行处理检测，识别路面破损并实现对路面破损的自动检测和分类。该技术在缓解劳动力的同时，也排除了人的主观因素的干扰，能够快速、准确地进行公路路况的评价，但其检测识别的结果在很大程度上取决于图像处理算法的选择。因此，研究改进合适的图像处理算法对实现高精度的路面破损检测及自动化的路面破损识别分类具有重要意义。本章在国内外路面破损检测研究成果的基础上，开展了基于线阵 CCD 图像的路面破损自动检测及分类方法研究，以实现路面破损的自动化检测识别及分类。

　　直观上，路面破损图像往往具有以下显著特点：

　　（1）路面破损位置的灰度较破损位置周围正常路面的灰度要暗；

　　（2）路面破损处会出现灰度梯度跳变；

　　（3）路面破损具有局部连通性。

基于路面破损图像的上述三个特性，国内外研究机构和学者相继开展了一系列路面破损检测方法的研究。

6.1 路面图像预处理技术研究现状

由于采集的路面图像受路面材料和路面环境的影响，往往存在沙砾、碎石、杂物等噪声的影响，且受光照影响较大。因此，在对路面图像进行检测工作之前，均要对路面图像进行预处理及图像增强，以达到消除路面图像噪声、强化路面破损的效果，为路面破损检测提供基础。

Jitprasithsiri 和 Sun 提出了采用非线性滤波的方法对图像进行增强处理[1, 2]，前者利用中值滤波算法对路面破损图像进行增强，在去除一定噪声的同时，保证了图像中裂缝目标的边缘不会失真，后者考虑到存在噪声的图像裂缝与背景之间的低对比度，利用原始图像与高斯低通滤波图像做差分运算实现图像去噪处理。孙波成等[3]提出了空间域滤波及掩膜平滑法等图像增强方法，其所利用的空间域滤波是通过小区域模板卷积的方法，实现将模板中心和图像中待处理的某像素点重合，并将模板各元素与模板下各自的对应像素值相乘，最后将模板输出响应作为当前模板中心所在像素的灰度值。为了更好地突出图像线形特征的方向性，通常的做法是对上述单模板进行扩展，构造 8 个方向的模板以实现对图像的增强。Koutsopoulos 等[4]利用差影法，对于路面破损图像，将其与不含破损的路面图像做差分，使得图像中的破损信息突显出来，实现了破损图像中目标的增强。

上述几种方法只有当路面破损图像内容较简单时，才能取得较好的效果。但一般情况下路面破损图像较为复杂，因此基于模糊、数学形态学和信息量等人工智能技术的路面病害图像增强方法，受到了许多研究人员的关注。Chou[5]、Cheng[6]和 Li 等[7]提出了基于模糊理论的图像增强方法，在传统模糊理论的基础上对其加以改进，提出了最大模糊熵阈值、模糊掩盖处理及灰度熵模糊法等方法。郭宝良[8]和欧阳琰[9]也通过对传统模糊理论的模糊隶属度函数进行改进处理，实现了图像增强的效果，但模糊增强方法的缺点是容易在模糊背景的同时，对路面破损也有一定程度的削弱，不利于对检测后期目标特征的提取。Cheng等[10]根据路面图像的灰度特征，提出了针对路面破损图像的增强算法，其处理的路面破损图像包括三类像素：一种是低频、宽幅值信号，代表的是亮度不均匀的背景像素；一种是宽幅值且边缘具有高频分量的幅值信号，代表图像中的破损目标；还有一种是高频窄幅信号，代表噪声像素。根据三类像素信号频谱的不同对图像中破损目标像素进行增强处理，取得了较好的效果。Nejad 等[11]利用直方图均衡化和快速傅里叶变换对图像进行增强处理，其快速傅里叶变换是针对图像的像素块（32×32）进行的傅里叶变换，但使用该方法处理后的图像有一定的边际效应。陈利利[12]提出了一种基于多尺度图像分析的路面病害研究方法，其基于多尺度分析，从形态学多尺度分析和非线性扩散多尺度分析两个方面对路面图像进行平滑处理，并基于形态学的各向异性扩散方程，利用形态学算子简化图像数据，保存必要的形状特征及消除不相关性的特点，对图像进行形态学多尺度去噪处理，该方法能较好地保持图像边缘和细节，抑制边界移动，同时能有效地去除噪声。类似于小波变换去噪，许多学者通过将图像转换至频率域对图像频谱进行频域变换以实现图像增强，Wang 等[13]和 Wu 等[14]提出了一种利用 Shearlet 变换对图像进行去噪的处理方法，该方法采用低频率部分的背景匹配和在多层阈值分割下对高频率部分的大尺度 Shearlet 变换，实现图像中噪声信息的去除。李刚[15]和胡士昆等[16]提出了一种基于 Contourlet 变换的图像增强去噪方法，该方法采用基于完全冗余的 Contourlet 变换、基于数学形态学的 Contourlet 变换和非下采样轮廓变换（NSCT）对路面裂缝图像实现增强。吕岩[17]提出了一种基于 Beamlet 变换的裂缝图像匀光算法。董立文等[18]提出了一种利用小波系数尺度间相关性的局部自适应去噪方法来实现路面破损图像增强，针对小波系数估计中硬阈值方法和软阈值方法的缺点，通过对双重量收缩函数得到的阈值乘以一个合适系数进行折中。

综上所述，各研究机构和学者提出的方法都通过实验得到验证，但是，由于实验数据格式不同，这些图像增强技术在具体实践中往往存在偏差。本章所研究的路面图像数据由高分辨率线阵 CCD 相机采集，能够实现毫米级裂缝的图像采集，但易受光照和道路环境影响，采集的路面图像中存在阴影且亮度较低。因此，本章在上述研究成果的基础上，对线阵 CCD 图像增强技术进行研究，以实现路面病害图像的高可靠性增强。

6.2　路面破损检测技术研究现状

路面破损检测是路面破损识别的基础，近些年来，国内外学者在路面破损检测技术方面进行了大量的研究探索。Huang 等[19]提出了一种利用直方图分析检测路面破损的方法。假设含有裂缝区域的路面破损图像的灰度直方图具有双峰特性，并据此确定一个阈值对路面破损图像进行分割。该方法对路面破损明显的图像较为有效，裂缝与路面背景对比度较低时该方法的检测效果较差。Li 等[20]提出了一种利用 Sobel 边缘检测路面破损的方法。其假定路面噪声区域的像素点周长小于 20 像素，而路面破损区域的像素点周长大于 20 像素，从而根据周长的大小实现噪声信息的去除，并得到路面破损图像分割结果，该方法的缺点是当图像中破损信息较为丰富时，采用硬阈值判断容易导致破损的误判，会影响后续对裂缝的识别分类。Grivas 等[21]提出了一种利用区域生长技术对路面破损图像进行分割处理的方法。Yan 等[22]探讨了利用数学形态学进行路面破损识别的可行性。

在分析路面破损图像几何相关性的基础上，冯永安[23]、李莉[24]和李晋惠等[25]提出了对 Sobel 算子模板进行改进后的 8 方向的 Sobel 算子模板，该方法利用图像边缘附近的亮度跃变这一特性，把在邻域内灰度变化超过某个适当阈值的像素点当作边缘点，以此来检测路面破损，但利用该方法检测到的路面破损边缘较粗，并且有时会产生伪边缘，且对噪声的影响较为敏感。唐磊等[26]通过对路面裂缝构建三维曲面模型，将裂缝视为模型中的山谷，通过三维曲率的计算检测到"山谷"位置及裂缝位置来实现对裂缝的检测，该方法存在的缺陷是由于算法的局限性导致检测到的裂缝往往出现断裂的现象，且需要结合其他算法使用。2003 年，Huo 等[27]提出了一种对细小特征运用复杂图表进行多尺度检测的方法，该方法是利用 Beamlets 对线性分段进行并行组织的多尺度系统，建立与 Beamlets 分析相关的算法，以从含噪声图像中复原线性片段。

统计学的新进展，形成了从噪声图像中提取细小片段或细小特征的多尺度方法来对路面破损进行检测。Kumar 等[28]采用 Gabor 滤波及其变形来检测路面图像纹理破损。张雷等[29]利用 Hear 变换对路面破损图像进行低通滤波处理，并对图像进行分块处理及自适应阈值，以实现路面破损区域的自动分割。李刚等[30]基于大津法对路面破损图像进行分割，并依据轮廓跟踪原理计算出路面破损区域的面积、周长等参数，并利用互信息量求取最优阈值，从而对路面破损区域提取特征。赵吉广[31]针对路面破损图像，对比研究了全局阈值与动态阈值相结合的最大类间方差法和基于直方图阈值分割阈值插值算法。Zhang[32]提出了一种将人工生命系统理论应用于路面病害的检测的方法，该方法通过使用不同结构的人造生物结构对图像进行卷积处理，以实现对裂缝的检测，该方法对路面上的油污黑点等有很好的去除作用，但算法结构较为复杂，不适用于对大量图像的检测。

综上所述，上述路面破损检测方法的主要局限性在于方法的普适性不高，针对各种不同路面破损的检测精度不高。本章针对线阵CCD路面破损图像，研究高精度的路面破损检测方法。

6.3 路面破损分类技术研究现状

路面破损区域目标分类的前提是对路面破损目标的特征描述，常用的特征描述子有灰度特征、纹理特征和几何形状特征等，目前，对于路面破损图像的特征描述，使用较多的是采用区域及几何特征描述子，路面图像的区域特征包括傅里叶变换特征和矩描述特征等。对此，国内外研究学者提出了诸多特征描述方法，例如，Haralick 等[33]提出了一种利用统计学的路面破损图像特征提取方法，该方法利用灰度级协方差矩阵或灰度的自相关性对裂缝信息进行特征提取。Paquis 等[34]从结构学的角度出发，提出了一种基于多分辨率协方差矩阵的形态学金字塔变换的特征提取方法。Jain 等[35]和 Mallat 等[36]分别提出了基于 Gabor 变换和快速傅里叶变换的路面图像破损特征提取方法。欧阳琰[9]提出了一种基于几何距离可分性的特征提取方法。肖旺新[37]提出了一种基于破损密度因子的路面破损特征提取方法，并利用该方法对路面破损图像进行了分类实验。储江伟等[38]利用原始灰度值的直方图特征作为子块路面图像特征，并进行了实验研究。

路面破损类型的自动识别是实现智能化路面破损检测系统的关键技术之一，国内外学者相继开展了探索研究。Wang 等[39]在对图像进行背景光照均衡化后，对图像进行 Shearlet 变换去噪处理，然后利用 Radon 变换对图像进行分类。Radon 变换是利用不同角度的裂缝所对应形成的 Radon 变换方向与位置的不同这一特点对路面裂缝进行分类，该方法的缺点是只适用于裂缝类病害，对于坑槽等形状不规则的路面破损类型则不适用。Nejad 等[11]提出了一种基于 Wavelet-Radon 变换和动态神经网络（DNN）的路面病害检测和分类方法，该方法通过 Wavelet-Radon 变换对路面破损进行分割特征提取，再利用 DNN 实现对路面破损的分类。欧阳琰[9]提出了一种基于聚类分析的路面破损分类方法，该方法采用 C-均值聚类算法实现对路面破损的识别分类。李刚[30]基于裂缝的投影性质，依据投影量的大小和方向初步判定路面破损的程度和类型，再对线性裂缝与不规则网状裂缝进行初步区分，并利用欧拉数（图像目标连接体数与其中的孔洞数之差）的大小对裂缝进行分类处理。该方法仅对裂缝类病害进行分类，且仅适用于对单个目标的分类。孙奥[40]提出了一种利用支持向量机对路面病害进行分类的方法。

综上所述，上述各种方法的局限主要有：各种算法往往只适用于裂缝类病害，而对于非裂缝类不规则破损分类效果较弱；各类方法在分类实验时采用的数据样本数量都比较小。在上述研究成果的基础上，本章针对线阵CCD路面破损图像，研究高效率的路面破损图像特征提取及分类方法。

参考文献

[1] Jitprasithsiri S, Lee H and Robert G. Development of a New Digital Pavement Image Processing Algorithm for Unified Crack Index Computation[C]. A Dissertation Submitted to the Faculty of the University of Utah, 1997.

[2] Sun Y, Salari E and Chou E. Automated Pavement Distress Detection Using Advanced Image Processing Techniques[C]. IEEE International Conference on Electro/information Technology, 2009.

[3] 孙波成, 邱延峻. 路面裂缝图像处理算法研究[J]. 公路交通科技, 2008, 25 (2): 64-68.

[4] Koutsopoulos H N and Downey A B. Primitive-based Classification of Pavement Cracking Images[J]. Journal of Transportation Engineering, 1993, 19 (3): 136-143.

[5] Chou J, Neill O and Cheng H. Pavement Distress Evaluation Using Fuzzy Logic and Moment Invariants[J]. Transportation Research Record, 199: 39-46.

[6] Cheng H, Chen J and Glazier C, etc. Novel Approach to Pavement Cracking Detection Based on Fuzzy Set Theory[J]. Journal of Computing in Civil Engineering, 1999, 13 (4): 270-280.

[7] Li G, Tong Y and Xiao X. Adaptive Fuzzy Enhancement Algorithm of Surface Image based on Local Discrimination via Grey Entropy[J]. Advanced in Control Engineering and Information Science, 2011, 15: 1590-1594.

[8] 郭宝良. CCD 图像处理及算法在沥青路面破损检测中的研究[D]. 山东: 山东理工大学, 2011.

[9] 欧阳琰. 道路信息自动检查中的路面破损识别方法及其实现研究[D]. 武汉: 武汉理工大学, 2009.

[10] Cheng H. Automated Real-time Pavement Distress Detection Using Fuzzy Logic and Neural Network [C]. SPIE Proceeding, 1996.

[11] Nejad F M and Zakeri H. An optimum feature extraction method based on Wavelet-Radon Transform and Dynamic Neural Network for pavement distress classification[J]. Expert Systems with Applications, 2011, 38 (9): 9442-9460.

[12] 陈利利. 基于多尺度图像分析的路面病害检测方法研究与分析[D]. 南京: 南京理工大学, 2009.

[13] Wang X and Feng X. Pavement distress detection and classification with automated image processing[C]. 2011 International Conference on Transportation, Mechanical, and Electrical Engineering, 2011.

[14] Wu C, Lu B and Chen D, etc. Pavement Image Denoising Based on Shearlet Treansform[C]. 2011 International Conference on Electronics and Optoelectronics, 2011.

[15] 李刚. 基于图像工程的路面破损自动识别算法研究[D]. 西安: 长安大学, 2010.

[16] 胡士昆. 基于数字图像处理技术的路面裂缝算法研究[D]. 南京: 南京邮电大学, 2012.

[17] 吕岩, 曲仕茹. 基于 Beamlet 变换的路面裂缝图像匀光算法[J]. 交通运输系统工程与信息, 2011, 11 (5): 123-128.

[18] 董立文, 贾朱植, 谢元旦, 等. 一种基于小波变换的图像去噪方法[J]. 鞍山科技大学学报, 2004, 27 (3): 212-215.

[19] Huang Y and Xu B. Automatic Inspection of Pavement Cracking Distress[J]. Journal of Electronic Imaging, 2006, 15 (1): 92-98.

[20] Li L, Chan P and Rao A, et al. Flexible Pavement Distress Evaluation Using Image Analysis [J]. Journal of Transportation Engineering, 1993, 119 (3): 402-418.

[21] Grivas D A, Bhagvati C and Skolnick M M, et al. Feasibility of Automating Pavement Distress Assessment Using Mathematical Morphology[J] .Transportation Research, 1994, 1435 (8): 52-58.

[22] Yan M, Bo S and Xu K. Pavement Crack Detection and Analysis for High-grade Highway[C]. The Eighth International Conference on Electronic Measurement and Instruments, 2007.

[23] 冯永安, 刘万军. 边缘检测改进算法在路面破损检测中的应用[J]. 辽宁工程技术大学学报, 2007, 26: 176-178.

[24] 李莉, 孙立军, 陈长. 适于路面破损图像处理的边缘检测方法[J]. 同济大学学报, 2011, 39 (5): 688-692.

[25] 李晋惠. 用图像处理的方法检测公路路面裂缝类病害[J]. 长安大学学报（自然科学版）, 2004, 24 (3): 24-29.

[26] 唐磊, 赵春霞, 王鸿南, 等. 基于图像分析的路面裂缝检测和分类[J]. 工程图学学报, 2008, 3: 99-104.

[27] Huo X, Chen J, and Donoho D L. Multiscale detection of filamentary features in image data[J]. Wavelets: Applications in Signal and Image Processing, 2003: 592-606.

[28] Kumar A and Pang G K H. Defect detection in textured materials using Gabor filters[J]. IEEE Trans. Appl. Ind., 2002, 38 (2): 425-440.

[29] 张雷, 马建, 宋宏勋. 小波域内基于块的路面破损检测算法[J]. 郑州大学学报, 2009, 30 (3): 48-51.

[30] 李刚, 贺昱曜, 赵妍. 基于大津法和互信息量的路面破损图像自动识别算法[J]. 微电子学与计算机, 2009, 26 (7): 241-243.

[31] 赵吉广. 基于视频图像的路面性能参数采集方法研究[D]. 南京: 东南大学, 2006.

[32] Zhang H G, and Wang Q. Use of Artificial Living System for Pavement Distress Survey[C]. The 30th Annual Conference of the IEEE Industrial Electronics Society, 2004.

[33] Haralick R M and Bosley R. Texture features for image classification[J]. IEEE Transactions on Systems, Man and Cybernetics, 1973, 3 (6): 610-621.

[34] Paquis S, Legeay V and Konik H. Road Surface Classification by Thresholding Using Morphological Pyramid[C]. International Conference on Pattern Recognition, 2000.

[35] Jain A K and Farrokhnia F. Unsupervised texture segmentation using Gabor filters[J]. Pattern Recognition, 1991, 24 (12): 1167-1186.

[36] Mallat S G. A theory for multiresolution signal decomposition: The wavelet representation[J]. IEEE Trans. PAMI, 1989 (11): 674-693.

[37] 肖旺新. 路面破损图像自动识别关键技术研究[D]. 南京: 东南大学, 2004.

[38] 储江伟, 初秀民, 王荣本, 等. 沥青路面破损图像特征提取方法研究[J]. 中国图像图形学报, 2003, 8 (10): 1211-1217.

[39] Wang X and Feng X. Pavement distress detection and classification with automated image processing[C]. International Conference on Transportation, Mechanical, and Electrical Engineering, 2011.

[40] 孙奥. 路面病害图像自动分类方法研究[D]. 南京: 南京理工大学, 2008.

第7章
路面信息感知的方法

随着我国道路交通运输事业的不断发展，车辆超载化、大型化的现象日益严重，为保证车辆行驶的安全性与舒适性，路面养护管理工作已成为公路管理部门工作的重中之重，而路面破损检测作为路面养护管理工作的依据，在公路养护事业中占据着重要地位。传统的路面破损检测主要依靠人工检测，但其存在较大的弊端，如工作效率低、劳动强度大、主观程度高和作业危险等。近些年来，随着科技和信息化的发展，如何实现智能化的路面破损检测是公路管理部门实施路面养护工作中亟待解决的问题。本章基于线阵 CCD 路面图像，以实现自动化的路面破损检测及识别分类为宗旨，对路面破损的检测及分类方法进行了相关研究，具体研究内容如下。

首先，基于线阵 CCD 路面图像，提出了一种基于联合检测器的路面破损自动检测方法。针对路面破损图像中破损像素较正常路面像素灰度较低这一基本特征，对比分析了邻域灰度差分法、局部灰度最小分析法和分块标记法的优势和劣势，基于级联分类器的思想，提出了用于路面破损检测的联合检测器，理论分析和实验结果表明联合检测器的性能优于邻域灰度差分法、局部灰度最小分析法和分块标记法，其检测率达到 96.7%。同时研究了基于连通域融合的路面破损目标精确定位方法，并通过实验验证了该方法的有效性。

其次，研究了路面破损图像的特征提取及分类方法，提出将 Contourlet 变换用于路面破损特征提取，并采用支持向量机进行路面破损自动化分类。对比分析了 Contourlet 变换（Contourlet Transform，CT）、边缘方向直方图（Edge Orientation Histogram，EOH）、梯度方向直方图（Histogram of Orientation Gradients，HOG）和分层梯度方向直方图（Pyramid of Histogram of Orientation Gradients，PHOG）四种特征提取方法，构建了东南大学路面破损图像数据库，采用支持向量机（SVM）分类器对提取的四种特征进行了对比实验，其识别率分别为 84.32%、75.14%、73.25%和 51.93%，实验结果表明 Contourlet 特征提取方法优于其他三种方法。

最后，提出了一种基于联合特征及随机子空间交叉内核支持向量机分类器集成的路面破损自动化分类方法。研究了图像联合特征的融合策略，利用串行融合策略构造了路面破损图像的 Contourlet 变换和 EOH 联合特征，并基于分类器集成的构造原则实现了交叉内核支持向量机分类器的集成方案，采用东南大学路面图像数据库进行了实验，实验结果表明 Contourlet 变换和 EOH 联合特征及随机子空间交叉内核支持向量机分类器集成优于单一 Contourlet 变换特征和 EOH 特征，分类正确率达到 86.61%。

7.1 基于联合检测器的路面破损检测方法

路面破损状况评价是公路管理部门进行路面养护管理的重要依据，并在养护管理决策中占据重要地位，而路面破损检测是实现路面破损状况评价的前提。传统的路面破损检测方法存在着劳动强度大、工作效率低等缺点，为了更好地实施路面养护管理，公路管理部门迫切需要智能化的路面破损检测方法。因此，本节主要研究基于线阵 CCD 图像的路面破损自动检测方法，以实现对路面破损的高精度检测。

7.1.1 路面破损图像采集

本节采用自主研发的 DN-2011 型车载便携式公路路面病害检测设备采集路面破损图像，如图 7.1 所示，该设备由高精度 GPS 接收机提供的瞬时速度驱动高分辨率的线阵 CCD 相机，以实现对公路路面进行扫描并获取高精度线阵图像。

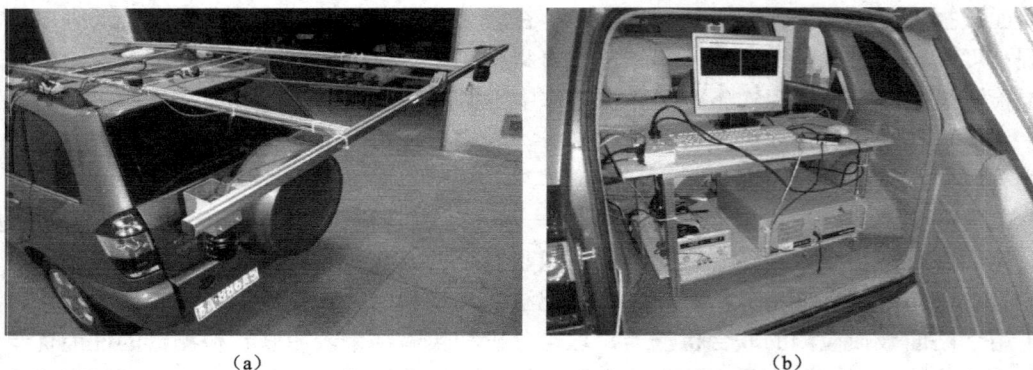

(a)　　　　　　　　　　　　　　　　　(b)

图 7.1　DN-2011 型车载便携式公路路面病害检测设备

路面破损线阵图像采集的路面图像的分辨率为 2 048×1 024 像素，如图 7.2 所示，图 7.2（a）～（d）分别为呈现横裂、纵裂、网裂和正常四种类型。从图 7.2 中可以看出，对于路面破损图像，其裂缝位置的灰度值较正常位置的图像灰度值暗，且图像中含有阴影、砂砾等噪声，因此，图像处理算法应充分考虑图像噪声的处理及细小破损的检测识别。

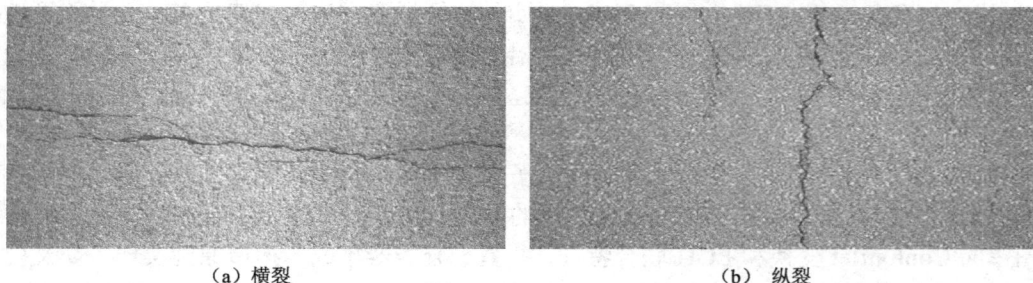

（a）横裂　　　　　　　　　　　　　　　（b）纵裂

图 7.2　路面破损线阵图像

（c）网裂　　　　　　　　　　　　　　　　（d）正常

图 7.2　路面破损线阵图像（续）

7.1.2　图像预处理

路面破损图像易受道路环境及光照因素的影响，并且路面破损图像中往往存在沙砾、油污和阴影等噪声，干扰噪声的存在导致路面破损图像中的灰度及光照不均匀，严重影响了路面图像中破损信息的检测。因此，需要对路面图像进行预处理，以消除图像中的噪声信息，并对路面破损信息进行增强。

1）道路标线信息去除

为保障车辆行驶的安全性，往往会在道路路面上添加道路标线对车辆驾驶进行引导。由于道路标线的存在，使得正常路面的背景相对道路标线而言灰度较暗，将影响对破损信息的检测，因此在图像预处理中首先需要消除道路中的道路标线。对于路面图像中的道路标线而言，由于道路标线一般为白色或黄色，其灰度值与路面背景灰度存在较大的差异，因此通过对图像进行灰度约束即可去除路面中的道路标线信息。灰度处理如图 7.3 所示。

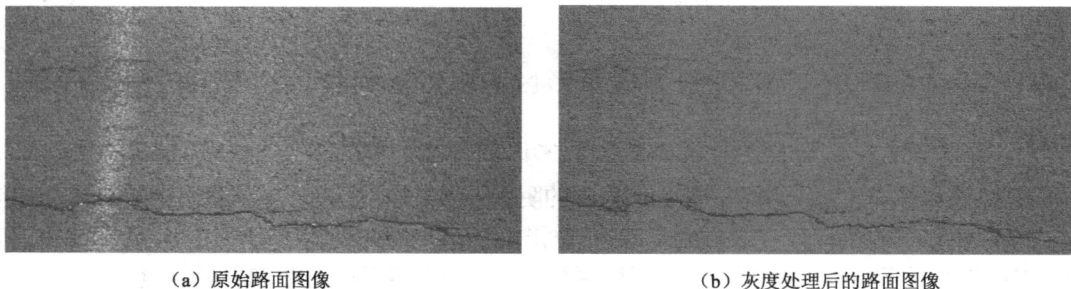

（a）原始路面图像　　　　　　　　　　　　（b）灰度处理后的路面图像

图 7.3　灰度处理

对于图 7.3（a）中的任意像素点 $I(i,j)$，有：

$$I'(i,j) = \begin{cases} \mu & , I(i,j) > \mu \\ I(i,j) & , I(i,j) \leqslant \mu \end{cases} \qquad (7\text{-}1)$$

式中：μ 为整幅图像的均值。通过式（7-1）约束可实现对图像中道路标线信息的去除，其处理效果如图 7.3（b）所示。

2）图像阴影去除

路面破损图像易受道路两旁树木、栅栏和建筑物等遮挡影响而形成阴影，阴影的存在造成图像中阴影区域的像素灰度较暗，从而严重影响了路面图像中破损信息的检测。针对图像中阴影的去除，参考文献[1]、[2]采用人机交互的方法人工标定图像中的阴影区域，再对标定区域进行亮度的补偿；基于阴影区域的光谱不变性，Salvador 等[3]结合阴影区域的几何特征对阴影区域进行划分并进行亮度补偿。前者需要人工的干预，而后者对阴影的检测补偿主要是针对目标的影子引起的阴影的去除，对于路面图像中由外部物体引起的阴影则无法消除。

由于图像阴影区域的灰度深度自区域中心向周围逐步缩减，本章将基于亮度高程模型的图像阴影去除方法应用于路面图像，以实现图像中阴影的去除[4]。基于亮度高程模型的图像阴影去除法是基于地理地图中的等高线模型提出来的，由于图像中阴影的强度是由阴影中心向阴影边界逐渐递减的，因此模型将阴影强度按照强度的不同划分为不同的等级，然后再对各等级进行相应的灰度补偿，以实现阴影的去除。具体方法如下。

（1）对图像进行形态学闭运算。由于裂缝亮度与阴影区域的亮度较为接近，为了避免将裂缝划入阴影区内而执行亮度补偿，需要在阴影区域划分前将裂缝去除，因此采用灰度形态学闭运算对原始路面图像进行处理。

（2）高斯平滑。对上述处理后的路面图像进行平滑处理，消除路面纹理对后续阴影区域划分的影响。

（3）亮度等高区域划分。首先计算图像每一像素所应含有的平均像素数 ng，并计算图像各个灰度级所含有的像素数，按照灰度级大小对各级像素数进行求和相加，当像素数之和 ≥ ng 时，将当前所加像素对应的灰度级分为一个区域，依次对整幅图像的灰度级进行划分，最终图像分为 N 个区域。根据经验阈值 $L = 7/8N$ 对图像进行区域划分，将图像分为阴影区域和非阴影区域。

（4）具有纹理平衡的亮度补偿。对于非阴影区域 B 和阴影区域 S，分别按照式（7-2）对该区域像素进行变换，实现亮度的补偿，即：

$$I'_{i,j} = \begin{cases} \alpha \cdot I_{i,j} + \lambda & ,(i,j) \in S \\ I_{i,j} & ,(i,j) \in B \end{cases} \tag{7-2}$$

式中：$\alpha = \dfrac{D_B}{D_S}$；$D_B$、$D_S$ 分别为非阴影区和阴影区的像素亮度值的标准方差；$\lambda = \hat{I}_B - \alpha \cdot \hat{I}_S$，$\hat{I}_B$、$\hat{I}_S$ 分别为非阴影区和阴影区的平均亮度。采用高程模型消除图 7.4（a）阴影的结果如图 7.4（b）所示，路面图像中的阴影得以去除。但是，在消除阴影的同时，也削弱了路面图像的破损目标，主要原因是原始路面图像光线较暗，阴影的灰度特性与路面图像中破损的灰度特性过于相似，从而导致在对阴影区域的灰度增强的同时，也对破损的灰度进行了增强。

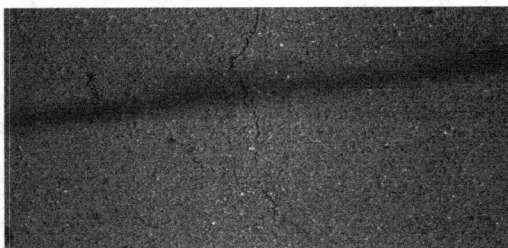

(a) 原始含阴影路面图像　　　　　(b) 阴影去除后路面图像

图 7.4　高程模型阴影去除

3）图像频域滤波处理

路面图像中的噪声主要是沥青路面不平整性及路面沙砾的离散性造成的，此类噪声信息的纹理特性与路面图像的纹理特性类似，因此，仅从纹理特性对路面破损图像进行降噪处理容易造成路面图像中破损目标信息的缺失。图像去噪的关键是在去除噪声的同时，能完整保留图像的原有细节信息，小波阈值去噪是由 Donoho 等[5]提出来的，该方法的特点是方法简单和计算量较小，近年来在图像去噪领域得到了广泛应用。对于路面破损图像而言，图像中的破损信息较少而背景信息较多，这恰恰符合小波阈值去噪的特性，因此，本书采用小波阈值去噪的方法来消除路面破损图像中的噪声。

在小波阈值去噪中，对于经小波变换后的图像，包含有信号重要信息的小波系数其幅值较大，但数量较少，而噪声对应的小波系数幅值小。通过选取适当的阈值，将小于阈值的小波系数置零，保留大于阈值的小波系数，从而抑制信号中的噪声。对于小波阈值去噪，主要包括以下步骤：

（1）对噪声图像 $\{I_{ij}, i, j = 1, 2, \cdots, N\}$ 做小波变换，得到小波系数 $\{W_{ij}, i, j = 1, 2, \cdots, N\}$；

（2）对上一步得到的小波系数 W_{ij} 进行阈值处理，$\overline{W_{ij}} = \eta_T(W_{ij})$，$i, j = 1, 2, \cdots, N$，其中，$\eta_T(\bullet)$ 为阈值函数，T 为选取的阈值；

（3）对小波去噪处理后的小波系数 $\overline{W_{ij}}$ 进行小波逆变换，得到去噪后的图像。

由上述步骤可知，小波阈值去噪的关键是阈值函数及阈值的选择。常见的阈值函数可以分为硬阈值函数、软阈值函数和半软阈值函数，它们的基本思想都是认为代表图像中噪声信息的小波系数较小，应将其去除，而对较大的小波系数进行保留。对于本书的路面图像去噪，由于图像尺寸较大，考虑到图像预处理耗费的时间及对后续破损检测的影响，本书选取小波阈值去噪函数中的硬阈值函数去噪，而其阈值选用通用 Visushrink 阈值，以期在实现图像去噪的同时，不增加图像处理算法的复杂度，提高处理算法的效率。硬阈值函数表达为：

$$\eta_T(w_{ij}) = \begin{cases} 0 & , |w_{ij}| \leqslant T \\ w_{ij} & , |w_{ij}| > T \end{cases} \qquad (7\text{-}3)$$

式中：阈值 T 的选取为 $T = \sigma_n \sqrt{2\log(N)}$。采用小波硬阈值函数及 Visushrink 阈值对图 7.5（a）进行去噪处理，处理结果如图 7.5（b）所示。小波去噪处理后的路面图像较原始图像而言，其路面破损背景部分由于沥青路面不平整性造成的毛刺噪声得到了有效的削弱，图像中离散的白色噪声点也得以去除，且实现了在去除噪声的同时，较为完整地保留了图像中的目标破损信息。

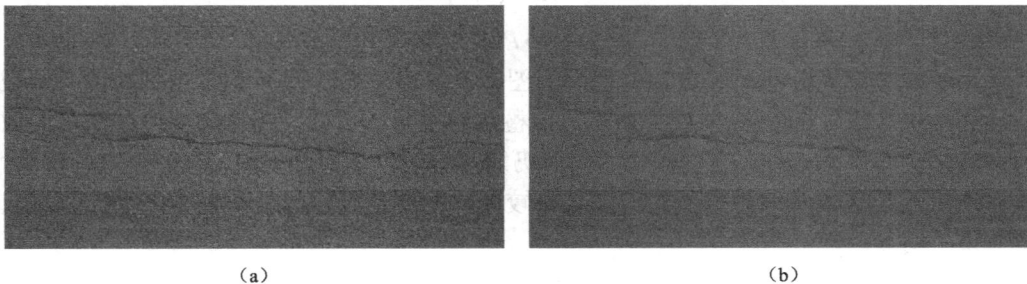

（a）   （b）

图 7.5 小波硬阈值函数及 Visushrink 阈值去噪

7.1.3　基于灰度分析的路面破损检测

在数字图像处理领域，图像的灰度即图像的深度。路面破损图像的显著特点是路面破损位置的图像比正常路面位置的深度暗，即路面破损位置的像素灰度比正常路面的像素灰度值小，基于这一事实，本章开展基于灰度分析的路面破损检测方法研究。

1）邻域灰度差分法

传统阈值分割是通过对图像设定阈值将图像像素分为若干类，其考虑的是图像的全局灰度特征，往往忽略图像的局部细节信息，邻域灰度差分法是对传统阈值分割的改进。邻域灰度差分法是利用图像的局部灰度特征，通过对像素点周边邻域像素灰度值与中心像素的灰度差分确定中心像素的灰度特征，其优点是充分考虑了图像的局部细节特征，且能够削弱图像中离散噪声的影响。

对于路面灰度图像中任意一像素点，其灰度值为 $p(x,y)$ ，其整幅图像的像素灰度级为 $\mathrm{val}(1,2,\cdots,L)$ ，则对于该点像素周边 W 邻域内像素，其灰度差分值为 $a_{\mathrm{val},p(x,y)}$ ，即：

$$a_{\mathrm{val},p(x,y)} = \sum_{j=1}^{W}[p_j - p(x,y)] \tag{7-4}$$

对于灰度值为 val 的像素点 $p(x,y)$ ， $a_{\mathrm{val},p(x,y)}$ 反映了其 W 邻域内各像素点与该中心像素的灰度差分。 $a_{\mathrm{val},p(x,y)}$ 值表征在该像素点位置的灰度梯度值的大小，能有效地反映图像中的灰度梯度变化。对于一张图像而言，其灰度值的变化范围为 $(1,2,\cdots,L)$ ，则对于每一灰度级 val ，统计图像中具有相同灰度值 val 的差分值 A_{val} ，即：

$$A_{\mathrm{val}} = \iint a_{\mathrm{val},p(x,y)} \mathrm{d}x\mathrm{d}y \tag{7-5}$$

则对于大小为 $X \times Y$ 的图像， $x \in (1,2,\cdots,X), y \in (1,2,\cdots,Y)$ ，则 A_{val} 为：

$$A_{\mathrm{val}} = \sum_{x=1}^{X}\sum_{y=1}^{Y}a_{\mathrm{val},p(x,y)} \tag{7-6}$$

由于路面破损图像中破损位置灰度较正常路面灰度较低，因此，破损位置像素灰度与其邻域像素灰度差分值较大。对于一幅图像取其最大差分值 A_{val} 的灰度级 val 代表的就是破损位置的像素灰度，因此，邻域灰度差分的阈值选取规则为：

$$t = \max_{i=1}^{L} A_i \tag{7-7}$$

利用灰度阈值 t 将路面破损图像中的裂缝区域与背景区域进行分割，即：

$$p(x,y) = \begin{cases} 1, & p(x,y) \leqslant t \\ 0, & p(x,y) > t \end{cases} \tag{7-8}$$

采用邻域灰度差分法对经过预处理后的图 7.2（a）～（d）进行破损区域检测，领域差分法检测结果如图 7.6（a）～（d）所示。由检测结果分析可知，邻域灰度差分法对图像光照因素的影响不敏感，对于亮度较暗的图像仍能取得较好的检测结果，具有一定的健壮性，但该算法对网裂破损及细微破损的检测效果较差，主要是因为网裂和细微破损的邻域灰度梯度效果不明显。

（a）横裂　　　　　　　　　　　　　（b）纵裂

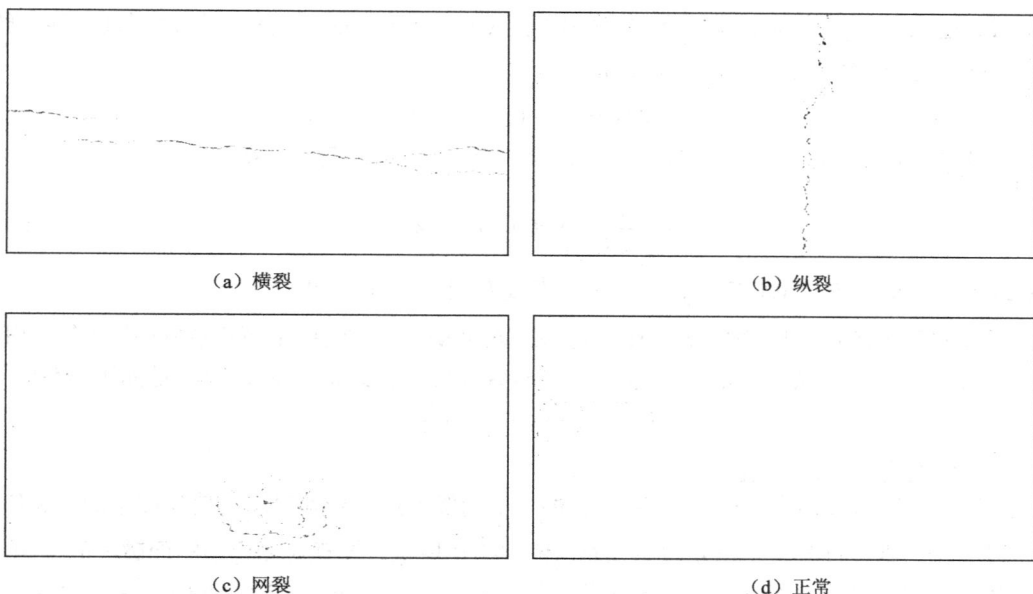

（c）网裂　　　　　　　　　　　　　（d）正常

图 7.6　邻域差分法检测结果

2）局部灰度最小分析法

路面破损图像通常存在沙砾和阴影，从而导致并不是所有灰度值较周围小的像素点都是裂缝点，局部灰度最小分析法可以在利用路面破损灰度特征的同时，兼顾考虑裂缝的局部联通性。局部灰度最小分析法通过对图像中的像素进行遍历搜索，获取图像各行各列的最小灰度像素，并据此对图像中各像素点进行判定。其判定原则为：对于大小为 $M \times N$ 的图像 I 中的任意像素点 $I(x,y)$，如果该点像素灰度在像素所在行（列）中为灰度最小值，则标记该像素点行（列）标记为 1，否则标记为 0，即：

$$\left. \begin{aligned} \boldsymbol{L}_x[x,y] &= \begin{cases} 1 & , \forall_{j\in\{1,2,\cdots,N\}}: I[x,y]=\min\left\{I[x,j]\,|\,x\in\{1,2,\cdots,M\}\right\} \\ 0 & , 其他 \end{cases} \\ \boldsymbol{L}_y[x,y] &= \begin{cases} 1 & , \forall_{j\in\{1,2,\cdots,M\}}: I[x,y]=\min\left\{I[j,y]\,|\,y\in\{1,2,\cdots,N\}\right\} \\ 0 & , 其他 \end{cases} \end{aligned} \right\}$$

（7-9）

对于图像 I 中各像素点的行标记和列标记矩阵 $\boldsymbol{L}_x$ 和 $\boldsymbol{L}_y$，对 $\boldsymbol{L}_x$ 和 $\boldsymbol{L}_y$ 进行求和得到矩阵 $\boldsymbol{L}[x,y]$，即：

$$\boldsymbol{L}[x,y] = \boldsymbol{L}_x[x,y] + \boldsymbol{L}_y[x,y]$$

（7-10）

对于 $\boldsymbol{L}:\{1,2,\cdots,M\}\times\{1,2,\cdots,N\}$，其取值为 $\{0,1,2\}$。当 $\boldsymbol{L}[x,y]=0$ 时，代表像素点 $I(x,y)$ 不是局部最小值像素点；当 $\boldsymbol{L}[x,y]=1$ 时，代表像素点 $I(x,y)$ 仅在水平或垂直方向是最小值点；当 $\boldsymbol{L}[x,y]=2$ 时，代表像素点 $I(x,y)$ 在水平和垂直方向均为最小像素点；在矩阵 $\boldsymbol{L}[x,y]$ 中，其非零元素的个数最大为 $(N+M)$，最小为 $\sqrt{N^2+M^2}$。对于标记的矩阵 $\boldsymbol{L}[x,y]$，其非零元素对应的图像像素灰度为局部灰度最小像素，但由于在路面图像中存在沙砾、阴影等噪声，导致所有标记的灰度最小值点并不都是破损像素，因此需要对标记点做进一步的标定确认，其判定过程为：

（1）选取 $L[x, y]$ 中两非零元素对应的像素点 $L[x_1, y_1]$、$L[x_2, y_2]$，则由两像素点可确定一条直线 $l_{1,2}$，对于 $\forall_{x \in (x_1, x_2), y \in (y_1, y_2)}$，有：

$$l_{1,2} : (y - y_1)(x_2 - x_1) - (y_2 - y_1)(x - x_1) = 0 \qquad (7\text{-}11)$$

（2）则当 $l_{1,2}$ 满足一定条件时，可判定该直线为破损，其判定条件为：

$$M_e \geq \frac{1}{l_{1,2}(S)} \sum_{a,b \in S} (I[a,b] - M_e) - \tau \qquad (7\text{-}12)$$

式中：$M_e = \mathrm{mean}(I[x_1, y_1], I[x_2, y_2])$；$S$ 为直线 $l_{1,2}$ 上所有点的集合。

（3）相对于图像中噪声像素的离散特性，路面破损图像中，路面破损往往具有局部连通性，因此，为了缩减算法的计算量，定义两备选像素点之间的距离应满足如下条件：

$$d = \sqrt{(x_2 - x_1)^2 + (y_2 - y_1)^2} < r \qquad (7\text{-}13)$$

式中：r 为设定的距离阈值。

（4）对于同时满足上述两个条件的直线 $l_{1,2}$ 上的像素点，令其对应二值化图像的像素值为 1，否则为 0，则经过判定，可获取图像对应的二值化图像，实现对图像中路面破损的检测。

采用局部灰度最小分析法对经过预处理后的图 7.2（a）～（d）进行破损区域检测，局部灰度最小分析法检测结果如图 7.7（a）～（d）所示。由检测结果分析可知，局部灰度最小分析法可有效地检测路面破损图像中的细小裂缝，但对网裂破损的检测效果不明显，并且该方法检测结果中含有较多的噪声信息，且检测到的二值化目标像素较为离散。

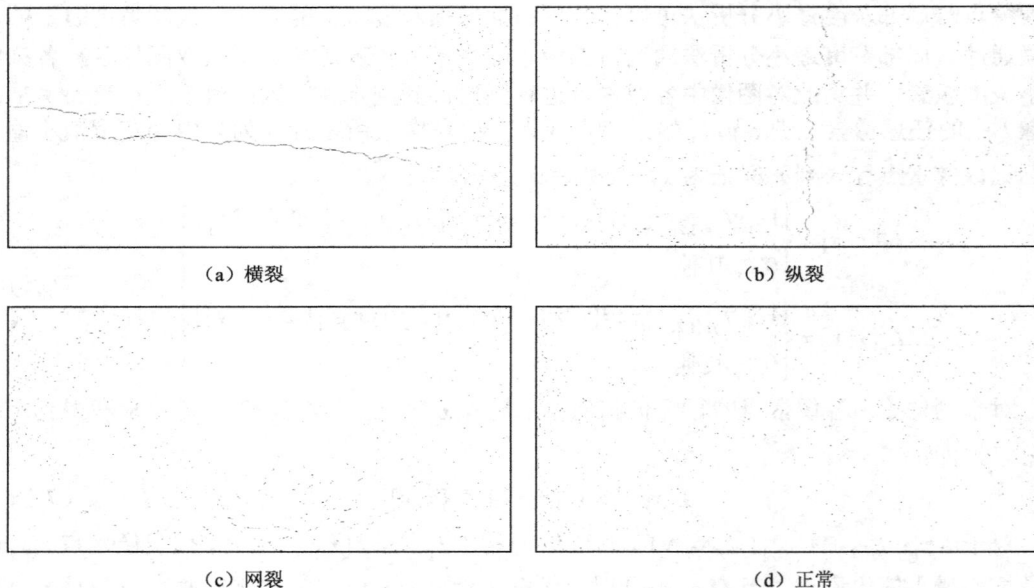

（a）横裂   （b）纵裂

（c）网裂   （d）正常

图 7.7 局部灰度最小分析法检测结果

3）分块标记法

通常，路面破损图像中的破损像素所占整幅图像的像素比例较小，而图像中绝大部分信息是背景信息，因此，可以对路面破损图像进行分块检测，统计各子块图像的特征，进而再对图像各子块进行细分处理。对于输入大小为 $M \times N$ 的图像，网格化为 $W \times L$ 的子块，其子块的大小选择应考虑原图大小及待检测目标的大小，子块太小容易导致错误的裂缝检测，太大则易丢失微裂缝。本书中原始图像大小为 2 048×1 024 像素，构建的子块大小为 128×64 像素，则图像被分为 16×16 个子块。对分割后的各子块图像建立均值特征矩阵 M_m 和方差特征矩阵 std_m 两个特征矩阵，分块标记法的具体步骤如下。

（1）初始标记。本节采用初始标记法来区分路面破损图像中的背景和目标，以实现图像增强。图像初始标记的原则为对于每一子块 (i,j)，根据子块的特征矩阵，建立子块标记的标记原则，即：

$$\text{label}^{(i,j)} = \text{label}_H^{(i,j)} \vee \text{label}_V^{(i,j)} \qquad (7\text{-}14)$$

$$\left.\begin{array}{l} \text{label}_H^{(i,j)} = [\text{std}(Ah^{(i,j)}) > (k_1 \times \text{std}(Bh^i) + k_2 \times \text{std}(Bh^i))] \\ \qquad\qquad \wedge [(Ah^{(i,j)}[1] - Ah^{(i,j)}[2]) > 0] \\ \text{label}_V^{(i,j)} = [\text{std}(Av^{(i,j)}) > (k_1 \times \text{std}(Bv^j) + k_2 \times \text{mean}(Bv^j))] \\ \qquad\qquad \wedge [(Av^{(i,j)}[1] - Av^{(i,j)}[2]) > 0] \end{array}\right\} \qquad (7\text{-}15)$$

式中：$Ah^{(i,j)} = [\dfrac{M_m(i,j-1) + M_m(i,j+1)}{2}, M_m(i,j)]$；$Bh^i = [0, \text{std}(Ah^{(i,2)}), \cdots, \text{std}(Ah^{(i,15)}, 0)]$；

$Av^{(i,j)} = \left[\dfrac{M_m(i-1,j) + M_m(i+1,j)}{2}, M_m(i,j)\right]^T$；$Bv^j = \left[0, \text{std}(Av^{(2,j)}), \cdots, \text{std}(Ah^{(i,15)}, 0)\right]^T$；参数 k_1 和 k_2 的取值采用线性规划在人为监督的情况下获取。

（2）加权处理。对于初始标记后的各子块的标记值 label 进行加权处理，即：

$$I'(i,j) = I(i,j) \times \text{nc} \qquad (7\text{-}16)$$

其中，参数 nc 由下式计算：

$$\text{nc} = \begin{cases} \dfrac{\text{val}_{\text{back}}}{M_m(i,j)^{'0'}} & , \text{label} = 0 \\[4mm] \dfrac{\text{val}_{\text{back}}}{\dfrac{1}{k^{'0'}}\displaystyle\sum_{p=-a}^{a}\sum_{q=-b}^{b} M_m(i+p, j+q)^{'0'}} & , \text{label} = 1 \end{cases} \qquad (7\text{-}17)$$

当 label 值标记为 0 时，则该子块图像为背景；当 label 值标记为 1 时，则该子块图像为破损区域。参数 val_{back} 为所有标记为 0 的子块的像素均值，$M_m(i,j)^{'0'}$ 为标记为 0 的子块的均值，$k^{'0'}$ 为子块 $I(i,j)$ 邻域内 label 标记值为 '0' 的子块个数，$M_m(i,j)^{'0'}$ 为 label 标记值为 0 的子块的均值，a、b 为邻域的范围，例如，子块 3×3 邻域内对应的 $a=b=1$，子块 5×5 领域内对应的 $a=b=2$。

（3）目标检测。对于存在破损的路面图像，其背景部分子块图像的均值较破损子块图像的均值较大，并且其方差反而较小，因此，可利用不同子块特征的差异对图像子块特征矩阵进行聚类分析，以实现对图像中目标（破损）子块的检测，本书采用无监督学习的 K 均值聚类算法进行路面破损检测。

K 均值聚类算法的主要思想是通过迭代把数据集划分成不同的类别，例如，对于路面图像 $I(i,j)$，计算图像各子块的均值特征和方差特征以构建特征矩阵，通过对图像特征的 K 均值聚类，将图像各子块分成 K 类以实现对路面图像中破损区域的检测。本书中取 K=2，采用分块标记法对图 7.2（a）～（d）进行破损区域检测，分块标记法检测结果分别如图 7.8（a）～（d）所示。由图 7.8 分析可知，分块标记法对网裂的检测效果较好，且算法的处理速度较快，但易受图像中阴影的影响。

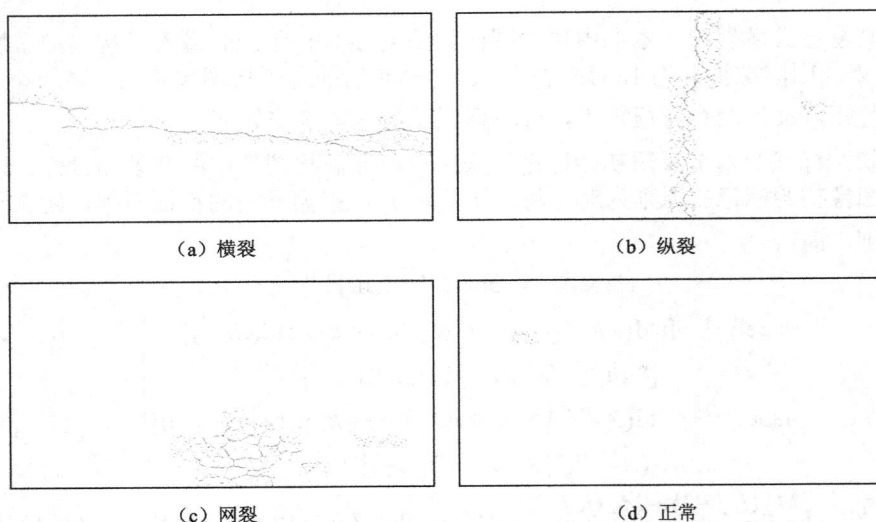

（a）横裂　　　　　　　　　　（b）纵裂

（c）网裂　　　　　　　　　　（d）正常

图 7.8　分块标记法检测结果

7.1.4　基于联合检测器的路面破损检测

由 7.1.3 节的理论及实验分析可得：邻域灰度差分法对图像光照因素的影响不敏感，对于亮度较暗的图像仍能取得较好的检测结果；局部灰度最小分析法对路面破损图像中细小裂缝具有较好的检测效果，但对网裂破损的检测不明显；分块标记法对网裂具有较好的检测效果，且算法的处理速度较快。上述三种路面破损检测方法各具有不同的优势和缺点，本节基于级联分类器的思想，采用邻域灰度差分法、局部灰度最小分析法和分块标记法构建一种路面破损联合检测器，用于提高路面破损检测率。

基于联合检测器的路面破损检测流程如图 7.9 所示。

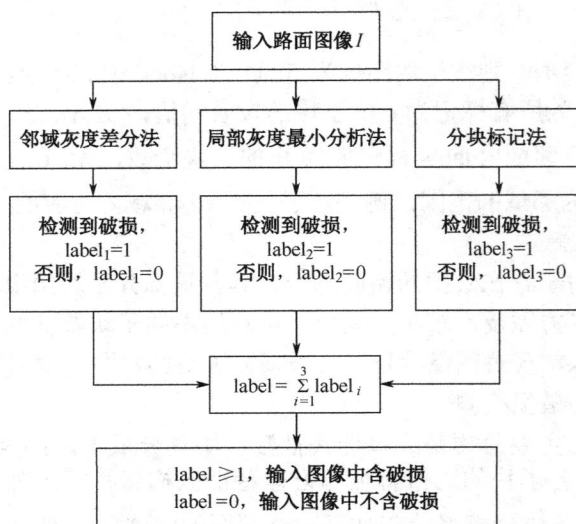

图 7.9　基于联合检测器的路面破损检测流程图

（1）对于输入图像 I 采用邻域灰度差分法进行破损检测，检测结果为 $label_1$，如果检测

126

到路面破损，则 $label_1=1$；否则，$label_1=0$；

（2）对于输入图像 I 采用局部灰度最小分析法进行破损检测，检测结果为 $label_2$，如果检测到路面破损，则 $label_2=1$；否则，$label_2=0$；

（3）对于输入图像 I 采用分块标记法进行破损检测，检测结果为 $label_3$，如果检测到路面破损，则 $label_3=1$；否则，$label_3=0$；

（4）计算上述三种方法对输入图像 I 的检测结果 label，即：

$$label = \sum_{i=1}^{3} label_i \tag{7-18}$$

如果 label≥1，则输入图像 I 中存在破损区域；否则，输入图像 I 为正常路面图像。为验证本书所提出的基于联合检测器的路面破损检测方法，分别采用邻域灰度差分法、局部灰度最小分析法、分块标记法和联合检测器对图 7.10 中的 36 张线阵路面图像进行检测处理，检测结果统一如表 7.1 所示。

图 7.10　实验图像

表 7.1　检测结果统计

检 测 方 法	检 测 率
邻域灰度差分法	80%
局部灰度最小分析法	60%
分块标记法	83.3%
联合检测器	96.7%

由表 7.1 可得，联合检测器的性能优于邻域灰度差分法、局部灰度最小分析法和分块标记法，其检测率分别为 96.7%、80%、60% 和 83.3%。联合检测器检测率提高的主要原因是三种检测方法的联合较好地弥补了各自的不足，分块标记法对网裂检测的优势弥补了其他两种方法在网裂检测方面的不足，而局部灰度最小分析法对细小裂缝检测的优势弥补了其他两种方法对细小破损的检测效果较差的缺点，而邻域灰度差分对噪声、阴影不敏感的

优势也较好弥补了其他两种方法对噪声敏感的缺点，因此本书提出的应用于路面破损图像检测的联合检测器具有较高的检测率。

7.1.5 路面图像破损区域定位

路面破损图像经过联合检测器处理后得到二值化图像，计算二值化图像目标连通域的外接矩形以实现破损区域的定位。由于路面图像破损裂缝的分散性，需要对破损图像的连通区域进行合并，路面图像破损区域定位的具体方法如下。

（1）连通区域标记。对于二值图像 I_{ij} $(i=0,1,2,\cdots,M;j=0,1,2,\cdots,N)$，计算二值图像中目标像素的连通度，并构建连通区域，计算并标记各连通区域的质心位置 $Q_{ij}(i,j)$。

（2）连通区域融合。由于路面破损图像中裂缝的分散性造成二值化图像目标的整体连通性较差，需要对各连通区域进行融合，其连通域融合过程如图 7.11 所示。

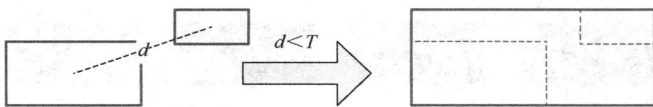

图 7.11　连通域融合过程

首先计算各连通区域的质心位置，当两连通区域位置小于限定的距离长度时，将两连通区域进行融合。对于任意两连通区域质心位置 $Q_1(x_1,y_1)$、$Q_2(x_2,y_2)$，其质心距离 d 为：

$$d=\sqrt{(x_2-x_1)^2+(y_2-y_1)^2} \tag{7-19}$$

设定允许融合的阈值 T，当两质心间距离满足 $d<T$ 时，对两连通区域进行融合，构建新的连通区域；反之，则对两连通区域不做融合处理，保持连通区域的独立性。

（3）目标定位。根据连通区域的外接边界进行路面破损图像区域的精确定位。

对图 7.2（a）～（b）采用联合检测器进行破损检测，根据上述步骤进行目标定位，路面破损定位结果如图 7.12 所示。

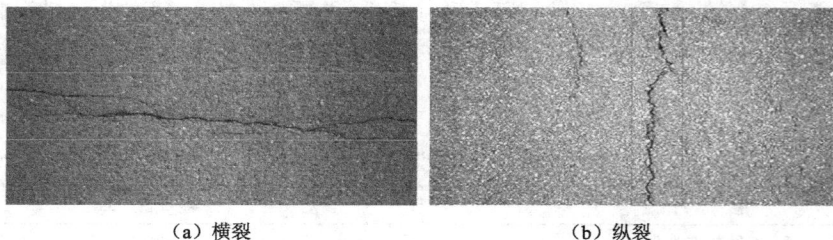

（a）横裂　　　　　　　　　　　　　（b）纵裂

图 7.12　路面破损定位结果

7.2　基于 Contourlet 变换的路面图像特征提取方法

为实现路面破损类型的自动化识别，需要研究路面破损图像的特征提取方法，特征提取方法优良程度的判别标准主要有：所提取的图像特征能否有效地表征目标图像，使得分类的错误率降低；提取的图像特征应具有较低的维数；提取的图像特征应对噪声和不相关的图像转换不敏感。因为路面破损图像具有丰富的边缘纹理特征，即其灰度纹理特征显著，因此，本节研究基于 Contourlet 变换的路面破损图像特征提取方法，并与边缘方向直方图（Edge Orientation Histogram，EOH）、梯度方向直方图（Histogram of Orientation Gradients，HOG）和分层梯度方向直方图（Pyramid of Histogram of Orientation Gradients，PHOG）三种特征提取方法进行对比分析，最后，采用支持向量机（SVM）分类器进行路面破损类型识别实验。

7.2.1 Contourlet 变换

Contourlet 变换是由 Do, et al. [6]提出的一种多尺度几何分析工具，具有良好的多分辨率、局部化和方向性等优良特性。与 Wavelet 变换相比，Contourlet 变换采用类似于轮廓段（Contour Segment）的基结构来逼近曲线，可在高频上做任意多个方向的分解，并提供各个方向的细节信息。Contourlet 变换基函数的支撑区间具有随尺度变化长宽比的"长条形"结构，具有方向性和各向异性，而二维小波是由一维小波张量积构建得到的，只能限于用正方形支撑区间描述轮廓，不同大小的正方形对应小波的多分辨率结构，因而缺乏方向性且不具有各向异性，对曲线描述的形式如图 7.13 所示。Contourlet 变换将小波的优点延伸到高维空间，能够更好地刻画高维信息的特性，更适合处理具有超平面奇异性的信息。Contourlet 变换的基本思想是：首先，采用拉普拉斯金字塔（Laplacian Pyramid，LP）分解得到边缘的孤立断点，然后，使用二维方向滤波器组（Directional Filter Bank，DFB）将方向一致的断点连接成线，从而形成基本的轮廓段。

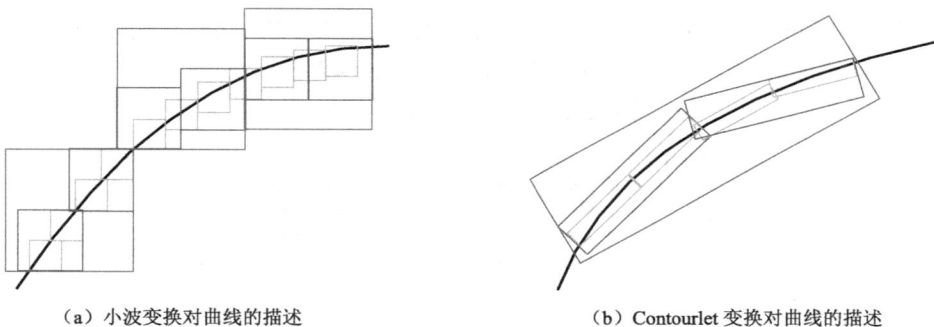

（a）小波变换对曲线的描述   （b）Contourlet 变换对曲线的描述

图 7.13 对曲线描述的形式

拉普拉斯金字塔分解与重构如图 7.14 所示，H 和 G 分别为分解和合成滤波，M 为采样矩阵。经过拉普拉斯分解的下采样图像为图像的低频信息 a，而下采样图像与预测图像的差图像为图像的高频信息 b。这种处理可以在下采样的低通信号 b 循环进行下去，最后形成第 n 层低通部分和 N 个细节部分（高频部分），组成金字塔式的图像分解。

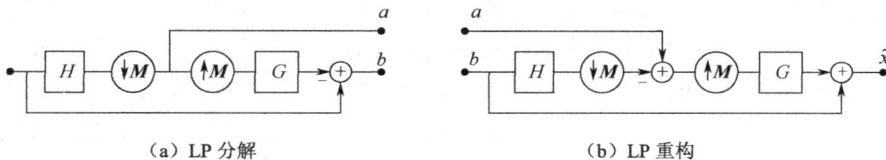

（a）LP 分解   （b）LP 重构

图 7.14 拉普拉斯金字塔分解与重构

方向滤波器（DFB）是对图像的多方向性分析，即通过一个 l 层的二叉树分解，将输

入图像分解成 2^l 个子带。经 LP 分解的高频信息经过 DFB 的处理可逐渐将点奇异连成线结构，从而形成图像的轮廓。DFB 包括两通道的梅花滤波器组和平移操作两个模块，梅花滤波器组（Quincunx 滤波器，如图 7.15 所示）是用扇形滤波器将 2-D 光谱分成垂直和水平两个方向。H 和 G 分别为分解和合成滤波器；Q 为采样矩阵，$Q_0 = \begin{pmatrix} 1 & -1 \\ 1 & 1 \end{pmatrix}$ 和 $Q_1 = \begin{pmatrix} 1 & 1 \\ -1 & 1 \end{pmatrix}$ 的不同在于图像反转的角度不同，分别为 45°和-45°。

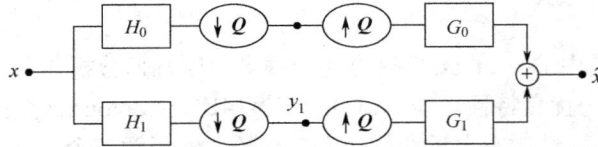

图 7.15　Quincunx 滤波器

平移操作（Shearing）是在 Quincunx 滤波分解阶段之前进行的，其作用是重新排序图像的采样。实施平移操作后图像被旋转并且宽度变为原来的 2 倍，在合成阶段再进行一个反 Shearing 操作对图像进行合成，Shearing 操作可采用 $R_0 = \begin{pmatrix} 1 & 1 \\ 0 & 1 \end{pmatrix}$、$R_1 = \begin{pmatrix} 1 & -1 \\ 0 & 1 \end{pmatrix}$、$R_2 = \begin{pmatrix} 1 & 0 \\ 1 & 1 \end{pmatrix}$ 和 $R_3 = \begin{pmatrix} 1 & 0 \\ -1 & 1 \end{pmatrix}$ 四种采样矩阵。实际上，DFB 分解过程可以等效为如图 7.16 所示的并行结构，即每个方向子带是由图像通过对应的方向滤波器 E 后再进行下采样 S 而得到的，右半部分为其对应的合成部分。对于多通道滤波器组 E，具有下列对角形式：

$$S_k^l = \begin{cases} \text{diag}(2^{l-1}, 2) & , 0 \leqslant k < 2^{l-1} \\ \text{diag}(2, 2^{l-1}) & , 2^{l-1} \leqslant k < 2^l \end{cases} \tag{7-20}$$

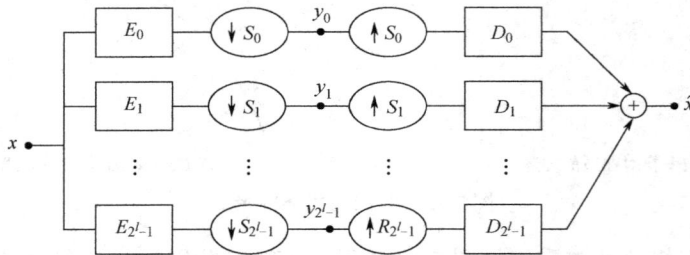

图 7.16　DFB 分解过程

Contourlet 变换将金字塔分解和方向滤波器结合起来，弥补了金字塔分解不具有方向性和方向滤波器对低频分解性能差的弱点，Contourlet 变换过程如图 7.17 所示。

路面破损图像的三层 Contourlet 分解如图 7-18 所示，对图 7.18（a）图像进行三层 Contourlet 分解，其中第 l 层分解的方向子带数为 2^l，最细致层上的方向子带数为 16，其各层子带图像如图 7.18（b）所示。对于每一个细节矩阵，计算各矩阵的列均值及矩阵方差作为各层细节矩阵的特征，则图像的特征可由各细节矩阵的特征组合构成。对于输入的 512×512 的路面图像，经过 Contourlet 特征提取后，获得图像的特征向量为 1×2 318 维。

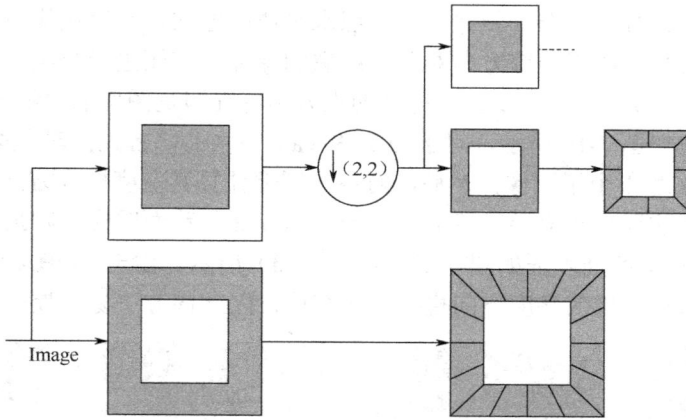

图 7.17　Contourlet 变换过程

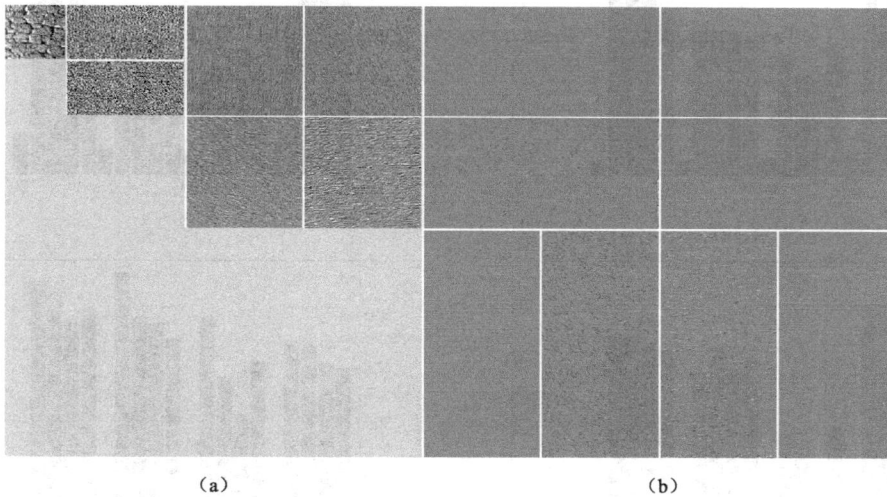

（a）　　　　　　　　　　　（b）

图 7.18　路面破损图像的三层 Contourlet 分解

7.2.2　其他纹理特征提取方法

1）边缘方向直方图

边缘方向直方图（Edge Orientation Histogram，EOH）特征是对图像边缘信息及梯度信息的综合描述，其基本思想是图像的局部形状特征可以由局部灰度梯度和边缘方向来表征。

首先，将一副图像划分为多个子图像，并按照水平边缘方向、垂直边缘方向、对角边缘方向（包括两个斜对角）和无边缘方向对各子图像的梯度直方图进行分类；然后，对各梯度直方图按照划分的分类方向进行统计，得到的直方图特征即是图像的边缘方向直方图特征。

路面破损图像如图 7-19 所示，对于图 7.19（a）～（d），首先，对图像进行边缘处理，并将边缘图像划分为 4 个子图像；然后，对各子图像计算其灰度梯度方向直方图的列均值及方差作为子图像的局部灰度梯度特征，对于 512×512 的路面图像，则最终获得 4×5 = 20 维的特征向量，EOH 特征表征如图 7.20（a）～（d）所示。由于 EOH 特征在统计的过程中是对图像各子部分图像的梯度方向直方图的统计，因此该方法易受噪声的影响。

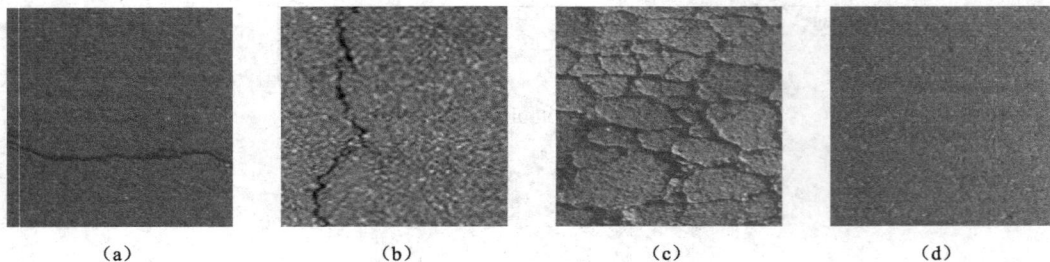

(a)　　　　(b)　　　　(c)　　　　(d)

图 7.19　路面破损图像

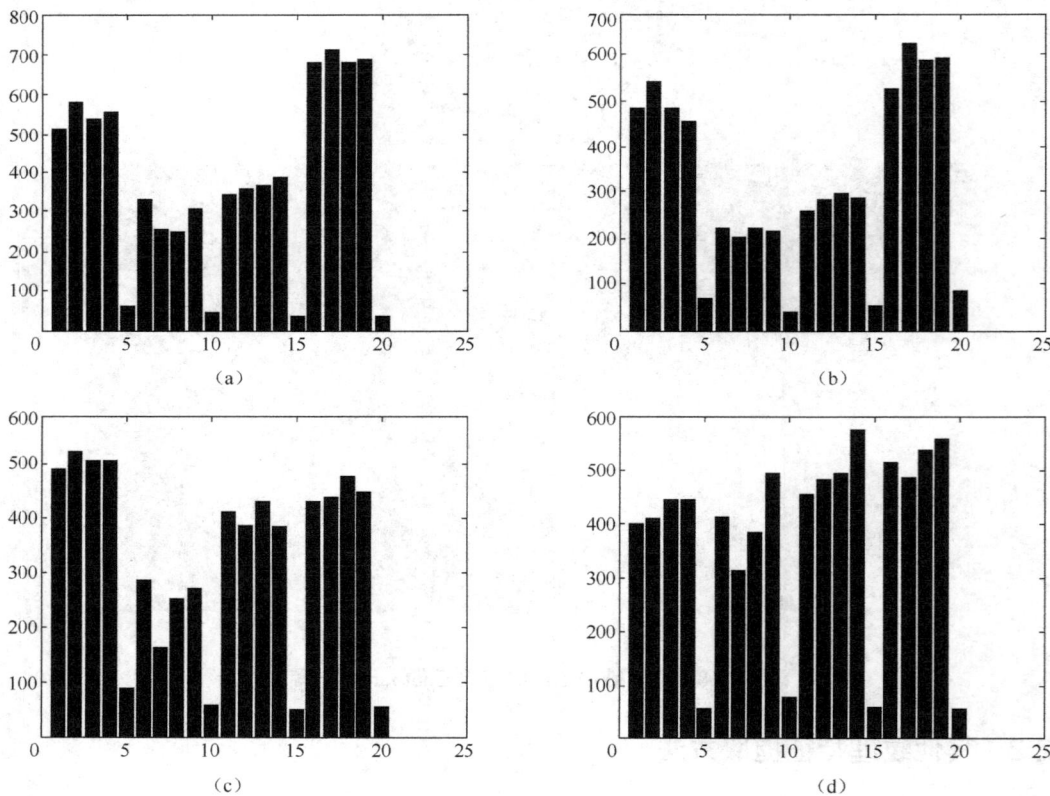

图 7.20　EOH 特征表征

2）梯度方向直方图

梯度方向直方图（Histograms of Oriented Gradient，HOG）特征[7]的主要思想是在梯度

（或边缘）的确切位置不确定的情况下，利用图像的局部梯度（或边缘）方向的分布能够实现对图像中对象的局部外观和外形的描述。首先，将图像划分为小的单元格（cell），并在各单元格内统计该单元格子图像的一维梯度方向直方图；然后，将所有单元格的直方图统计结果连接起来，继而形成整个图像的 HOG 特征表示。对于图 7.21 中 512×512 的路面图像，首先，设置其细胞单元大小为 256×256，并在每个细胞单元内统计 9 个直方图通道的无向梯度（即将 0°～180° 的梯度方向划分为 9 个区间）；然后，设置归一化块（Block）的大小为 256×256（各细胞单元作为独立的一个块），块在水平和竖直方向的步进大小均为 128；最后，将所有细胞单元的直方图组合起来形成 HOG 特征描述子，得到的特征描述子大小为 9×3×3=81 维，HOG 特征参数如图 7.21 所示。

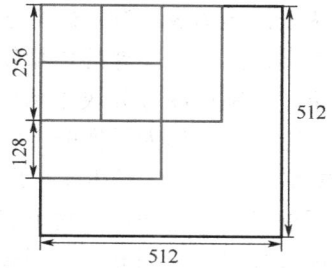

图 7.21　HOG 特征参数

对于图 7.19 中的路面破损图像进行 HOG 特征提取，动块的大小与细胞单元大小相同，移动步长为 128，路面破损图像的 HOG 特征直方图结果分别如图 7.22（a）～（d）所示。

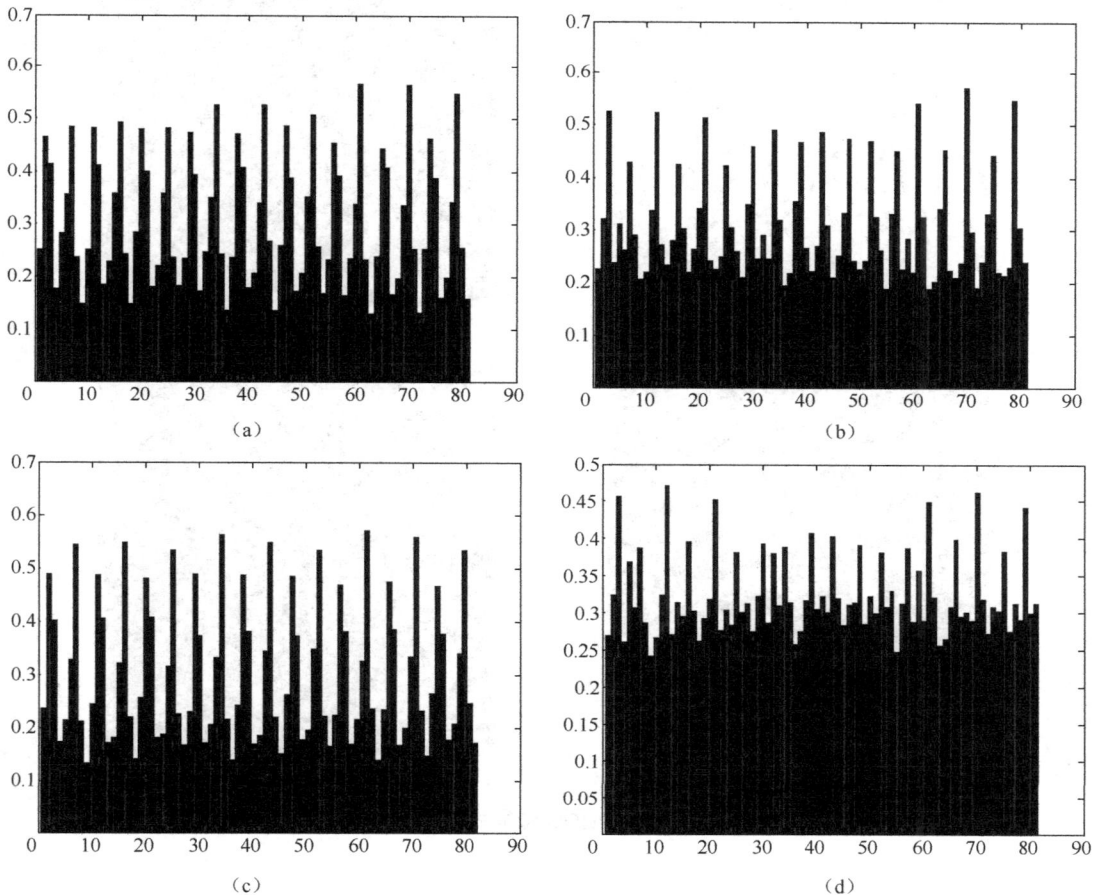

图 7.22　路面破损图像的 HOG 特征直方图结果

3）分层梯度方向直方图

分层梯度方向直方图（Pyramid of Histogram of Orientation Gradients，PHOG）特征[8]的主要思想是采用金字塔结构的梯度方向直方图描述特征的方法，该方法是通过使用空间四叉树分解形成图像的多分辨率表示，并连接从低分辨率到高分辨率的多级梯度方向直方图来描述图像，PHOG 特征提取过程如图 7.23 所示。首先，对输入的图像提取图像的边缘轮廓；然后将图像的边缘轮廓进行分层，每一层将上一层的各块按宽和高等分成更小的分块，分别提取各分块轮廓点的梯度方向直方图；最后，按权值合并成一个大的梯度方向直方图金字塔作为图像的形状特征。对于图 7.23（a）的路面破损图像进行 3 层 PHOG 特征提取，其 PHOG 描述就是由 3 个梯度方向直方图顺序连接而成的特征向量。第一层 $l=0$ 时，不进行空间划分，将整个图像作为 1 个单元计算其梯度方向直方图；第二层 $l=1$ 时，将图像进行四叉树划分，将图像划分为 4 个矩形单元计算其 HOG 特征；第三层 $l=2$ 时，将图像分解为 16 个矩形单元计算 HOG，最终形成的直方图是 $l=0,1,2$ 时各 HOG 直方图的顺序组合，则 PHOG 特征维数为 $4+16+64=84$，PHOG 特征如图 7.24 所示。

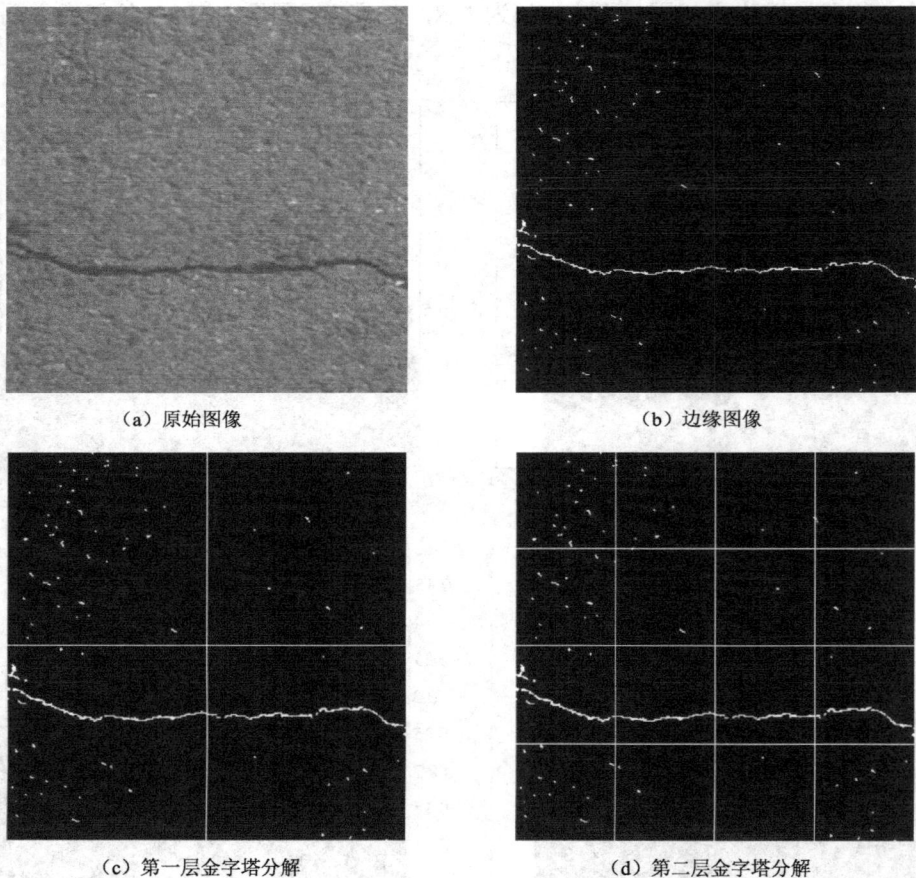

（a）原始图像　　　　　　　　　　　　　　（b）边缘图像

（c）第一层金字塔分解　　　　　　　　　　（d）第二层金字塔分解

图 7.23　PHOG 特征提取过程

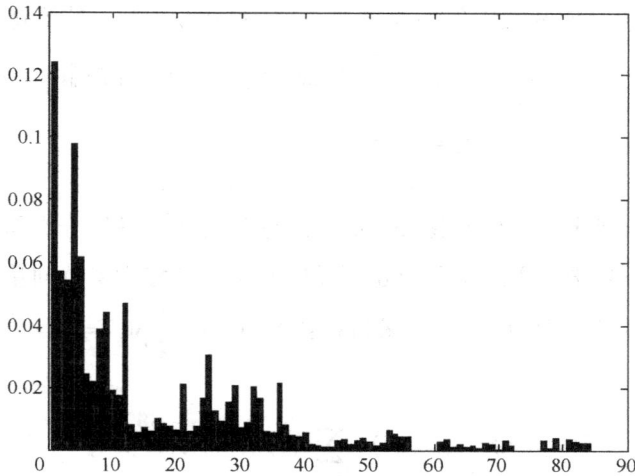

图 7.24　PHOG 特征

7.2.3　支持向量机分类器

支持向量机（SVM）分类器是由 Vapnik 等[9]于 1995 年提出的一类新型机器学习方法，该方法通过把低维空间中线性不可分的数据集映射成高维空间中线性可分的数据集，进而实现数据的分类，能够较好地解决小样本、非线性及高维数等模式识别问题。SVM 是从线性可分情况下的最优分类面发展而来的，所谓最优分类线就是要求分类面不但能够将两类样本正确分开，而且使两类样本的分类间隔最大，推广至高维空间，最优分类线就变成了最优分类面。最优分类线如图 7.25 所示，实心点和空心点表示两类样本，H 为正确分开两类样本的分类线，H_1，H_2 分别为过各类中离分类线最近的样本且平行于分类线的直线，它们之间的距离称为分类空隙或分类间隔。

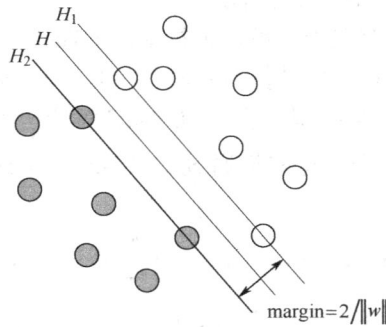

图 7.25　最优分类线

1）最优分类面

设线性可分的样本集 (x_i, y_i)，$i = 1, 2, \cdots, n, x \in R^d$，$y \in \{+1, -1\}$ 为类别标号，d 维空间中线性判别函数的一般形式为

$$g(x) = w \cdot x + b \tag{7-21}$$

分类面方程可以描述为

$$w \cdot x + b = 0 \tag{7-22}$$

将判别函数归一化使两类中的所有样本均满足 $|g(x)| \geq 1$，即离分类平面最近的样本 $|g(x)| = 1$，则分离间隔等于 $\dfrac{2}{\|w\|}$，因此，间隔最大等价于使 $\|w\|$ 或 $\|w\|^2$ 最小，而要求判别分界面对所有样本正确分类，则要求其满足：

$$y_i[(w \cdot x) + b] - 1 \geq 0 , \quad i = 1, 2, \cdots, n \tag{7-23}$$

由上述可得：满足上述条件且使 $\|w\|^2$ 最小的分类面就是最优分类面。过两类样本中离最优超平面最近的点且平行于最优分类超平面的样本就被称为支持向量，则最优分类平面的问题可以归结为约束条件（7-22），求目标函数 $\phi(w) = \dfrac{1}{2}\|w\|^2 = \dfrac{1}{2}(w \cdot w)$ 的最小值，定义 Lagrange 函数：

$$L(w, b, a) = \frac{1}{2}(w \cdot w) - \sum_{i=1}^{n} a_i \{y_i[(w \cdot x) + b] - 1\} \tag{7-24}$$

式中：a_i（$a_i > 0$）为 Lagrange 系数，则问题转化为对 w 和 b 求 Lagrange 函数的极小值。对式（7-24）分别求 w 和 b 的偏微分，并分别令其为零，则原问题转化为以下对偶问题，约束条件为：

$$\sum_{i=1}^{n} y_i a_i = 0 \tag{7-25}$$

式中：$a_i \geq 0, i = 1, 2, \cdots, n$，对 a_i 求解式（7-26）函数的最大值：

$$Q(a) = \sum_{i=1}^{n} a_i - \frac{1}{2} \sum_{i,j=1}^{n} a_i a_j y_i y_j (x_i \cdot x_j) \tag{7-26}$$

上式中，如果 a_i^* 为最优解，则有

$$w^* = \sum_{i=1}^{n} a_i^* y_i x_i \tag{7-27}$$

由上式可得：最优分类面的权系数向量是训练样本向量的线性组合，这是一个不等式约束下的二次函数极值问题，存在唯一解。根据 Kuhn-Tucker 条件，该优化问题的解满足：

$$a_i[y_i(w \cdot x_i + b) - 1] = 0 , \quad i = 1, 2, \cdots, n \tag{7-28}$$

因此，对于多数样本 a_i^* 将为 0；取值不为 0 的 a_i^* 对应于使式（7-23）等号成立的样本，即为支持向量。b^* 可由任意一个支持向量通过式（7-23）等式成立求得，求解上述问题后得到的最优分类函数为：

$$f(x) = \text{sgn}[(w^* \cdot x) + b^*] = \text{sgn}[\sum_{i=1}^{n} a_i^* y_i (x_i \cdot x) + b^*] \tag{7-29}$$

式中：$\text{sgn}(\ )$ 为符号函数。由于非支持向量对应的 a_i 均为 0，因此式（7-29）中的求和实际上只对支持向量进行。将上述讨论的基于线性可分样本问题推广到非线性可分样本的分类问题，即广义最优化分类平面问题。所谓线性不可分的情况，就是某些训练样本不能满足式（7-23）的条件。为此，添加一个松弛项，则 $\xi_i > 0$ 为：

$$y_i[(w \cdot x) + b] - 1 + \xi_i \geq 0 \tag{7-30}$$

对于足够小的 $\sigma > 0$，只要使式（7-31）成立，即：

$$F_\sigma(\xi_i) = \sum_{i=1}^{n} \xi_i^\sigma \tag{7-31}$$

对应线性可分情况下使分离间隔最大，在线性不可分情况下可引入约束 $\|w\|^2 \leqslant c_k$ ，在约束式（7-28）和 $\|w\|^2 \leqslant c_k$ 的条件下，求式（7-29）的极小值，就得到了线性不可分情况下的最优分类平面，该平面称为广义最优分类平面。取 $\sigma = 1$ ，则经过简化计算，广义最优分类平面问题可进一步演化为在条件（7-28）下求下列函数的极小值，即：

$$\phi(w,\xi) = \frac{1}{2}(w \cdot w) + C(\sum_{i=1}^{n} \xi_i) \qquad (7-32)$$

式中：C 为常数。用求解最优分类面时同样的方法求解这一最优化问题，同样可以得到一个二次函数极值问题，其结果与可分情况下得到的判别函数相同，只是其 a_i 的约束变为：

$$0 \leqslant a_i \leqslant C, i = 1, 2, \cdots, n \qquad (7-33)$$

2）核函数

非线性支持向量机在映射的过程中首先采用一个非线性的变换 ϕ 将输入映射到一个特征空间 Z ，即 $X \xrightarrow{\phi R^m \to R^m} F$ 。设 $\{\phi_j(X)\}_{j=1}^{m_1}$ 为输入空间 R^m 到输出空间 R^m 的一组非线性变换，则映射可表示为：

$$\phi(X) = [\phi_1(X), \phi_2(X), \cdots \phi_{m_1}(X)] \qquad (7-34)$$

在特征空间 F 中，数据线性可分，则在 F 中可以找到一个线性判别函数对应于 X 中的一个非线性判别函数。支持向量机可以通过训练来构造一个线性判别函数 $w^T \phi(X) + b = 0$ ，使得分离间隔最大，根据 Hilbert-Schmidt 原理，只要满足 Mercer 条件，可以找到一个核函数 $K(x, x')$ ，使式（7-35）成立，即：

$$K(x, x') = \varphi^T(x)\varphi(x) \qquad (7-35)$$

因此，在最优分类面中采用适当的点积函数 $K(x, x')$ 就可以实现某一非线性变换后的线性分类，相应的优化函数为：

$$Q(a) = \sum_{i=1}^{n} a_i - \frac{1}{2} \sum_{i,j=1}^{n} a_i a_j y_i y_j K(x_i, x_j) \qquad (7-36)$$

而相应的判别函数为：

$$f(x) = \text{sgn}\left(\sum_{i=1}^{n} a_i y_i K(x_i, x) + b \right) \qquad (7-37)$$

对于一个特定的核函数，给定的样本集中的任意一个样本都可能成为一个支持向量，因此，采用不同核函数 $K(x_i, x_j)$ 可以构造实现输入空间中不同类型的非线性决策面的学习机。

7.2.4 实验分析

本节采用 DN-2011 型车载便携式公路路面病害检测设备采集路面图像，并利用同态滤波[10]对采集的路面图像进行光照均衡处理，以构建东南大学路面图像数据库，如图 7.26 所示。同态滤波是把频率过滤和灰度变换结合起来的一种图像处理方法，该方法首先对图像进行对数变换，实现对图像的灰度拉伸，然后对经过对数处理后的图像进行傅里叶变换将图像转换到频率域，并通过对图像进行频域滤波实现图像的去噪处理，最后对图像进行傅里叶逆变换和指数运算即得到同态滤波处理后的图像。构建的东南大学路面图像数据库中图像共 140 幅，图像大小为 512×512，包括横裂、纵裂、网裂和正常路面 4 种类型，每种类型 35 张，保证了数据库中样本的均衡性。随机选取东南大学路面数据库中 80%的图像（112 张）作为训练样本，其余的 20%的图像（28 张）做测试样本，分别采用 Contourlet 变换、EOH 特征提取、PHOG 特征提取和 HOG 特征提取 4 种方法提取样本图像的特征向量，并采用 SVM 进行分类识别，SVM 核函数选取实时性较好的线性核函数 $k(x,y)=x \cdot y$。进行 100 次随机试验，并将 100 次随机试验的结果作为最终试验结果，4 种特征提取方法并采用 SVM 识别的结果如表 7.2 所示。

（a）横裂

（b）纵裂

（c）网裂

图 7.26   东南大学路面图像数据库

（d）正常

图 7.26　东南大学路面图像数据库（续）

表 7.2　四种特征提取方法识别结果

特 征 种 类	识 别 率
Contourlet	84.32%
EOH	75.14%
PHOG	51.93%
HOG	73.25%

　　由表 7.2 可得：针对东南大学路面数据库，采用 Contourlet 变换、EOH 特征提取、PHOG 特征提取和 HOG 特征提取 4 种方法进行特征提取，并选用线性核函数的 SVM 进行识别实验，平均识别率分别为 84.32%、75.14%、51.93% 和 73.25%。100 次随机试验结果表明 Contourlet 变换特征优于其他三种特征提取方法，达到 84.32%；EOH 特征提取方法次之，达到 75.14%；PHOG 特征提取方法最差，仅为 51.93%。PHOG 分类结果较低的主要原因是路面图像中的破损目标区域相对于非破损区域所占整幅图像的比例较小，则获取的边缘图像中破损目标所占区域较小，细分为各子块图像后，子块图像的边缘特征不明显，受噪声边缘的影响较为严重，从而导致最终的 PHOG 组合边缘梯度方向直方图特征对路面破损的描述不够详尽，造成最终的识别分类结果较低。

7.3　基于联合特征及分类器集成的路面破损类型分类方法

　　传统的模式识别通常只使用样本中的单一特征或某个特定分类器进行分类，由于不同的特征描述及不同的分类器在性能上存在彼此互补性[11, 12]，因此，采用联合特征及分类器集成可有效地提高路面破损类型的分类正确率。由 7.2 节的研究结论可得：Contourlet 变换和边缘方向直方图适合用于路面破损图像的特征表征，因此，本节研究基于 Contourlet 变换和边缘方向直方图联合特征及支持向量机集成的路面破损类型分类方法，以提高路面破损图像的分类正确率。

7.3.1　联合特征

　　联合特征（Combined Features，CF）即多特征的融合，图像的多特征融合通常集中在像素级融合、特征级融合和决策级融合这 3 个不同层次上进行，目前应用较广泛的是特征级融合，通常采用简单易行的特征组合来实现图像的特征级融合，特征组合是指直接对特征进行组合构成新的特征向量，目前常用的有串行融合和并行融合两种策略。串行特征联合是对于模式样本空间 Ω 上存在两个不同的特征空间 A、B，对于任意模式样本 $\xi \in \Omega$，设它对应的两个特征向量分别为 $\alpha \in A$ 和 $\beta \in B$，则组合后的串行特征为 $\gamma = (\alpha, \beta)$，由组合原理可知，若特征向量 α 和 β 分别为 n 维和 m 维，则其组合后的串行特征空间为 $(n+m)$ 维。

并行特征联合策略是相对串行特征联合而言的，对于模式样本空间 Ω 上两个不同的特征空间 A、B，设它对应的两个特征向量分别为 $\alpha \in A$ 和 $\beta \in B$，则 $\gamma = \alpha + i\beta$ 表示特征向量的组合，其中 i 为虚数单位，即对两特征向量进行复数运算实现的特征联合，对于新的组合特征，其维数为：

$$n = \max\{\dim A, \dim B\} \tag{7-38}$$

组合后的特征空间为：

$$C = \{\alpha + i\beta \mid \alpha \in A, \beta \in B\} \tag{7-39}$$

定义该特征空间的内积为：

$$(X,Y) = X^H Y \tag{7-40}$$

式中：$X, Y \in C$；H 为共轭转置符号。在特征的组合过程中，当两组特征 α 与 β 的维数不等时，低维的特征向量用零补足。

由于 Contourlet 变换和边缘方向直方图特征能较好地表征路面破损图像，因此，基于 Contourlet 变换特征和边缘方向直方图特征，本书提出采用串行特征联合策略构建联合特征来表征路面破损图像。

7.3.2 分类器集成

在模式识别领域，以多分类器集成为代表的融合技术也受到越来越多的关注。分类器集成是指将多个分类器集成起来，通过对多个分类器的分类结果进行某种组合来决定最终的分类结果，以取得比单个分类器更好的性能。如果把单一分类器看作一个决策者的话，那么集成分类器就相当于多个决策者共同进行一项决策。

不同分类器的集成有并行构造、序列构造、选择性构造和树状构造 4 种类型。并行构造是分类器集合中的个体分类器相互之间不存在依赖关系，相互之间的构造过程完全独立，其过程可以并行完成，目前研究较多的并行构造方法是 Bagging 算法；序列构造与并行构造方法相反，序列构造是分类器集合中的个体分类器在构造生成的过程中存在前向依赖关系，即当前个体分类器的构造实现必须以之前构造的个体分类器为基础，生成的集成分类器呈现一种序列关系，例如，Boosting 系统就是典型地采用序列构造方法进行分类器集成；选择性构造方式是通过对分类器进行筛选择优，产生最终参与集成的基分类器子集合，进而达到优化集成的目的，如 GASEN 算法；树状构造是一种复合构造方法，可以看作前几种结构的复合，如同层为并行构造，不同层为序列构造，或相反，如扩展的 Boosting 系统。

对于同类型分类器的集成，其构造相对不同分类器的集成简单，通常是通过对样本的随机取样，生成不同的训练样本集合，再利用同类型分类器对不同训练样本集合进行训练，实现集成构造方式。对样本的取样可采用可重复的随机取样或先按照分类难易程度分别赋予不同的权值，再根据权重进行取样或者根据样本的模糊隶属度取样，以生成多个训练样本集，通过对不同训练样本的训练从而实现分类器之间的多样性。

根据 Maji 等[13]提出的快速交叉内核支持向量机组（Intersection Kernel Support Vector Machines，IKSVM）的思想，本书提出了基于随机子空间的交叉内核支持向量机分类器集成方案。交叉内核支持向量机是一种核函数为交叉检验核函数的支持向量机，该分类器组的算法效率及复杂度完全不受分类器数目的限制，且表现出了较好的识别分类效果。对于构建交叉内核支持向量机组最关键的问题即训练样本的多样性生成，对此本书采用随机子空间技术（Random Subspace，RS）[14, 15]，其基本思想是：对于一个 d 维的训练样本集，按照均匀分布随机从中选取 n 维训练样本构成子训练集，则原始的 d 维训练集转化为了 n 维子空间，通过对产生的特征子空间进行训练产生分类器集成的基分类器。按照上述过程重复 m 次，则产生的 m 个基分类器对随机选取的测试样本进行训练测试，并根据投票表决的方法实现对样本的最终分类。

假定训练样本集为 $X = \{X_1, X_2, \cdots, X_n\}$，对于训练集中的任一样本 $\boldsymbol{X}_i$ 是 p 维的特征向量，即 $\boldsymbol{X}_i = (x_{i1}, x_{i2}, \cdots, x_{ip}), (i = 1, 2 \cdots, n)$，其随机子空间的构成流程为：

（1）For $r = 1, 2, \cdots, R$。

① 从 p 维特征空间集合 X 中随机选取新的 p 维特征子空间 X^r，定义子空间中的特征向量为 $\boldsymbol{x}$；

② 在选取的子特征空间 X^r 中利用选取的随机样本进行分类器训练，最终生成的分类器为 $C^r(x)$；

③ 定义分类器集成过程中其投票权重为：

$$c_r = \frac{1}{2} \log(\frac{1 - \text{err}_r}{\text{err}_r}) \tag{7-41}$$

式中：$\text{err}_r = \frac{1}{n} \sum_{i=1}^{n} w_i^r \xi_i^r$ 表示所有被错误分类的样本的权重和，如果 X_i 能被正确分类，则 $\xi_i^r = 0$，反之 $\xi_i^r = 1$；w_i^r 表示各分类器的权重，通常情况下，对于构成的 m 个分类器 $w_i^r = \frac{1}{m}$；n 为训练样本的个数。

（2）对生成的多个分类器 $C^r(x)$，$r = 1, 2, \cdots, R$，按照其投票权重形成最终的分类器判别规则：

$$\beta(x) = \arg \max_{y \in \{-1, 1\}} \sum_{r=1}^{R} \delta_{\text{sgn}(C^r(x)), y} \tag{7-42}$$

式中：当 $i = j$ 时，$\delta_{i,j} = 1$；否则，$\delta_{i,j} = 0$。

7.3.3 实验分析

基于构建的东南大学路面图像数据库，根据上述联合特征的实现过程和集成分类器的集成原则，本书构建 5 个交叉内核支持向量机分类器作为基分类器，并对建立的联合特征训练集进行了 100 次随机抽样实验，随机抽样实验中分别抽取 Contourlet 变换和边缘方向直方图特征联合特征的 60%作为特征向量，联合特征及分类器集成分类结果如图 7.27 所示。由图 7.27 可得：Contourlet 变换特征、EOH 特征和联合特征及随机子空间分类器集成的分类正确率分别为 84.82%、72.86%和 86.61%，实验结果表明，Contourlet 特征与 EOH 特征之间存在特征的互补，两种特征的联合实现了对图像特征更为细致的描述，从而提高了图像的识别分类率。

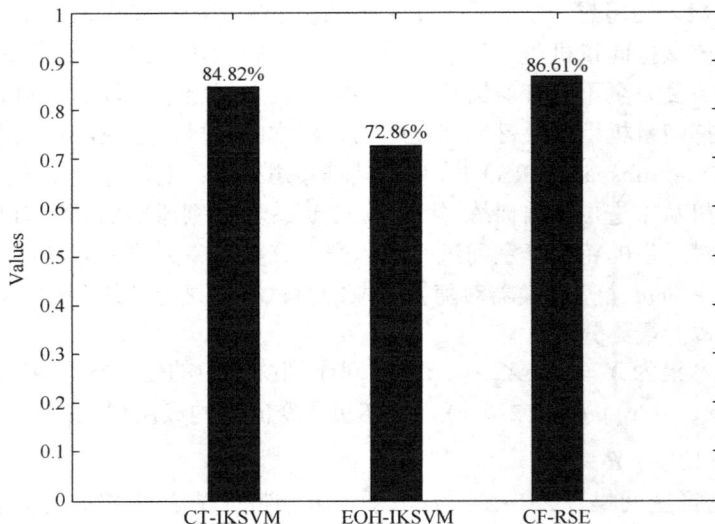

图 7.27　联合特征及分类器集成分类结果

7.4　小结

为了实现路面养护管理的信息化与智能化，本书研究了基于线阵 CCD 图像的路面破损自动检测及分类方法，具体研究成果如下。

（1）提出了一种基于联合检测器的路面破损自动检测方法。针对路面破损图像中破损像素较正常路面像素灰度较低这一基本特征，对比分析了邻域灰度差分法、局部灰度最小分析法和分块标记法的优势和薄弱点。基于级联分类器的思想，提出了用于路面破损检测的联合检测器，理论分析和实验结果表明联合检测器的性能优于邻域灰度差分法、局部灰度最小分析法和分块标记法，其检测率达到 96.7%，并研究了基于连通域融合的路面破损目标精确定位方法，通过实验验证了该方法的有效性。

（2）提出将 Contourlet 变换用于路面破损特征提取，并采用支持向量机进行路面破损自动化分类的方法。对比分析了 Contourlet 变换、边缘方向直方图、梯度方向直方图和分层梯度方向直方图 4 种特征提取方法，基于构建的东南大学路面图像数据库，采用线性核函数的 SVM 作为分类器进行了路面破损识别实验，实验结果表明：Contourlet 变换优于边缘方向直方图、梯度方向直方图和分层梯度方向直方图，达到 84.32%。因此，采用 Contourlet 变换进行路面破损特征提取及线性核函数的 SVM 作为分类器可以实现路面破损类型的有效识别。

（3）提出了一种基于联合特征及随机子空间交叉内核支持向量机分类器集成的路面破损自动化分类方法。研究了图像联合特征的融合策略，基于串行融合策略构造了路面破损图像的 Contourlet 变换和 EOH 联合特征，并基于分类器集成的构造原则实现了交叉内核支持向量机分类器的集成方案，采用东南大学路面图像数据库进行了实验，实验结果表明

Contourlet 变换和 EOH 联合特征及随机子空间交叉内核支持向量机分类器集成优于单一 Contourlet 变换特征和 EOH 特征，分类正确率达到 86.61%。

参考文献

[1] Li Y, Gong P and Sasagawa T. Integrated shadow removal based on photogrammetry and image analysis[J]. International Journal of Remote Sensing, 2005, 26 (18): 3 911-3 929.

[2] Wu T P and Tang C K. A bayesian approach for shadow extraction from a single image[J]. Proc. of the International Conference on Computer Vision, 2005: 480-487.

[3] Salvador E, Cavallaro A and Ebrahimi T. Cast shadow segmentation using invariant color features[J]. Computer Vision and Image Understanding, 2004, 95 (2): 238-259.

[4] 邹勤. 低信噪比路面裂缝增强与提取方法研究[D]. 武汉: 武汉大学, 2012.

[5] Donoho D L and Johnstone I M. Ideal spatial adaptation by wavelet shrinkage[J]. Biometrika, 1994, 81 (3): 425-455.

[6] Do M and Vetterli M. Contourlets: a directional multiresolution image representation [C]. International Conference on Image Processing, New York, 2002, 1:357-360.

[7] Dalal N and Triggs B. Histogram of oriented gradients for human detection[C]. IEEE Computer Society Conference on Computer Vision and Pattern Recognition, 2005,1: 886-893.

[8] Bosch A, Zisserman A and Munoz X. Representing Shape with a Spatial Pyramid Kernel[C]. ACM International Conference on Image and Video Retrieval, 2007: 401-408.

[9] Zhang P, Bui T D and Suen C Y. A novel cascade ensemble classifier system with a high recognition performance on handwritten digits[J]. Pattern Recognition, 2007, 40 (12): 3415-3429.

[10] Heusch G, Cardinaus F and Marcel S. Lighting normalization algorithms for face verification[J], Tech. Rep., IDIAP-Com, 2005,5 (3): 1-38.

[11] 韩宏, 杨静宇. 神经网络分类器的组合[J]. 计算机研究与发展, 2000, 37 (12): 1488-1492.

[12] 王伟, 盛立东. 基于级联分组 BP 网络高精度手写数字识别[J]. 中文信息学报, 1998, 14 (2): 60-64.

[13] Maji S, A. Berg C and Malik J. Classification Using Intersection Kernel Support Vector Machines is efficient[J]. Proceeding CVPR, Anchorage, Alaska, 2008: 1-8.

[14] Skurichina M, Robert P and Duin W. Bagging, boosting and the random subspace method for linear classifiers[J]. Pattern Analysis & Applications, 2002, 5 (2): 121-135.

[15] Ho T K. The random subspace method for constructing decision forest[J]. IEEE Transactions on Pattern Analysis and Machine Intelligence, 1998, 20 (8): 832-844.

下 篇

驾驶人信息感知理论与技术

Chapter 8

Introduction of Driver's Information Perception

8.1 Introduction of driver's fatigue detection

The phenomenon of fatigue refers to a combination of symptoms such as impaired performance and a subjective feeling of drowsiness. Studies show that 25% – 30% of driving accidents are fatigue related[1, 2]. The European Transport Safety Council (ETSC) defines four levels of sleepiness based on behavioral terms as follows: completely awake, moderate sleepiness, severe sleepiness, and sleep[3]. In an attempt to avoid having an accident, most sleepy drivers will try to fight against sleep with moderate sleepiness, severe sleepiness. The purpose of the Driver Fatigue Monitoring System (DFMS) is to monitor the attention status of the driver. If driver fatigue is detected, different countermeasures should be taken to maintain driving safety, depending on the types and levels of fatigue. When a driver is fatigued, certain physical and physiological phenomena can be observed, including changes in brain waves or EEG, eye activity, facial expressions, head nodding, body sagging posture, heart rate, pulse, skin electric potential, gripping force on the steering wheel, and other changes in body activities.

Biological measures of driver's fatigue include EEG, electrocardiogram (ECG), electro-oculography (EOG), and surface electromyogram (SEMG). These signals are collected through electrodes in contact with the skin of the human body. Recent research has proposed various methods of extracting features from a segment of raw EEG data for fatigue detection. Lin et al. established a linear regression model to estimate the drowsiness level from the independent component analysis (ICA) of 33-channel EEG signals and could estimate the drowsiness level with 87% accuracy[4]. They then implemented a real-time embedded EEG-based driver drowsiness estimate system[5], which adopted only four channels of EEG data. Damousis et al. selected eight eye activity features, extracted from EOG, to develop a fuzzy expert system (FES) for the detection of hypovigilance[6]. Jap et al. accessed four electroencephalography (EEG) activities for 52 subjects during a monotonous driving session, and the results showed an increase in the ratio of slow wave to fast wave EEG activities over time[7]. Yeo et al. trained SVM to classify EEG signals into four principal frequency bands and then to predict the transition from alertness to drowsiness[8]. Hu and Zheng employed an SVM to perform drowsiness prediction with 11 eyelid-related features extracted from EOG[9]. In [10], kernel principal component analysis (KPCA) algorithm was employed to extract nonlinear features from the complexity parameters of EEG and improve the generalization performance of an HMM. Yang et al. employed a dynamic BN with EEG and ECG to estimate fatigue, and a first-order HMM was employed to compute the dynamics of a BN at two different time slices[11]. Sibsambhu et al. presents a method based on a class of entropy measures on the recorded Electroencephalogram (EEG) signals of human subjects for relative quantification of fatigue during driving[12]. Rami et al. developed an efficient fuzzy mutual-information-based wavelet packet transform feature-extraction method for classifying the driver drowsiness state into one of predefined drowsiness levels[13].

Physical measures of driver's fatigue include eye closure duration (ECD), blink frequency, nodding frequency, fixed gaze, and frontal face pose. In [14], the different linguistic terms and their corresponding fuzzy sets were distributed in each of the inputs using induced knowledge based on the hierarchical fuzzy partitioning method, and three variables (fixed gaze, PERCLOS, and ECD) were determined to be crucial cues for detecting a driver's fatigue. Suzuki et al. derived the following three factors from the blinking waveform[15], and these factors were then weighted using a multiple regression analysis for each individual to calculate the drowsiness level. Orazio et al. used a mixture Gaussian model to model the "normal behavior" statistics from the ECD and frequency of eye closure (FEC) for each person to identify anomalous behaviors[16]. Friedrichs and Yang explored 18 features of eye movement for drowsiness detection[17], and chose the sequential floating forward selection (SFFS) algorithm to select the most promising features to construct a classifier. In [18], it also reported that sleep deprived drivers have a lower frequency of steering reversals, a deterioration of steering performance, a decrease in the steering-wheel reversing rate, more frequent steering maneuvers during wakeful periods, no steering correction for a prolonged period of time followed by a jerky motion during drowsy periods, low-velocity steering, large amplitude steering-wheel movements, and large standard deviations in the steering-wheel angle.

Most of the above measures techniques require that sensor devices must be attached to driver's clothing or body, which is not a natural way to monitor a driver's activities. It is unlikely that drivers would accept any tethered sensing solution, i.e. using wired sensors or wireless sensors attached to their bodies. Image-based fatigue detection would be more applicable in a consumer car without the requirement of special markers or user intervention. Eskandarian et al. utilized artificial neural network (ANN) to analyze vehicle parameter data and eye-closure data to infer driver fatigue, and then, they analyzed the data to identify the potential variables that were correlated with drowsiness[19]. Fan et al. utilized a gabor features representation of the face for fatigue detection[20], and then AdaBoost algorithm was used to extract the most critical features from the dynamic feature set and construct a strong classifier for fatigue detection. But a few of recent works attempt to recognize and classify fatigue degrees of vehicle's drivers using image-based technologies.

8.2　Introduction of driver's abnormal activities detection

The driver's behaviours reflect his or her driving conditions, such as fatigue levels, attention and other unsafe information. Automatic understanding and characterizing driver behaviours is one of the key aspects for the development of human-centered driver assistance systems, in which Intelligent Transportation System (ITS) Community has been very interested. The driver's unsafe behaviours such as eating, talking on a cellular telephone and fatigue, will reduce a driver's alertness to the vehicle's surrounding environment. Nadeau et al.[21] carried out an epidemiological study on two large cohorts, namely non-users and users of cell phones, and the most significant finding is that the adjusted relative risks for heavy users were at least two times to those making minimal use of cell phones. To develop an effective driver behaviour recognition system, two important techniques have to be included, i.e., how to efficiently describe a driver's postures or maneuvers, and how to reliably classify the postures accordingly.

The driver's body information can be obtained in untethered manner by using vision sensors. Liu et al.[22] described a vision system that tracked the driver face and estimated his face pose in driving conditions using the yaw orientation angles. In order to address the problem of lacking the stable illumination in driving images captured by the colour camera, Kato et al.[23] developed an active capturing system with a far infrared camera for the detection of the driver face directions, such as rightward, frontward and leftward. Cheng et al.[24] used a commercial motion-capture system with the retroreflective markers placed on the driver's head, left hand and right hand, to predict and recognize the driver's left and right intersection-turn behaviours. Watta et al.[25] presented a vision system to recognize the driver's seven poses including looking over the left shoulder or over the right shoulder, at the road ahead, down at the instrument panel, at the center rear view mirror, in the left rear view mirror or at the right rear view mirror. Cheng et al.[26] introduced a multiple camera views (i.e., thermal infrared and colour) and multi-modal video-based system to recognize the driver activities including going forward, turning left or turning right. Demirdjian et al.[27] used an infrared time-of-flight (TOF) camera to estimate the orientation and location of a driver's limbs, including hands, arms, head and torso, and the articulated ICP algorithm and 3D model fitting approach were applied to incorporate the uncertainty in visual observation and model data in the driving pose estimation framework. Also, Yang et al.[28] presented an ECG system to monitor the driver's sitting postures (forward movement, back movement, left back movement or right back).

Most of the current research literature for driver activity recognition focused on the detection of driver head orientation, face direction and gaze, etc. Although many other kinds of motion-capture technologies exist in the literature to recover body pose by using different kind of sensors like magnetic, mechanical or optical marker-based sensors to provide either three degrees-of-freedom position of a point on the subject's body or full six DOF body-part orientation and position, such techniques have the biggest disadvantage that a subject is required to attach the sensor device or markers with his/her body or cloth, which is not a natural way of monitoring a driver's activities. So, it is unlikely that drivers would accept any tethered sensing solution, i.e. using wireless sensors or wired sensors attached to the driver's body. For this reason, image-based motion capture would be more applicable in a consumer car, as it does not require special markers or user intervention. A few of recent works attempted to understand and recognize the driver's postures, such as grasping the steel wheel, operating the shift lever, eating a cake and talking on a cellular telephone by using the image-based system. Only Veeraraghavan et al.[29] proposed an agglomerative clustering and a Bayesian Eigen-image classifier to recognize two types of a driver postures: unsafe type and safe type with a side-mounted camera capturing the driver's profile.

References

[1] Ranney T. A., Mazzae E., Garrott R. and Goodman, M. J. NHTSA driver distraction research: Past, present, and future[R]. Transp. Res. Center Inc., East Liberty, OH, Tech. Rep., Jul. 2000.

[2] The Royal Society for the Prevention of Accidents. Driver fatigue and road accidents: A literature review and position[D]. Birmingham, U. K., 2001.

[3] Croo H. D., Bandmann M. and Mackay G. M., et al. The role of driver fatigue in commercial road transport crashes[R]. Eur. Transp. Safety Council, Brussels, Belgium, Tech. Rep., 2001.

[4] Lin C. T., Wu R. C. and Liang S. F., et al. EEG-based drowsiness estimation for safety driving using independent component analysis[J]. IEEE Trans. Circuits Syst. I, Reg. Papers, 2005, 52 (12): 2726-2738.

[5] Lin C. T., Chen Y. C. and Huang T. Y., et al. Development of wireless brain computer interface with embedded multitask scheduling and its application on real-time driver's drowsiness detection and warning[J]. IEEE Trans. Biomed. Eng., 2008, 55 (5): 1582-1591.

[6] Damousis I. G. and Tzovaras D. Fuzzy fusion of eyelid activity indicators for hypovigilance-related accident prediction[J]. IEEE Trans. Intell. Transp. Syst., 2008, 9 (3): 491-500.

[7] Jap B. T., Lal S., and Fischer P., et al. Using EEG spectral components to assess algorithms for detecting fatigue[J]. Expert Syst. Appl., 2009, 36 (2): 2352-2359.

[8] Yeo M. V. M., Li X. P. and Shen, K. Can SVM be used for automatic EEG detection of drowsiness during car driving? [J]. Safety Sci., 2009, 47 (1): 115-124.

[9] Hu S. and Zheng G. Driver drowsiness detection with eyelid-related parameters by support vector machine[J]. Expert Syst. Appl., 2009, 36 (4): 7651-7658.

[10] Liu J., Zhang C. and Zheng C. EEG-based estimation of mental fatigue by using KPCA–HMM and complexity parameters[J]. Biomed. Signal Process. Control, 2010, 5 (2): 124-130.

[11] Yang G., Lin Y. and Bhattacharya P. A driver fatigue recognition model based on information fusion and dynamic Bayesian network[J]. Inf. Sci., 2010, 180 (10): 1942-1954.

[12] Sibsambhu K., Mayank B. and Aurobinda R. EEG signal analysis for the assessment and quantification of driver's fatigue[J]. Transportation Research Part F Traffic Psychology and Behaviour. 2010, 13 (5): 297-306.

[13] Khushaba R. N., Kodagoda S. and L. Sara, et al. Driver drowsiness classification using fuzzy wavelet-packet-based feature extraction algorithm[J]. IEEE Transactions on biomedical engineering, 2011, 58 (1): 121-131.

[14] Bergasa L., Nuevo J., and Sotelo M., et al. Real-time system for monitoring driver vigilance[J]. IEEE Trans. Intell. Transp. Syst., 2006, 7 (1): 63-77.

[15] Suzuki,M., Yamamoto, N., Yamamoto, O., et al. Measurement of driver's consciousness by image processing—A method for presuming driver's drowsiness by eye-blinks coping with individual differences[J]. Proc. IEEE Int. Conf. Syst., Man, Cybern., 2007 (4): 2891-2896.

[16] Orazio T. D., Leo M. and Guaragnella C. A visual approach for driver inattention detection[J]. Pattern Recognit., 2007, 40 (8): 2341-2355.

[17] Friedrichs F. and Yang B. Camera-based drowsiness reference for driver state classification under real driving conditions. Proc[J]. IEEE Intell. Veh. Symp., 2010: 101–106..

[18] Dong Y. C, Hu Z. C. and Uchimura K., et al. Driver inattention monitoring system for intelligent vehicles: a review[J]. IEEE Transactions on intellignet transportation systems, 2011, 12 (2): 596-614.

[19] Eskandarian A., Sayed R., and Delaigue P., et al. Advanced driver fatigue research[R]. U.S. Dept. Transp., Fed. Motor Carrier Safety Admin., Washington, DC, Tech.Rep. 2007.

[20] Fan X., Sun, Y. and Yin B. Gabor-based dynamic representation for human fatigue monitoring in facial image sequences[J]. Pattern Recognit. Lett., 2010, 31 (3): 234-243.

[21] Nadeau C. L., Maag U. and Bellavance F., et al. Wireless telephones and the risk of road crashes[J]. Accident Analysis and Prevention, 2003, 35 (5): 649-660.

[22] Liu X., Zhu Y. D. and Fujimura, K. Real-time Pose Classification for Driver Monitoring[C]. Proceedings of the IEEE 5th International Conference on Intelligent Transportation Systems, Singapore, 2002.

[23] Kato T., Fujii T. and Tanimoto M. Detection of driver's posture in the car by using far infrared camera[J]. IEEE Intelligent Vehicles Symposium, Parma, Italy, 2004: 339–344.

[24] Cheng S. Y. and Trivedi M. M. Turn-Intent Analysis Using Body Pose for Intelligent Driver Assistance[J]. IEEE on Pervasive Computing, 2006, 5 (4): 28-37.

[25] Watta P., Lakshmanan S. and Hou Y. L. Nonparametric approaches for estimating driver pose. IEEE Transactions on Vehicular Technology, 2007, 56 (4): 2028-2041.

[26] Cheng S. Y., Park S. and Trivedi, M. M. Multi-spectral and multi-perspective video arrays for driver body tracking and activity analysis[J]. Computer Vision and Image Understanding, 2007, 106 (2-3): 245-257.

[27] Demirdjian D. and Varri C. Driver poses estimation with 3D time-of-flight sensor[J]. IEEE Workshop on Computational Intelligence in Vehicles and Vehicular Systems, 2009: 16–22.

150

[28] Yang C. M., Wu C. C. and Chou C. M., et al. Vehicle driver's ECG and sitting posture monitoring system[C]. Proceedings of the 9th International Conference on Information Technology and Applications in Biomedicine, Larnaca, Cyprus, 2009.

[29] Veeraraghavan H., Bird, N. and Atev S., et al. Classifiers for driver activity monitoring[J]. Transportation Research Part C: Emerging Technologies, 2007, 15 (1): 51-67.

Chapter 9

Perception of Driver's Fatigue Information Using Curvelet transform

A decisive step in developing image-based driver fatigue degree recognition system is to extract suitable features from the driver's images and characterize differences between different driver fatigue expressions. In this book, we proposed an efficient features extraction of driver fatigue expression based curvelet transform, and Support Vector Machines (SVM) was then exploited in classification fatigue expression, compared with Linear Perception (LP) Classifier, k-Nearest Neighbor (k-NN) classifier, Multilayer perception (MLP) classifier and parzen classifier.

9.1 SEU fatigue expression data acquisition

Traffic accidents are often related with moderate sleepiness and severe sleepiness. The symptoms of moderate sleepiness is that vehicle drivers repeat yawning, and the symptoms of severe sleepiness is that vehicle drivers have difficulties in keeping eyes open and nodding off at the wheel. So our SEU fatigue expression dataset, created in southeast university using a side-mounted Logitech C905 CCD camera, consists of three kinds of facial expressions, i.e., awake expressions, moderate fatigue expressions, and severe fatigue expressions. There are 20 male drivers and 20 female drivers in SEU fatigue expression dataset, and the lighting conditions varied under the natural conditions, as the car was in an outdoor parking lot. The Fig. 9.1 shows example images of a driver inside the vehicle.

| (a) | (b) | (c) |

Fig. 9.1　Example images of a driver inside the vehicle

In this book, Viola-Jones face detection algorithm was used to detect the vehicle driver's faces[1]. The basic principle of the Viola-Jones algorithm is to scan a sub-window capable of detecting faces across a given input image, and the standard image processing approach would be to rescale the input image to different sizes and then run the fixed size detector through these images. The major contributions of Viola-Jones face detection algorithm consist of rectangular feature extraction, classification using AdaBoost learning algorithm, and multi-scale detection algorithm. The face detection result of one example images of a driver inside the vehicle is shown in Fig. 9.2.

(a) Example image (b) result image

Fig. 9.2 Face detection and segmentation of a vehicle driver

9.2 Curvelet transform for image feature description

In order to address the problem of illumination variations in images of SEU fatigue facial expression dataset, we adopted the well-known normalization technique called homomorphic filter (HOMOF) to enhance the image quality. With HOMOF, the images are first transformed into logarithm and then a frequency domain to emphasize the high frequency components. Then the images are transformed back into spatial domain by applying the inverse Fourier transform, followed by appropriate exponential operation. One example image of SEU fatigue facial expression dataset, before and after preprocessed by HOMOF is shown in Fig. 9.3.

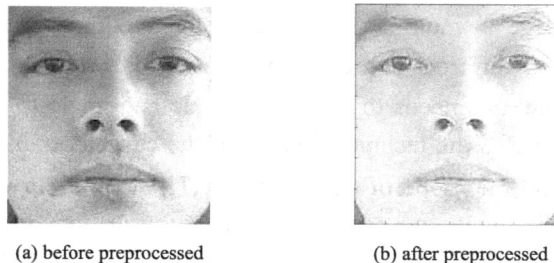

(a) before preprocessed (b) after preprocessed

Fig. 9.3 Example image before and after preprocessed by HOMOF

Curvelet transform[2, 3] is one of the latest developments of non-adaptive transforms.

Compared to wavelet, curvelet provides a more sparse representation of the image, with improved directional elements and better ability to represent edges and other singularities along curves. Compared to methods based on orthonormal transforms or direct time domain processing, sparse representation usually offers better performance with its capacity for efficient signal modelling.

While wavelets generalize the Fourier transform by using a basis that represents both location and spatial frequency, the curvelet transform provides the flexibility that the degree of localization in orientation varies with scale. In curvelet, fine scale basis functions are long ridges, and the shape of the basis functions at scale j is 2^{-j} by $2^{-j/2}$. So the fine-scale bases are skinny ridges with a precisely determined orientation. The curvelet coefficients can be expressed by

$$c(j,k,k) = \int_{R^2} f(x)\phi_{j,l,k}(x)\,dx \tag{9-1}$$

where $\varphi_{j,l,k}(\cdot)$ denotes curvelet function, and j, l and k are the variable of scale, orientation, and position respectively. In the last few years, several discrete curvelet and curvelet-like transforms have been proposed. The influential approach is based on the Fast Fourier Transform (FFT)[4]. In the frequency domain, the curvelet transform can be implemented with φ by means of the window function U. Defining a pair of windows $W(r)$ (a radial window) and $V(t)$ (an angular window) as below

$$\sum_{j=-\infty}^{\infty} W^2(2^j r) = 1, \quad r \in (3/4,\ 3/2) \tag{9-2}$$

$$\sum_{j=-\infty}^{\infty} V^2(t-1) = 1, \quad r \in (-1/2,\ 1/2) \tag{9-3}$$

where variables W as a frequency domain variable, and r and θ as polar coordinates in the frequency domain, then for each $j \geqslant j_0$, U_j is defined in the Fourier domain by

$$U_j(r,\theta) = 2^{3j/4}\omega(2^{-j}r)\nu\left(\frac{2^{\lfloor j/2 \rfloor}\theta}{2\pi}\right) \tag{9-4}$$

where $\lfloor j/2 \rfloor$ denotes the integer part of $j/2$. The above brief introduction of the frequency plane partitioning into radial and angular divisions can be explained by Fig. 9.4, where the shaded area is one of the polar wedges represented by U_j, which is supported by the radial and angular windows W and V. The radial divisions (concentric circles) are responsible for decomposition of the image in multiple scales (used for bandpassing the image) and angular divisions corresponding to different angles or orientation. Therefore when we consider each wedge like the shaded one, one needs to define the scale and angle to analyze the bandpassed image at scale j and angle θ. The technical details of the curvelet transform implementation is much involved and beyond the scope of current paper. The fastest curvelet transform currently available is curvelets via wrapping[5], which will be used for our work. If $f([t_1,t_2])$, $0 \leqslant t_1, t_2 \leqslant n$ is taken to be a Cartesian array and $\hat{f}[n_1,n_2]$ to denote its 2D Discrete Fourier Transform.

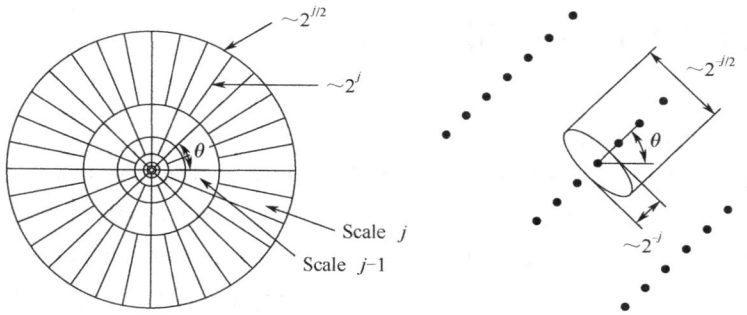

Fig. 9.4　Curvelet transform: Fourier frequency domain partitioning (left)

and spatial domain representation of a wedge (right)

From the curvelet coefficients, some statistics can be calculated from each of these curvelet sub-bands as image descriptor. The mean μ and standard deviation μ are the convenient features[6]. If n curvelets are used for the transform, $2n$ features $G = \left[G_\mu, G_\delta \right]$ are obtained, where $G_\mu = [\mu_1, \mu_2, \cdots, \mu_n]$, $G_\delta = [\delta_1, \delta_2, \cdots, \delta_n]$. The $2n$ dimension feature vector can be used to represent each image in the dataset. Curvelet transform of one example image of Fig. 9.3 is shown in Fig. 9.5, and Fig. 9.5 (b) is the approximate coefficients, and Fig. 9.5 (c)~Fig. 9.5 (j) are detailed coefficients at eight angles from three scales. All the images are rescaled to same dimension for demonstration purpose. From each of the detail coefficient matrices, the first-order and second-order statistics mean and standard deviation were calculated as features vectors of fatigue expressions of vehicle drivers in this book.

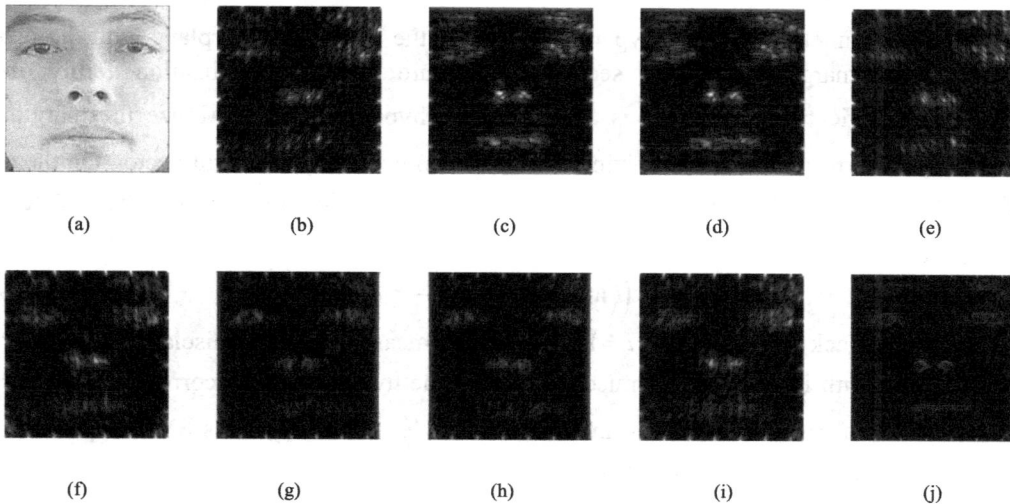

(a)　　(b)　　(c)　　(d)　　(e)

(f)　　(g)　　(h)　　(i)　　(j)

Fig. 9.5　Curvelet transform of example image

9.3 Support Vector Machine (SVM)

SVM was originally designed for binary-class classification problems[7], based on the idea of structural risk minimization. The basic principle of binary-class SVM is to find an optimal separating hyperplane (OSH) and separate two classes of patterns based on the training set and the decision boundary, which can be formulated as a quadratic programming (QP) problem in the feature space[8]. Consider a problem of separating training data $\left\{(x_i, y_i)\right\}_{i=1}^{N}$ into two separate classes, where $x_i \subset \Re^n$ is an ith input vector in n-dimensional input space, and $y_i \in \{-1, +1\}$ is a specified binary target vector. The main goal of SVM approach is to find a hyperplane as following

$$f(x_i) = \langle w \cdot x_i \rangle + b \qquad (9\text{-}5)$$

where w is the weight vector and b is a bias term. The hyperplane is able to separate the class linearly so that all the points with the same class are on the same side of the hyperplane. According to the hyperplane, all the training data must satisfy the following constrains

$$\begin{cases} \langle w \cdot x_i \rangle + b \geqslant +1 & \text{,for} \quad y_i = +1 \\ \langle w \cdot x_i \rangle + b < -1 & \text{,for} \quad y_i = -1 \end{cases} \qquad (9\text{-}6)$$

Each sample is classified into +1 or -1 which side of the hyperplane lies on. The constraint of the hyperplane can be written as:

$$y_i (w \cdot x_i) + b \geqslant 1, \quad i = 1, 2, \cdots, N \qquad (9\text{-}7)$$

The distance from the closest point to the hyperplane equals to $1/\|w\|$, where $\|\cdot\|$ is the Euclidean Norm function, and the hyperplane realizes the maximal hyperplane with the margin $\rho = 2/\|w\|$. The margin ρ can be seen as a measure of the generalization ability of the hyperplane classification. The OSH is the separating hyperplane to maximize the margin ρ. Accordingly, it corresponds to minimizing the Euclidean norm of the weight vector. On the other hand, for the non-separable case, the slack variables ξ_i allowing the margin to be violated can be introduced

$$y_i \left(\langle w^{\mathrm{T}} \cdot x_i \rangle + b \right) \geqslant 1 - \xi_i \qquad (9\text{-}8)$$

where the slack variable ξ_i, $i = 1, \cdots, N$, is a measure of the misclassification errors, namely when the ith input vector is misclassified by the hyperplane, the corresponding $\xi_i > 0$. From the structural risk minimization inductive principle, the binary-class SVM approach is to minimize the guaranteed risk bound as follows:

$$\min_{w,b,\xi} \frac{1}{2} \langle w^{\mathrm{T}} \cdot w \rangle + C \sum_{i=1}^{N} \xi_i \qquad (9\text{-}9)$$

where C is a user-defined positive finite constant, controlling a compromise between maximizing the margin and minimizing the number of training set error. A larger C means that a higher penalty is assigned to empirical errors. The solution to the optimization problem of equation (9-9) is a convex QP, which can be solved by using the langrage multipliers method and the Karush-Kuhn-Tucher theorem in the optimization theory. Accordingly, the coefficient α_i can be found by solving the flowing convex QP problem

$$\alpha^* = \arg\max\left[\sum_{i=1}^{N}\alpha_i - \frac{1}{2}\sum_{i=1}^{N}\sum_{j=1}^{N}\alpha_i\alpha_j y_i y_j\left(x_i \cdot x_j\right)\right]$$ (9-10)

with constraints as following

$$\sum_{i=1}^{N}\alpha_i y_i = 0, \quad C \geqslant \alpha_i \geqslant 0, \quad i = 1,2,\cdots,N$$ (9-11)

Therefore the decision boundary function of the classifier can be expressed as

$$f(x) = \text{sign}\left[\sum_{i=1}^{N}\alpha_i y_i \langle x_i \cdot x\rangle + b\right]$$ (9-12)

The formulated binary-class SVM is called the hard margin SVM. However, the hard-margin SVM do not work well, while the training data are linearly inseparable. One improvement is the nonlinear SVM that maps the training data from the input space into a high-dimensional feature space via a non-linear mapping function $\Phi(\cdot)$, also called the kernel function such that

$$K\left(x_i,x_j\right) = \langle x_i,x_j\rangle = \langle\Phi(x_i)\cdot\Phi(x_j)\rangle$$ (9-13)

The interesting property of nonlinear SVM is that, once a valid kernel function has been selected, one can practically work in spaces of any dimension without any significant additional computational cost, since feature mapping is never effectively performed. The most commonly applied nonlinear kernel is linear kernel, polynomial kernel, RBF kernel, sigmoid kernel, and intersection kernel are described as follows.

Linear kernel

$$K\left(x_i,x_j\right) = x_i^{\text{T}}\cdot x_j$$ (9-14)

Polynomial kernel

$$K\left(x_i,x_j\right) = \left(\gamma\cdot x_i^{\text{T}}\cdot x_j + r\right)^d, \quad \gamma > 0$$ (9-15)

RBF kernel

$$K\left(x_i,x_j\right) = \exp\left(-\gamma\|x_i - x_j\|^2\right), \quad \gamma > 0$$ (9-16)

Sigmoid kernel

$$K\left(x_i,x_j\right) = \tan\left(\gamma\cdot x_i^{\text{T}}x_j + r\right), \quad \gamma > 0$$ (9-17)

Intersection kernel

$$K\left(x_i,x_j\right) = \min(x_i,x_j)$$ (9-18)

where γ, r and d and are kernel parameters. The decision boundary function can be rewritten as

$$f(x) = \text{sign}\left[\sum_{i=1}^{N}\alpha_i y_i K\left(x_i,x\right) + b\right]$$ (9-19)

Therefore, the dual objective function in a non-linear SVM becomes as follows:

$$\alpha^* = \arg\max\left[\sum_{i=1}^{N}\alpha_i - \frac{1}{2}\sum_{i=1}^{N}\sum_{j=1}^{N}\alpha_i\alpha_j y_i y_j K\left(x_i \cdot x_j\right)\right] \tag{9-20}$$

The Karush–Kuhn–Tucker (KKT) conditions are necessary and sufficient conditions for an optimal point of a positive definite dual problem. The dual problem is as follows

$$\begin{cases} \alpha_i = 0 \Rightarrow y_i f(x_i) \geq 1 \\ 0 < \alpha_i < C \Rightarrow y_i f(x_i) = 1 \\ \alpha_i = C \Rightarrow y_i f(x_i) \leq 1 \end{cases} \tag{9-21}$$

The dual objective function is usually solved by the sequential minimization optimization (SMO) algorithm[9]. Even though binary-class SVM shows the excellent performance in pattern classification applications, it is required to formulate a multi-class SVM method since most of classifying applications are considered as the multi-category problems in the real world. Multi-class pattern recognition problems are commonly solved using a combination of binary-class SVM and a decision strategy to decide the multi-class of the input pattern. This implementation of k-class OAO SVM is converted into k binary SVM problems[10, 11], and then combine k binary classifiers. The ith SVM is trained with all samples in the ith class with positive label, and all other samples with negative label. Considering the training set $\{(x_i, y_i)\}_{i=1}^{N}$, where $x_i \in R^n$ is given a class label $y_i \in \{1, \cdots, k\}$. The k-class OAA SVM of the ith class can be expressed into the following problem:

$$\underset{w^i, b^i, \xi_j^i}{\text{Min}}\left\{\frac{1}{2}\|w^i\|^2 + C\sum_{j=1}^{N}\xi_j^i\right\} \tag{9-22}$$

subject to

$$\begin{array}{ll} \left(w^i\right)^{\mathrm{T}}\varphi\left(x_j\right) + b^i \geq 1 - \xi_j^i & ,if \quad y_j = i \\ \left(w^i\right)^{\mathrm{T}}\varphi\left(x_j\right) + b^i \leq -1 + \xi_j^i & ,if \quad y_j \neq i \end{array} \quad \xi_j^i \geq 0, j = 1, \cdots, N \tag{9-23}$$

We can assign the data x_j belongs to the class c_i with the maximal value of the decision function based on the following equation.

$$c_i = \underset{i=1,\dots,k}{\arg\max}\left(\left(w^i\right)^{\mathrm{T}}\varphi_i\left(x_j\right) + b^i\right) \tag{9-24}$$

9.4 Other classification methods compared

9.4.1 Linear Perception (LP) classifier

The linear perceptron (LP) classifier can be seen as a simplest kind of feedforward neural network[12], which is shown in Fig. 9.6. A feature representation function $f\left(x_i, Y_j\right)$ maps each possible input/output pair to a finite-dimensional real-valued feature vector.

$$\hat{Y}_j = \arg\max_{Y_j} f(x_i, Y_j) \cdot w \qquad (9\text{-}25)$$

where w is a weight vector. Learning again iterates over the samples, predicting an output for each, leaving the weights unchanged when the predicted output matches the target, and changing them when it does not. The update becomes

$$w_{t+1} = w_t + f(x_i, Y_j) - f(x_i, \hat{Y}_j) \qquad (9\text{-}26)$$

This multi-class formulation reduces to the original perception when x_i is a real-valued vector, Y_j is chosen from $\{0,1\}$, and $f(x_i, Y_j) = Y_j \cdot x_i$. For certain problems, input/output representations and features can be chosen so that $\arg\max_{Y_j} \{f(x_i, Y_j) \cdot w\}$ can be found efficiently even though Y_j is chosen from a very large or even infinite set.

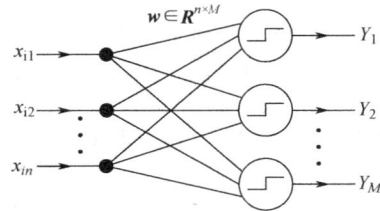

Fig. 9.6　Linear perceptron classifier network

9.4.2　*k*-Nearest Neighbor (*k*-NN) classifier

k-nearest neighbor (*k*-NN) classifer[13] is a method for classifying objects based on closest training examples in the feature space.*k*-NN is a type of instance-based learning, or lazy learning where the function is only approximated locally and all computation is defered until classification. The *k*-nearest neighbor algorithm is amongst the simplest of all machine learning algorithms: an object is classified by a majority vote of its neighbors, with the object being assigned to the class most common amongst its *k* nearest neighbors (*k* is a positive integer, typically small).　If *k*=1, then the object is simply assigned to the class of its nearest neighbor. The *k*-NN rule is optimal in the asymptotic case, i.e., the error tends to the Bayes error when the size of the training set tends to infinity. The major drawback of the *k*-NN algorithm is the computational complexity, caused by the large number of distance computations.

9.4.3　Multilayer Perception (MLP) classifier

Multilayer perception (MLP) classifier is a modification of the standard linear perceptron, which can distinguish data that is not linearly separable. A multilayer perceptron is a feedforward artificial neural network model that maps sets of input data onto a set of appropriate output, and consists of a set of source nodes forming the inputlayer, one or more hidden layers of computation nodes, and an output layer of nodes [14].

The MLP utilizes a supervised learning technique called backpropagation for training the network and constructs input-output mappings that are a nested composition of nonlinearities with the form

$$y = f\left(\sum g\left(\sum(\cdot)\right)\right) \qquad (9\text{-}27)$$

where he number of function compositions is given by the number of network layers. An MLP can be trained by gradient descent using the back-propagation algorithm to optimize any derivable criterion, such as the Mean Squared Error, Here, an MLP is trained to classify an input to be one of the given class labels. The input of the MLP is a vector corresponding to the features extracted from gait patterns. The output of the MLP is either 1 (if the input corresponds to a control group) or -1 (if the input corresponds to children with CP). Though MLP has been proved to be able to virtually approximate any function with any desired accuracy, there is a common criticism for MLP that is very difficult to interpret the trained discriminant function.

9.4.4 Parzen classifier

Parzen classifier is a kernel density estimator, with which a nonlinear function is approximated by the superposition of a set of kernels[15]. For pattern X_j, a Gaussian kernel-based Parzen classifier is determined by N training samples $X = [X_1, X_2, \cdots, X_N]$ as follows

$$f(x_j, s) = \frac{1}{N} \sum_{i=1}^{N} \frac{1}{\left(s\sqrt{2\pi}\right)^n} \exp\left(-\frac{\|x_j - x_i\|^2}{2s^2}\right) \tag{9-28}$$

where x_i is an n-dimensions training feature vector of training sample x_i, and s is a kernel width. The Parzen classifier design means to estimate the relevant kernel width s using the training feature set $\{x_1, \cdots, x_i, \cdots, x_N\}$. A maximum likelihood principle was adopted to estimate the kernel width s which is as follows

$$s = \sqrt{\frac{1}{n \cdot N} \sum_{j=1}^{N} \sum_{i \neq j}^{N} \frac{\|x_j - x_i\|^2}{N-1}} \tag{9-29}$$

9.5 Experiments

Two standard experimental procedures, named the holdout approach and the cross-validation approach, are used to compare the performance of SVM with five different kernels and other four classifiers, namely, LP classifier, k-NN classifier, MLP classifier, and parzen classifier by using HP Elite Book 6 930p computer. In the holdout approach, certain amounts of fatigue facial expression features extracted from images in SEU fatigue facial expression dataset (shown in Fig. 9.7) are reserved for testing, and the rest are for training. In k-fold cross-validation approach, SEU fatigue facial expression dataset is partitioned into k sub-datasets. Of them, the kth sub-dataset is retained for testing the classification model and the remaining $k-1$ sub-datasets are used for training the classification model. The cross-validation experiments are then repeated k times, with all of the k sub-samples used exactly once as the validation dataset[16]. The k experiment results from the folds are then averaged to produce a single classification rate.

(a) awake expressions

(b) moderate fatigue expressions

(c) severe fatigue expressions

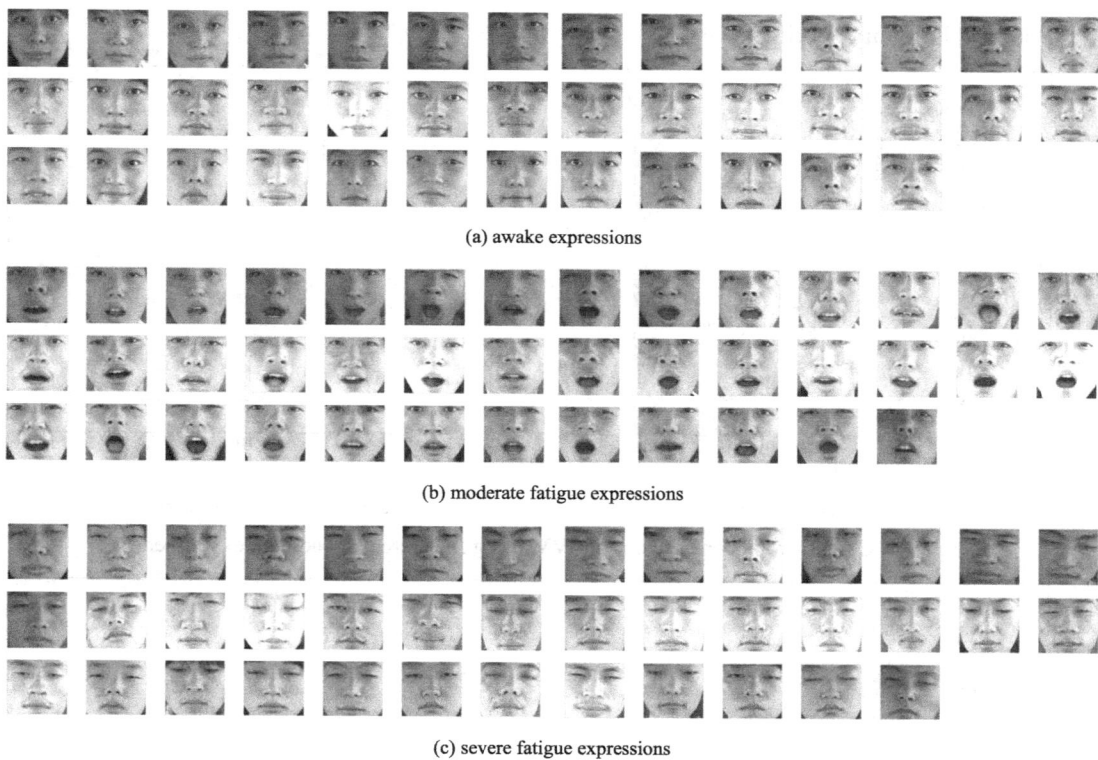

Fig. 9.7　Fatigue facial expression of vehicle drivers in SEU fatigue facial expression dataset

1) Holdup experiments

Holdout experiments are based on randomly dividing fatigue expressions features into a training dataset (80% of fatigue expression features extracted from the images in SEU fatigue expression dataset) and a test dataset (20% of fatigue expression features extracted from the images in SEU fatigue expression dataset). Using the holdout experiment approach, only the test dataset is used to estimate the generalization error. We repeated the holdout experiment 100 times by randomly splitting the fatigue expression dataset, and recorded the classification results.

In the first holdout experiment, the same set of training and testing are applied to SVM with five different kernels, and their classification performances are simultaneously compared. The results of classification rate for fatigue expressions by SVM with five different kernels are displayed in the bar plots of Fig. 9.8 (a) and box plots of Fig. 9.8 (b). The average classification accuracies of linear kernel, polynomial kernel, RBF kernel, sigmoid kernel and intersection kernel are 82.96%, 85.21%, 33.79%, 25.04% and 84.08%, respectively. From Fig. 9.9, it is obvious that SVM with polynomial kernel offers the best performance among the five kernels in the first holdout experiments.In the second holdout experiment, the same set of training and testing are applied to SVM with polynomial kernel and the other four classifiers, and their classification performances are simultaneously compared. The results of classification rate for the fatigue expression are displayed in the bar plots of Fig. 9.9 (a) and box plots of Fig. 9.9 (b). It is obvious that SVM with polynomial kernel offers the best performance rate among five classifiers in the second holdout experiments.

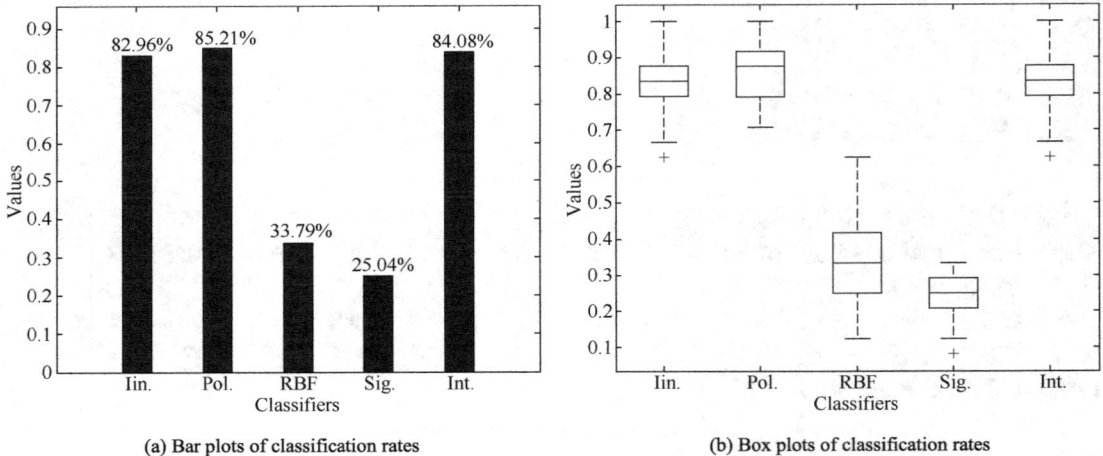

(a) Bar plots of classification rates

(b) Box plots of classification rates

Fig. 9.8　Classification performance of SVM using five kernels in holdout experiment

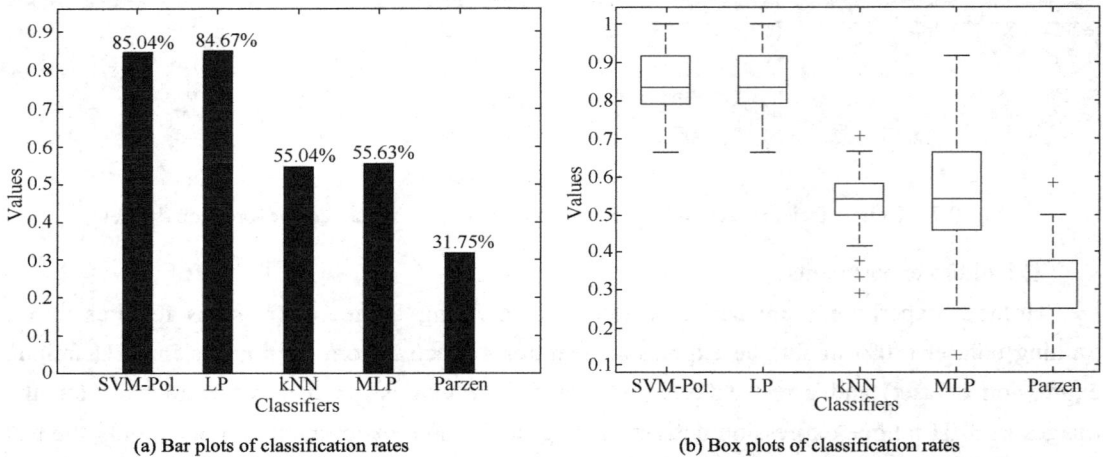

(a) Bar plots of classification rates

(b) Box plots of classification rates

Fig. 9.9　Classification performance of SVM with polynomial kernel and other four methods in holdout experiment

To further measure the classification performance regarding the information about actual and predicted classifications acquired, confusion matrix is often used. A confusion matrix is a square matrix or table that represents the number/proportion of examples from one class classified into another (or same) class. In the holdout experiment, the confusion matrix that summarizes the detailed performance of the SVM with polynomial kernel is shown in Table 9.1. In a confusion matrix, the rows and columns indicate true and predicted class, respectively. The diagonal entries represent correct classification, while the off-diagonal entries represent incorrect ones. The rows and columns of the confusion matrices express the fatigue expression classes of awake expressions, moderate fatigue expressions, and severe fatigue expressions. The corresponding classification accuracies are 80.87%, 85.30%, and 84.08%, respectively. From confusion matrix of the holdout experiments, it is clear that the class of moderate fatigue expression has the most recognition accuracy of three classes in the holdout experiments.

Table 9.1   Confusion matrix for the result from SVM classifier with polynomial kernel in holdout experiments.(I) awake expressions, (II) moderate fatigue expressions and (III) severe fatigue expressions.

class	I	II	III
I	80.87%	12.23%	6.90%
II	12.29%	85.30%	2.41%
III	13.38%	2.55%	84.08%

2) Cross-validation experiments

The k-fold cross validation approach is another commonly used technique that takes a set of m examples and randomly partitions them into k folds of size m/k. For each fold, the classifier is tested on one fold (consists of m/k examples) and trained on the other $k-1$ folds (consisting of $m(1-1/k)$ examples). In the first cross-validation experiment, 10-fold cross validation was used when comparing SVM with five different kernels. The 120 sets of fatigue expression features extracted from the images in SEU fatigue facial expression dataset are randomly divided into 10 disjoint subsets of approximately equal size (every subset consists of 12 fatigue expression features). Nine of these ten disjoint subsets are trained and then tested on the one left out, each time leaving out a different one. The average classification accuracies of the 100 cross-validation experiments are displayed in the bar plots of Fig. 9.10 (a) and box plots of Fig. 9.10(b). The average classification accuracies of the five kernels, i.e., linear kernel, polynomial kernel, RBF kernel, sigmoid kernel and intersection kernel, are 83.26%, 85.99%, 34.08%, 16.96% and 84.97%, respectively. From the bar plots and box plots of the classification rates, the polynomial kernel outperforms the other four kernels, because it achieves the highest classification rates among the five kernels in the first cross-validation experiments.

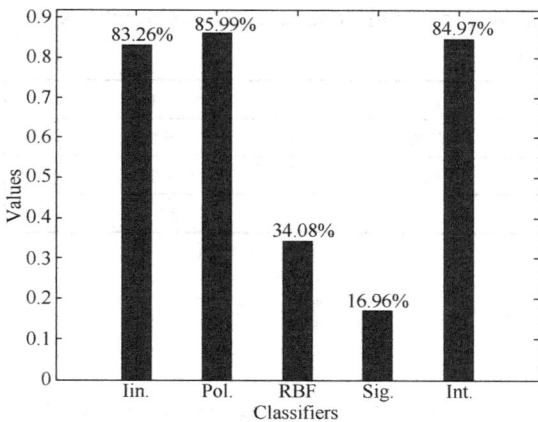

(a) Bar plots of classification rates

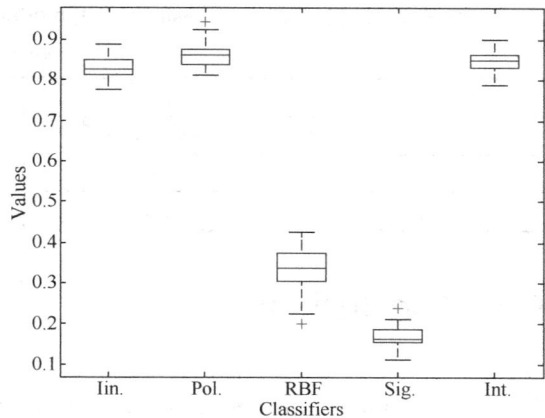

(b) Box plots of classification rates

Fig. 9.10   Classification performance of SVM using five kernels in Cross-validation experiment

In the second cross-validation experiment, 10-fold cross validations are applied to SVM with polynomial kernel and the other four classifiers, and their classification performances are simultaneously compared. The results of classification rate for the fatigue expressions are displayed in the bar plots of Fig. 9.11 (a) and box plots of Fig. 9.11 (b). From Fig. 11, it is obvious that SVM with polynomial kernel offers the best performance rate of five classifiers in the second cross-validation experiments. In the cross-validation experiment, the confusion matrix that summarizes the detailed performance of SVM with polynomial kernel is shown in Table 9.2. The accuracies of the three classes, (i.e., awake facial expression, etc.) are 85.10%, 88.60%, and 85.38%, and once again, it is clear that the class of moderate fatigue expression has the most recognition accuracy of three classes in the cross-validation experiments.

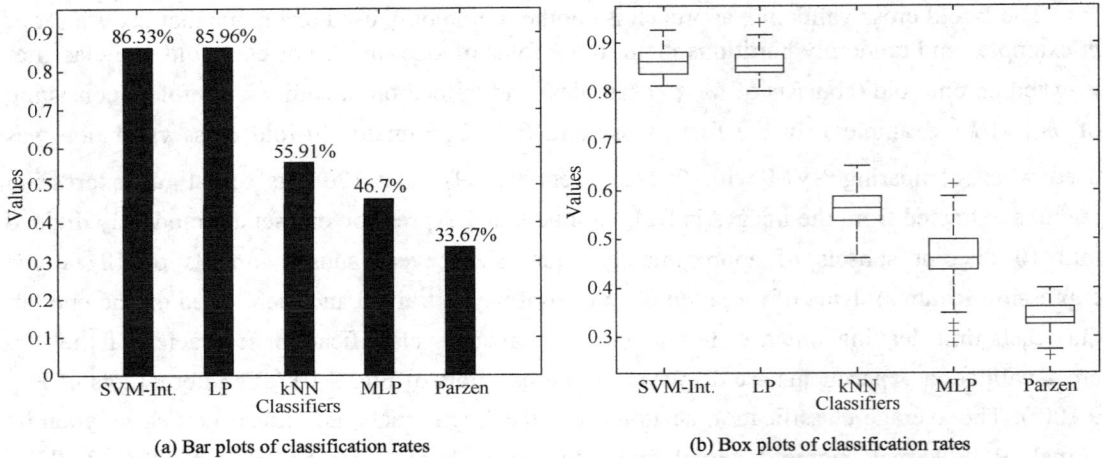

(a) Bar plots of classification rates   (b) Box plots of classification rates

Fig. 9.11　Classification performance of SVM with polynomial kernel and other four methods in Cross-validation experiment

Table 9.2　Confusion matrix for the result from SVM classifier with polynomial kernel in Cross-validation experiments. (I) awake expressions, (II) moderate fatigue expressions and (III) severe fatigue expressions.

class	I	II	III
I	85.10%	8.40%	6.50%
II	10.30%	88.60%	1.09%
III	14.42%	0.20%	85.38%

9.6　Conclusions

With features extracted by curvelet transform from SEU fatigue facial expression dataset, consisting of awake expressions, moderate fatigue expressions and severe fatigue expressions, we comparatively studied SVM using five different kernels, with other four commonly used classification methods, namely, LP classifier, k-NN classifier, MLP classifier and parzen classifier, in the classification of three pre-defined classes of driver fatigue expressions. The holdout and cross-validation experiments were conducted, which indicated that polynomial kernel outperforms the other four kernels, and SVM with polynomial kernel offers the best classification performance rate of five classifiers. Our experiments also showed that moderate fatigue expression has the most recognition accuracy of the three classes. With SVM using polynomial kernel, the classification accuracies of moderate fatigue expression are over 85% in both of the holdout and cross-validation experiments, which shows the effectiveness of the proposed feature extraction method and the importance of SVM classifier in developing DFMS.

References

[1] Paul V. and Michael J. J. Robust real-time face detection[J]. International journal of computer vision, 2004, 57 (2): 137-154.

[2] Starck J., Candes E., and Donoho D. L. The curvelet transform for image denoising[J], IEEE transactions image processing, 2002 (11): 670-684.

[3] Candes E., Donoho D. L. Curvelets - a surprisingly effective nonadaptive representation for objects with edges, in Curves and Surfaces[M]. Vanderbilt University Press, 1999.

[4] Candes E. L., Demanet D. and Donoho L., et al. Fast discrete curvelet transforms[J]. Multiscale Modeling and Simulation. 2006 (5): 861-899.

[5] Geback T. and Koumoutsakos P. Edge detection in microscopy images using curvelets[J]. BMC Bioinformatics, 2009 (10): 1-14.

[6] Sumana I., Islam M. and Zhang D. Content based image retrieval using curvelet transform[C], IEEE 10th Workshop on Multimedia Signal Processing, Cairns, Australia, 2008.

[7] Cortes C, Vapnik V. Support-Vector Networks [J]. Machine Learning, 1995, 20 (3): 2973-2979.

[8] Vapnik V. N. Statistical Learning Theory[M]. New York: John Wiley & Sons , 1998.

[9] Platt J. Fast training of SVM using sequential minimal optimization[M]. In advances in kernel methods Support Vector Machine. Cambridge: MIT Press , 1999.

[10] KreBel U. Pairwise classification and support vector machines[M]. In Advances in kernel methods: Support vector learning, Cambridge, MA.:MIT Press, 1999.

[11] Milgram J, Cheriet M and Sabourin R. One against one or one against all: which one is better for handwriting recognition with SVM? [C]. International workshop on Frontiers in handwriting recognition, Montreal, Canada, 2006.

[12] Collins M. Discriminative training methods for hidden markov models: theory and experiments with perceptron algorithms[J]. proceedings of conferences on empirical methods in natural language processing, Philadelphia, 2002 (10): 1-8.

[13] Bremner D., Demaine. E., Erickson, J., et al. Output-sensitive algorithms for computing nearest-neighbor decision boundaries[J]. Discrete and computational geometry, 2005, 33 (4): 593-604.

[14] Simon H. Neural Networks: a comprehensive foundation ,2ed. [M]. Prentice Hall, 1998.

[15] Kraaijveld M. A. A parzen classifier with an improved robustness against deviations between training and test data[J]. Pattern Recogn. Lett., 1996, 17 (7): 679-689.

[16] Zhang B., L., Zhang Y., C. Classification of cerebral palsy gait by kernel fisher discriminant analysis[J]. International journal of hybrid intelligent systems, 2008, 5 (4): 209-218.

Chapter 10

Recognition of Driver's Fatigue Expression Using Local Multiresolution Derivative Pattern

Most of the above techniques require that sensor devices must be attached to driver's clothing or body, which is not a natural way to monitor a driver's activities. It is unlikely that drivers would accept any tethered sensing solution, i.e. using wired sensors or wireless sensors attached to their bodies. Image-based fatigue detection would be more applicable in a consumer car without the requirement of special markers or user intervention. A decisive step in developing image-based driver fatigue degree recognition system is to extract suitable features from the driver's images and characterize differences between different driver fatigue expressions. When being fatigue, the drivers will repeat yawning, and have difficulties in keeping eyes open. The key features of fatigue expression images are locations and contours of mouth, eyes and eyebrows, which are localized in both location and direction. The images of fatigue expressions contain intrinsic geometrical structure (locations and contours of mouth, eyes and eyebrows), which are key features in visual information for fatigue expression recognition. Recently, a powerful operator, called Local Derivative Pattern (LDP) was proposed by Zhang for face recognition[2]. LDP encodes directional pattern features based on local derivative variations, and captures more detailed discriminative information of face. But LDP can't obtain the relationship information of local high pattern for the intrinsic geometrical structures (locations and smoothed contours of mouth, eyes and eyebrows. This disappointing behaviour of LDP in fatigue expression indicates that more powerful representations are needed in higher dimensions. With the aim to explore the intrinsic geometrical structure of fatigue expression images, we propose a novel, efficient features extraction approach, named Local Multiresolution Derivative Pattern (LMDP) for fatigue expressions descriptions of vehicle drivers.

The paper is organized as follows. In section 2, the background of SEU (Southeast University) fatigue facial expression dataset is outlined. In section 3, Local Multiresolution Derivative Pattern (LMDP) for image feature description of fatigue expressions is introduced. Intersection Kernel Support Vector Machines (ISKVMs), compared with k-Nearst Neighbor (k-NN), Multilayer Perceptron (MLP) and Dissimilarity classifier are presented in Section 4. Section 5 details the experiments and reports on the classification results for the fatigue expressions of vehicle drivers. Section 6 presents our conclusions.

10.1　Fatigue expression data acquisition

Traffic accidents are often related to moderate sleepiness and severe sleepiness. The sign of moderate sleepiness is that vehicle driver's repeat yawning, and the sign of severe sleepiness is that vehicle drivers have difficulties in keeping eyes open and nodding off at the wheel[1]. We created a fatigue expressions dataset, named Southeast (SEU) fatigue expressions dataset, which consists of three kinds of fatigue expressions images, i.e., awake expressions, moderate fatigue expressions. The SEU fatigue expression dataset was created using a side-mounted Logitech C905 CCD camera and includes 120 fatigue expressions images. There are 20 male drivers and 20 female drivers in SEU fatigue expression dataset, and the lighting conditions varied under the natural conditions, as the car was in an outdoor parking lot. In this book, Viola-Jones face detection algorithm was used to detect the vehicle driver's faces[3]. The major contributions of Viola-Jones face detection algorithm include the exploitation of Haar-like feature expression and AdaBoost learning. In our data acquisition and normalization, Viola-Jones face detection algorithm offers excellent performance in detecting the driver's face even when a driver turns his/her face to look at rear-mirrors, or lower his/her head to operate the shift lever. At finally, SEU fatigue expression dataset consists of 40 subjects with 3 different sessions per subject and in total 120 sessions. The Fig. 10.1 (a) shows example images of a driver inside the vehicle, and the corresponding face detection result is shown in Fig. 10.1 (b).

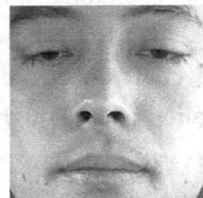

(a) Example image　　　　　　　　　　　　　(b) Gray image of Viola-Jones face detection

Fig. 10.1　Example image of a driver inside the vehicle driver

10.2　Local multiresolution derivative pattern

In this section, a brief review of Local Derivative Pattern (LDP) is presented, and then Local Multiresolution Derivative Pattern (LMDP) is introduced in details.

10.2.1 Local Derivative Pattern(LDP)

Local Derivative Pattern (LDP) encodes the higher-order derivative information of an image[2], which is derived from a general definition of texture in a local neighbourhood. Given an image $I(Z)$, the first-order derivative is denoted as $I'(Z)$. Let Z_0 be a point in $I(Z)$, and Z_i, $i=1,\cdots,8$ be the neighboring point around Z_0. The first-order derivatives in at $Z=Z_0$ can be written as

$$I'(Z_i)=I(Z_0)-I(Z_i) \tag{10-1}$$

The second-order local derivative pattern, LDP^2 at $Z=Z_0$ is defined as

$$\text{LDP}^2(Z_0)=\{f(I'(Z_0),I'(Z_1)),f(I'(Z_0),I'(Z_2)),\cdots,f(I'(Z_0),I'(Z_8))\} \tag{10-2}$$

where $f(\cdot,\cdot)$ is a binary coding function determining the types of local pattern transitions, and encodes the co-occurrence of two directions at different neighboring pixels as

$$f(I'(Z_0),I'(Z_i))=\begin{cases}0, & \text{if } I'(Z_0)\cdot I'(Z_i)>0 \\ 1, & \text{if } I'(Z_0)\cdot I'(Z_i)\leqslant 0\end{cases} \quad i=1,2,\cdots,8 \tag{10-3}$$

From Eq. 10-3, it can be seen that the second-order LDP encodes the change of the neighbourhood derivative directions, which represents the second-order pattern information in the local region. To calculate the nth-order Local Derivative Pattern, the nth-order LDP is a binary string describing gradient trend changes in a local region of directional $(n-1)^{\text{th}}$-order derivative images $I^{n-1}(Z)$ as

$$\text{LDP}^n(Z_0)=\{f(I^{n-1}(Z_0),I^{n-1}(Z_1)),f(I^{n-1}(Z_0),I^{n-1}(Z_2)),\cdots,f(I^{n-1}(Z_0),I^{n-1}(Z_8))\} \tag{10-4}$$

where $I^{n-1}(Z_0)$ is the $(n-1)^{\text{th}}$-order derivative in at $Z=Z_0$, and $f(I^{n-1}(Z_0),I^{n-1}(Z_i))$ is defined as

$$f(I^{n-1}(Z_0),I^{n-1}(Z_i))=\begin{cases}0, & \text{if } I^{n-1}(Z_0)\cdot I^{n-1}(Z_i)>0 \\ 1, & \text{if } I^{n-1}(Z_0)\cdot I^{n-1}(Z_i)\leqslant 0\end{cases} \quad i=1,2,\cdots,8 \tag{10-5}$$

The high-order local patterns provide a stronger discriminative capability in describing detailed texture information than the first-order local pattern. The higher the order is, the more details the local pattern operator can extract from the image, but over-detailed patterns tend to be noise instead of identity information.

10.2.2 Local Multiresolution Derivative Pattern(LMDP)

For a human visual system to capture the essential information of a natural scene, it is well-known that a computational image representation based on a local, directional and multiresolution expansion will be efficient. With this insight, the sparse expansion for fatigue expression image can be obtained by applying a Laplacian Pyramid (LP) with orthogonal filters[4], followed by a Directional Filter Bank (DFB) [5]. The LP with orthogonal filters is used to capture the point discontinuities, and the DFB is used to link point discontinuities into linear structures. In the frequency domain, the structure of LP with orthogonal filters, followed by a two-dimensional DFB, provides a multiscale and directional decomposition to obtain sparse expansions for images having smooth contours. And then a high-order Local Multiresolution Derivative Pattern (LDP) can be used for capturing the detailed discriminative information of contours of mouth, eyes and eyebrows in sparse representation images of fatigue expressions. The structure of Local Multiresolution Derivative Pattern (LMDP) with 2 levels is presented in Fig. 10.2. Bandpass images from LP are fed into a DFB so that directional information can be captured. The scheme can be iterated on the coarse images, which can be decomposed into directional subbands at multiple scales. With orthogonal filters, the BFB is an orthogonal transform.

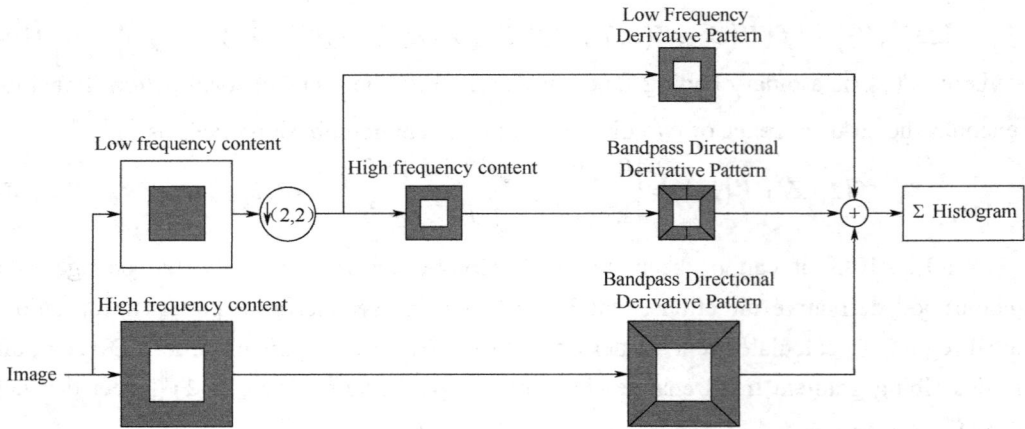

Fig. 10.2   The structure of Local Multiresolution Derivative Pattern (LMDP) with 2 levels

The Laplacian Pyramid (LP) decomposition with orthogonal filters at each level generates a downsampled lowpass version of the original and the difference between the original and the prediction, resulting in a bandpass image. In this book, the "9-7" biorthogonal filters is adopted in the LP stage. Fig. 10.3 depicts this decomposition process, where H, G and M are called (lowpass) analysis filter, synthesis filter and sampling matrix respectively. This process can be iterated on the coarse (downsampled lowpass) image, and the outputs are a coarse approximation a[n] and a difference b[n] between the original image and the prediction.

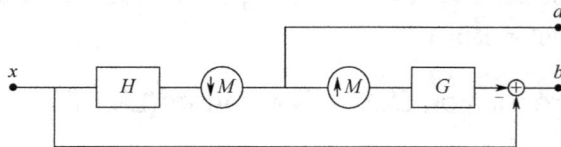

Fig. 10.3   One level of LP decomposition

The orthogonal lowpass filter G in a multilevel LP is an orthogonal scaling function $\phi(t) \in L^2(R)$ that generates a multiresolution analysis (MRA) represented by a sequence of nested subspaces $\{V_j\}_{j \in Z}$, $\cdots V_2 \subset V_1 \subset V_0 \subset V_{-1} \subset V_{-2} \cdots$ with $\text{Closure}\left(\bigcup_{j \in Z} V_j\right) = L^2(R)$ and $\bigcap_{j \in Z} V_j = \{0\}$.

The scaling function ϕ is specified from the filter G via the two-scale equation:

$$\phi(t) = |M|^{1/2} \sum_{n \in Z} g[n] \phi(Mt - n) \tag{10-6}$$

where $\phi_{j,n}(t) = |M|^{-j/2} \phi(M^j t - n)$, $j \in Z$, $n \in Z$. Then the family $\{\phi_{j,n}\}_{n \in Z}$ is an orthonormal basis of V_j for all $j \in Z$. Define W_j to be the orthogonal complement of V_j in V_{j-1}:

$$V_{j-1} = V_j \oplus W_j \tag{10-7}$$

Denote $F_i (0 \leqslant i \leqslant |M| - 1)$ the highpass filters, and associate to each of these filters a continuous function $\psi^{(i)}$ where

$$\psi^{(i)}(t) = |M|^{1/2} \sum_{n \in Z} f_i[n] \phi(Mt - n) \tag{10-8}$$

These functions also generate families of scaled and translated functions as

$$\psi_{j,n}^{(i)} = |M|^{-j/2} \psi^{(i)}(M^{-j} t - n), \quad j \in Z, \quad n \in Z \tag{10-9}$$

Using the two-scale equations for $\phi(t)$ and $\psi(t)$, the coarser image $c^{(j)}[n]$ and the detail image $d^{(j)}[n]$ in j-th scale of the LP decomposed image using the "10-7" symmetric biorthogonal filters is the inner product of the input sequence $c^{(j-1)}[n]$ at the j-1 scale can be written as

$$c^{(j)}[n] = \sum_{k \in Z} c^{(j-1)}[k] \cdot g[k - Mn] \tag{10-10}$$

$$d^{(j)}[n] = \sum_{k \in Z} c^{(j-1)}[k] \cdot f_i[k - Mn] \tag{10-11}$$

The directionality, which is a crucial feature for an efficient image representation, is supported by recent studies to identify the sparse components of natural images. A simplified construction for the two Dimensional Filter Bank (DFB) was proposed[5], which is efficiently implemented via an l-level binary tree decomposition that leads to 2^l subbands with wedge-shaped frequency partitioning. The simplified DFB is intuitively constructed from two building blocks, which are a two-channel quincunx filter bank with fan filters and a shearing operator. Using multirate identities, it is instructive to view an l-level tree-structured DFB equivalently as a 2^l parallel channel filter bank with overall sampling matrices, as shown in Fig. 10.4.

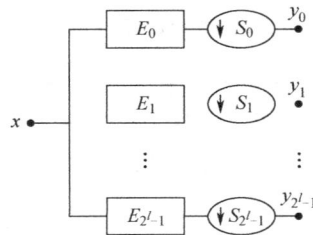

Fig. 10.4 The multichannel view of an l-level tree-structured DFB

Consider a Multi-channel Directional Filter Bank (MDFB), which results from 2^l channels with equivalent filters and diagonal sampling matrices $S_k^{(j)}$. Obviously, all the channels in the

MDFB have the same sampling density, which is equal to the number of channels, as $\det(S_k) = 2^l$, for $k = 0, \cdots, 2^l - 1$. Each bandpass image $d^{(j)}[n]$ is further decomposed by the 2^j level DFB into the bandpass directional images $y_k^{(j)}[m]$, $k = 0, 1, \cdots, 2^j - 1$. The "23-45" biorthogonal quincunx filters is adopted in the DFB stage.

$$y_k^{(j)}[m] = \left\langle d^{(j)}[n], E_k^{(j)}[S_k^{(j)} m - n] \right\rangle \tag{10-12}$$

where k and m are the direction and location indices, respectively. And the corresponding diagonal sampling matrices is shown to have the following diagonal forms.

$$S_k^{(j)} = \begin{cases} \text{diag}(2^k, 2), & \text{for } 0 \leqslant k < 2^l - 1 \\ \text{diag}(2, 2^k), & \text{for } 2^{l-1} \leqslant k < 2^l \end{cases} \tag{10-13}$$

The family $\left\{ E_k[S_k^{(j)} - \cdot] \right\}_{0 \leqslant k \leqslant 2^l, m \in Z}$ obtained from the time-reversed version of the analysis filters E_k, $k = 0, \cdots, 2^l - 1$. The directional filter bank is a powerful mechanism for decomposing images into local and directional expansions. The filter bank is implemented efficiently with a tree structure.

Let $c_0^{(j)}[n]$ is a center point in low frequency content of LP image, and $c_i^{(j)}[n]$, $i = 1, \cdots, 8$, is the 8 neighboring points around $c_0^{(j)}[n]$, among which the point $c_8^{(j)}[n]$ is the right side point of $c_0^{(j)}[n]$. Let $d_{k,0}^{(j)}[n]$ is a center point in high frequency content of DFB image in k direction, and $d_{k,i}^{(j)}[n]$, $i = 1, \cdots, 8$, is the 8 neighboring points around $d_{k,0}^{(j)}[n]$, among which the point $d_{k,8}^{(j)}[n]$ is the right side point of $d_{k,0}^{(j)}[n]$. The first order Derivative Patterns (DP) of 8 neighboring points along the horizontal direction at point $c_0^{(j)}[n]$ and point $d_{k,0}^{(j)}[n]$ can be written as

$$\text{DP}_i' = \sum_{k \in Z} c_i^{j-1}[k] \cdot g[k - Mn] - \sum_{k \in Z} c_8^{j-1}[k] \cdot g[k - Mn], \quad i = 0, \cdots, 7 \tag{10-14}$$

$$\text{DP}_{k,i}' = \left\langle \sum_{k \in Z} d_i^{(j-1)}[k] \cdot f[k - Mn], E_k^{(j)}[S_k^{(j)} m - n] \right\rangle \\ - \left\langle \sum_{k \in Z} d_8^{(j-1)}[k] \cdot f[k - Mn], E_k^{(j)}[S_k^{(j)} m - n] \right\rangle, \quad i = 0, \cdots, 7 \tag{10-15}$$

The first-order Low Frequency Derivative Pattern (LFDP) at point $c_0^{(j)}[n]$ and the first-order High Frequency Derivative Pattern (HFDP) at point at point $d_{k,i}^{(j)}[n]$ are defined as the concatenation of the first-order derivatives at 8 neighboring points

$$\text{LFDP}'\left(c_0^{(j)}\right) = \left\{ \text{DP}_0', \text{DP}_1', \cdots, \text{DP}_7' \right\} \tag{10-16}$$

$$\text{HFDP}'\left(d_{k,0}^{(j)}\right) = \left\{ \text{DP}_{k,0}', \text{DP}_{k,1}', \cdots, \text{DP}_{k,7}' \right\} \tag{10-17}$$

The second-order LFDP and the second-order HFDP are defined as

$$\text{LFDP}^2\left(c_0^{(j)}\right) = \left\{ f\left(\text{DP}_0', \text{DP}_8'\right), f\left(\text{DP}_1', \text{DP}_8'\right), \cdots, f\left(\text{DP}_7', \text{DP}_8'\right) \right\} \tag{10-18}$$

$$\text{HFDP}^2\left(d_{k,0}^{(j)}\right) = \left\{ f\left(\text{DP}_{k,0}', \text{DP}_{k,8}'\right), f\left(\text{DP}_{k,1}', \text{DP}_{k,8}'\right), \cdots, f\left(\text{DP}_{k,7}', \text{DP}_{k,8}'\right) \right\} \tag{10-19}$$

where $f(\cdot, \cdot)$ is a binary coding function determining the types of local pattern transitions. It encodes the co-occurrence of two derivative directions at different neighboring pixels as

$$f(A,B) = \begin{cases} 0, & \text{if } A \cdot B > 0 \\ 1, & \text{if } A \cdot B \leqslant 0 \end{cases} \quad i = 0, \cdots, 7 \tag{10-20}$$

In a general formulation, the nth-order LFDP^n and the nth-order HFDP^n are a binary string describing gradient trend changes in a local region of directional $(n-1)^{\text{th}}$-order derivative images LFDP^n and HFDP^{n-1}

$$\text{LFDP}^n\left(c_0^{(j)}\right) = \left\{ f\left(\text{DP}_0^{n-1}, \text{DP}_8^{n-1}\right), f\left(\text{DP}_1^{n-1}, \text{DP}_8^{n-1}\right), \cdots, f\left(\text{DP}_7^{n-1}, \text{DP}_8^{n-1}\right) \right\} \tag{10-21}$$

$$\text{HFDP}^n\left(d_{k,0}^{(j)}\right) = \left\{ f\left(\text{DP}_{k,0}^{n-1}, \text{DP}_{k,8}^{n-1}\right), f\left(\text{DP}_{k,1}^{n-1}, \text{DP}_{k,8}^{n-1}\right), \cdots, f\left(\text{DP}_{k,7}^{n-1}, \text{DP}_{k,8}^{n-1}\right) \right\} \tag{10-22}$$

where LFDP^{n-1} is the $(n-1)^{\text{th}}$-order derivative along the horizontal direction at point $c_0^{(j)}[n]$ in scale j, and HFDP^{n-1} is the $(n-1)^{\text{th}}$-order derivative along the scale j and k direction at point $d_{k,0}^{(j)}[n]$.

To extract the discriminative LMDP features of a fatigue expression image, the spatial histograms can be used to model the distribution of the high-order LMDP, because it is more robust against variations in an illumination than the holistic methods. In this book, taking the spatial histograms of the subregions and concatenating them into an enhanced feature vector as the fatigue expression image descriptor. The special histogram of a fatigue expression image is represented as

$$H_{\text{LMDP}} = H_{\text{LFDP}^n}\left(c^{(j)}\right) + \sum_{k=0}^{2l-1} H_{\text{HFDP}^n}\left(d_k^j\right) \tag{10-23}$$

To balance the identification accuracy and feature length, we selected the parameters of the 16×16 sub-regions with 32 histogram bins for representing the LMDP images. And the joint feature of histogram is 1×8 192(16×16×32) dimension. LMDP offers a much richer set of directions and shapes, and thus they are more effective in capturing smooth contours and geometric structures in images. The visualized feature results of the 2th-order LDP and the 2-th-order LMDP for a fatigue expression image Fig. 10.1 (b) are shown in Fig. 10.5.

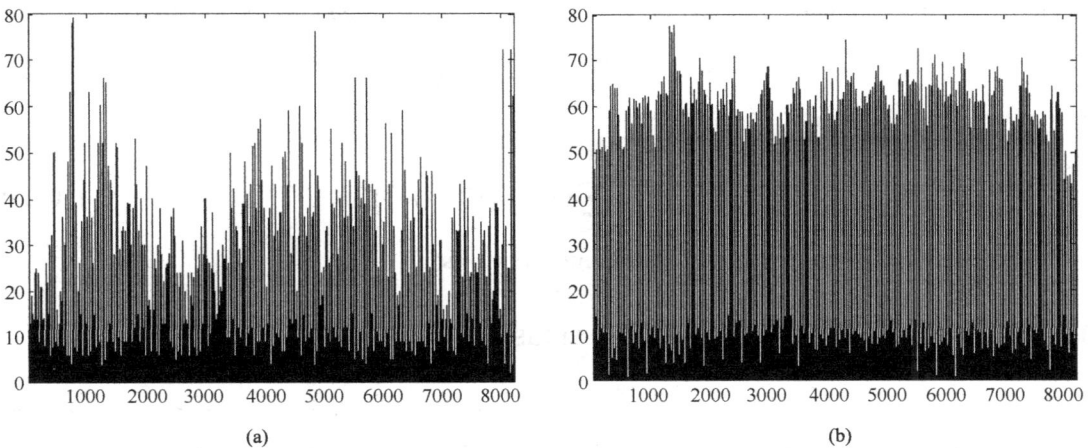

(a)

(b)

Fig. 10.5   Histogram of LMDP versus LDP for an example image.

(a) histogram of LDP, and (b) histogram of LMDP.

10.3 Classification methods compared

Support vector machine (SVM) is supervised learning models with associate learning algorithms that analyse data and recognize patterns, used for classification[6]. The k-nearest neighbour algorithm (k-NN) is a method for classifying objects based on closest training examples in feature space[10]. Multilayer perception (MLP) classifier is a modification of the standard linear perceptron[11], which can distinguish data that is not linearly separable. In Dissimilarity-based classifier[12], the dissimilarities computed between an object and its prototypes are used for object's classification. The above four classifiers are most commonly used in pattern classification, and adopted to classify fatigue expressions in our study.

10.3.1 Intersection kernel support vector machines

Support Vector Machines (SVM) was originally designed for binary-class classification problems, and the basic principle of binary-class SVM is to find an optimal separating hyperplane (OSH) and separate two classes of patterns based on the training set and the decision boundary[6]. In order to solve the multi-class problem, a variety of schemes have been proposed in the literature[7, 8], such as One Against All (OAA), One Against One (OAO), Directed Acyclic Graph (DAA), Error Correcting Output Coding (ECOC), and Multiclass objective function by adding bias to the objective function.

Recently, Maji et al. proposed a fast IKSVM with an approximation scheme whose time and space complexity is $O(n)$, independent of the number of support vectors, and have been shown to be successful for the objects' detection and recognition [9]. In this book, we adopt the fast IKSVM for the classification of fatigue expressions of vehicle drivers. The key idea of fast IKSVM proposed by Maji et al. is that for a class of kernels including the intersection kernel, the classifier can be decomposed as a sum of functions, one for each histogram bin, each of which can be efficiently computed. For feature vectors X, $z \in \Re_+^n$, the intersection kernel is

$$k(\boldsymbol{x}, \boldsymbol{z}) = \sum_{i=1}^{n} \min(x(i), z(i)) \tag{10-24}$$

and classification is based on evaluating

$$h(\boldsymbol{x}) = \sum_{l=1}^{m} \alpha_l y_l \left(\sum_{i=1}^{n} \min(x(i), x_l(i)) \right) + b \tag{10-25}$$

Thus the runtime complexity of computing $h(\boldsymbol{x})$ is $O(n \log m)$.

10.3.2 k-Nearest Neighbor (k-NN) classifier

k-nearest neighbor (k-NN) classifier[10] is a method for classifying objects based on closest training examples in the feature space. k-NN is a type of instance-based learning, or lazy learning where the function is only approximated locally and all computation is deferred until classification. The *k*-nearest neighbor algorithm is amongst the simplest of all machine learning algorithms: an object is classified by a majority vote of its neighbors, with the object being assigned to the class most common amongst its *k* nearest neighbors (*k* is a positive integer, typically small). If $k=1$, then the object is simply assigned to the class of its nearest neighbor. The *k*-NN rule is optimal in the asymptotic case, i.e., the error tends to the Bayes error when the size of the training set tends to infinity. The major drawback of the *k*-NN algorithm is the computational complexity, caused by the large number of distance computations.

10.3.3　Multilayer Perception (MLP) classifier

A Multilayer perception (MLP) classifier is a feedforward artificial neural network model that maps sets of input data onto a set of appropriate output, and consists of a set of source nodes forming the inputlayer, one or more hidden layers of computation nodes, and an output layer of nodes [11]. The MLP utilizes a supervised learning technique called backpropagation for training the network and constructs input-output mappings that are a nested composition of nonlinearities with the form

$$y = f\left(\sum g\left(\sum(\cdot)\right)\right) \tag{10-26}$$

where the number of function compositions is given by the number of network layers. An MLP can be trained by gradient descent using the back-propagation algorithm to optimize any derivable criterion, such as the mean squared error, Here, an MLP is trained to classify an input to be one of the given class labels. The input of the MLP is a vector corresponding to the features extracted from gait patterns. The output of the MLP is either 1 (if the input corresponds to a control group) or -1 (if the input corresponds to children with CP). Though MLP has been proved to be able to virtually approximate any function with any desired accuracy, there is a common criticism for MLP that is very difficult to interpret the trained discriminant function.

10.3.4　Dissimilarity-based classifier

In the dissimilarity-based classification, the dissimilarity measure $D(x_i,R) = \{d(x_i,p_1),\cdots,$ $d(x_i,p_r)\}$ between an object $x_i \in T$, $1\leqslant i\leqslant n$, and the prototypes $R=\{p_1,\cdots,p_r\}$, is a vector with *r* distance that associates x_i with all objects in the representation set R [12]. Therefore, the proximity $D(T,R)$ is a dissimilarity matrix of size *n×r*, which refers objects in the training set to all objects in the representation set. Given a test set *S*, its representation $D(S,R)$ is obtained by calculating the distances between its objects and prototypes in *R*. The dissimilarity measure is small when the objects x_i and p_h are similar, but it should be larger when the objects are more different. The distance $d(x_i,p_h)=0$ when x_i and p_h are identical. In this book, the Euclidean distances are used for the dissimilarity representation between the objects and prototypes.

10.4 Experiments

Two standard experimental procedures, named the holdout approach and the cross-validation approach, are used to evaluate the performance of LMDP versus LDP using IKSVM classifier, compared with other three commonly used classifiers, namely, *k*-NN classifier, MLP classifier and Dissimilarity-based classifier. SEU fatigue facial expression dataset, which is shown in Fig. 10.6, is used for the performance evaluation of the above two feature extraction approaches and four classifiers in the holdout and cross-validation experiments. There are 3 classes of fatigue expressions, i.e., awake, moderate fatigue and severe fatigue in SEU fatigue facial expression dataset. Each class of fatigue expressions consists of 40 images, which are captured in different time under the natural lighting conditions, as the car was in an outdoor parking lot.

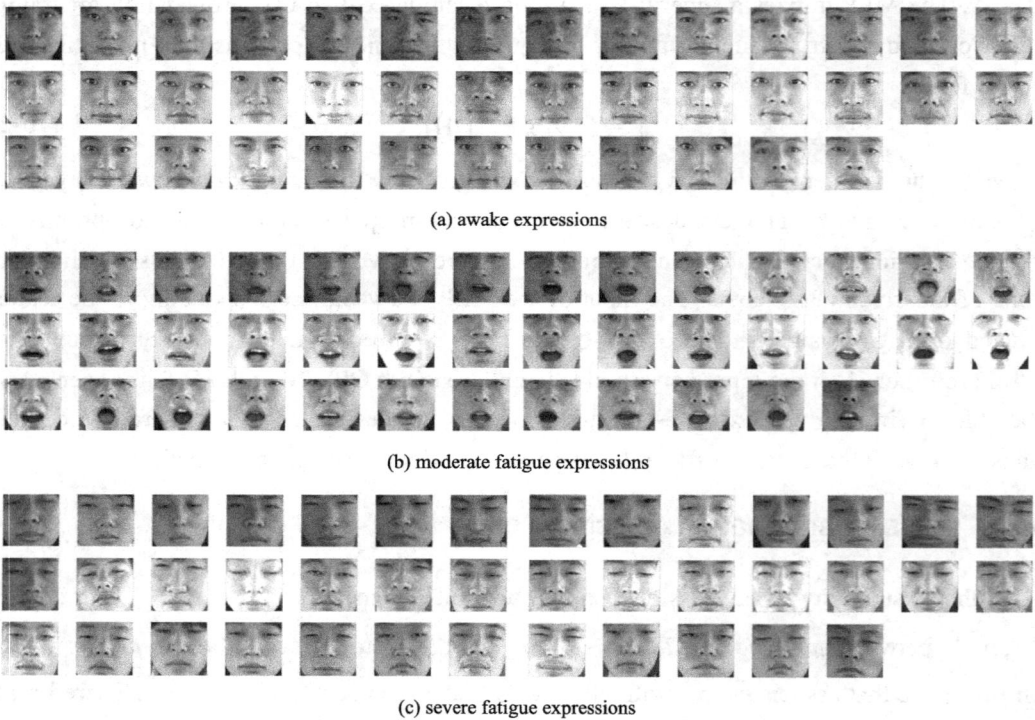

(a) awake expressions

(b) moderate fatigue expressions

(c) severe fatigue expressions

Fig. 10.6   Fatigue facial expression of vehicle drivers in SEU fatigue facial expression dataset

10.4.1 Holdout experiments

Holdout experiments are based on randomly dividing feature vectors of fatigue expression images, extracted from images in SEU fatigue facial expression dataset, into a training dataset (80% feature vectors of fatigue expression extracted from images in SEU fatigue expression dataset) and a test dataset (the rest 20% feature vectors of fatigue expression extracted from the images in SEU fatigue expression dataset). Using the holdout experiment approach, only the test dataset is used to estimate the generalization error. We repeat the holdout experiment 100 times by randomly splitting the fatigue expression dataset, and recorded the classification results.

The comparative experiments between LMDP and LDP are first conducted in the first holdout experiments. The results of classification rate for fatigue expressions using LMDP versus LDP by IKSVM classifier are displayed in the bar plots of Fig. 10.7 (a) and box plots of Fig. 10.7 (b). From Fig. 10.7, it is obvious that the average recognition accuracy of fatigue expressions is significantly improved using LMDP than using LDP. The experimental results in Fig. 7 also demonstrated that the high-order LMDP offers the better performance than the first-order LMDP, but the performance drops when the order of LMDP reach to the third-order and four-order. The experimental results reveal that the high-order local patterns, such as the second-order LMDP, can extract more detailed information than the first order, but it is incapable of dealing with further detailed information contained in the higher-order LMDP, such as the third-order and four-order LMDP.

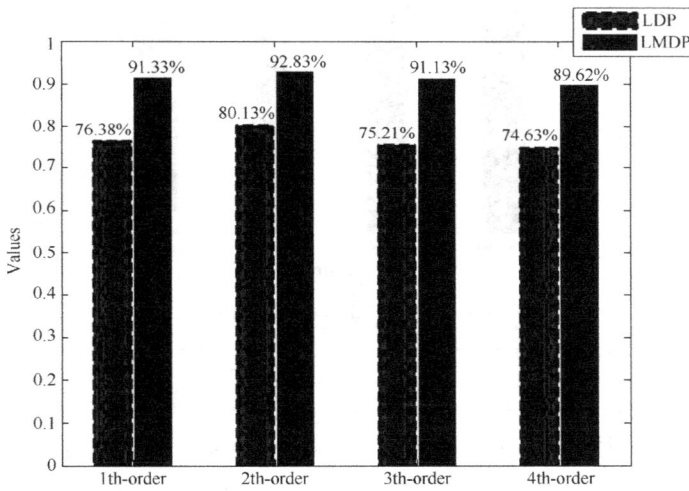

(a) Bar plots of classification rates

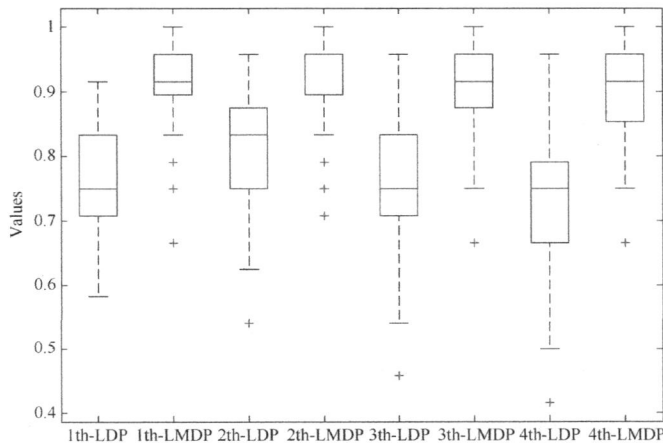

(b) Box plots of classification rates

Fig. 10.7   Classification performance of IKSVM with other four classifiers in holdout experiment

In the second holdout experiment, the same set of training and testing are applied to IKSVM, compared with *k*-NN classifier, MLP classifier and Dissimilarity-based classifier, and their classification performances are simultaneously compared. The results of classification rate in average for fatigue expressions by IKSVM with other three classifiers are displayed in the bar plots of Fig. 10.8 (a) and box plots of Fig. 10.8 (b). The average classification accuracies of IKSVM classifier, *k*-NN classifier, MLP classifier and Dissimilarity-based classifier, are 92.92%, 81.83%, 92.79% and 89.08%, respectively. From Fig. 10.8, it is obvious that IKSVM classifier offers the best performance among the four classifiers in the second holdout experiments.

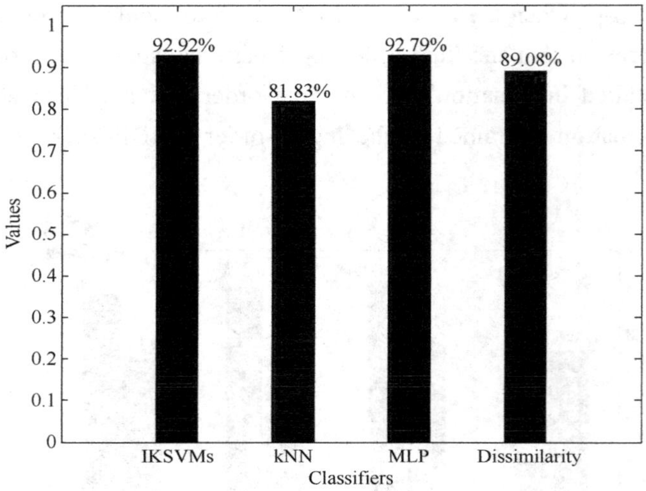

(a) Bar plots of classification rates

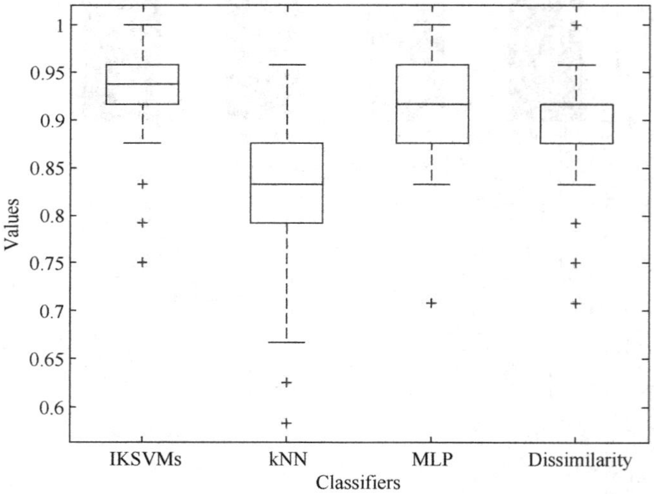

(b) Box plots of classification rates

Fig. 10.8 Classification performance of IKSVM with other four classifiers in holdout experiment

The confusion matrix, which represents the proportion of examples from one class classified into another class, is often used for further measuring the classification performance regarding the information about actual and predicted classifications acquired. In the holdout experiment, the confusion matrix that summarizes the detailed performance using the second-order LMDP and IKSVM classifier is shown in Table 10.1. In the confusion matrix, the rows and columns indicate true and predicted class, respectively. The diagonal entries represent correct classification, while the off-diagonal entries represent incorrect ones. The rows and columns of confusion matrices express the fatigue expression classes of awake expressions, moderate fatigue expressions, and severe fatigue expressions. The corresponding classification accuracies are 88.24%, 98.77% and 90.46%, respectively. From confusion matrix of the holdout experiments, it is clear that the class of awake expression has the most recognition accuracy of three classes in the holdout experiments.

Table 10.1 Confusion matrix for the result using LMDP and IKSVM classifier in holdout experiments. (I) awake expressions, (II) moderate fatigue expressions, and (III) severe fatigue expressions.

Class	I	II	III
I	88.24%	0	11.76%
II	0	98.77%	1.23%
III	9.41%	0.13%	90.46%

10.4.2 Cross-validation experiments

The k-fold cross validation approach is another commonly used technique that takes a set of m examples and randomly partitions them into k folds of size m/k. For each fold, the classifier is tested on one fold (consists of m/k examples) and trained on the other k-1 folds (consisting of $m(1-1/k)$ examples)[13]. The cross-validation experiments are then repeated k times, with all of the k sub-samples used exactly once as the validation dataset, and the k experiment results from the folds are then averaged to produce a single classification rate. In this book, 5-fold cross validation was used when comparing LMDP versus LDP using IKSVM classifier and other three classifiers, i.e., k-NN classifier, MLP classifier and Dissimilarity-based classifier. One set of feature vector corresponds to one fatigue expression image, and there are 120 sets of feature vectors extracted from the images of SEU fatigue facial expression dataset. The 120 sets of feature vectors of fatigue expression images are randomly divided into 5 disjoint subsets of equal size, and each subset consists of 24 sets of feature vectors. The cross-validation experiments were repeated 100 times by randomly splitting the fatigue expression dataset, and recorded the classification results in average.

In the first cross-validation experiment, the classification rates for fatigue expressions using LMDP versus LDP by IKSVM classifier are displayed in the bar plots of Fig. 10.9 (a) and box plots of Fig. 10.9 (b), which shows again that the recognition accuracy of fatigue expressions in average is significantly improved using the proposed LMDP than using LDP. The experimental results in Fig. 10.9 also demonstrated that the performance of LMDP drops when the order reaches the third-order and four-order, and it reveals that the high-order LMDP can extract more detailed information than the first order. But the third-order and four-order LMDPs aren't incapable of dealing with the further detailed information contained in a fatigue expression image.

(a) Bar plots of classification rates

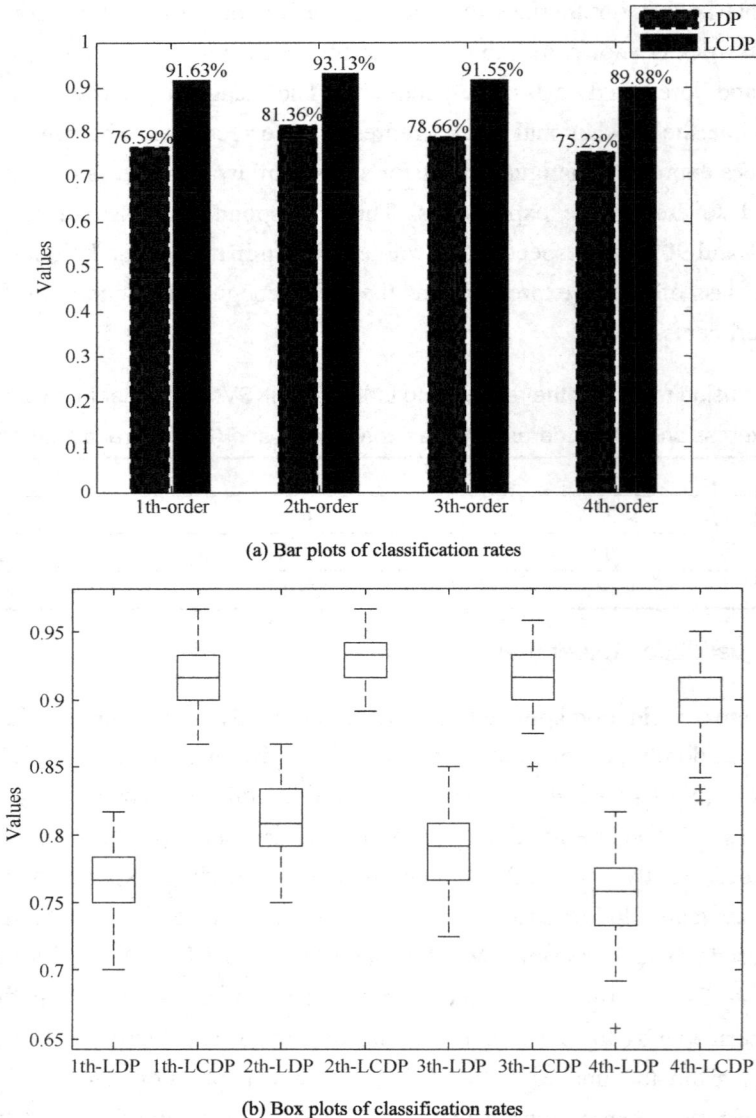

(b) Box plots of classification rates

Fig. 10.9   Classification performance of IKSVM with other four classifiers in holdout experiment

In the second cross-validation experiment, the same set of training and testing are applied to the second-order LMDP and IKSVM, compared with k-NN classifier, MLP classifier and Dissimilarity-based classifier, and their classification performances are simultaneously recorded. The average classification accuracies of the 100 cross-validation experiments using the proposed LMDP and IKSVM classifier, compared with k-NN classifier, MLP classifier and Dissimilarity-based classifier, are displayed in the bar plots of Fig. 10.10 (a) and box plots of Fig. 10.10 (b). From Fig. 10.10, it is obvious IKSVM classifier outperforms the other three classifiers, because it achieves the highest classification rates in the second cross-validation experiments. In the cross-validation experiment, the confusion matrix that summarizes the detailed performance of the proposed second-order LMDP and IKSVM classifier is shown in Table 10.2. The accuracies of three classes, (i.e., awake facial expression, etc.) are 89.80%, 99.57%, and 90.02%, and once again, it is clear that the class of awake expression has the most recognition accuracy of three classes in the cross-validation experiments.

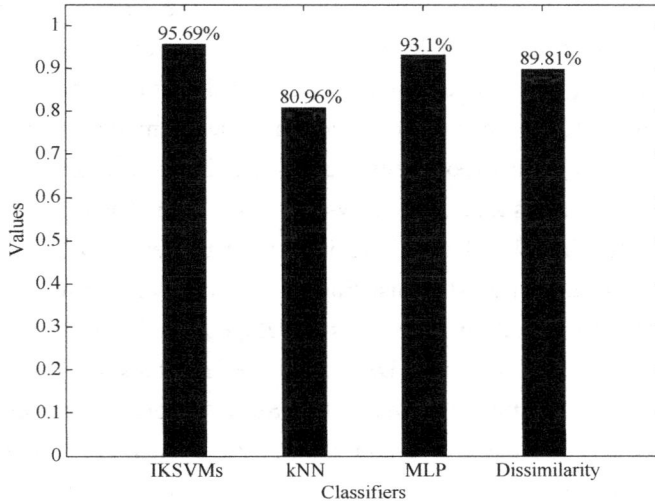

(a) Bar plots of classification rates

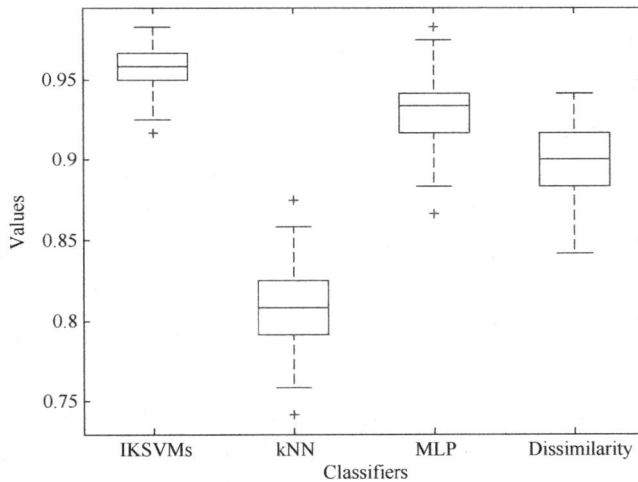

(b) Box plots of classification rates

Fig.10.10　Classification performance of IKSVM with other four classifiers in Cross-validation experiment

Table 10.2　Confusion matrix for the result using LMDP and IKSVM classifier in cross-validation experiments. (I) awake expressions, (II) moderate fatigue expressions, and (III) severe fatigue expressions.

Class	I	II	III
I	89.80%	0	10.20%
II	0	99.57%	0.43%
III	9.90%	0.08%	90.02%

10.4.3　Discussions

Most of the noninvasive technological approaches for detecting driver's fatigue are only based on the local features of driver images, such as eye closure, eyelid movement, blink measurement, head pose and gaze direction. Single local features are not reliable in driver fatigue detection. Take eye blinks as an example. DD850 Driver Fatigue Monitor (DFM) designed by Attention Technology Inc., is a video-based drowsiness detection system for measuring slow eyelid closure, and the field of view is large enough to accommodate normal head movement. The device has a visual gauge that represents the driver's drowsiness level and emits an audible warning when the driver reaches a present drowsiness threshold. The disadvantages of DFM are that every driver has the individual eyes and it is hard to determine a universal drowsiness threshold. Driver State Monitor (DSM) consisting of the ForeWarn Drowsy Driver Alert system and the ForeWarn Driver Distraction Alert, was developed by Delphi Inc., and upon detecting and tracking the driver's facial features, DSM analyses eye closures and head pose to infer fatigue or distraction level. InSightTM developed by SensoMotoric Instruments GmbH (SMI), is a noninvasive computer-vision based operator monitoring system that measures head position and orientation, gaze direction, eyelid opening, and pupil position and diameter. InSightTM calculates PERCLOS to determine a driver's state of alertness. Video-based Eye Tracking Systems ETS-PCⅡ, developed by Applied Science Laboratories, and Eye gaze Analysis System developed by LC Technologies Inc., are both the eye trackers-based systems utilizing the pupil reflection technique for measuring eye movements. Drowsy Driver Detection System designed by Johns Hopkins University Applied Physics Laboratory, can monitor and quantitatively measure the speed, frequency, and duration of eyelid closure, rate of heartbeat and respiration, and pulse rate by analyzing the Doppler components in the reflected signal. RPI computer vision system for monitoring driver vigilance by Rensselaer Polytechnic University can simultaneously and unobtrusively monitor in real time several behaviors that typically characterize a driver's level of alertness, and these visual cues include eyelid, gaze movements, pupil movement, head movement and facial expression. And these parameters computed from these visual cues are subsequently combined probabilistically using a Bayesian Networks model to form a composite index that can characterize the driver's alertness level. Drowsiness Detecting System based on Artificial Neural Network (ANN) developed by George Washington University (GWU), and the ANN observes the steering angle patterns and classifiers them into drowsy and non-drowsy driving intervals. GWU researchers trained and tested the ANN by conducting a driving simulator experiment, and twelve drivers, each under different levels of sleep, were tested, and the results showed that the ANN method detected drowsiness with an accuracy of 90%.

Different drivers have individual differences on eye blinking. Moreover, it is also affected by environment factors such as outside road lighting and oncoming headlights. Therefore, it is hard to determine the preset drowsiness threshold on eye blinking. In this book, we presented a more reliable fatigue monitoring system based on comprehensive characterization of driver's facial expressions, including eyes closure, position of eyelid, motion of cheek muscle and mouth movement. An efficient feature extraction approach, named as Local Multiresolution Derivative Pattern (LMDP), was proposed to describe fatigue expressions of vehicle drivers. From the experimental results of the holdout and cross-validation, it is observed that the recognition rates of driver's fatigue expressions in average are above 92%, which shows that effectiveness of the proposed feature extraction approach in developing Human-centric Driver Fatigue Monitoring System (DFMS).

The severe fatigue is the most dangerous situation since the driver may lose control of the vehicle and the chances of accidents could dramatically increase. Although our fatigue monitoring system obtains higher average recognition rates of driver's fatigue expressions, the severe fatigue classification accuracy of 90% is lower than the class of moderate fatigue expressions. It is observed that the main difference between awake expressions of SEU image database is the openness of the eyes. So that the two types of driver's expressions are likely to be misclassified to each other. In the future work, we will continue our investigations on feature extraction approaches of drivers' fatigue expressions to enhance the eyes-around or eye-related features to further improve the performance of detecting the severe fatigue.

10.5　Conclusions

Fatigue expressions recognition of vehicle drivers are investigated, and three contributions are presented in this book. Firstly, in order to investigate the approach of recognizing the driver's fatigue degree using comprehensive characterization of driver's facial expressions, a fatigue expression dataset, named Southeast (SEU) fatigue expressions dataset, is presented, and the SEU fatigue expression dataset consists of 40 subjects with 3 different sessions per subject and in total 120 sessions. Secondly, we proposed a novel local descriptor, named Local Multiresolution Derivative Pattern (LMDP), to describe fatigue expression images, and the experimental results show the more feasibility and effectiveness of high-order LMDP than high-order LDP for fatigue expression recognition. Thirdly, the confusion matrixes of the holdout and cross-validation experiments show that the class of moderate fatigue expressions has the most recognition accuracy of three, and the severe fatigue classification accuracy of 90% is lower than the class of moderate fatigue expressions.

References

[1]　Croo H. D., Bandmann M. and Mackay G. M., et al. The role of driver fatigue in commercial road transport crashes[C]. Eur. Transp. Safety Council, Brussels, Belgium, Tech. Rep., 2001.

[2]　Zhang B., Gao S. and Zhao S., etc. Local derivative pattern versus local binary pattern: face recognition with high-order local pattern descriptor[J]. IEEE Transactions on Image

Processing, 2010, vol. 19 (no.2): 533-544.

[3] Paul V., and Michael. J. J. Robust real-time face detection[J]. International Journal of Computer Vision, 2004, vol. 57 (no.2): 137-154.

[4] Minh N. D. and Martin V. Framing pyramids[J]. IEEE Transactions on Signal Processing. 2003, vol. 51 (no. 9): 2329-2342.

[5] Park S. I., smith M. J. T. and Mersereau R. M. Improved structures of maximally decimated directional filter banks for spatial image analysis[J]. IEEE Transactions on Signal Processing. 2004, vol. 13 (no. 9): 1424-1434.

[6] Cortes C., Vapnik V. Support-vetor networks[J]. Machine Learning, 1995, 20 (3): 273-297.

[7] Platt J. Fast training of SVM using sequential minimal optimization, in: Advances in Kernel Methods Support Vector Machine[M], MIT Press, Cambridge, 1999.

[8] Milgram J, Cheriet M, Sabourin R. One Against One or One Against All: Which One is Better for Handwriting Recognition with SVM? [C]. International workshop on Frontiers in handwriting Recognition, Montreal, Canada, 2006.

[9] Maji S., Berg, A. C., Malik J. Classification using Intersection Kernel Support Vector Machines is efficient[J]. IEEE Conference on Computer Vision and Pattern Recognition, Anchorage, 2008: 1-8.

[10] Bremner D., Demaine. E. and Erickson J., et al. Output-sensitive algorithms for computing nearest-neighbor decision boundaries[J]. Discrete and computational geometry, 2005, vol.33 (no.4): 593-604.

[11] Haykin S. Neural Networks: a comprehensive foundation (2ed.) [M]. Prentice Hall, 1998.

[12] Pekalska E., Paclik P. and Duin R. P. W. A generalized kernel approach to dissimilarity-based classification[J]. Journal of Machine Learning Research, 2001 (vol. 2): 175-211.

[13] Zhang B., L., Zhang Y. C. Classification of cerebral palsy gait by kernel fisher discriminant analysis[J]. International journal of hybrid intelligent systems, 2008, vol.5 (no.4): 209-218.

Chapter 11

Perception of Driver's Abnormal Activities Information Using Nonsubsampled Contourlet Transform

A crucial step in developing image-based driving postures recognition is to extract suitable feature representation of the driver's images and characterize the differences between the different driving postures. In the paper, we proposed an efficient feature to describe a driver's postures by Nonsubsampled Contourlet Transform (NSCT), and k-Nearest Neighbour (k-NN) classifier is then used to classify the features vectors into one of the four predefined classes of driving postures: grasping the steel wheel, operating the shift lever, eating a cake and talking on a cellular telephone. The rest of the paper is organized as follows.

11.1 Data acquisition and features extraction of driving postures

We designed a driving posture dataset by using a side-mounted Logitech C905 CCD camera. There are 10 female drivers and 10 male drivers in the driving postures dataset (Southeast University (SEU) dataset afterward), and the lighting conditions varied under the natural conditions, as the car was in an outdoor parking lot. The SEU driving posture dataset consists of four driving postures, i.e., grasping the steering wheel, operating the shift lever, eating a cake and talking on a cellar phone.

Fig. 11.1 shows samples of our SEU driving posture dataset consisting of 80 driving posture images, each with resolution 480×640 pixels. In order to address the problem of illumination variations in images of SEU driving postures dataset, we adopted the well-known normalization technique called Homomorphic Filter (HOMOF)[1] to enhance the image quality. With HOMOF, the images are first transformed into logarithm and then a frequency domain to emphasize the high frequency components. Then the images are transformed back into spatial domain by applying the inverse Fourier transform, followed by appropriate exponential operation. One example image of SEU driving posture dataset before and after preprocessed by HOMOF is shown in Fig. 11.2.

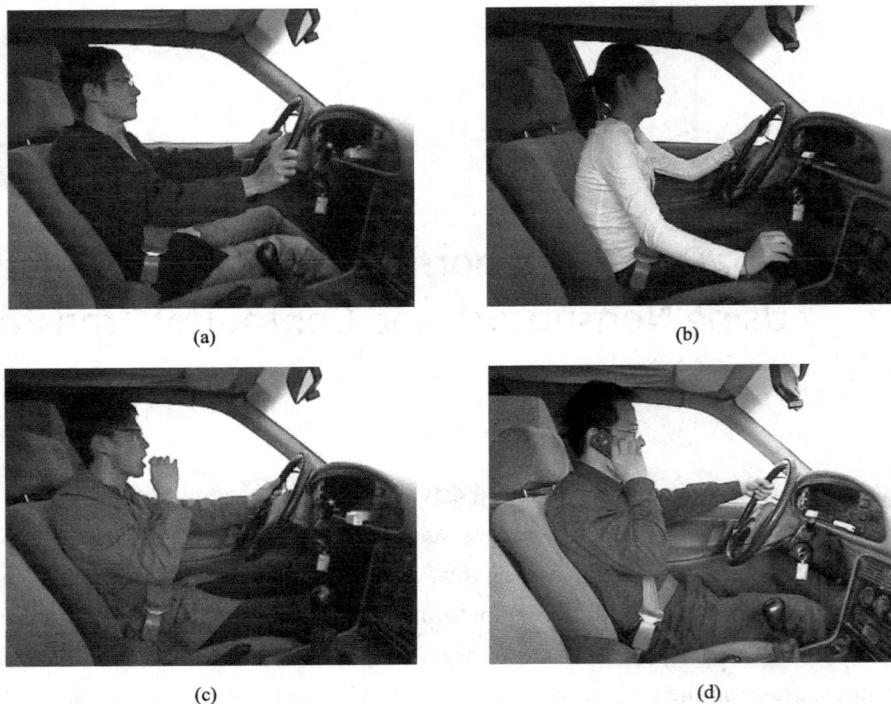

(a)

(b)

(c)

(d)

Fig. 11.1 Example images of SEU driving posture dataset. (a) Grasping the steering wheel,
(b) Operating the shift lever, (c) Eating a cake and (d) Talking on a cellular phone.

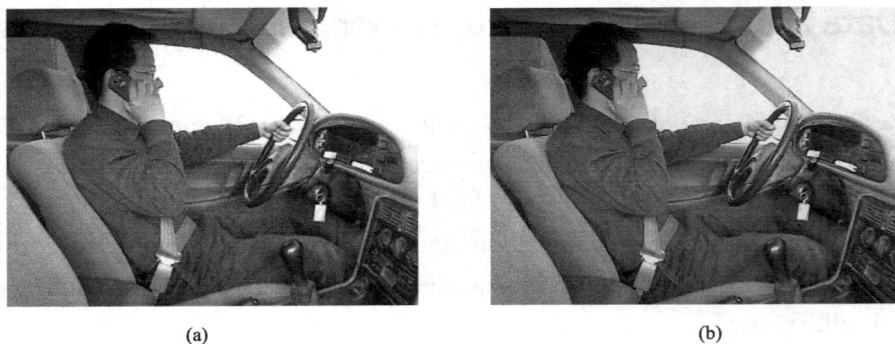

(a)

(b)

Fig. 11.2 Example image before and after preprocessed by HOMOF.
(a) before preprocessed and (b) after preprocessed.

The objects of interest in the driving images are the skin-like regions, such as the left hand, right hand and driver's head. It is a fact that human skin tones have very similar chromatic properties regardless of race, and skin colour detection can be fairly robust under certain illumination conditions. The classification of colour pixels into non-skin tones and skin tones can be performed by working in the normalized RGB space. An RGB triplet (r, g, b) with values for each primary colour between 0 and 255 is normalized into the triplet (r', g', b') by using the following relationships:

$$r' = \frac{255r}{r+g+b}, g' = \frac{255g}{r+g+b}, b' = \frac{255b}{r+g+b} \tag{11-1}$$

The normalized colour (r', g', b') is classified as a skin colour if it lies within the region of the normalized RGB space described by the following rules.

$$\begin{cases} r' > 95, \quad g' > 45, \quad b' > 20 \\ \max\{r', g', b'\} - \min\{r', g', b'\} > 15 \\ r' - g' > 15, \quad r' > b' \end{cases} \tag{11-2}$$

Fig. 11.3 shows the skin-colour segmentation results of the four example images preprocessed by HOMOF.

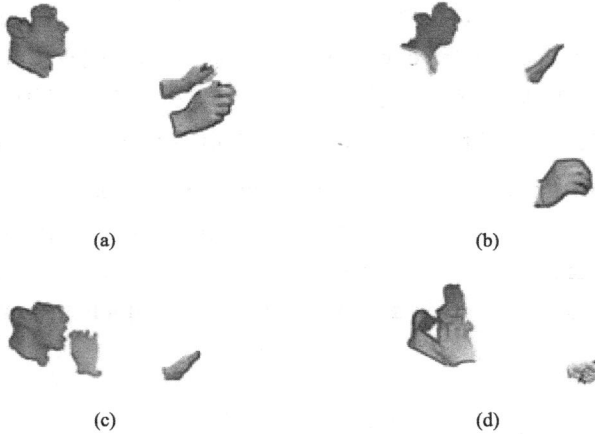

(a)   (b)

(c)   (d)

Fig. 11.3   Skin-colour segmentation preprocessed by HOMOF. (a) Grasping the steering wheel,
(b) Operating the shift lever, (c) Eating a cake and (d) Talking on a cellular phone.

11.2   Features extraction by Nonsubsampled Contourlet Transform (NSCT)

The Nonsubsampled Contourlet Transform (NSCT)[2], which allows redundancy, is a new development of contourlet transform. Allowing redundancy would make NSCT represent images more completely and more flexibly, and Fig. 11.4 illustrates an overview of NSCT. NSCT is implemented by nonsubsampled filter bank structures. More specifically, it is constructed by combining the nonsubsampled pyramid structure that ensures the multiscale property and the nonsubsampled directional filter bank structure that gives varying directions. Denote f_j as the input signal in the jth level ($1 \leqslant j \leqslant J$). Nonsubsampled pyramid first splits f_j into a high-pass subband f_j^1 and a lowpass subband f_j^0 using high-pass filter h_1 and low-pass filter h_0:

$$f_j^i = h_i * f_j, \quad i = 0, 1 \tag{11-3}$$

where $*$ is convolution operator. Specially, the convolution formula is

$$f_j^i[n] = \sum_{k \in \sup p(h_i)} h_i[k] f_j[n - k \cdot S], \quad i = 0, 1 \quad n \in N \times N \tag{11-4}$$

where $S = 2^{j-1} I$ is the sampling matrix, I is the identity matrix, and supp(h_i) is the compactly supported function of h_i. Then the highpass subband f_j^1 is decomposed into several directional subbands by nonsubsampled directional filter bank and f_j^0 is for the next-stage decomposition. The nonsubsampled directional filter bank is constructed in cascade by combining two-channel fan filter banks and parallelogram filters without upsamplers and downsamplers. Consequently, the number of the directional subbands at a specific level is a power of two. We denote the equivalent filter for the k-th direction as u_k^{eq}, then the directional subbands can be obtained by

$$y_{j,k} = u_k^{eq} * f_j^1, \quad k = 1, \ldots, 2^{l_j} \tag{11-5}$$

where 2^{l_j} is the number of directional subbands at the j-th level. This procedure would repeat on the low-pass subband by setting $f_{j+1} = f_j^0$ for the next level decomposition and the final low-pass subband is f_j^0, so that directional subbands of different levels are generated. For the next level, all filters of pyramid are upsampled by 2 in both dimensions and this operation has been implied in the Eq. (11-4). It should be noted that filtering with the upsampled filters does not increase computational complexity. In this book, the 'dmaxflat7' filters and the 'maxflat' filters are, respectively, selected for nonsubsampled directional and nonsubsampled pyramid filter bank.

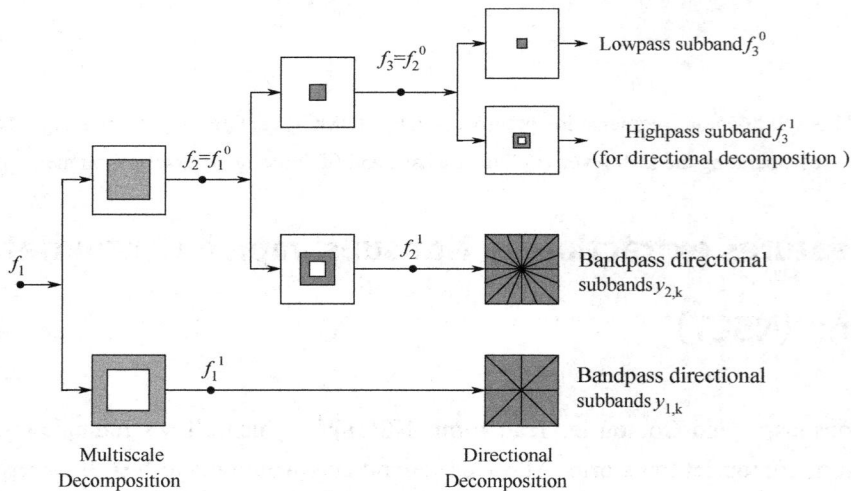

Fig. 11.4   Three-stage pyramid decomposition of NSCT

The reconstruction of NSCT is also based on filtering operation according to the invert procedure of decomposition. Assume g_0 and g_1 are the corresponding synthesis filters of h_0 and h_1, respectively, and v_k^{eq} is the synthesis filter of u_k^{eq}. Then reconstruction of NSCT can be described as follows:

$$\begin{cases} \hat{f}_j^0 = \hat{f}_{j+1} \\ \hat{f}_j^1 = \sum_{k=1}^{2^{l_j}} v_k^{eq} * y_{j,k} \quad , j = 1, \cdots, J \\ \hat{f}_j = g_0 * \hat{f}_j^0 + g_1 * \hat{f}_j^1 \end{cases} \tag{11-6}$$

Given directional subbands $\{y_{j,k}\}_{j,k}$ and the low-pass subband f_J^0, by setting $\hat{f}_{J+1} = f_J^0$ and iterating the procedure in Eq. (11-6) from the J-th level to the first level, the input signal can be reconstructed by $\hat{f} = \hat{f}_1$. NSCT differs from other multi-scale analysis methods in which the contourlet transform allows for different and flexible number of directions at each scale. According to the direction information, directional filter bank can concatenate the neighboring singular points into (local) contours in the frequency domain, and therefore the detection of contours is obtained. By combination of nonsubsampled directional and nonsubsampled pyramid filter bank, NSCT is constructed as a fully shift-invariant, multi-scale and multi-direction decomposition. One example image decomposed into 3 levels by nonsubsampled contourlet transform is shown in Fig. 11.5, and the coefficients of lowpass subband f_3^0 are used as the features of the driving postures in the following experiments.

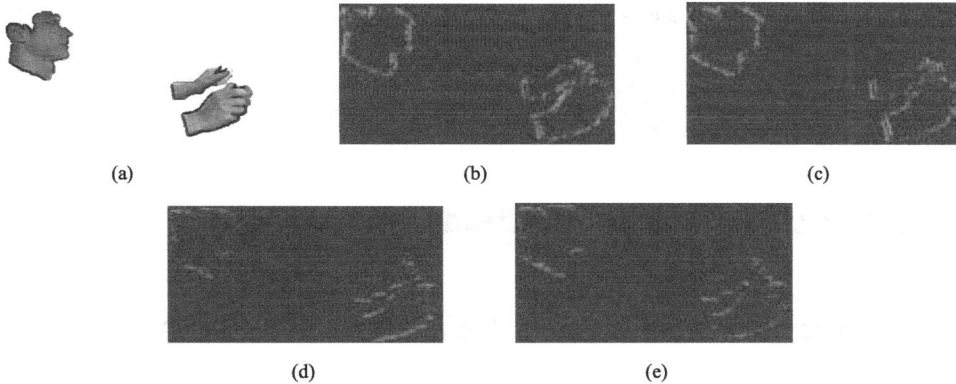

(a)   (b)   (c)

(d)   (e)

Fig. 11.5   Nonsubsampled contourlet transform of one example image in SEU driving postures dataset.
(a) Example image of SEU driving postures dataset, (b) Lowpass subband f_3^0, (c) Howpass subband f_3^1,
(d) Bandpass directional subband $y_{2,k}$ and (e) Bandpass directional subband $y_{1,k}$.

11.3   *k*-Nearest Neighbor (*k*-NN) classifier

In pattern recognition, k-Nearest Neighbor (k-NN) is a method for classifying objects based on closest training examples in the feature space[3]. Let $X = [x_1, \cdots, x_N]$ be the training data with N points of dimensionality D, and $X_i = [x_{i1}, \cdots, x_{ik}]$ be the k nearest neighbors of x_i. The testing data are denoted as X_t with N_t points. x_0 is an arbitrary testing data point, and $X_0 = [x_{01}, \cdots, x_{0k}]$ contains its k nearest neighbors from training data, with labels denoted as $[l_1, \cdots, l_k]$. Suppose there are C classes in the data denoted as $\Omega = [\Omega_1, \cdots, \Omega_C]$. The k-NN classifier finds the k nearest neighbors of a testing point in the training data and assigns the testing point to the most frequently occurring class of its k neighbors. The k-NN classifies x_0 with the following majority voting rule:

$$j^* = \arg \max_{j=1,\cdots,C} \sum_{i=1}^{k} \delta(l_i, j) \tag{11-7}$$

where δ is the Kronecker delta, and satisfies

$$\delta(l_i, j) = \begin{cases} 1 & \text{,if } l_i = j \\ 0 & \text{,otherwise} \end{cases} \tag{11-8}$$

The k-NN classification can potentially be improved by learning a distance metric derived from the training data, e.g.,

$$\text{dis}(x_i, x_j) = \left\| T(x_i - x_j) \right\|^2 \tag{11-9}$$

where T represents a linear transformation[4]. Because nonlinear dimensionality reduction is associated with some transformation of the original data, it can also be regarded as an approach to obtain a new distance metric. In k-NN, the k neighbors of a testing point are assumed to have equal weights. It is appealing to assign different weights to the neighbors and then classify the testing point as the class for which the weights set to its neighbors sum to the largest value. The corresponding decision rule of the k-NN is

$$j^* = \arg \max_{j=1,\dots,C} \sum_{i=1}^{k} \omega_i \cdot \delta(l_i, j) \tag{11-10}$$

where w_i is the weight of x_{0i}.

11.4 Other classification methods compared

11.4.1 Intersection Kernel Support Vector Machine (IKSVM)

Support vector machine (SVM) were originally designed for binary-class classification problems, based on the idea of structural risk minimization. The basic principle of binary-class SVM is to find an Optimal Separating Hyperplane (OSH) and separate two classes of patterns based on the training set and the decision boundary, which can be formulated as a Quadratic Programming (QP) problem in the feature space. A variety of schemes have been proposed in the literature for solving multi-class problem by using techniques including one-against-all strategy, one-against-one strategy, and multiclass objective function by adding bias to the objective function. Tuning the hyperparameters of a SVM classifier is a crucial step in order to establish an efficient classification system. Generally, at least two parameter values have to be chosen carefully in advance. They concern respectively the regularization parameter C, which sets the trade-off cost between the training error and the complexity of the model, and the kernel function parameter, reduced to the bandwidth in the classical case of a radial basis function kernel.

The problem of choosing these parameters values is called model selection in the literature and its results strongly impact the performance of the classifier. In this book, we followed the conventional grid search method which selects the parameters empirically by trying a finite number of values and keeping those that provide the least test error. The histogram intersection kernel, $k_{HI}(h_a, h_b) = \sum_{i=1}^{n} \exp\min(h_a(i), h_b(i))$ has been used as a measurement of similarity between histograms h_a and h_b. Due to the positive definite property, it can be used as a kernel for discriminative classification using SVM. Recently, IKSVM has been shown to be successful for a number of tasks, for instance, detection and recognition. However, the earlier successful application of IKSVM often comes at great computational cost compared to simpler linear SVM, because non-linear kernels require memory and computation linearly proportional to the number of support vectors for classification. Recently Maji et al proposed a fast IKSVM[5] with an approximation scheme whose time and space complexity is $O(n)$, independent of the number of support vectors. The key idea is that for a class of kernels including the intersection kernel, the classifier can be decomposed as a sum of functions, one for each histogram bin, each of which can be efficiently computed.

11.4.2 Multilayer Perception (MLP) classifier

Multilayer Perception (MLP) classifier is a modification of the standard linear perceptron, which can distinguish data that is not linearly separable. A multilayer perceptron is a feedforward artificial neural network model that maps sets of input data onto a set of appropriate output, and consists of a set of source nodes forming the inputlayer, one or more hidden layers of computation nodes, and an output layer of nodes[6]. The MLP utilizes a supervised learning technique called backpropagation for training the network and constructs input-output mappings that are a nested composition of nonlinearities with the form

$$y = f\left(\sum g\left(\sum(\cdot)\right)\right) \tag{11-11}$$

where he number of function compositions is given by the number of network layers. An MLP can be trained by gradient descent using the back-propagation algorithm to optimize any derivable criterion, such as the Mean Squared Error, Here, an MLP is trained to classify an input to be one of the given class labels. The input of the MLP is a vector corresponding to the features extracted from gait patterns. The output of the MLP is either 1 (if the input corresponds to a control group) or -1 (if the input corresponds to children with CP). Though MLP has been proved to be able to virtually approximate any function with any desired accuracy, there is a common criticism for MLP that is very difficult to interpret the trained discriminant function.

11.4.3 Parzen classifier

Parzen classifier is a kernel density estimator, with which a nonlinear function is approximated by the superposition of a set of kernels. For pattern x_j, a Gaussian kernel-based Parzen classifier is determined by N training samples $X = [X_1, X_2, \cdots, X_N]$ as follows

$$f(x_j, s) = \frac{1}{N} \sum_{i=1}^{N} \frac{1}{\left(s\sqrt{2\pi}\right)^n} \exp\left(-\frac{\|x_j - x_i\|^2}{2s^2}\right) \tag{11-12}$$

where x_i is an n-dimensions training feature vector of training sample X_i, and s is a kernel width. The Parzen classifier design means to estimate the relevant kernel width s using the training feature set $\{x_1, \cdots, x_i, \cdots, x_N\}$. A maximum likelihood principle proposed by Kraaijveld[7] was adopted to estimate the kernel width s which is as follows

$$s = \sqrt{\frac{1}{n \cdot N} \sum_{j=1}^{N} \sum_{i \neq j}^{N} \frac{\left\| x_j - x_i \right\|^2}{N-1}} \tag{11-13}$$

11.5 Experiments

Two standard experimental procedures, namely the holdout approach and the cross-validation approach, are used to compare the performance of proposed features extraction method and k-NN classifier, compared with other three classifiers, namely, IKSVM, MLP classifier and Parzen classifier. In the holdout approach, certain amounts of features extracted by NSCT from SEU driving postures dataset (shown in Fig. 11.6) are reserved for testing, and the rest are for training.

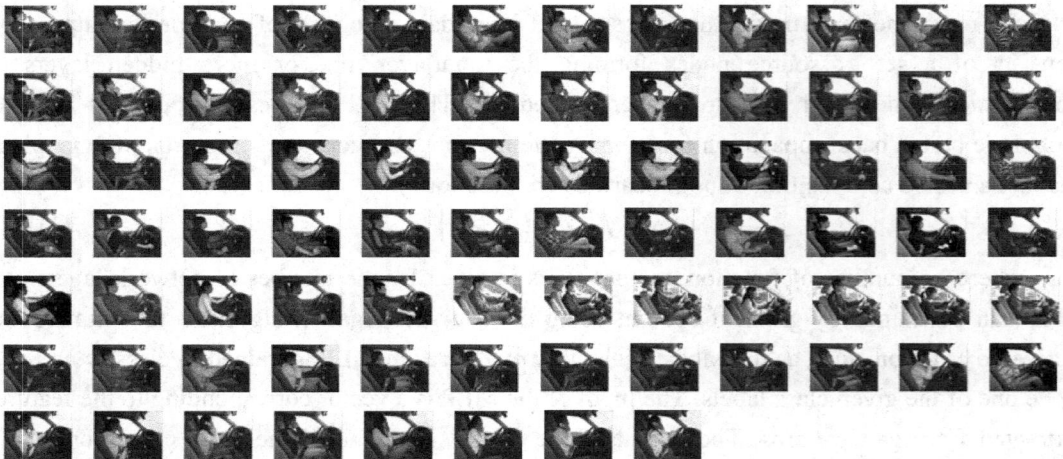

Fig. 11.6   SEU driving postures dataset

In k-fold cross-validation approach, the driving posture datasets are partitioned into k sub-datasets. Of them, the kth sub-dataset is retained for testing the classification model, and the remaining k–1 sub-datasets are used for training the classification model. The cross-validation experiments are then repeated k times, with all of the k sub-samples used exactly once as the validation dataset[7]. The k experiment results from the folds are then averaged to produce a single classification rate.

1) Holdout experiments

Holdout experiments are based on randomly dividing driving posture features into a training dataset (80% of driving postures features extracted from the images in the SEU driving posture dataset) and a test dataset (20% of driving postures features extracted from the images in the SEU driving posture dataset). Using the holdout experiment approach, only the test dataset is used to estimate the generalization error. We repeated the holdout experiment 100 times by randomly splitting the driving posture datasets, and recorded the classification results. For each random testing, the same set of training and testing are applied to the four classifiers and their classification performances are simultaneously compared.

The classification rate is first simple performance indicator for a classifier accuracy. The results of classification rate for the driving postures are displayed in the bar plots of Fig. 11.7 (a) and box plots of Fig. 11.7 (b), which are the averaged classification results from the 100 random splits of the driving posture dataset into training and testing sets. The average classification accuracies of IKSVM, MLP classifier, Parzen classifier, and k-NN classifier, are 70.5%, 33.25%, 70.94%, and 88.06%, respectively. From Fig. 11.7, it is obvious that k-NN classifier offers the best performance of the three classifiers in the holdout experiments.

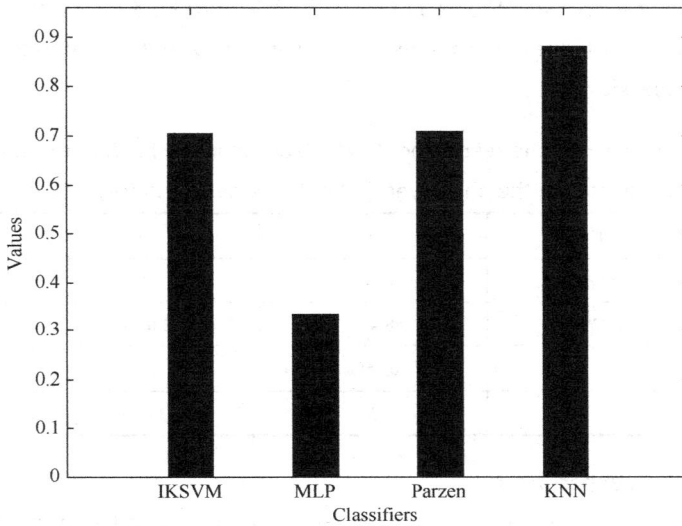

(a) Bar plots of classification rates and

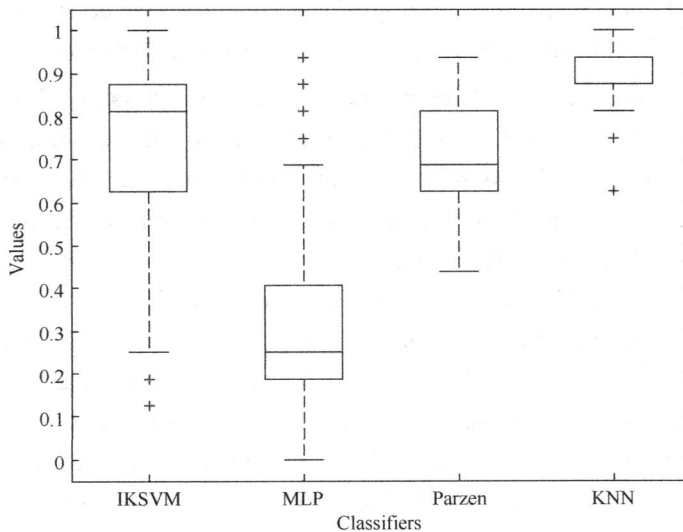

(b) box plots of classification rates.

Fig. 11.7   Classification performance of four classifiers in holdout experiments.

To further measure the classification performance regarding the information about actual and predicted classifications acquired, confusion matrix is often used. A confusion matrix is a square matrix or table that represents the number/proportion of examples from one class classified into another (or same) class. In the holdout experiment, the confusion matrix that summarizes the detailed performance of k-NN, is shown in Table 11.1. In a confusion matrix, the rows and columns indicate true and predicted class, respectively. The diagonal entries represent correct classification, while the off-diagonal entries represent incorrect ones. The rows and columns of the confusion matrices express the posture classes of grasping the steering wheel, operating the shift gear, eating a cake and talking on a cellular phone. The corresponding classification accuracies are 99.76%, 88.46%, 77.89% and 86.34%, respectively. From the confusion matrix of the holdout experiments, it is clear that of the four classes, eating a cake is the most difficult to classify.

Table 11.1 Confusion matrix for the result from k-NN classifier in the holdout experiments. (I) grasping the steering wheel, (II) operating the shift lever, (III) eating a cake and (IV) talking on a cellar phone.

class	I	II	III	IV
I	99.76%	0.24%	0	0
II	8.72%	88.46%	2.05%	0.77%
III	0	0.75%	77.89%	21.36%
IV	0	0	13.66%	86.34%

2) Cross-validation experiments

The k-fold cross validation approach is another commonly used technique that takes a set of m examples and randomly partitions them into k folds of size m/k. For each fold, the classifier is tested on one fold (consists of m/k examples) and trained on the other $k-1$ folds (consisting of $m(1-1/k)$ examples). In the following experiments, 10-fold cross validation was used when comparing IKSVM, MLP classifier, Parzen classifier and k-NN classifier. The 80 sets of driving posture features extracted by NSCT from the images in the SEU driving posture dataset are randomly divided into 10 disjoint subsets of approximately equal size (every subset consists of 8 driving postures features). Nine of these ten disjoint subsets are trained and then tested on the one left out, each time leaving out a different one.

The comparisons of k-NN classifier with other three classification methods are processed similarly as in the above. The driving postures features extracted from the 80 images in the SEU driving posture dataset are randomly divided into 10 folds for 100 times, and 100 cross-validation experiments are carried out. The average classification accuracies of the 100 cross-validation experiments are displayed in the bar plots of Fig. 11.8 (a) and box plots of Fig. 11.8 (b). The average classification accuracies of IKSVM, MLP classifier, Parzen classifier and k-NN classifier, are 75.29%, 30.11%, 68.06%, and 88.25%, respectively. From the bar plots and box plots of the classification rates, k-NN classifier outperforms the other three classifiers, because it achieves the highest classification rates among the four classifiers in the cross-validation experiments. In the cross-validation experiment, the confusion matrix that summarizes the detailed performance of k-NN classifier is shown in Table 11.2. The accuracies of the four classes, (i.e., grasping the steering wheel, etc.) are 99.79%, 88.24%, 78.22% and 89.65%, and once again, it is clear that eating a cake is the most difficult posture to classify of the four classes in the cross-validation experiments.

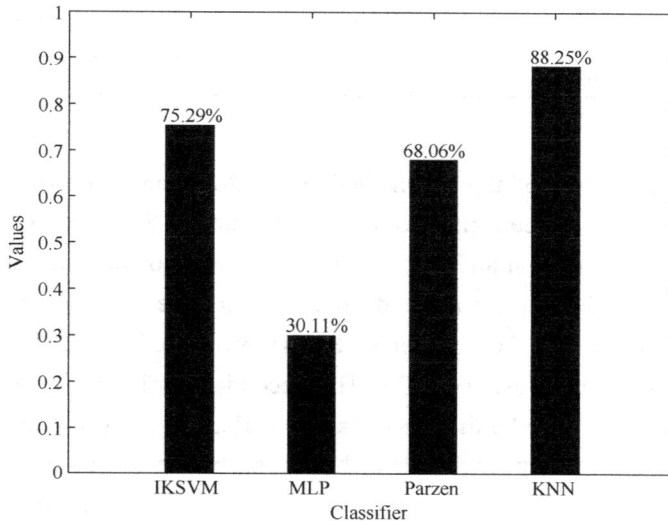

(a) Bar plots of classification rates and

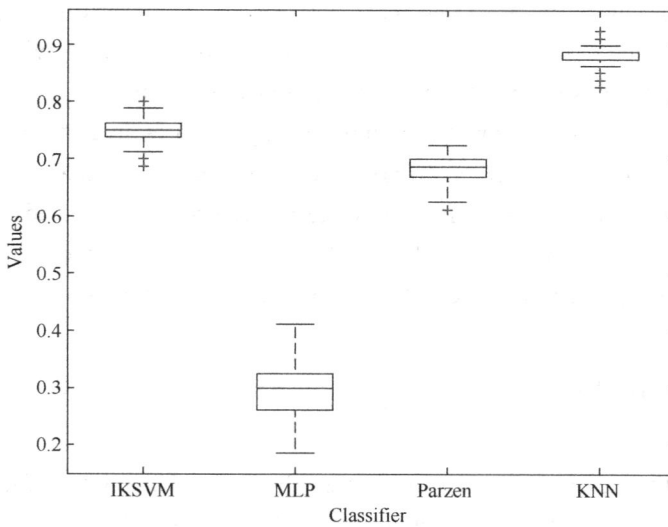

(b) box plots of classification rates.

Fig. 11.8   Classification performance of four classifiers in cross-validation experiments.

Table 11.2 Confusion matrix for the result from *k*-NN classifier in the cross-validation experiments. (I) grasping the steering wheel, (II) operating the shift lever, (III) eating a cake and (IV) talking on a cellar phone.

class	I	II	III	IV
I	99.79%	0.16%	0	0.04%
II	9.31%	88.24%	2.44%	0
III	0	1.42%	78.22%	20.36%
IV	0	0	10.35%	89.65%

3) Discussions

Compared to other state of the art methodologies for monitoring driver's behaviours in current research literature[8], three contributions are presented in this book. With the potential for flexible multiscale, multidirection and shift-invariant image decomposition, the Nonsubsampled Contourlet Transform (NSCT) has the good ability for feature description of driving posture images. The first contribution of this paper is that we proposed an effective feature extraction approach for driving postures using NSCT. The second contribution is that *k*-NN classifier compared with IKSVM, MLP classifier and Parzen classifier, is exploited in classifying four pre-defined classes of driving postures. The third contribution is our empirical proof of the effectiveness of the proposed feature extraction method and *k*-NN classifier in the recognition of driving postures. Some special issues have been identified from the experiments. Particularly we showed that eating a cake is the most difficult situation to be automatically recognized among the four driving posture classes studied. The most obvious advantage of our proposed approach is that the four predefined classes of driving postures can be classified with a relatively high accuracy using static images taken from a cheap CCD vision sensor.

The methodology proposed for recognizing driving postures in this book is limited by the fact that it is more sensitive to the skin-like color areas in the vehicles. For example, if the driving posture is eating a cake, but only one hand of the driver is detected, then this would be incorrectly classified as talking on a cellular phone. In the future, we will further study the relevant issues and hand detection under adverse conditions in particular.

11.6　Conclusions

To automatically understand and characterize the driver behaviours, four different pattern classification paradigms are studied in the automatically understanding and characterizing driver behaviours. With features extracted by NSCT from a driving posture dataset consisting of grasping the steering wheel, operating the shift lever, eating a cake and talking on a cellular phone, created at Southeast University, we comparatively studied *k*-NN classifier with other three commonly used classification methods, including IKSVM, MLP classifier, and Parzen classifier, in the classification of four pre-defined classes of driving postures. With the features extracted by

NSCT, the holdout and cross-validation experiments were conducted, which indicated that k-NN classifier outperforms the other three classifiers. Our experiments also showed that eating a cake is the most difficult one among the four classes studied. With the proposed features extraction method and k-NN classifier, the classification accuracies of eating a cake are over 88% in both of the holdout and cross-validation experiments, which shows the effectiveness of the proposed feature extraction method and the importance of k-NN classifier in automatically understanding and characterizing driver behaviours towards human-centric driver assistance systems.

References

[1] Heusch G., Cardinaus F. and Marcel S. Lighting normalization algorithms for face verification[J]. Tech. Rep., IDIAP-Com, 2005, 5 (3): 1-38.

[2] Cunha L., Zhou J. P. and Do M. N. The nonsubsampled contourlet transform: theory, design, and applications[J]. IEEE Transactions on Image Processing, 2006, 15 (10): 3089-3101.

[3] Darrell S. and Ed I. Nearest-Neighbor Methods in Learning and Vision[M]. MIT Press, 2005.

[4] Hall P., Park B. U., Samworth R. J. Choice of neighbor order in nearest-neighbor classification[J]. The Annals of Statistics, 2008, 36 (5): 2135-2152.

[5] KreBel U. Pairwise classification and support vector machines. In Advances in kernel methods: Support vector learning[M]. MIT Press, Cambridge, MA., 1999.

[6] Kraaijveld M. A. A parzen classifier with an improved robustness against deviations between training and test data[J]. Pattern Recogn. Lett., 1996, 17 (7): 679-689.

[7] Zhang B. L., Zhang Y. C. Classification of cerebral palsy gait by kernel fisher discriminant analysis[J]. International journal of hybrid intelligent systems, 2008, 5 (4): 209-218.

[8] Veeraraghavan H., Bird N. and Atev, S., et al. Classifiers for driver activity monitoring[J]. Transportation Research Part C: Emerging Technologies, 2007, 15 (1): 51-67.

Chapter 12

Recognizing Driving Postures by Combined Features of Contourlet Transform and Edge Orientation Histogram

A decisive step in developing image-based driver posture recognition system is to extract suitable features from driver images and to discriminate different driving postures. In this book, we propose an efficient Combined Feature (CF) extraction approach from contourlet transform and Edge Orientation Histogram (EOH) for driving posture descriptions. For classification of driving postures, this paper exploits a novel Random Subspace Ensemble (RSE) of Intersection Kernel Support Vector Machine (IKSVM). In Section 12.1, the establishment of SEU-DP database is outlined and preprocessing of image normalization is reported. In Section 12.2, CF for image features description of driving postures is introduced. RSE of IKSVM for classification is presented in Section 12.3. Section 12.4 details the experiments and reports the classification results for driving postures of vehicle drivers. Section 12.5 draws the conclusions.

12.1 SEU-DP database and image normalization

The proposed approach was tested on the Southeast University Driving Posture (SEU-DP) database. The driving posture images were captured at a frame rate of 2 Hz using a side-mounted Logitech C905 CCD camera. SEU-DP database contains 10 male drivers and 10 female drivers with natural lighting condition of an outdoor parking lot. For each driver, we captured four different driving postures, two of which are distractive driving inattention[1]. These four postures are ① grasping the steering wheel, ② operating the shift lever, ③ eating a cake, and ④ talking on a cellar phone. In total, SEU-DP database consists of 80 driving posture color images, each with a resolution of 480×640 pixels. Fig. 12.1 shows the four example images of the four different postures in SEU-DP database. The experimentations of the proposed CF+RSE approach were conducted on all the images of SEU-DP database, which will be reported in Section 12.4.

(a) Grasping the steering wheel

(b) Operating the shift lever

(c) Eating a cake

(d) Talking on a cellular phone

Fig. 12.1   Example images of the SEU-DP database

Because the driving posture images are under natural lights, there are inevitably illumination variations which would affect both image segmentation and feature extraction. To address this problem, images are preprocessed using homomorphic filter (HOMOF) normalization technique to enhance the quality[2]. First, an image is transformed into logarithm frequency domain and the high frequency components are emphasized. Then the frequency "image" is transformed back into spatial domain by applying the inverse fourier transform, followed by appropriate exponential operation. The objects of interest in the driving image are the skin-like regions, such as the driver head and two hands. Human skins have similar chromatic properties regardless of races. Thus skin detection can be robustly performed based on an appropriate color-based segmentation. The classification of color pixels into skin tones and non-skin tones is performed in a normalized RGB space. An RGB triplet (r, g, b) with values for each primary color between 0 and 255 is normalized into the triplet (r', g', b') using the equations expressed as

$$r' = \frac{255r}{r+g+b}, g' = \frac{255g}{r+g+b}, b' = \frac{255b}{r+g+b} \tag{12-1}$$

The normalized color (r', g', b') is classified as a skin color if it lies within the region of the normalized RGB space described by the following equations[3].

$$\begin{cases} r' > 95, \quad g' > 45, \quad b' > 20 \\ \max\{r',g',b'\} - \min\{r',g',b'\} > 15 \\ r' - g' > 15, \quad r' > b' \end{cases} \tag{12-2}$$

Fig. 12.2 shows the skin-color segmentation results of the four example images of Fig. 12.1 preprocessed by HOMOF. It is observed that most skin regions of the images were correctly detected with small non-skin regions. Hairs and cellular phones were classified as non-skin region and hence were excluded.

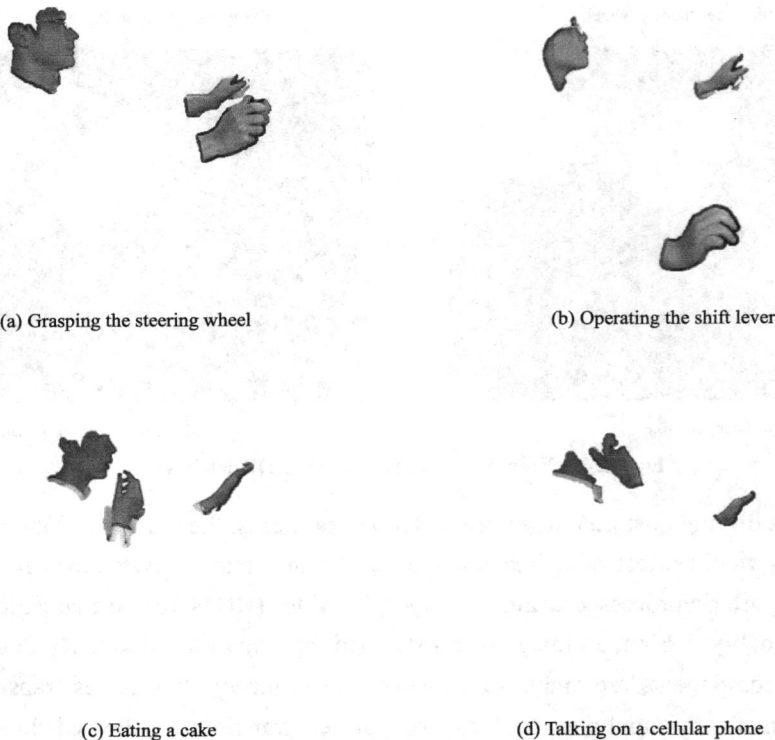

(a) Grasping the steering wheel

(b) Operating the shift lever

(c) Eating a cake

(d) Talking on a cellular phone

Fig. 12.2   Skin-color segmentation results of Fig. 12.1 preprocessed by HOMOF.

12.2   Combined features for driving posture description

The multiscale decomposition of Contourlet Transform (CT) is handled by a Laplacian Pyramid (LP), and the directional decomposition is handled by a directional filter bank[4]. The information of smooth contours can be captured using contourlet transform. On the other hand, the Edge Orientation Histogram (EOH) is efficient in detecting edge information from images[5]. In this book, we propose to use combined features from contourlet transform and EOH for describing driving postures of vehicle drivers.

12.2.1　Contourlet transform for image feature description

Contourlets form a multiresolution directional tight frame designed to efficiently approximate images made of smooth regions separated by smooth boundaries. The CT has a fast implementation based on a LP decomposition followed by directional filterbanks applied on each bandpass subband. A filter bank structure that can deal effectively with piecewise smooth images with smooth contours, was proposed by Do and Vetterli[4]. Implementing the idea of combining subband decomposition with a directional transform, consists of two major stages: the subband decomposition and the directional transform. LP filters are used as the first stage and Directional Filter Banks (DFB) as the second stage.

First, for the multiscale decomposition it uses LP filters. The LP decomposition at each level generates a downsampled lowpass version of the original and the difference between the original and the prediction, resulting in a bandpass image. The directional decomposition stage is also constructed based on the idea of using an appropriate combination of shearing operators together with two-direction partition of quincunx filter banks at each node in a binary tree-structured filter bank, to obtain the desired 2-D spectrum division, it is instructive to view an l level tree-structured DFB equivalently as a 2^l parallel channel filter bank with equivalent filters and overall sampling matrices, where the equivalent (directional) synthesis filters are represented by $D_k^{(l)}, 0 \leqslant k \leqslant 2^l$. The corresponding overall sampling matrices have the following diagonal forms:

$$S_k^{(l)} = \begin{cases} \text{diag}\left(2^{l-1}, 2\right) & \text{,for } 0 \leqslant k < 2^{l-1} \\ \text{diag}\left(2, 2^{l-1}\right) & \text{,for } 2^{l-1} \leqslant k < 2^l \end{cases} \tag{12-3}$$

This basis exhibits both directional and localization properties. Combining the LP and DFB into a double filter bank structure the contourlet transform is developed. Fig. 12.3 (a) shows the decomposition used in the contourlet filter bank. Bandpass images from the LP are fed into a DFB to capture the directional information. By iterating this scheme on the coarse image, the image decomposes into directional subbands at multiple scales. This cascade structure helps the user to decompose different scales into different directions. An example of frequency partition of CT is shown in Fig. 12.3 (b). This type of frequency partitioning leads to the sparsity of the contourlet coefficients, i.e., only the coefficients with both direction and location on the original image edges has significant values.

The contourlet transform sub-bands of the example image Fig. 12.2 (d) is in Fig. 12.4, where the image is decomposed into two pyramidal levels. From each of the detail coefficient matrices, the first-order and second-order statistics mean and standard deviation are calculated as features vectors of images of driving postures, and 1×906 dimension feature vector is extracted for a given image in this book.

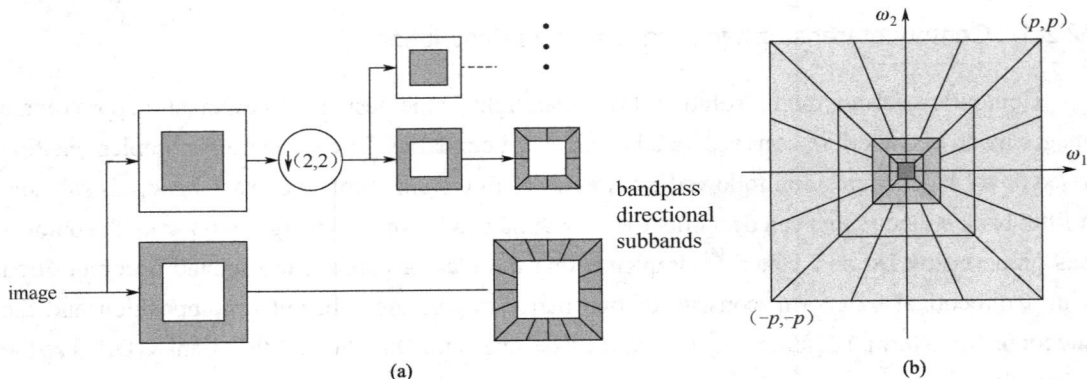

Fig. 12.3　Contourlet filter bank: Laplacian pyramid as the first stage and
directional filter bank as the second stage.

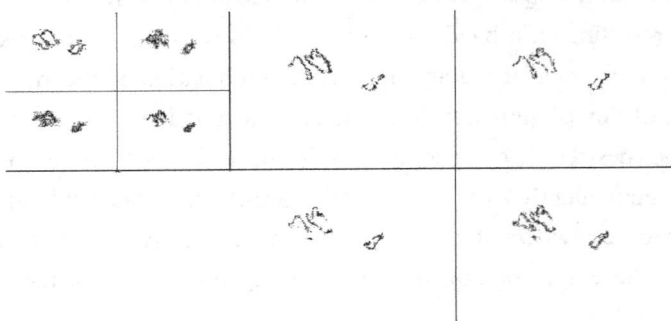

Fig. 12.4　Contourlet transform result of Fig. 12.2 (d) with two pyramidal levels

12.2.2　Edge Orientation Histogram (EOH) for image features description

Edge Orientation Histogram (EOH)[5] is applied to extract driving posture features of skin-color segmentation images. The basic idea of EOG is that local object shape can be characterized rather well by the distribution of local intensity gradients or edge directions. In practice this is implemented by dividing the image window into small spatial regions, for each cell accumulating a local 1-D histogram of gradient directions or edge orientations over the pixels of the cell. The EOH is very flexible because it consists of the local-edge histograms only. More specifically, histograms are created by categorizing edges in all subimages into five types: vertical, horizontal, diagonal and nondirectional edges. Each subimage can be further divided into nonoverlapping square image blocks with particular size which depends on the image resolution. Each of the image blocks is then classified into one of five mentioned edge categories or as a nonedge block. In this book, EOH represents the local edge distribution by dividing image space into 4 × 4 subimages and then the statistics means and second-order standard deviations of the sub-image local intensity gradients were calculated as image features. For a given image of driving posture, a 1×20 dimension vector is extracted. The EOH features of Fig. 12.2 (d) is shown in Fig. 12.5.

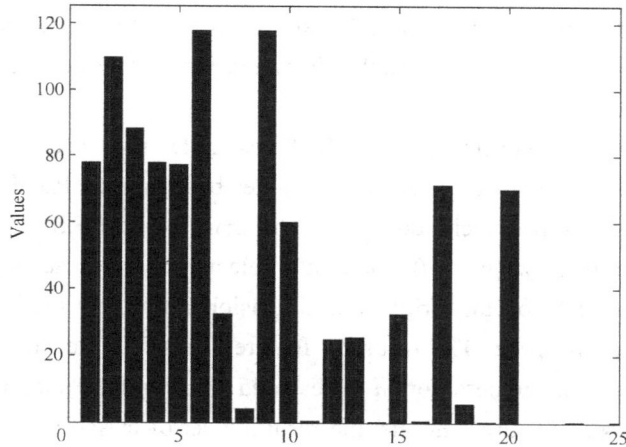

Fig. 12.5   EOH feature extraction result of Fig. 12.2 (d)

12.2.3   Combined features

Each feature extracted from the above two different methods characterizes only certain aspects of driving postures. The joint exploitation of CT feature and EOH feature is then necessary to provide a more comprehensive description in order for a classification system with a higher accuracy. For a given image, a feature vector of $1\times(906+20)$ dimension is extracted from combined features of CT and EOH. One of the difficulties of multiple feature aggregation lays in the high dimensionalities of the features vectors. To resolve this problem, we chose the Random Subspace Ensemble (RSE) of Intersection Kernel Support Vector Machine (IKSVM) as the classifier which has great dimension reduction capability. The proposed RSE of IKSVM will be elaborated in Section 12.3.

12.3   Random subspace ensemble of intersection kernel support vector machines for classification

The idea of classifiers ensemble is to individually train a set of classifiers and appropriately combine their component decisions[6], and classifier ensembles generally offer improved performance. A mainstream methodology, which form classifiers ensemble, is to train the ensemble members on different subsets of the training data, which can be implemented by re-sampling (bagging)[7] and re-weighing (boosting)[8] the available training data. Recently, Maji et al proposed a fast Intersection Kernel Support Vector Machine (IKSVM) with an approximation scheme whose time and space complexity is $O(n)$ [9], independent of the number of support vectors. And the fast IKSVM has been shown to be successful for a number of tasks, for instance, detection and recognition. The key idea of the fast IKSVM is that for a class of kernels including the intersection kernel, the classifier can be decomposed as a sum of functions,

203

one for each histogram bin, each of which can be efficiently computed. Despite different classifier solutions can be applied in ensemble learning, we will exploit the fast IKSVM as the base learner in this book.

An important issue in constructing IKSVM ensemble is to create the diversity of the ensemble. In this book, we focus on IKSVM ensembles based on the Random Subspace (RS), a successful ensemble generation technique[10, 11]. The main idea of RS is: for a d-dimensional training set, choose a fixed n ($n < d$), randomly select n features according to the uniform distribution. Thus, the data of the original d-dimensional training set is transformed to the selected n-dimensional subspace. The resulting features subset is then used to train a suitable base classifier. Repeat this process for m times, and then m base classifiers are trained on different randomly chosen features subsets, the resulting set of classifiers are then combined by using majority voting. Consider a training set $X = \{X_1, X_2, \cdots, X_n\}$, each training sample X_i is described by a p-dimensional vector, $X_i = \{x_{i1}, x_{i2}, \cdots, x_{ip}\}, (i = 1, \cdots, n)$. The details of RSE is formally described as follows:

Step 1: Repeat for $r = 1, 2, \cdots, R$.

(1) Select the P^* dimensional random subspace X^r from the original dimensional feature space X. Denote each p^* dimensional feature vector by x.

(2) Construct a classifier $C^r(x)$ with a decision boundary $C^{r(x)} = 0$ in X^r.

(3) Compute combining weights

$$c_r = \frac{1}{2}\log\left(\frac{1 - \text{err}_r}{\text{err}_r}\right) \tag{12-4}$$

where $\text{err}_r = \frac{1}{n}\sum_{i=1}^{n}\omega_i^r \xi_i^r \sum$, $\xi_i^r = 0$ if X_i is classified correctly, and otherwise $\xi_i^r = 1$.

Step 2: Combine classifiers $C^r(x)$, $r = 1, \cdots, R$, by the weighted majority vote with weights c_r to a final decision rule

$$\beta(x) = \arg\max_{y \in \{-1,1\}} \sum_{r=1}^{R} \delta_{\text{sgn}(C^r(x)), y} \tag{12-5}$$

Where $\delta_{i,j} = 1$, if $i = j$, otherwise $\delta_{i,j} = 0$.

12.4 Experiments

Two standard experimental procedures, named the holdout protocol and the cross-validation protocol, were used to evaluate the proposed CF + RSE of IKSVM. In RSE, two parameters need to be determined, which are ensemble size L and dimensionality of feature subsets M, respectively. L is the number of base classifiers in the ensemble. Recently, the selection of L and M has been addressed in the classification of the brain images of fMRI[12] and the text categorization[13], which show that relatively medium M and small L yield an ensemble which could improve the performance. In the experiments, we set $L = 5$ and the fixed feature subspace accounts for 80% of the CF dimension. In the holdout and cross-validation protocols, certain amounts of driving posture features extracted from the SEU-DP images (shown in Fig. 12.6) were reserved for testing, and the rest were for the training.

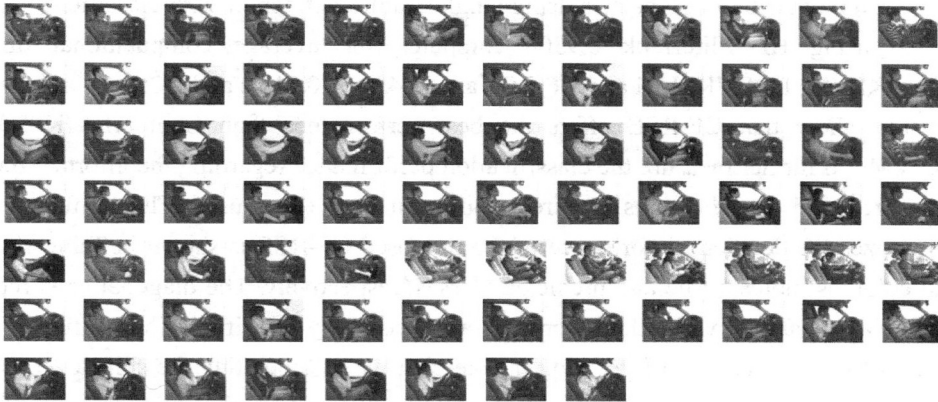

Fig. 12.6   The 80 images of the Southeast University Driving Posture (SEU-DP) database.

12.4.1   Holdout experiments

The holdout experiments were conducted on randomly splitting the dataset into a training subset (80% of driving posture features extracted from SEU-DP database) and a test subset (20% of driving posture features extracted from SEU-DP database). Using the holdout approach, only the test subset is used to estimate the generalization error. We repeated the holdout experiment 100 times by randomly splitting the dataset into 100 different pairs of training subsets and test subsets. The classification results were recorded correspondingly. The results of classification for driving postures dataset by Contourlet features by IKSVM (Contourlet-IKSVM), EOH features by IKSVM (EOH-IKSVM), CF by RSE of IKSVM (CF-RSE) were compared as box plots in Fig. 12.7.

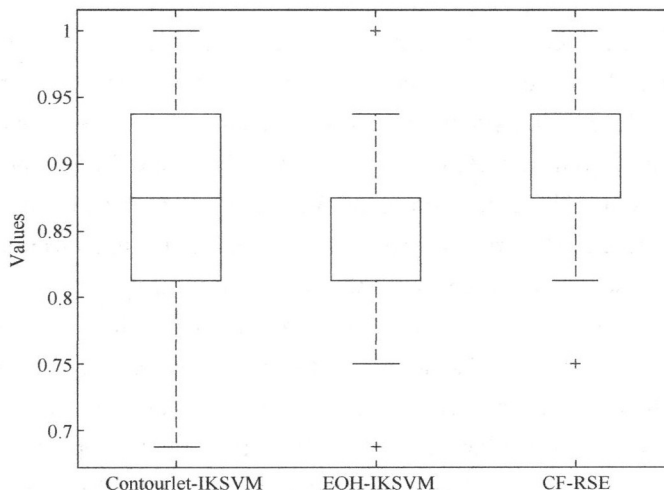

Fig. 12.7   Classification performance of three classifiers in the holdout experiments

Fig. 12.7 shows that the average classification accuracies of Contourlet-IKSVM, EOH-IKSVM, and CF-RSE are 88.75%, 84.06% and 90.16%, respectively. It can be observed that CF-RSE has the highest accuracy value, including of upper quartile, sample maximum and median, over the other two approaches using single feature extraction with classifiers. Tested in Matlab 7.0 using HP EliteBook 6 930p computer, the average computational times of Contourlet-IKSVM, EOH-IKSVM and CF-RSE are 0.049 8 s, 0.014 s and 0.253 6 s, respectively. These results show that CF-RSE offers the best performance than Contourlet-IKSVM and EOH-IKSVM. To further measure the classification performance regarding the information about actual and predicted classifications acquired, confusion matrix was used. The confusion matrix that summarizes the detailed performance of the proposed CF-RSE is shown in Table 12.1. The rows and columns indicate true and predicted classes, respectively. The diagonal cells represent the correct classifications, while the other cells are incorrectly classified. The confusion matrix contains all of the four classes of grasping the steering wheel, operating the shift lever, eating a cake and talking on a cellular phone. From Table 12.1, the corresponding classification accuracies are 85.86%, 87.53%, 92.53% and 91.56%, respectively. It indicates that the class of grasping the steering wheel is the most difficult to recognize among the four driving postures.

Table 12.1. Confusion matrix for the result from CF by RSE of IKSVM in the holdout experiments ((I) grasping the steering wheel, (II) operating the shift lever, (III) eating a cake , (IV) talking on a cellar phone.)

class	I	II	III	IV
I	85.86%	11.41%	0.50%	2.23%
II	12.23%	87.53%	0.24%	0
III	0	0	92.53%	7.47%
IV	0	0	8.44%	91.56%

12.4.2 Cross-validation experiments

In the second experiment, 10-fold cross validation was used to evaluate the proposed CF-RSE approach. The 80 sets of driving posture feature vectors extracted from SEU-DP images were randomly divided into 10 disjoint subsets with equal sizes, i.e., each subset has 8 driving postures vectors. Nine disjoint subsets were used for training the CF-RSE and it was then tested on the tenth subset. With different choices of the testing subset and random divisions, this experiment was repeated 100 times. The average classification accuracies of the 100 cross-validation experiments are shown as the box plots in Fig. 12.8.

Fig.12.8 shows that the average classification accuracies of Contourlet-IKSVM, EOH-IKSVM and CF-RSE are 89.35%, 84.9%, and 90.65%, respectively. CF-RSE has the higher performance, including of upper quartile, sample maximum and median, over Contourlet-IKSVM and EOH-IKSVM. Tested in Matlab 7.0 using HP EliteBook 6 930p computer, the average computational times of Contourlet-IKSVM, EOH-IKSVM and CF-RSE are 0.519 7 s, 0.025 2 s and 2.669 0 s, respectively. The results show that the proposed CF-RSE approach offers the best performance over Contourlet-IKSVM or EOH-IKSVM in the cross-validation experiments. The confusion matrix that summarizes the detailed performance of the proposed CF-RSE approach is shown in Table 12.2. The accuracies of four classes are 89.10%, 90.45%, 92.56% and 90.91%, respectively. The class of grasping the steering wheel is the most difficult to recognize among the four classes in the cross-validation experiments. However, the proposed approach managed to achieve a high accuracy of 89.10%.

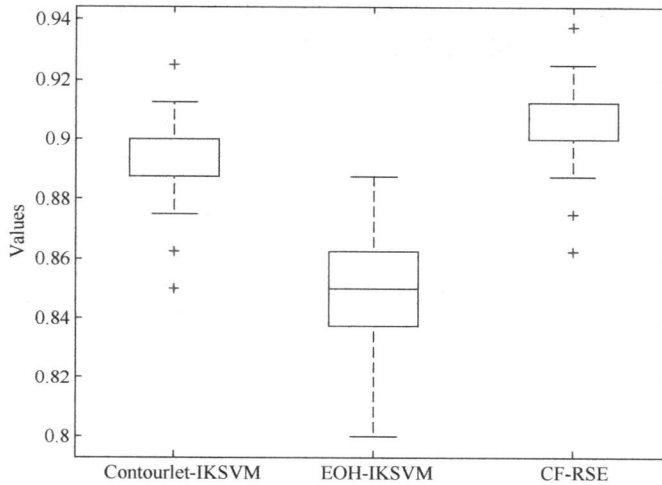

Fig. 12.8   Average classification performance of three classifiers in the cross-validation experiments

Table 12.2. Confusion matrix for the result from the proposed CF-RSE

in the cross-validation experiments

((I) grasping the steering wheel, (II) operating the shift lever, (III) eating a cake ,

(IV) talking on a cellar phone.)

class	I	II	III	IV
I	89.10%	8.61%	0.64%	1.65%
II	8.90%	90.45%	0.65%	0
III	0.20%	1.01%	92.56%	6.23%
IV	0	0	9.09%	90.91%

12.4.3   Discussions

Compared to other state of the art methodologies for monitoring driver's behaviors in current research literatures, we present a more reliable monitoring system of driver's postures based on comprehensive characterization of two hand areas and head area. This paper also proposed an efficient combined feature extraction approach from CT and EOH to describe driving postures. An RSE of IKSVM as the base classifiers was then exploited for classification of predefined four classes of driving postures, i.e., grasping the steering wheel, operating the shift lever, eating a cake and talking on a cellar phone.

Another state of the art gradient descriptor Histograms of Oriented Gradients (HOG) is based on evaluating a dense grid of well-normalized local histograms of image gradient orientations over the image windows. Specifically, an image is first divided into non-overlapping pixel regions or cells. For each cell a 1-dimension HOG over pixels in that cell is accumulated. In this book, the 100 times holdout experiments were conducted to compare the performance of the proposed combined feature extraction approach and HOG feature extraction. Fig. 12.9 shows that the average classification accuracies of CF-RSE and HOG-IKSVM are 90.38% and 89.19%, respectively. It can be observed that CF-RSE has the highest accuracy value, including of upper quartile, sample maximum and median, than HOG feature extraction.

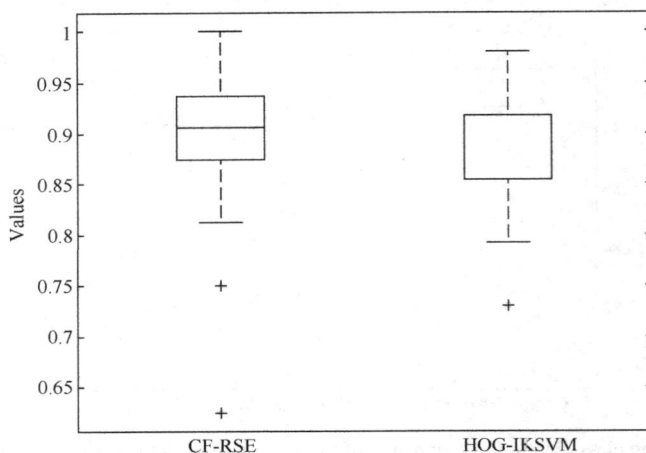

Fig. 12.9　Performance of CF-RES compared with HOG-IKSVM

A Receiver Operating Characteristic (ROC) curve is a plot of the true positive rate against the false positive rate for the different possible cut-points of a diagnostic test. The ROC curves of the four classes using the classification model trained by the proposed CF-RSE approach is shown in Fig. 12.10. From Area Under Curves (AUC) of ROC in Fig. 12.10, it can be observed that the class of grasping the steering wheel is the most difficult to recognize among the four classes, and the class of eating a cake has the highest accuracy value among the four classes using the classification model trained by the proposed CF-RSE approach.

Our study is limited by the fact that the proposed method for recognizing driving postures is more sensitive to the skin-like color areas in the vehicles. When a driver dressed in skin-like colors, the recognition system of driving postures will detect not only two hands and faces of drivers, but also body the area of skin-like color clothes. When a driver dressed in gloves of non-skin color, the area of two hands will be missed using our recognition system of driving postures. In the future, we will also continue the investigation on the hand detection methods of drivers under bad conditions.

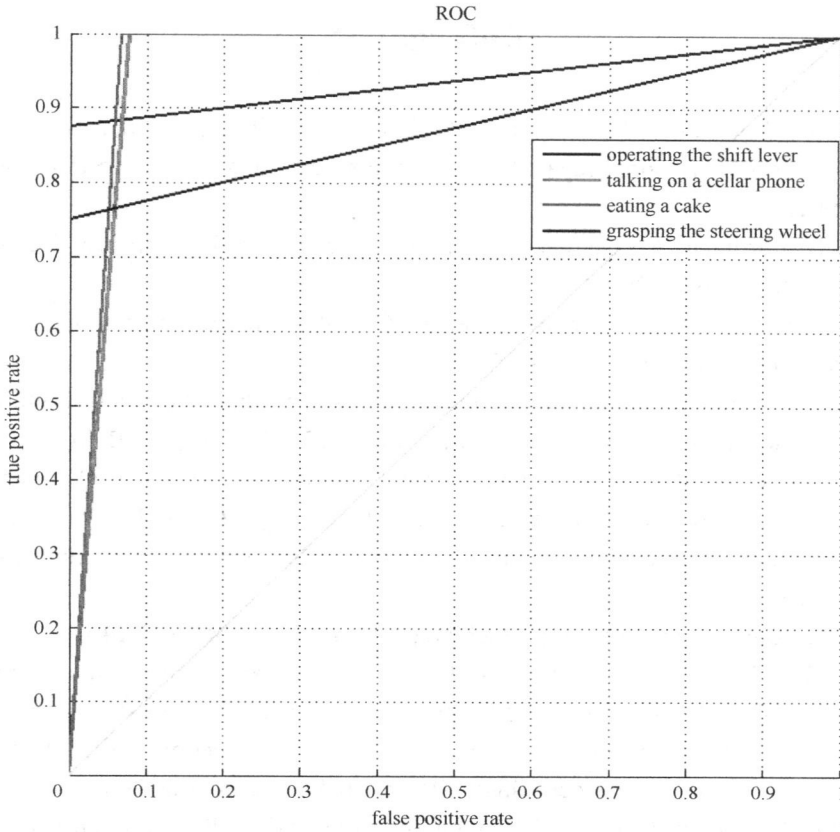

Fig. 12.10   ROC curve of CF-RES

12.5   Conclusions

Driving postures recognition of vehicle drivers was investigated and the following three contributions were presented in this book. Firstly, we proposed to combine two different features from Contourlet transform and Edge Orientation Histogram (EOH) to describe image features of driving postures. Secondly, we exploited a Random Subspace Ensemble (RSE) of IKSVM as base classifiers in classifying four classes of driving postures. Thirdly, the holdout and cross-validation experiments were conducted, which show that the proposed CF-RSE outperforms recognition strategies with single feature extractions and without RSE. It was observed among the four classes of driving postures, the class of grasping the steering wheel is the most difficult to recognize and over 85% in both of holdout and cross-validation experiments, which shows the effectiveness of the proposed feature extraction method and RSE of IKSVM in developing human-centered driver assistance systems.

References

[1] Stutts J. C., Reinfurt D.W., Staplin L., Rodgman E. A. The Role of driver distraction in traffic crashes[R]. Report Prepared for AAA Foundation for Traffic Safety. Washington, DC. , 2001.

[2] Heusch G., Cardinaux F. , Marcel S. Lighting normalization algorithms for face verification [R]. Tech. Rep., IDIAP, 2005.

[3] Veeraraghavan H., Bird N., Atev S., et al. Classifiers for driver activity monitoring[J]. Transport. Res. Part C, 2007, 15 (1): 51-67.

[4] Do M. N. and Vetterli M. The Contourlet transform: An efficient directional multiresolution image representation[J]. IEEE Trans. Image Process., 2005, 4 (12): 2091-2106.

[5] Sikora T. The MPEG-7 Visual Standard for Content Description-An Overview[J], IEEE Transactions on Circuits and Systems for Video Technology, 2001 (11): 696-702.

[6] Kuncheva L. I. Combining Pattern Classifiers: Methods and Algorithms[M]. Wiley-Interscience, 2004.

[7] Breiman L. Bagging predictors[J], Machine Learning, 1996 (24): 123-140.

[8] Freund Y., Schapire R. E. A Decision-theoretic generalization of on-line learning and an application to boosting[J], Journal of Computer and System Sciences, 1997 (55): 119-139.

[9] Maji S., Berg A. C., Malik J. Classification Using Intersection Kernel Support Vector Machines is efficient[J]. In Proceedings, CVPR, Anchorage, Alaska, 2008: 1-8.

[10] Skurichina M., Robert P., Duin W. Bagging, boosting and the Random Subspace Method for Linear Classifiers[J], Pattern Analysis & Applications, 2002 (5): 121-135.

[11] Ho T. K. The random subspace method for constructing decision forest[J], IEEE Trans PAMI, 1998 (20): 832-844.

[12] Kuncheva L. I., Rodriguez J. J. Plumpton C. O. et al. Random subspace ensembles for fMRI classification[J]. IEEE Trans Med Imaging. 2010, 29 (2): 531-42.

[13] Gangeh M. J., Kamel M. S., Duin P. W. Random Subspace Method in Text Categorization [C]. International Conference on Pattern Recognition, 2010.